LAND-SAVING ACTION

LAND-SAVING ACTION

A WRITTEN SYMPOSIUM BY 29 EXPERTS ON PRIVATE LAND
CONSERVATION IN THE 1980s

Edited by Russell L. Brenneman
and Sarah M. Bates

ISLAND PRESS, COVELO, CALIFORNIA

Library of Congress Cataloging in Publication Data

Land-saving action.
    Bibliography: p. 239
    Includes index.
    1. Land use—United States—Addresses, essays, lectures. 2. Land trusts—United States—Addresses, essays, lectures. 3. Soil conservation—United States—Addresses, essays, lectures. I. Brenneman, Russell L., 1928–   . II. Bates, Sarah M., 1949–
HD205.L353   1984   333.73'16'0973   83-22803
ISBN 0-933280-23-8
ISBN 0-933280-22-X (pbk.)

Text and cover designer: Diana Fairbanks

Editor: Barbara Youngblood

Production coordinator: Linda Gunnarson

Proofreaders: Frances Haselsteiner, Russell Fuller

Typesetter: Graphic Typesetting Service, Los Angeles

Printer and binder: BookCrafters, Chelsea, Michigan

Grateful acknowledgment is made to the following for permission to reprint material previously published (some of which has been edited for this volume):

Hank Goetz, "A Cooperative Approach to River Management: The Blackfoot Experience," adapted from article originally published in *Western Wildlands: A Natural Resources Journal*, Vol. 4, No. 2, Fall 1977, published by Montana Forest and Conservation Experiment Station, University of Montana, Missoula.

Chart entitled "States Using Farmland Protection Tools," compiled by National Association of State Departments of Agriculture Farmland Project, 1982.

Ross D. Netherton, "Environmental Conservation and Historic Preservation Through Recorded Land-Use Agreements," reprinted by permission of the Real Property, Probate, and Trust Law Section from 14 *Real Property, Probate and Trust Journal*, Fall 1979. Copyright 1979, American Bar Association, Chicago, Illinois.

The Uniform Conservation Easement Act is authored by the National Conference of Commissioners on Uniform State Laws, Chicago, Illinois.

Glenn F. Tiedt, "An Introduction to Conservation Easements for Colorado Archaeologists," reprinted by permission from *Southwestern Lore*, Vol. 48, No. 2, June 1982. Copyright 1982, Colorado Archaeological Society, Boulder, Colorado.

Glenn F. Tiedt, "Easements and Artifacts: An Archaeological Investigation of the Internal Revenue Code," reproduced by permission of the Society for American Archaeology from *American Antiquity* 47(2):376–381, 1982. Footnotes added.

Russell L. Brenneman, "Charitable Contributions (Not in Trust) of Less Than the Contributor's Entire Interest in Property; Land Conservation and Historic Preservation Restrictions; Contributions of Undivided Portions of the Contributor's Interest; Time Allocated Contributions; Retained Life Estates (Personal Residence or Farm)." Proceedings of the New York University Thirteenth Conference on Charitable Organizations. Copyright 1983, New York University. Reprinted as "Gifts of Partial Interests in Real Property" in this volume.

Thomas A. Coughlin III, "Increased Tax Penalties for Valuation Overstatements," reprinted by permission from 2 *PLR* 2034, May 1983. Copyright 1983, National Trust for Historic Preservation.

Janet E. Milne, "The Landowner's Options," adapted from *The Landowner's Options, A Guide to the Voluntary Protection of Land in Maine*, jointly sponsored by the Maine State Planning Office and the Maine Coast Heritage Trust, November 1978.

Roger E. Koontz, "How to Form a Land Trust"; Roger E. Koontz and Marion R. Fremont-Smith, "Becoming and Remaining a Tax-Exempt Organization"; Roger E. Koontz and Russell K. Osgood, "Summary of Forms and Consequences of Land Acquisition by a Charity"; and Suzanne C. Wilkins, "How to Manage Land Acquired by a Trust," republished or adapted from the *Connecticut Land Trust Handbook*. Copyright 1982, The Nature Conservancy and the Conservation Law Foundation of New England, Inc.

*This book is dedicated to the memory of
James R. Etter and to his belief in the civilized
stewardship of nature's bounty.*

Contents

Preface

A fortunate few who read these pages will recall an autumn afternoon in Cambridge, Massachusetts, in 1981. Outside, golden leaves, brisk air, gray clapboard, and crisp, white trim. Inside, the meeting rooms provided by the Lincoln Institute of Land Policy overflowing with people. Excitement. The excitement of land saving *in action.*

This gathering of land conservationists was unique. It was a colloquium, or, as it called itself, a "consultation" of conservation organizations. These organizations were not large national foundations whose names are household words and that are served by large professional staffs and fueled by national fund drives; to the contrary, these were small, community-based charities that are saving land close to home through the work of volunteers and local fundraising.[1]

The excitement was generated by the encounter of these enthusiastic, and in some cases inexperienced, practitioners of the land-saving ethic. Organizations with such nationally uncelebrated names as the Ottauquechee Regional Land Trust, the Yakima River Regional Greenway Foundation, and the Brandywine Conservancy learned that they are all in the same business and that they have a great deal to teach and learn from one another. Many participants believed the meeting heralded a significant shift of emphasis in the history of the land-saving movement.

Thomas Jefferson, looking west from Monticello, saw the North American continent as possessed of land and resources sufficient unto the "thousandth generation." The business of the nation in the nineteenth century became the exploitation of the public domain in a process that led one contemporary scholar to observe: "The United States are primarily a commercial society, and only secondarily a nation."[2] President Woodrow Wilson was to reflect sadly, a century after Jefferson's words, on the wasteful way in which wealth had been wrested from the "wilderness." The roots of the American land conservation movement lie in that wasteful experience and in the way thoughtful, ethical citizens perceive the consequences of that experience.

It is well known that conservation emerged into national prominence through the movement to establish the national parks. While not overlooking the significance of the efforts to establish urban parks, it still can be said that land conservation in the first instance was identified primarily with the management of federal public lands. Whether focusing on discrete monuments such as Mount Rainier or on the vast lands protected by the Wilderness Act, the American land conservation movement has been centered on public law, federal policy, and the protection of what remains of the national public domain.

There is no reason that this should not continue to be important. However, in the twentieth century there emerged the phenomenon of land conservation by charitable organizations that had nothing to do with the government as such. These charities often adopted the mission of protecting particular parcels for specific purposes—for example, to preserve wildlife habitat or natural areas. Although not funded by the federal government, these tax-exempt organizations were substantially benefited by federal tax law incentives that encouraged taxpayers to make contributions to them. Over the years some enjoyed great success and developed large staffs and sophisticated management skills.

In the latter part of the twentieth century a significant new development has occurred. Small, community-based, "grass roots" charities have emerged whose goal is to protect the land with which they are most familiar—the land close to home. Responsive to local challenges, reliant on local resources, and shaped by regional idiosyncrasies, these charities have developed distinctively. The significance of that autumn afternoon in 1981 is that it was the first time a large number of these small land-saving organizations had gotten together and perceived themselves to be a significant collective part of the modern American conservation movement.

The premise of *Land-Saving Action* is that a great many resources are needed by this movement that now is less centered on national issues than on local efforts and is less concerned with public law than with private initiative. *Land-Saving Action* collects the most advanced learning on many of the subjects that are important to people and organizations who are trying to save land that, without their intervention, would be at risk. The collection is not an academic exercise but, it is hoped, a useful addition to the armory of both small and large organizations and the individuals who serve and support them. It joins a distinguished predecessor, published by Island Press under the auspices of the Montana Land Reliance and the Land Trust Exchange, entitled *Private Options: Tools and Concepts for Land Conservation*.

This book is a written symposium containing contributions from many experts (because it is felt that no one author can supply all that is needed), in effect a one-volume library of reference materials for the multitude of actors present in the land-saving arena. *Land-Saving Action* discusses tax issues, the administration of land-saving organizations, the management of protected land, and the choices open to landowners. It considers the legal issues that may be present in many protection arrangements. We hope the contents are understandable to nonlawyers as well as to legally trained advisors.

Land-Saving Action will succeed only if it is useful to landowners, organizations, and the advisors who help them—naturalists, appraisers, lawyers, financial advisors, among others. It is not an end in itself. It is only one more *means* to the end of stewardship. The book will not serve its purpose unless the ideas and information in it are put to good use. Thinking back to that autumn afternoon in Cambridge, we have no doubt that they will be.

RUSSELL L. BRENNEMAN
SARAH M. BATES

Notes

1. An account of this seminal meeting will be found in *Proceedings, 1981 National Consultation, Local Land Conservation Organizations*, Allan Spader, ed., Bar Harbor, Maine: Land Trust Exchange.

2. Turner, Frederick Jackson, *The Frontier in American History* (H. Holt and Co.: New York, 1920), p. 211, quoting a Professor Boutmy.

Acknowledgments

Land-Saving Action was made possible by grants from the Conservation and Research Foundation and the Richard King Mellon Foundation. In particular, we wish to thank Dr. Richard H. Goodwin, president of the Conservation and Research Foundation, for his unflagging enthusiasm and enterprise in seeing this volume to publication. We wish also to thank the Conservation Law Foundation of New England for its administrative assistance and Island Press for its dedication to the literature of land conservation. To the contributing authors, whose book this truly is, and to our many unnamed colleagues, we can only express our gratitude for this opportunity at collaboration. Mistakes are solely ours; credit for this endeavor goes to those for whom stewardship has been the only practical response to questions of land use.

LAND-SAVING ACTION

PART I
CASE STUDIES

As the Big Blackfoot River winds through western Montana, it becomes a part of many worlds: that of the ranchers who own a great portion of its banks; that of the timber companies who also control access to much of the river; that of the boaters and fishermen who seek out its channel for recreation; that of the local, state, and federal agencies involved in land-use management; and that of private conservation organizations seeking to protect key natural resources. Unlike the river system, these different interests once did not exist in harmony with one another; indeed, by the mid-seventies, they seemed primed for collision. Hank Goetz tells the story of the Blackfoot's evolution into a coherently managed resource where private and public uses have been accommodated and the river protected. The story is one of private involvement in land saving, and the results show how dedicated individuals can design creative transactions and produce a cooperative management enterprise.

Frightened by the prospect of losing control over its character and resources, a small community in northern California decided to tackle the state's coastal management program. Trinidad's vision of stewardship through a local land trust eventually persuaded state legislators, and the Humboldt North Coast Land Trust was born. Steele Wotkyns describes the power of this notion and shows how influential a tool the local land trust can be in managing natural areas in a manner that accommodates the public need for conservation and that satisfies the desire for local responsibility for the community's resources.

On the East Coast, Lincoln, Massachusetts, has long preserved the rural assets of its historic com-munity through private efforts. The Codman estate transactions, described by Robert Lemire, illustrate a diverse and complex series of arrangements that protect a 200-acre parcel. The disposition of this property, the uses to which it was put, the various financial agreements, and the role of public and private agencies indicate the sophistication of private land saving and the somewhat astonishing number of tools at its disposal.

Hundreds of thousands of dollars and hours of labor are generated by the land-saving community for conservation; even so, individuals working to save a particular area are often unaware of the successes of their colleagues. These stories illustrate the diversity of efforts made by the private sector to protect treasured natural resources and the remarkable degree of success achieved through the tenacity and ingenuity of private citizens. Their relevance is not so much in expounding specific techniques; rather, it is in demonstrating the spirit of private land saving and in banishing the isolation felt by many conservationists. Recounting what others have attempted and accomplished is the greatest encouragement we can offer to those who work to safeguard the places dear to them and their communities.

Simple or complicated, embattled or harmonious, the circumstances of private land saving run the gamut of political, social, and economic conditions; but the compelling motivation to save valued land is central to every example of private action. The force of this purpose creates new solutions over and over again across the country. The following stories show the paths of three such endeavors; equally important, however, are the unsung successes that occur daily.

A Cooperative Approach to River Management: The Blackfoot Experience

Hank Goetz

As leisure time and disposable income increase, more and more people are discovering the satisfactions and challenges of outdoor activities, including those associated with rivers. This expanding demand, in conjunction with developments limiting public use of many streams, has placed increasing pressure on remaining free-flowing waterways. Many rivers, although the water per se is public, flow through private land; thus the public must cross private land to gain access to the water, leading to inevitable conflict with landowners.

A case in point is the Big Blackfoot River in western Montana, where recreationists and landowners were, at least until a few years ago, on a collision course. At that time a number of people recognized the impending crisis and took steps to preserve the thirty-mile recreational heart of the river for public use. In a spirit of compromise, federal, state, and county agencies worked cooperatively with corporate timberland owners, ranchers, and rural property owners to develop a plan that would protect the natural, scenic, and recreational integrity of the Blackfoot River corridor. The plan emphasizes local management, voluntary landowner participation, and self-imposed restrictions on ecologically incompatible uses and development. At the same time the landowners retain all the essential rights to pursue both present and future agricultural and forestry activities. After eight years of successful implementation, this approach on the Blackfoot River appears to be a viable alternative to a more formal program, such as Wild and Scenic Rivers designation.

History of Recreational Use on the Blackfoot

Historically the thirty-mile reach of the Blackfoot River in question was open for recreational use, even though 90 percent of its banks were in private ownership. Many people, in fact, considered the land to be public ground. The Anaconda Company, a predecessor of Champion Timberlands, allowed unrestricted access to the river. In addition the company leased river frontage to the Blackfoot Valley Garden Club, which maintained a locally popular camping area in the lower end of the corridor. People could also gain access to the river through private ranch property; the ranchers traditionally used the river frontage very little for agricultural purposes. The relatively few overnight campers and fishermen, many of whom knew the ranchers personally, had little impact on the resources. The nature and amount of recreational use were such that they did not interfere with agricultural and forestry activities or cause undue concern among the landowners.

However, in the late 1960s and early 1970s the situation changed in the Blackfoot Valley. The number of recreationists increased dramatically, as did the range and scope of their river activities. The rapid increase in recreational use coincided with the accelerated growth rate in both the City and County of Missoula and with the boom in rural recreational land sales. People were buying small acreages in the country, including choice waterfront property; these soon were posted with No Trespassing signs. As a result, more people shifted their recreational activities to large timber-company holdings and the larger ranches, since these property owners either permitted unlimited access or were unable to effectively channel or prohibit public use, except in isolated circumstances.

In addition to experiencing increased numbers of people, the landowners perceived an attitude change among the river users. People no longer stopped and asked permission for river access. Some (those most easily remembered by the landowner) implied that it was their inherent right to use private land for recreational purposes, particularly for access to a public resource such as the river.[1]

3

The pattern of use on the river also began to change. Whereas fishing with occasional overnight stays had previously been the most popular activity, intensified camping and floating were becoming more popular. The availability of pickup-camper and trailer units made riverside camping more pleasant than the "rural ghetto" conditions prevalent in many public campgrounds. With intensified overnight use, the now-familiar litany of landowner complaints increased: litter, human waste, gates blocked, shooting, and vandalism. To compound the problem for the private landowner, river floaters, ranging from the whitewater kayak enthusiast to the rubber rafter—with or without the cooler of beer—discovered the Blackfoot. The tubers and swimmers continued to use the lazy stretches of calm water for their leisurely sport. Floaters required access to the river for put-in and take-out; and as it happened, the most convenient and popular places for those were located on private land. In addition the kayakers would often shoot the same rapids time after time, and they preferred a riverbank free of obstructions for moving their crafts back upstream.

In short, the number of people seeking access to the river was increasing rapidly, and more and more users were not familiar with the landowners and did not seek permission to cross private land. Plus there were the militant few who believed they had the God-given right to do anything they pleased anywhere. The floaters, whose numbers appeared to grow in geometric progression, needed good vehicle access points at convenient locations along the river. The ranchers and other private landowners were faced with a definite problem: Should they throw their land wide open? Lock everything up? Lease? Sell?

Alternative Solutions to the Problem

Over the course of two to three years, many alternatives for responding to increased recreational pressure were considered—and ultimately rejected—by the landowners. On the one hand, landowners who allowed relatively unrestricted public access found that they could not deal effectively with the growing numbers of people; just enough individuals took unfair advantage to make this solution unfeasible. On the other hand, landowners who erected fences, bought a gross of No Trespassing signs, and denied public access to the river discovered this option was really not appealing. The landowners had to enforce the restrictions, which led to potentially serious confrontations and extreme frustration. At minimum, patrolling was a time-consuming and unpleasant task. Then, too, many of the ranchers felt that eventually the public would gain access through private land to the river, quite possibly by legislative dictate. Naturally the residents were hesitant to take any action that would hasten forced access through their property.

The landowners also discussed less extreme solutions to the problem. One alternative was to classify the river under the federal Wild and Scenic Rivers Act (the Blackfoot was

on the original list of fifty-five study rivers) or to incorporate the river into a state system. (The latter assumed, of course, that Montana would soon have the necessary enabling legislation.) The landowners without exception rejected this approach. First of all, they did not want to relinquish managerial control of their land. Second, no federal agency had substantial land holdings in the river corridor. Third, they felt very strongly that they could continue to manage the land as well as a federal or state agency. Last, the local residents were hesitant to adopt any alternatives that might significantly increase recreational use, and they sensed that formal designation would be tantamount to hanging neon Welcome signs. For many of these same reasons the ranchers did not want to enter into sale or long-term lease agreements with either a federal or state agency.

Another possible middle-of-the-road approach would have been to lease the river frontage to a private club or fishing organization. The designated group would then have exclusive use of and patrol responsibility for the area. However, the landowners felt that this would not only run counter to the tradition of public use of the area, but also would not be economically worth the hassle.

The Landowners' Solution

It soon became apparent that the traditional approaches to management of public use on private land were not suitable in this situation and that a somewhat new and experimental tack would have to be taken.

As potential solutions to the problem were considered and rejected, a set of common goals and objectives gradually emerged from the diverse group of landowners. Of paramount importance was the landowners' desire to retain their agricultural way of life and to maintain the natural state of the river. As a group they did not want to be forced by escalating land values and accompanying taxes into selling their land for development purposes. Concurrently, the landowners wished to preserve the tradition of reasonable public use of private land. With a sense of enlightened self-interest, they perceived that if the private sector voluntarily provided recreation access to the river, the potential of imposed public access through governmental action would be blunted.

The ranchers and corporations thought it essential to retain their ownership rights and to make final decisions regarding the type, amount, location, and duration of public use on their property. However, they also felt that if they voluntarily allowed recreational use of their land, they should not have to bear the additional cost of serving as policemen and garbagemen for the public. Rather, a governmental agency or agencies should pay the costs of management.

The Formation of a Local Planning Group
These common objectives surfaced in 1975 when a task

force of interested landowners and representatives of public agencies and private organizations slowly evolved. Staff members from the University of Montana School of Forestry had been discussing use problems with Land Lindbergh of the Lindbergh Cattle Company and Bill Potter of the E-L Ranch. The Nature Conservancy, a national conservation organization, had shown interest in obtaining conservation easements to protect the natural and scenic qualities of the Blackfoot River. The Montana Department of Fish, Wildlife and Parks had been negotiating for fishing access points along this river with Champion Timberlands. Missoula County was in the process of developing a county-wide recreation plan. The efforts of all these parties were interrelated, but no single individual or agency had the resources to develop a plan that would encompass thirty miles of river frontage and involve some fourteen landowners and government agencies. Thus, assistance was solicited from the regional office of the Bureau of Outdoor Recreation in Denver, which assigned a representative to coordinate the work of the various parties and to assist in developing a management plan for the river.

With the invaluable aid of the BOR representative, a year of intensive planning began at the local level. Riparian landowners and representatives of state and county agencies met in small groups and in large gatherings, in formal sessions and in the hayfield, to develop a workable solution to the problem. After numerous revisions, a working-draft document emerged that would provide the framework for both the long-range protection of the river resource and the coordinated management of public use on both public and private lands within the corridor.

Conservation Easements

The landowners decided to use conservation easements as the tool to afford long-term protection of the river. Basically, a conservation easement is a legally binding document in which the landowner, either through gift or sale, grants certain ownership rights in his property to another.[2] Under the conservation easement concept the "landowner retains all the incidents of ownership not transferred by the easement. He may use, sell, lease, or otherwise convey the land, subject of course to the express terms and conditions of the easement."[3]

In this instance the landowner would donate those property rights along the river that could significantly impair the natural, scenic, or aesthetic quality of the resource, for example, the right to subdivide, to clearcut timber, to dredge, or to establish feedlots. However, the landowner would keep all other agricultural and forestry rights, such as the option to selectively harvest timber, to graze livestock, to cultivate crops, to irrigate, and so on. The conservation easement technique offers several advantages to the property owner. An important one is that ranch property cannot be taxed on subdivision potential because the rancher no longer owns the right to subdivide. Of course,

the rancher is still subject to taxation on the rights that he retains, such as agriculture.

In 1977 The Nature Conservancy designated a pilot area of approximately ten riverfront miles involving five different landowners to initiate this phase of the plan. An escrow concept, developed by Robert Knight, a local attorney representing The Nature Conservancy, is being employed in the project. Landowners agree individually to the specific terms of the conservation easement as it pertains to their property, and the document is put into escrow. If one so chooses, any of the five parties within the pilot area may inspect the documents signed by the other landowners to ensure that suitable flank protection will be afforded his property. At present, two landowners have already donated easements. The remaining private landowners have placed their documents in escrow, awaiting the acquisition of easement rights by the Montana Department of Fish, Wildlife and Parks from the Montana Department of State Lands. We expect this transfer to take place by the time this book appears in print, at which time the escrow agreement will close on the entire ten miles of the pilot area.

In the past few years, numerous conservation easements have also been donated by landowners outside the original pilot area. For example, just downstream, an easement on 450 acres has recently been donated to The Nature Conservancy, and the rights on an additional 300 acres are pending.

Management of Recreational Use

To manage recreational use within the river corridor, the landowners chose points where the public could gain access to the river. In addition, between the parking areas a public travel zone was established along each riverbank—temporarily defined as fifty feet above the high-river mark—where people could walk to fish, picnic, or carry river craft. Three of the fifteen access points in the corridor were designated as overnight campgrounds, while day-use activities only were permitted in the remaining areas.

The rules and regulations adopted for the corridor were kept simple. The users were asked to park only in designated areas, to pack out litter and garbage, to build campfires only in the overnight areas, and not to shoot along the river. Each property owner determined the location of access points and the permitted activities on his individual ownership. In general, the landowners determined that day-use activities such as fishing, floating, and picnicking would be compatible with private land, whereas overnight camping and firebuilding should be confined to public lands. The Montana Department of Fish, Wildlife and Parks and the Missoula county commissioners provided funds (which were administered by the School of Forestry) to employ a river researcher-manager. This individual not only made a formal study of the existing recreational use in the river corridor, but also directed the public to parking areas and ensured compliance with the plan.

Implementation of the Recreational Management Plan

The recreation management portion of the plan was implemented in the summer of 1976 under the auspices of the Blackfoot River Recreation Management Advisory Council. The council, composed of riparian landowners and public land managers, was formed by the Missoula Board of County Commissioners, which accepted final responsibility for enacting the plan. Although we experienced some problems in the initial weeks of the project, due in part to the ad hoc administrative structure of the program, this approach to public use of private land proved generally successful.

Through a program of signing, distributing printed brochures, and personal contact, the river manager obtained public compliance with the plan. Despite restrictions, most recreationists felt that the plan was a worthwhile step in resolving user-landowner conflicts. The public especially appreciated the fact that by using the signed parking areas and staying along the river they did not have to worry about trespass or confrontation with an irate landowner. The plan was revised in 1977 to better meet the needs of the recreationists, who desired some fence relocation and the addition of specially designated floater campgrounds.

The council considered the first two years as a trial period, emphasizing public information and cooperative compliance, with a minimum of site development and formal organizational structure. In 1978 the Montana Department of Fish, Wildlife and Parks assumed managerial responsibility for the project under a self-renewing annual agreement with the individual landowners. A full-time river warden has been assigned to the project during the summer season, with periodic patrolling during the remainder of the year.

The private landowners have been satisfied with the plan. They have been able to retain their ownership rights yet maintain the tradition of public access to the river. Furthermore, they do not have to pick up litter or patrol their property. Over the past eight years, thousands of visitors have used this thirty-mile reach of river without serious conflict between landowners and the public.

Applicability of This Approach to Other Rivers

Is this cooperative method of recreational management applicable to other river systems with large proportions of private riparian ownership? Or, for that matter, would it be appropriate to other natural resource situations? The answer is a definite yes. Although the specific problem and the resolution may have been unique to this portion of the Blackfoot River, the general approach should be applicable elsewhere. A number of factors and circumstances, however, can make this management technique more suitable.

First of all, timing is very important. In the case of the Blackfoot, there were sufficient public use and a significant threat of incompatible river development to alert the residents, land managers, and public agencies to the seriousness of the problem. The impetus for action was there. On the other hand, the problems had not yet reached the stage where the involved parties were so overwhelmed and frustrated that they considered the situation hopeless. The stage of problem development is critical because locally initiated planning, implemented by a diverse cross section of small landowners, large corporations, and public bodies, takes a long time—much longer than if plans are developed by "professionals," with minimal input from local property owners. Although cooperative on-the-ground planning unquestionably has the best chance of successful implementation, time is a necessity. In addition, the resources must be considered by everyone involved to be of such high value that the problem is worth resolving. Often time is required for individuals to overcome past disagreements with others, to truly listen to one another, and to simply trust one another.

The attitude of landowners toward the resource is a second important ingredient of cooperative management. Obviously, if the private landowners viewed their river-front property as strictly an economic commodity to be auctioned to the highest bidder, a voluntary approach would not be suitable. Two miles of river frontage developed into fifty-foot lots may have rendered the Blackfoot plan inoperative. Also, most landowners along the Blackfoot had reached the conclusion that public access across private land to the river was inevitable. Certainly, then, a locally conceived plan would be preferable to one developed by administrators in Missoula, Helena, Denver, or Washington, D.C. The landowners realized that for self-protection and decision-making authority they would have to be willing to commit the necessary time to the project. One advantage of this management approach is that the landowner may choose his level of commitment, and thus the degree to which his personal viewpoints are reflected in the final plan.

The third major component of local management is the attitude of public agencies and public officials. Most important, and this point cannot be overemphasized, the public agencies must treat the private landowners as true partners in the planning process. Partnership requires that resource agency personnel, on occasion, will have to suppress not only their personal professional egos, but also the professional egos of the agencies they represent. This approach may even require implementation of a solution that professionals feel will not work; but as true partners, agencies may be required to participate in failure as well as success.

In the Blackfoot project we were fortunate that key public officials and the public agencies—in this instance, the Missoula county commissioners and the Montana Department of Fish, Wildlife and Parks—were willing to invest public money in a locally directed program without extensive day-to-day supervision of the funds or establishment of strict guidelines dictating exactly when, where, and how the money was to be spent. This is not to advocate that we should throw blank checks at problems, but to suggest that public bodies, after examining the philosophy of a project, should be willing to contribute necessary seed money and trust the people on the ground to use it for the maximum good. In addition, a public agency such as the now-disbanded Bureau of Outdoor Recreation should be available to devote the necessary time and technical assistance to aid in the planning process. The agency personnel must have the capacity to tolerate the back-tracking and stutter-step planning often characteristic of grassroots effort. It is also important that this assistance be offered without a hard-sell approach, or even the appearance of a hard-sell manner.

The last, and perhaps most important, ingredient in the planning method is the recreational user. The recreationist must also be willing to compromise and accept restrictions, particularly for the privilege of using private land. In development of the Blackfoot plan the public was cooperative, and many people took the opportunity to meet in working sessions with the landowners and discuss mutual goals in a frank, yet courteous, manner. Some committed individuals even assumed the responsibility of personally informing other members of the public about the plan and assisted in clean-up campaigns and site-development projects. Although it was not necessary in our case, the public may also be required through a recreation license or user fee to actually contribute funding for a locally initiated project. To achieve ultimate success, a cooperative plan must elicit a voluntary positive response from the user groups.

Conclusion

In conclusion, although this cooperative, ad hoc approach is not a panacea for river management problems, there are instances where circumstances make it a viable alternative to more formal methods. Many private landowners, both as individuals and as corporations, are ready and willing to allow responsible public use of private land, provided they can receive assistance from the public agencies as equals in the stewardship of the resource. With a spirit of cooperation and commitment among private landowners, public agencies, and responsible recreationists, many resource problems can be resolved where they should be: on the ground at the local level.

Notes

1. Although the Blackfoot River has never been declared a navigable stream, under current interpretation of the law it appears to meet all the necessary criteria.

2. Montana's Open-Space Land and Voluntary Conservation Easement Act specifies that holders of conservation easements must be either qualified private organizations or public bodies.

3. *Conservation Easements in Montana*, Montana Department of Fish, Wildlife and Parks and the Bureau of Outdoor Recreation, Mid-Continent Region, Denver, Colo.

Trinidad and the Humboldt North Coast Land Trust: A Solution for Land-Use Conflict

Steele Wotkyns

Trinidad

Countering the decades-long trend that has tended to centralize and prescribe land-use planning, the establishment of the Humboldt North Coast Land Trust (HNCLT) is an early and dramatic example of the effectiveness of local volunteer responsiveness to land-use issues. This endows Trinidad's story with a special interest. Local volunteer land trusts occupy a "vacant niche" between private and local community interests and the more generalized public interest of large-scale government agencies. HNCLT's success in reducing the levels of conflict between these approaches heralds a renaissance of local responsibility. The side effects are as dramatic as the original impulse. Trinidad has rediscovered itself. This is the vital and sufficient reward the volunteers have worked so hard to achieve.

Trinidad is the smallest and second-oldest incorporated city in California. It is a semirural community on the fringes of Eureka. Located 300 miles north of San Francisco, Eureka is the only moderately large population center on the north coast. For most people who do not know the state, the vast north coast is a hidden and unknown land. Roads, rail, and air services are minimal. Humboldt County is a haven for adventurous travelers and exurbanites. It is home to a significant and remarkably stable native-born population whose ancestors came for gold and trees. Trinidad has been a minor port for the region's products in conjunction with Humboldt Bay and is an important local fishing center. It retains in large measure the virtues and vices of a traditional, independent, and self-sufficient small American town.

The city's character is inseparable from its physical environment. The several miles of coast which it and its hinterland command are incomparably beautiful. Rare on the western coasts of the Americas, the presqu'isle of Trinidad Head offers protection in the summer from the prevailing northwest winds. It was here in the eighteenth century that Spanish explorers sought refuge, named the town for the Feast of the Trinity, and gave the first accounts of the native American population, the Tsurai of Yurok stock. The prehistoric village site is within the city limits, and the descendants of its inhabitants are among our influential citizens. Huge, rocky sea-stacks dot the ocean, while the coast consists of a variety of pocket beaches nestled under the brooding palisades which are so characteristic of the California coast. The steep coastal mountain range rises behind, still covered in part with the redwood forest for which our region is famous.

One-third of the incorporated land within the city limits is a long-established state park. Within ten minutes of the city are two flanking state parks of generous proportions. Other parks, including the new Redwood National Park, are less than an hour's drive from the town. Nearly all of the other privately owned beaches and coves within the city limits and the hinterland have always been available to the public by a network of informal trails leading from the nearest coastal road. Development along the coast is relatively unobtrusive. Moderate private surveillance in the immediate past has managed to preserve the near-pristine quality of the coastal experience for visitors and the local population. In the dry summers there are morning fogs and brilliant afternoon sunshine; in the winter it rains and rains. A price for paradise!

Crab and salmon are the principal fisheries, while the coast is alive with birds and a rich tidal life. Sea lions and pods of harbor seals cover the offshore rocks within sight and sound of the city. Fishing boats anchored in the lee of the Head, with a fringe of white houses on the palisades above, rival the beauty of the most famous fishing villages of the Mediterranean coast.

California's Coastal Act of 1976

As a result of the Coastal Act of 1976, our community was suddenly overwhelmed by rigid demands for coastal preservation, conservation, and planning. We were also threatened with state purchases within the city limits and the city's adjoining hinterland. Had these purchases been made, considering the naturally limited land-base of the town, the "critical mass" necessary for a successful community might have disappeared.

You can imagine the consternation of a community of 300 souls suddenly beset by the two-pronged descent of powerful and remote state agencies: one, the California Coastal Commission, demanding rigid adherence to an elaborate and inflexible planning standard geared to the infrastructure of a large city; the other, the State Department of Parks and Recreation, planning to remove yet another third of the city's land by purchase. Our part-time city clerk and then-unsophisticated city council were overwhelmed. Threatened landowners, both within the city and nearby, faced the situation with a mixture of disbelief, resignation, and mounting anger.

Although the town and state eventually squared off, it all began fairly low key while the commission and the city council reviewed their respective parts in the process. Citizens were surveyed concerning their desires for the community. To all those participating, it seemed hopeful when the technical part of producing the planning document, known in California as the Local Coastal Program (general plan), began. Subsequently, however, the desultory public hearings, which probably satisfied the letter of the law, failed entirely to reach people in the community or to reflect their expressed desires. The commission's regulations clouded the issues, and neither the commission's regional and state staff nor the citizens could predict their ultimate effect on the social fabric of the community.

Finally, a document, foreign in many ways to the expressed desires of the citizens, was produced, and the certification hearings were upon us. Some of us began to suspect that the return of reasonable local jurisdiction, upon certification, was a chimera. However, exhausted and intimidated by endless wrangling with the commission's staffs, the planning consultant and city officials urged the adoption of the document. Fortunately, by vigorous citizen action, certification was delayed. Then the ax fell!

Thirty-three coastal landowners received notification from a subagency of the California State Department of Parks and Recreation that their lands were being considered for purchase by act of eminent domain in order to establish yet another park in our town and immediate vicinity. The shock to the landowners was paralleled by the shock registered in the community at large. Already surrounded and partly invaded by public parks, we were able to see immediately that the future economic and social structure of our community would be made subservient to the whims of a distant impersonal bureaucracy.

The rush to restudy the largely imposed plan was on. Threatened landowners created an informal association, The Concerned Citizens of Trinidad. At first, we felt at sea, without voice, without connections, and without access, confronted by a remote, unresponsive, and unaccountable bureaucracy. There appeared to be an unimpeachable power in the state capitol holding all the cards. Expensive consultation with leading attorneys in San Francisco suggested that we hold out for a maximum purchase price by forcing the state to go through complex condemnation procedures. Our unified stand, forcing the state to consider this cumbersome process, did buy our association some time. However, we soon recognized that legal proceedings offered no real solution. Our limited collective means precluded the endless costs of legal services that could gain for us only a maximum invasion of the public purse. As taxpayers and landowners this was not an attractive option. Moreover, the health of the community in which we had chosen to live would still have remained seriously threatened.

Political action, then, appeared the only recourse, even though the odds seemed insuperable. An aroused citizenry sharply questioned the proposed general plan. We called to the attention of the city council the implications of admitting the validity of further public purchase in our community. Others sought and documented wide public support through petition opposing unnecessary and costly state purchase of local land. Still others arranged for area-wide publicity, including television talk shows and newspaper articles, some as far away as San Francisco. Throughout we concentrated on reaching real decision-makers, avoiding a uniformly unresponsive bureaucracy.

The controversy between the town and state embodied a dilemma. On the one hand, a statewide public consensus (Proposition 20, which created the Coastal Commission by referendum) had expressed a new interpretation of private property rights in places of high resource value; while, on the other hand, it could unequivocally be shown that unlimited public use of those resources results in degradation of them along with a questionable invasion of private and community interests. Thus, under certain circumstances, there is a kind of built-in defeat in the very objectives of the Coastal Act of 1976. So we began an intensive search for a creative accommodation, for an alternative to the too-rigid strictures of regulation, an alternative that would satisfy the intent of the law while permitting the diversity of response needed to accommodate specific circumstances.

We also began to realize that the "doctrinaire" conservation community had missed something vital. Since the "conservation ethic" is a human idea, it cannot be isolated from other human responses to the environment, so it cannot be considered separately from other social and economic values that make up a community. Real conservation depends on people living with and in the environment who feel a keen personal responsibility for valuable natural resources. This caring level of stewardship is rarely achieved by the faceless mechanisms of a centralized government agency.

The question before us was refined: What kind of an alternative would balance the abstract public welfare against the specific character of our environment and local community? Whatever it was, it had to be attractive to private interests and reasonably palatable to more conservative private sensibilities as well.

As we worked to develop such an alternative, it became clear that legislative action would be required if we were to succeed. A reawakened legislature, led by our own assemblyman and now Senator Barry Keene, and a group of Trinidad citizens began searching for a specific alternative proposal. In the course of this search, a nonprofit corporation, The Trust for Public Land (TPL), offered a suggestion. "Why not," asked TPL as ombudsman, "set up a private, local nonprofit land trust that will let the people decide and do voluntarily what has proved very difficult in the heavy hands of public agencies?"

Humboldt North Coast Land Trust

Our legislators liked the idea of a local land trust, and so did we. Events moved rapidly. Senator Keene devised a special bill that withdrew appropriations from the Department of Parks and Recreation for the contended purchases, recognized the newly formed Humboldt North Coast Land Trust as an "appropriate entity" to serve the public interest, and granted it $100,000 as seed money for the partial purchase of lands where owners had been adversely affected by coastal regulation. The proposed bill then attracted wide support in the California assembly and senate, chiefly for its potential merit in resolving growing conflicts in the dangerously heated climate of coastal regulation.

Now that our land trust was recognized and granted seed funds by the legislature, we needed a bridge for cooperation between our local trust and state agencies. Happily, the more flexible California Coastal Conservancy has become this bridge. Meanwhile Trinidad, chosen as a pilot program under the Coastal Act, became the first trust to have a certified coastal plan under the coastal law of 1976.

Our trust is young. Yet in the five years of its existence, we have been given land appraised at more than $2 million. These gifts include easements and below-market-value purchases. The fiscal as well as environmental benefits of this approach have been substantial. The original appropriation for purchase in our area was $1,200,000, representing only a minor portion of the proposed parks and recreation project. In contrast, the trust has used only the original seed funds granted to it by the state legislature. Even so, we have succeeded in dramatically increasing protected areas. For example, one below-market-value purchase tripled the effective size of an adjacent county park.

The trust has also been able to act independently of state funding. For instance, it was able to sell a one-plus-acre parcel of already developed land within an eighteen-acre habitat preserve. This transaction assured permanent protection of seventeen acres of open space and precluded further potentially damaging development. The one-acre sale carried with it restrictive conditions that built in care and surveillance of the land. The increased value of the one-acre parcel compensates the county tax base, which is chronically in need. A moderate profit realized by the trust will finance other critical purchases and help maintain the trust's other activities. In coming years, other promised gifts, purchases, and granted easements will exceed in public benefit and cost much less than the original plans of the California State Department of Parks and Recreation.

The trust also has exciting plans in cooperation with the City of Trinidad and the County of Humboldt for the establishment and management of trails to beaches, the proposed establishment of a recycling septic tank management district, and various aspects of Trinidad's harbor development. All of this is being accomplished with relatively little pain in an improved atmosphere of cooperation, as opposed to confrontation—all in a way that strengthens the social fabric of the community rather than threatening its ultimate decline.

The decentralizing thrust of the volunteer land trust movement is reflected in HNCLT's belief that long-range conservation is best served by a diversity of ownership and management patterns. An early alert given the trustees informed them of the imminent transfer of Trinidad Head out of federal ownership. This triggered a quiet but intense campaign by the trust at federal, state, and local levels that resulted, in the winter of 1982/83, in an astonishingly rapid transfer of the Head to the ownership of the City of Trinidad. The city, the trust, and the Tsurai Ancestral Society will share in the management of this unique coastal feature.

HNCLT, like other local land trusts, has the enormous advantage of promoting the enlightened self-interest of our patrons in providing for genuine public needs. They, in turn, protect their residual rights after suitable gifts are made in the public interest, realize tax and estate-planning advantages, and, above all, have the ultimate satisfaction of real service to the community. That negotiations between the trust and its patrons can remain low keyed and unpressured is a great advantage in obtaining grants of easements or gifts of land from the more conservative members of the community who often control critical lands.

The trust is also able to be flexible and responsive to owners' attitudes and special circumstances. In one case, it was able to accept land that had been repeatedly offered to the state and repeatedly refused, ostensibly for budget reasons; in other cases because the owners were adamantly opposed to agency ownership.

Aside from the financial advantages that are often possible for land trust patrons, negotiations are conducted with friends and neighbors so emotional attachments to land are released gently. Patrons retain not only the sense of directing the destiny of their land, but also of a very real participation in the formulation of policy and active involvement in the continued management of their now-protected lands. In short, the implicit demand to continue caring promotes the best kind of social responsibility and community solidarity.

For example, HNCLT never makes an "acquisition." Instead, it receives a gift from a generous patron in circumstances where the gift is of benefit to the patron, the community, the public, and is at the same time a reasonable option for trust management. If any one of these ingredients is missing—no deal. HNCLT does not accept or promote a new accessway, open space easement, or habitat reserve unless there is a clear advantage both to its patron and to the "public." Sharing the resource builds in turn a reciprocal responsibility among the trust, its patron, and the community. Most important, HNCLT does not make prescriptive plans; instead, it is on the lookout to identify step by step, as the situation changes, ways to protect and preserve management options for both its patrons and the community at large.

Aside from its concrete objective to protect and make available coastal resources, the trust is having considerable success in areas of social influence not contemplated on its formation. Points of view and political orientations that were polarized by imposed regulation and the threat of acquisition have been resolved by local community action and organization, making possible the cooperative rapprochement between distant state agencies and local individuals.

Meanwhile, there have been a number of other bills passed by the state legislature that have strengthened the position of private and local nonprofit land trusts. One of these provisions has been to extend to trusts limited public liability for lands that they manage in the public interest. Sister land trusts are springing up all over the state. The diversity of these volunteer associations and their goals differ with the resources of their localities. As the volunteer trust network grows, there is both a greater sense of responsibility and a growing power to shape our own destinies. Conservation of our natural resources in a fashion appropriate to the local community and compatible with the needs of society as a whole follows.

In spite of all the organizational problems, political hurdles, and the sounds of distant thunder, what have we accomplished? As of 1983, HNCLT has received gifts and services in kind, land, conservation easements, and money valued at $2 million or more. But money is just a convenient way to count the accomplishments and means nothing in particular of itself. The real accomplishment is that we have learned how much we can do if we just begin to accept, and even demand, responsibility for that share of our affairs *that we can do better for ourselves.*

The Codman Estate Transactions, Lincoln, Massachusetts

Robert A. Lemire

The following is a brief history of a community's successful efforts to save what needed to be saved of a major estate when the last of a long line of family owners passed away in 1967. More than that, it is the story of how appropriate parts of the property were planned to meet community development needs. It is a study of close cooperation among the trustees of the Codman estate, community officials, and representatives of a nonprofit land trust, all of whom recognized the need to develop and implement practical plans that would allow the trustees to fulfill their responsibility for realizing full dollar value for 200 acres of prime land located in the center of Lincoln while striving to respond to a broad range of community interests.

In 1967 the Codman property was composed of a well-maintained Federal period mansion attributed in part to Bullfinch, servants' quarters, a carriage house, and a farmhouse near a cluster of three barns, all situated on 240 acres of beautiful Lincoln land. Included near the dwellings were handsomely landscaped pastures and the remains of a formal garden. The balance was made up of flat, rolling farm fields bordered by old stone walls and wooded hillsides with frontage along charming country roads.

When assembled in the early 1700s by Charles Chambers as a country estate, the property totaled 700 acres. By 1967 most of the larger portion had long since been sold and subsequently given to the Massachusetts Audubon Society, which now uses some of the land as its headquarters, the rest as a wildlife sanctuary and educational farm.

Long before the demise of Dorothy Codman, last of the Chambers-Russell-Codman family line, the future of the property loomed large in the minds of town officials and other members of the Lincoln community. Dorothy's affection for Lincoln and its residents was well known, and rumors abounded as to how she would leave her property. She was a quiet, private person, however, and it was not until the publishing of her will that her way of expressing this affection became known. It was then that the Lincoln community learned that she had left her mansion with two accessory buildings on 15 acres along with a modest endowment to the Society for the Preservation of New England Antiquities. An abutting wooded parcel of 25 acres was given to the Lincoln Land Conservation Trust. The balance, made up largely of open farm fields, including the farmhouse and cluster of barns, was left in trust to be sold with the proceeds to be invested and the income therefrom to be granted to the people of Lincoln. As generous and well received by the Lincoln community as the Dorothy Codman bequest was, the required disposition of the 200 acres posed serious land-use issues that needed careful community attention.

As described in my book *Creative Land Development: Bridge to the Future*, "Lincoln is a rural suburb located thirteen miles from Boston on its western fringe. Bordered by Lexington, Bedford, Concord, Sudbury, and Weston, Lincoln has a long history that predates the American Revolution. It was in Lincoln that Paul Revere was captured by the British as he rode to Concord to sound the alarm. A community of 5,200 people, Lincoln covers 9,500 acres and governs itself under a town meeting form of government with unpaid elected officials. Under this form of government all zoning and budgeting decisions are made by registered voters at annual and special town meetings."[1]

The use of land had also been a matter of broad community concern before the demise of Dorothy Codman. By 1967 the town had upgraded its residential zoning from 10,000 feet in 1929 to 40,000 feet in 1936, and then to 80,000 feet in 1955. There were cluster provisions and an apartment district. Through its conservation commission, the town had also embarked on a comprehensive program of defining its land of conservation interest, purchasing special properties with state and federal funding assistance and bonding much of the town's share to spread the cost over time. There was an active land conservation trust and a newly formed sister nonprofit trust empowered to undertake limited development as part of its efforts to protect open space. Known as the Rural Land Foundation, this latter organization was soon to be called upon to play a major role in shaping the future of 71 of the 200 acres of Codman property destined to be sold. Moreover, in 1965 Lincoln had held a town-wide conference to consider land to be saved and special development requirements, including affordable housing and commercial facilities. Sponsored by the League of Women Voters and led by Lincoln's hard-working and forward-looking planning board, this conference had produced an important consensus on land-use matters that gave town officials the confidence needed to make bold plans to shape the community's land-use destiny as major parcels were placed on the market.

It was in this context that the planning board responded to the news of the planned disposition of the 200 Codman acres by informing the Codman trustees of the town's wish to acquire, at fair market value, the entire 200 acres. Favoring the protection of the property through use, the planning board issued an invitation to architects and planners for suggestions to include some well-placed single-family houses, some moderate-income housing, and some conservation and recreation use.

The conservation commission responded to this notice and coincident news that the Commonwealth's Department of Natural Resources was about to lose $1 million in available federal funds for lack of a project to support by preparing plans to acquire 570 acres of land of conservation interest about to reach the market, including 122 acres of the Codman property, later found to be valued at $500,000. The overall package was valued at $1.8 million and was approved for purchase at the March 1969 annual town meeting. Federal and state funding totaled 75 percent, leaving the town with some $450,000 in debt obligations to pay off over a twelve-year period. At the time this amounted to roughly $50 per year for the average Lincoln household, a sum considered to be substantially less than the increased taxes that would have resulted from converting the 570 acres into 250 or more single-family houses. Nevertheless, this economy was not the principal reason for saving the 570 acres that had been designated as being of conservation interest and needing to be saved with the tools available at the time—public or private acquisition for conservation purposes.

Shortly after the so-called Mount Misery acquisition of 570 acres, the town voted to purchase 10 more Codman acres, including the farm cottage and cluster of three barns, for the appraised value of $150,000 as a next step in dealing with the Codman estate. This purchase was made on an unrestricted basis in order to convert the barns into a community recreational facility and to make the farmhouse available at low rent to town employees. Since this conversion was to benefit the people of Lincoln, it was

expected that its cost would be funded by the Codman trustees from income to be derived from the trust, then funded by the sale of the initial 122 acres.

It was not until the townspeople saw the initial conversion plans that provided for a swimming pool near the barns, which in turn were to be converted into meeting rooms, a small theatre, and the like, that the importance of the site as farm-related property was fully appreciated. Intense community debate produced a plan to restore the barns as working barns, convert four acres into 160 community gardens, encourage the founding of Codman Community Farms as a community-based organization to undertake a farm program for much of Lincoln's protected farmland—all as part of a general agricultural renaissance—and locate the needed swimming pool near the town's school facilities. To be sure, much of this was made possible through the funding support provided by the Codman trustees and a willingness of the town to appropriate funds against bonds to be repaid by grants to come from the Codman trust.

The remaining seventy-one Codman acres were located at the intersection of Lincoln's main road and the commuter rail line that runs to Boston. Across the road was a modest commercial center considered inadequate for Lincoln's growing commercial needs. Four of the seventy-one acres were zoned for commercial use, the remaining sixty-seven for residential use. These were made up of sixteen acres of wooded land fronting on Lincoln Road and fifty-one acres of rear land, including a beautiful, productive twenty-eight-acre farm field fully bordered by woods and twenty-six acres of wetlands. The Codman trustees decided to press this land on the market for $275,000 and thereby triggered one of Lincoln's most creative land-use responses.

By the time this happened, Lincoln's Rural Land Foundation was well on its way to successful completion of its first limited development project to secure open spaces. In 1966 it had been organized as a nonprofit trust in order to respond to the threat of overwhelming development of the Wheeler Farm. By finding thirty individuals willing to endorse notes of $10,000 each, it had acquired with bank cooperation a 109-acre farm with its two farmhouses, planned a limited development of ten additional houses configured to protect a historic colonial road, open fields, and land overlooking the Lincoln cemetery; then it extricated itself with a modest profit after deeding 54 acres to the Lincoln Land Conservation Trust. This group rose to the Codman challenge by soliciting new guarantees and purchasing the 71 Codman acres with the idea of holding them while town officials planned their best use. In short, they voluntarily served as a land bank while the town considered the possibility of creating a moderate-income housing development on some of the land and finding ways of rationalizing its commercial development. As long as progress was made toward a practical program that would allow the Rural Land Foundation to extricate itself from its purchase, it was willing to hold the land. It was understood that a breakdown of the planning process was to result in conventional treatment of the land, with the Rural Land Foundation doing its best to protect the dollar interest of its guarantors.

This urgency along with the consensus developed at the 1965 land-use conference resulted in the planning board's preparation of two new zoning options, one of which would permit dense housing linked to a package sewage treatment plant, provided rezoning received a two-thirds vote at an annual town meeting. This option made possible the creation of a nonprofit housing committee to work with state funding agencies, architects, the planning board, and others to bring forth a detailed housing plan. After much work and dedication, and a favorable town meeting, the result was Lincoln Woods: 125 units of low-income, moderate-income, and market housing located on 12.5 acres. Shortly thereafter, 55 acres, including the 28-acre farm field, were given to the town for conservation purposes. This left the Rural Land Foundation with the 4 acres of commercially zoned land.

Working closely with the planning board and the town's selectmen, the Rural Land Foundation developed a sense of the commercial facilities required by the town. It then interviewed potential developers and found one willing to address town needs and to work on a land rental, rather than purchase, basis. Working with the planning board, this developer prepared an acceptable plan that provided for a relocated post office, bank, supermarket, hardware store, and miscellaneous shops and offices. These were soon built and occupied. The Rural Land Foundation collects $9,000 in annual land rents and has the option of acquiring the buildings after they are depreciated. As a result of this arrangement, the town also has been able to develop a commuter parking lot and to improve the commuter train facilities so that trains no longer block Lincoln Road when stopped.

So it is that the Lincoln community was able to turn a potential land-use problem into a remarkable opportunity to save what needed to be saved of an important property while fostering what needed to be built there to meet long-term community needs. With the new and permanent ownership established for the Codman property's several elements, the community's attention is now directed to improving their use. The Friends of the Codman House are helping the Society for the Preservation of New England Antiquities make the mansion a living part of the community.

An ancillary group is raising funds to preserve the carriage house as a community facility linked to tourism, particularly as it relates to the Codman property. Two apartments created in one of the Codman buildings under Lincoln's accessory apartment by-law provide needed support for the Codman House and needed low-cost housing. All in all, 128 families live on carefully selected portions of the 240 Codman acres, which could so easily have been converted into 120 single-family houses that would have overwhelmed the property's historic legacy. In addition to providing an ongoing presence in the mansion, the apartment rentals help defray its maintenance and management costs. The protected farmland and woods are maintained by the town's conservation commission, which leases the farmland to local farmers while managing the balance for community passive recreation. Someday the town of Lincoln, as beneficiary of the Rural Land Foundation, will own the commercial center, which was developed with such great care to appropriate community scale and needs.

Looking back, the Codman case can be seen as one of close public sector/private sector cooperation. It demonstrates that a community is never without the power needed to shape its land-use future if it is willing to organize itself fully to anticipate and deal effectively with change and opportunities as they arise.

For a more complete account of the Codman case as it developed in its Lincoln context, readers may wish to refer to *Creative Land Development: Bridge to the Future*. For a detailed account of the Codman family and estate, readers are referred to "Old-Time New England," *The Bulletin of the Society for the Preservation of New England Antiquities*, Vol. LXXI, Serial No. 258, published in 1981. Details on the Rural Land Foundation and its Wheeler Farm Project were published as Case No. 1 by the New England Natural Resources Center in 1974 under the title "The Rural Land Foundation of Lincoln, Massachusetts: Partial Development Bootstraps Open Space Preservation," which was written by Kenneth W. Bergen, founder of the Rural Land Foundation. Details on Lincoln Woods are contained in a forty-four-page case study by that name published in 1979 by the Department of Urban Studies and Planning, Massachusetts Institute of Technology.

Note

1. Robert A. Lemire, *Creative Land Development: Bridge to the Future* (New York: Houghton Mifflin, 1979), 55.

PART II
LAND-SAVING ORGANIZATIONS

Much of the land preserved privately in this nation has gained its protected status through the intervention, at some stage of the negotiations, of land-saving organizations. These charitable entities range from small, voluntary, local land trusts to nationally active groups that have large staffs, budgets, and holdings. As diverse as land-saving organizations are, they share several key characteristics: their charitable status, their land management responsibilities, and their educational functions. Having a grasp of these common attributes is essential to improving the performance of land-saving organizations, both as vehicles for individuals to fulfill their land stewardship goals and as powerful, independent, and timely forces for land conservation.

The initial article in this section, "Portrait of Land Trusts," introduces the land trust community and provides answers to the who, what, where, and why so often asked when one speaks of voluntary associations to save land. The reaction to these answers is often one of surprise at the extent, success, and diversity of the land trust movement. Of importance to those with a general interest in the land trust as an agency of change, this article is of special concern to those newly embarked on the establishment of a land trust. As precarious a venture as the land trust may appear to be, the nationwide experience is one of achievement and stability under a wide range of circumstances.

The next two articles, "How To Form a Land Trust" and "Becoming and Remaining a Tax-Exempt Organization," deal with the corporate requirements of land-saving organizations. Often, with an intense focus on the business of land saving itself, organizations neglect to attend to their own need for administrative integrity. The first article discusses the various forms of land-saving organizations, the legal procedures governing the establishment of a land-saving organization, and internal administrative devices such as by-laws. The second article addresses the federal tax law as it relates to land-saving organizations. Under the Internal Revenue Code, a land-saving organization is entitled to tax-exempt status as a charitable organization if it meets certain criteria affecting both the substantive work of the organization, such as the type of gifts it accepts, and its procedural obligations. Familiarity with the relevant federal tax law will enable a land-saving organization to procure and keep the full benefits of its charitable status, a status that typically provides the financial incentives that make land saving possible.

Once a land-saving organization has attended to its corporate self, then it can fulfill its primary purposes: identifying and managing resources. While what should be saved and how and why and where are questions whose answers are so obvious to the initiated as to leave them too often unexamined, a land-saving organization cannot afford such a lack of self-scrutiny. The articles devoted to these issues cover the following topics: criteria for acquisition and management, subsequent land management, and the treatment of special resource lands.

In order for a land-saving organization to be able to articulate why it acquires certain tracts or interests and how it then manages them, it must first understand the need for such a statement of policies. That need is the subject of "Criteria for Acquisition and Management." In addition, articles concerning agricultural land protection, scenic areas preservation, and community and urban land trusts detail the criteria that can govern land saving in these specific instances. Although this selection describes only a few of the many varieties of land-saving organizations flourishing today, it is intended to give enough familiarity with particular issues to enable an organization with different purposes to articulate persuasively its goals and standards.

Once criteria are established and land or interests in land acquired, the actual task of management remains. The translation of documented management objectives into the actual condition of protected property requires a method of monitoring and evaluating land use. Three articles speak to this. The first, "How To Manage Land Acquired by the Trust," is a general overview of management priorities and techniques. The purpose of this article is to acquaint a land-saving organization with its management obligations so that it can attend to its holdings without incurring liabilities or jeopardizing its charitable status. The second, "Monitoring Protected Lands," discusses a monitoring system used by one private organization to make certain that its policies are in fact being fulfilled. The last, "Government Monitoring Program for Partial Interest Projects," gives the perspective of a government agency, which can be of assistance to private organizations faced with the management of easements and other restrictions on land use. This article places particular emphasis on the management of restricted forestland.

Special resource lands are the subject of the next two articles, the first on agricultural lands and the second on forestlands. These articles are included because while many land-saving organizations concentrate on natural areas of various sorts, an increasing number are concerned with economically productive land and must therefore deal with a series of issues outside traditional conservancy practices. Organizations involved in agricultural land preservation respond to a specific set of pressures on land that sustains food production. Consequently, they have had to develop protection devices that effectively counter the diversion of farmland to other uses but simultaneously allow it to remain in a productive, although not natural, condition. Forestland protection poses the similar challenge of meeting social, cultural, economic, and ecological concerns concurrently through a coherent program of land protection.

The last article in Part II, "Enabling Technical Assistance," describes how one organization fulfills its obligation to educate others in land saving. The motivation behind this program is to transfer the expertise of an existing organization to fledgling groups so that they themselves become independent and skilled forces for land preservation.

Portrait of Land Trusts

Terry Bremer

Introduction

The American land's diversity in nature is mirrored by the diversity of local land conservation organizations. Land trusts preserve land for food and shelter; land for wildlife, plants, and people; land for water quality, soil conservation, and water quantity; land to satisfy visual sensibilities and physical needs; land to learn from, to play on, and land to dream on—prairies, dunes, deserts and coastlines, marshes, rivers and floodplains—land for folks rich and poor, urban, suburban, and rural. And land for land's sake.

Information gathered from the first national survey of land trusts in 1981[1] documents the activities, techniques, and accomplishments of 423 organizations.[2] Representing nearly 300,000 members drawn from every region of the country, land trusts form a multifaceted group. They have gathered primarily private funds and have harnessed local volunteer initiative to preserve over 680,000 acres of resource lands in forty-one states.[3] Although preceded by four regional studies,[4] this was the first national survey, and therefore provides a basis for future comparative study. The different types of land trusts (LTs) and the kinds of land of concern can be described, along with their sources of revenue and how they spend it, how many there are, where and when they were formed, what problems and weaknesses they see hindering their work, and the techniques and activities they employ to protect land.

What Is a Land Trust?

According to the survey, a land trust is defined as a private, nonprofit entity directly involved in land transactions that protect open space, recreation, and resource lands. That involvement is shown by a trust's ability and inclination to own land or hold easements on it, or to work for the transfer of land to another conservation organization—private or public, local or national. Publicly funded organizations that use private funds for land acquisition and land management were included in the survey. Legal affiliates (not chapters) of national organizations such as the National Audubon Society were included if they were autonomously operated and funded. However, chapters of national land-holding groups such as Trout Unlimited, The Nature Conservancy, National Audubon, and others were excluded, as were organizations that administer single property preserves and have no intention of acquiring more land.

The Number of Land Trusts, Their Locations, and Dates of Formation

The formation of land trusts began in the late nineteenth century in the Northeast where urbanization forced early decisions for conservation. Although a handful of LTs emerged every decade after 1900, the real growth of the movement did not begin until the 1950s, when spreading urbanization, dramatically increasing population pressures, and technological growth began to exert tremendous strains on land. As these pressures rippled across the Middle West, South, and Far West during the '60s and '70s, land trusts formed to meet local needs.

Before 1950, 39 LTs were preserving land in twenty states; nearly half of those groups operated in Mid-Atlantic states and New England. (Thirteen early groups were founded by those whose primary interest was birds, not land.) By 1965, 97 LTs had formed (see chart on page 18). The most dramatic increase followed in the decade 1965 to 1975 when 174 new LTs emerged. From 1976 to 1981 another 97 LTs organized, bringing the total to 423. (Nineteen LTs did not report their dates of formation; see footnote 2.)

Growth of Local Land Trusts by Region and Time Period

Region	97 LTs formed through 1964		174 LTs formed 1965–1975		97 LTs formed 1976–1981	
Far West	7.2%	(7)	7.4%	(13)	17.5%	(17)
Rocky Mountains	1.3%	(1)	3.0%	(5)	6.2%	(6)
Southwest	1.3%	(1)	1.7%	(3)	2.1%	(2)
Plains	3.0%	(3)	.5%	(1)	5.1%	(5)
Great Lakes	13.0%	(13)	14.5%	(25)	20.6%	(20)
South	5.0%	(5)	9.2%	(16)	11.3%	(11)
Mid-Atlantic	27.0%	(26)	15.5%	(27)	6.2%	(6)
New England	42.2%	(41)	48.2%	(84)	31.0%	(30)
Total	100.0%	(97)	100.0%	(174)	100.0%	(97)

Note: 387 land trusts have been confirmed; another 36 are known to exist but were not included in this report because data on them was not available.
Far West: Alaska, California, Hawaii, Nevada, Oregon, Washington
Rocky Mountains: Colorado, Idaho, Montana, Utah, Wyoming
Southwest: Arizona, New Mexico, Oklahoma, Texas
Plains: Iowa, Kansas, Minnesota, Missouri, Nebraska, North and South Dakota

Great Lakes: Illinois, Indiana, Michigan, Ohio, Wisconsin
South: Alabama, Arkansas, Florida, Georgia, Kentucky, Louisiana, Mississippi, North and South Carolina, Tennessee, Virginia, West Virginia
Mid-Atlantic: Delaware, Maryland, New Jersey, New York, Pennsylvania
New England: Connecticut, Maine, Massachusetts, New Hampshire, Rhode Island, Vermont

The geographic range of the operations of land trusts breaks down as follows, revealing that more than half of them function within a single town or county:

Towns	151*	41%
County	64	17%
Two or more counties	76	21%
State	58	16%
Multistate	18	5%

*Lacking data on this subject for Connecticut land trusts, the author categorized all of that state's 77 groups under "Towns."

Hammocks, Swales, and Space for Soul and Sanity—The Diversity of Concern

Land trusts have as many varied concerns as there are diverse natural resources. To determine the similarities, differences, and range of interests, LTs were asked the question "Which types of land is your organization concerned with? Check *all* that apply." Nationally, the categories concerning the greatest number of LTs were wildlife habitat (84 percent); scenic and recreational land (79 percent); and wetlands, riparian lands, and/or coastal zone land (72 percent). For these three top resources, the national pattern and rough proportion were reflected in six out of eight regions. Apparently, alarms sounded by national conservation groups on the dangers of loss of habitats and salt and freshwater wetlands have been heard. However, interest in agriculture surpasses concern for wetlands in the Rockies, as do the categories of historic and archaeological sites and rights-of-way for hiking in both the Rockies and the Plains states. Following is a list of the categories surveyed and the percentage of land trusts concerned with them.

84	Wildlife habitats
79	Scenic and recreational land
72	Wetlands, riparian, and/or coastal zone land
40	Productive agricultural and forest land
33	Rights-of-way for hiking, etc.
30	Historic and archaeological sites
21	Community gardens and other neighborhood open space
18	Natural hazard areas
15	Other
13	Land base for social or economic alternatives
9	Low-cost housing sites

In the "Other" category, LTs expressed concern for plant habitats, parks, desert, and ranchland. Prairie grasslands in the Plains, sand dunes in the Great Lakes, hardwood hammocks and mangrove swamps in Florida arouse attention, as do bogs, ridges, and swales in Wisconsin. LTs are the watchdogs of Corps of Engineers permits, National Park in-holdings, wastewater treatment sites, and aquifer recharge areas. Also of interest are caves in Texas, mountain massifs in Tennessee, and, in Wisconsin, "space for soul and sanity."

Land trusts in six regions of the country have a similar number of interests. In the Mid-Atlantic region LTs are distinguished by the greatest number of concerns, while land trusts in the Rockies expressed the fewest.

Types of Land Trusts[5]

Multiresource Land Trusts

While a few land trusts focus their aims on a specific goal such as protection of productive farmland or the social fabric of urban and rural communities, most responding organizations (340, or 88 percent) expressed concern for many resources. These multiresource land trusts gave the following typical response to the narrative question on purpose of organization: "To serve as a means of preserving open spaces, natural resources, recreational lands, etc., as part of the orderly development of the town and for the benefit of and use by the people of the town."

Maintenance of genetic banks for native plant and animal life is the main purpose of a multiresource trust in California. For a trust in Ohio, preserving a hillside is the goal, protecting a unique resource of the land in that community. However, concern for resources that are naturally representative is far more common than concern for resources that are unique. The words "unique" and "rare" were mentioned only four times in the purposes or criteria of all responding LTs, underscoring the fact that local groups are doing a different job from that of national organizations such as The Nature Conservancy. Indeed, perhaps an underlying aim of LTs is to preserve representative or characteristic natural systems and features of the landscape before they become rare.

Although over half of the LTs reported that they did have specific criteria for the land selected, "specific" ranged from highly detailed evaluation forms to "we judge each parcel on its own merit." The most frequent response equated land selection criteria with the trust's purpose or geographic scope of operation; however, because so much depends on the clarity of purpose, those criteria seem nonspecific and misleading. The specific criterion cited most often is "property must be contiguous to other conservation land." One group requires that a new property be endowed before it is accepted. The overall response suggests that most land trusts see the breadth and diversity of their operations as precluding specific land selection criteria.

Agricultural and Forest Land Trusts

Farms and forests are two types of land that concern land trusts nationwide. While 155 LTs (40 percent of those responding) indicated concern for agricultural and forest land, making that category the fourth most frequently chosen, 9 of the LTs have it as their primary concern. (Since none of these agricultural land trusts checked off "community/neighborhood" on the questionnaire, they are not to be confused with community land trusts interested in agriculture.) Regionally, 4 of the 9 agricultural LTs are in New England, with 2 in Illinois, and 1 each in California, Montana, and West Virginia. All have organized since 1974. Six have paid staff and budgets over $20,000 a year, higher than the national average for all LTs. Five of the 9 are not membership organizations, differing significantly from the national trend, which shows only 8 percent of responding organizations as nonmembership oriented.

As a group, agricultural land trusts are concerned with farm- and forestland (100 percent), wildlife habitats (67 percent), scenic/recreational land (56 percent), and wetlands (44 percent), revealing a reordering of priorities but basic adherence to the national pattern of concern for wildlife (84 percent), scenic/recreational land (79 percent), wetlands (72 percent) and agricultural/forest lands (40 percent). Five of the nine try to develop and implement financing and programs to help provide farmlands to individuals. Seven of the nine would use easements and hold ownership to land, reflected in the 3,500 acres owned and the 24,610 acres under easements. In the ranking of their activities and conservation methods, limited development, education, and contract services were checked least often.

Although not disinterested in farmland, four LTs have forestland as their primary concern and differ from agricultural groups in several respects, including their generally earlier dates of organization: 1901, 1924, 1944, and 1979. The youngest is in Missouri and did not report a budget, while the three in New England are staffed, with annual budgets of $125,000, $476,000, and $500,000, making them among the best funded of all land trusts. Forest LTs protect 12,110 acres in ownership, 8,665 acres in easements, and 240 acres indirectly. Managing resources was indicated by all, reflecting the long history of conservation practices by forest LTs. Land ownership and easements are methods used by all four groups. Limited development and education were activities mentioned, a point of departure from the agricultural LTs, which were least interested in those two categories.

If trends continue, the future accomplishments of agricultural land trusts can be significant, as existing organizations mature and other LTs give more attention to farmland. Recent national interest in the subject of the country's agricultural and forest resources should assist these groups in developing public support and financial backing. Much depends on the IRS's forthcoming clarification of the use of easements and the development of creative financing to make farm- and forestland affordable. Forest- and farmland trusts do not operate to the exclusion of each other; their interests and activities often overlap.

Community Land Trusts

Departing from traditional ownership of land by individuals, community land trusts (CLTs) advocate the shared ownership and use of land. They combine productive and ecological land-use practices to achieve their egalitarian social and economic goals. CLTs use their land in several ways. Housing for low- and middle-income members is an objective of many urban and rural CLTs. In addition, urban CLTs improve the quality of life in city neighborhoods by providing community gardens and urban parks. Rural CLTs, often through nonprofit lease arrangements on agricultural and forest land, provide farming opportunities for those unable to afford direct purchase of land.

Representing 10 percent of the national total of land trusts, twelve urban and twenty-six rural CLTs are located in all regions of the country except the Rocky Mountains and the Southwest. Almost all were organized during the 1970s. As a group, the concerns of urban and rural CLTs differ from the national pattern. They express relatively little interest in wildlife habitats, scenic/recreational lands, or wetlands. CLTs are interested in social and economic alternatives (84 percent), productive agricultural and forest land (68 percent), community gardens and other neighborhood open space (55 percent), and housing sites (66 percent). Unlike their rural counterparts, however, urban trusts are understandably much less interested in farm- and forestland.

Most CLTs, because they are not tax-exempt, do not receive gifts of land. However, many rural CLTs do manage to generate some revenue from the sale of products and contract services for their nonprofit operations. On the other hand, traditional land trusts do receive gifts of land and are increasingly aware of the cost of managing it. Informal and formal associations between LTs and CLTs are now being explored for their mutual benefit.

Other Special-Interest Land Trusts

Six land trusts have rallied round the prairies and grasslands of the country's Plains region: four in Illinois, one in Kansas, and one in Missouri. As a group, all have budgets under $12,000, own 847 acres, and have indirectly protected 735 acres. While two groups formed in the 1960s, the other four have organized since 1974.

Trail development and protection along riverbanks and railroads, as well as in mountains and other scenic areas, are the primary focuses of 8 land trusts, representing nearly every region of the country. Nationally, 128 LTs are concerned with rights-of-way for hiking. Although the acreage (253) these groups protect through ownership and easement seems small, it is misleading to measure their success in acres. Many of these groups noted that the rights-of-

way they seek to keep open are often narrow swaths through land in private ownership. Their annual budgets, with the exception of one group with $100,000 a year, average well under $12,000.

Membership

Membership in the nation's land trusts has grown to nearly 300,000. In relation to membership in national conservation organizations such as National Audubon, which has 400,000 members, or The Nature Conservancy, which has 100,000, most trusts seem small and undeveloped by professional membership techniques. But, in the aggregate, land trusts represent a sizable body of support for the value of land conservation. Membership is greatest in New England (36 percent of the national total) and Mid-Atlantic states (21 percent). Also of note, thirty-four LTs (8 percent) have chosen not to be membership organizations.

Membership Distribution—Total: 280,935

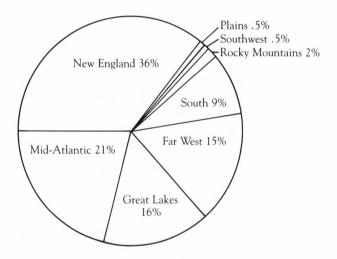

Funding

Nationally, 60 percent of the LTs reporting (235) have budgets under $20,000 a year; indeed, 36 percent of the total make do with less than $5,000. Regionally, the Mid-Atlantic and Southern LTs are the best funded; 50 percent of those have budgets exceeding $20,000. Nationally, the lowest budget reported was "nothing to speak of," while the highest was $3,000,000 for one group in New England.

Budget statistics may be misleading because responses were sketchy regarding sources and expenditures of funds. In addition, many of the best-funded groups, while avidly saving land, are not solely land trusts. Natural history museums with natural areas programs and Audubon affiliates are among those groups likely to have much larger budgets than the more typical land trust.

Land trusts have tried a variety of money-making ventures, ranging from annual dinners, bird-a-thons, and boat races to bluegrass concerts and pig roasts. T-shirt sales have been surprisingly lucrative, as have native plant and shrub sales. An adopt-a-tree program in Alabama raised $12,000 in six weeks to ensure the down payment on a threatened property. Direct solicitation, limited development schemes, sales of publications, technical services, and promotional films to present their message have raised substantial funds. A mail-order business of desert ceramics and jewelry netted $59,000 for a California land trust. All of these demonstrate an ability to use local customs and needs to raise money, usually for specific projects, although only rarely do they bring the long-term return that might be expected from professionally planned and assisted fundraising campaigns.

Problems and Weaknesses Hindering Land Trusts

Financial difficulties were cited as the principal problem for land trusts by a three-to-one margin. Most respondents simply cited lack of money as the problem, but a few pointed to specific impediments such as the anticipated demise of the Land and Water Conservation Fund, the skyrocketing price of land in coastal zones and certain areas of the West, or the general state of the economy. Often noted was the pressure of reconciling large goals with limited time and money: "We're just doing the best we can in our small area, with no resources to speak of." A common belief was that without money to buy it, land cannot be saved; many seemed unfamiliar with nonmonetary protection techniques or the possibilities of creative financing.

Frustrated by lack of administrative continuity and yearning for greater local participation, many all-volunteer groups are discouraged by their inability to afford paid staff. Some groups expressed a need for more education of their board members on complex land conservation issues. Although embattled, they frequently voiced their enthusiasm, conviction, and willingness to persevere.

The indifference and occasional hostility of the public are a problem for some groups. The public's general lack of understanding of the value of land preservation, as well as its failure to grasp the specific tax benefits, seems to hinder the efforts of some LTs. Relationships with state and federal government were easier for some than was interaction with "short-sighted, bickering" local officials, who were sometimes perceived as having "love affairs with developers." However, federal policy can be a problem for local conservation efforts; for example, in Louisiana where floodplains and wetlands are "reclaimed."

General development pressures, inability to compete with developers financially and politically, as well as a dwindling supply of available open space, seem of special concern to groups in areas of high population concentration. Surprisingly, only a few LTs mentioned specific land management problems such as vandalism or control of erosion.

In sum, then, lack of money, staff, and sufficient support from the public and local officials were the three most common problems, summarized by a Pennsylvania group as "money, apathy, staffing—same old thing." Additional comments reveal that most land trusts are heartened to discover so many similar organizations operating in or near their own areas. While many had been assisted by national conservation organizations, they were unaware that other groups are working at the local level.

Conservation Methods and Related Activities

Nationally, owning land through purchase, donation, or bargain sale is the conservation technique used by the most land trusts—316 organizations, or 82 percent. Aiding the transfer of land ownership or easements to another conservation organization (public or private) is the next tool, which was selected by 204 (53 percent), followed by holding conservation easements/restrictions (through purchase, donations, etc.), with 159 LTs (41 percent) reporting their use. Open space preservation through limited development is used by 20 percent, or 76 LTs.

All regions of the country reflect the national pattern of 82 percent, 53 percent, 41 percent, and 20 percent, except the Rocky Mountains. There, holding easements or conservation restrictions (75 percent) is the technique preferred over land ownership (67 percent). Trusts in the Plains states chose land transfer as often as land ownership (78 percent), in contrast to New England where 97 percent of reporting trusts indicated their use of land ownership as a technique, with less than half that choosing easements (38 percent) and 49 percent facilitating transfers. Following is a list of the conservation techniques surveyed and the percentage of land trusts selecting each.

82	Land ownership
54	Manages land
53	Facilitates transfer
50	Education
41	Easements/restrictions
39	Participates in public policy
28	Technical assistance to landowners
22	Technical assistance to others
20	Limited development
17	Other
12	Contracts services
8	Farmland to individuals

The breakdown of acres preserved by land protection technique is shown in the following national and regional charts. "Indirectly protected" refers to aiding the transfer of land ownership or easements to another conservation organization, public or private.

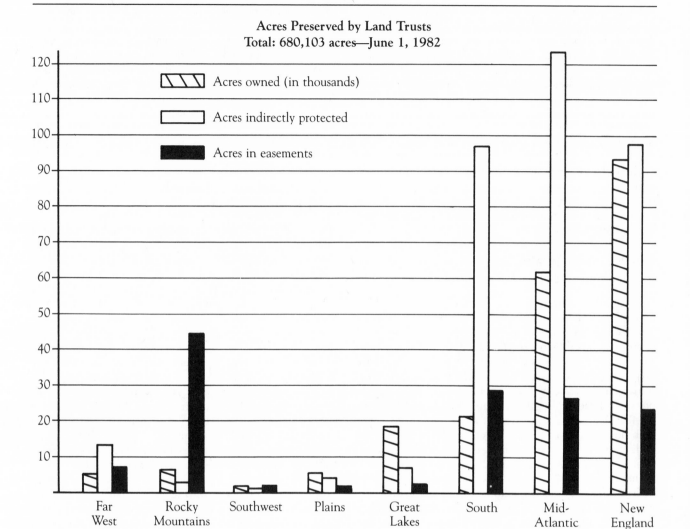

Acres Preserved by Land Trusts
Total: 680,103 acres—June 1, 1982

Region	Total acres preserved	Percent in easement	Acres in easement	Average size parcel in easement (acres)
Far West	22,900	26	5,966	199
Rocky Mountains	52,184	85	44,080	3,149
Southwest	558	11	60	60
Plains	8,345	0.5	35	35
Great Lakes	25,988	4	1,019	39
South	146,602	20	29,075	190
Mid-Atlantic	211,396	12	26,186	125
New England	212,130	11	23,218	63

Use of Conservation Easements by Land Trusts

The chart on page 22 shows acres and percentages of land protected by using conservation easements, which cover 129,639 acres in 802 parcels, representing 19 percent of the total acres (680,103) protected by private local land trusts. Twenty-five percent (98 groups) have actually used easements, although 155 LTs (40 percent of 387) indicated that they would use easements to protect land.

Most Americans live far from wilderness, but the quality of their daily lives is enhanced by the conservation land preserved by land trusts close to home. Raymond F. Dasmann, author of *Environmental Conservation*, noted in "The Country In Between":

> Not too long ago I was one of those who were interested only in the extremes of land use, the city and the wilderness. Everything in between was just space to be passed through as quickly as possible. I did know, intellectually, that the country in between was important, but emotionally I had no attachment to it. Now it seems to me that the fringe lands, the farmlands, the ranges, pastures, and managed forests are the areas where the real conservation issues of the next two decades will be faced.[6]

In that "country in between," land trusts buy and receive gifts of land, hold easements on it, and take responsibility for managing it. They help transfer land to other conservation organizations, educate the public, assist landowners who might otherwise need help from public agencies, play a role in influencing public policy on land conservation, act as intermediaries between government officials and private citizens, and research land use and ecological communities. All, all of this is done at minimal cost to the American public, beneficiary of the natural heritage now being preserved by local land trusts.

Notes

1. The survey, funded by the Lincoln Institute of Land Policy and others, was compiled during the summer of 1981 by Terry Bremer and Russell Cohen. Results of the survey are in the *1981 National Directory of Local Land Conservation Organizations*, published by the Land Trust Exchange, Bar Harbor, Maine.

For the survey the term "local land conservation organization" was used because it was intended to include many groups preserving land at the local level that did not seem to fit comfortably within the term "land trust." For example, twenty-three bird clubs, eighteen natural history museums or nature centers, and eight watershed associations conduct continuing programs of land protection in their communities and were included in the national survey. However accurate the term may be, "local land conservation organization" makes for tedious reading and is a mouthful besides; "land trust" (LT) will be used in this report.

2. The analysis in this portrait is based on information received from 387 organizations. Another 36 land trusts are known to exist, bringing the total to 423, but were not included here because data on them were not available.

3. States without confirmed land trusts are Arizona, Arkansas, Hawaii, Louisiana, Nebraska, Nevada, New Mexico, North Dakota, and South Dakota.

4. Previous surveys of selected land conservation organizations were made by The Trust for Public Land, the Institute of Community Economics, the Massachusetts Audubon Society, and the Connecticut Land Trust Service Bureau, a joint project of The Nature Conservancy and Conservation Law Foundation.

5. Classification of land trusts by type was not made by the land trusts; it is the judgment of the researchers based on several factors, including which resources were checked off, literature submitted about the land trust, criteria for land selection, and narrative response to "purpose of your organization."

6. Raymond F. Dasmann, "The Country In Between," in the Sierra Club Engagement Calendar, 1982.

How To Form a Land Trust

Suzanne C. Wilkins
and Roger E. Koontz

Interested citizens and/or town officials can help preserve local natural areas and open space by forming a land conservation trust. The formation process is not a difficult one, requiring only committed persons and the completion of some necessary paperwork.

A. Human Resources

1. *Initial focus*

Local citizens, perhaps members of the conservation commission or of existing local community groups unable to hold land, may first become aware of the need to form a land trust because of several different situations:

(1) intensive local development or pressure for improper development,

(2) a series of poor local zoning decisions,

(3) lack of government funding for acquisition of local open space, or

(4) lack of interest in land preservation on the part of local government or any other community group.

In any case, a group of citizens decides to try to preserve remaining local natural resources. Included in this list may be green belts, coastal resources, areas of historic or scenic value, habitats of wildlife (especially of rare or endangered species), land important to protect the quantity or quality of the local water supply, and areas for public education and recreation.

Before proceeding, this group should evaluate the local government, existing community bodies, and neighboring groups to determine if any other organization could function as a land trust. If none can serve in that capacity, the group may decide to form a new organization to preserve local open space. A land conservation trust, as a nonprofit organization that can act independently and hold and manage land for the benefit of the public, will provide the necessary vehicle.

2. *Developing local support*

The group of citizens interested in forming a land trust should compile local land-use statistics and point out land-use trends.

Identifying a particular parcel in need of protection will help develop a base of public support and participation. If the initial protection effort is successful, it will help ensure the future of the trust.

The group must also analyze whether or not there is enough volunteer interest to sustain the trust. In an effort to determine interest and to expand it, the group should identify and contact key persons, urging them to support the land trust concept and to participate in the operation of the trust. Such key persons might include representatives of historical societies, church groups, garden clubs, local businesses, volunteer and civic organizations, scouting groups, service organizations (Kiwanis, Rotary, Elks, Moose), school parent-teacher groups, fishing and other sports groups, and bird clubs. Others might include potential donors, local scientists and teachers, people living near an initial land acquisition, community leaders (bankers, businesspersons, real estate agents, sympathetic developers), and town officials.

It is important to demonstrate from the beginning the participatory nature of the land trust, so the group should keep the general public informed of its concerns and plans. The best way to obtain general acceptance and receive additional participation and support is by means of the media.

3. *Preliminary steps*

As the group continues to examine the viability of a land trust, it should draw up a statement of purpose, hold several public meetings, and secure a financial base. It may also seek legal advice.

a. *Statement of purpose*

A statement of purpose for the land trust clarifies the organization's direction for the public and for potential land donors. The wording of the statement is important since it sets the tone for the trust's whole operation. The statement should be the basis for the trust's founding documents.

b. *Public meetings*

The group should call a series of public meetings, at an accessible and familiar location, to explain the purpose of the trust and to obtain broader support. Good press coverage of the meetings helps ensure visibility and community understanding and support. The group should invite to the meetings people whose participation in the trust is vital to its success and members of nearby trusts who can help answer questions.

In addition to explaining the goals of the trust, these meetings are a good time to assign specific tasks. On the agenda should be (1) reaching a consensus on whether or not to form a trust at that time; (2) determining whether or not adequate volunteer power is available; (3) choosing a temporary chairperson; (4) selecting a small committee to draw up the incorporation papers and bylaws and obtaining general approval of these documents; (5) choosing a nominating committee to select a slate for the board of directors and officers and voting on the candidates; and (6) obtaining volunteers for certain activities and information on preferred public activities and potential acquisition parcels, possibly by means of a questionnaire.

c. *Financial base*

As the group forms the land trust, it will need money for filing fees and initial publicity, including meeting notices, press releases, and an informative flyer. The amount of money needed depends on the amount of volunteer participation and free services the group can obtain, and the elaborateness of its effort, but $200 to $1,000 should suffice. If even this amount is not immediately available, more can be raised as it is needed. Charter members, for instance, may be asked for contributions.

d. *Legal advice*

While it may be possible for a layman to complete the initial paperwork with the information contained in this article, a trust may wish to consult a lawyer. This person should understand how a private nonprofit organization operates and should be interested in land conservation. The group should make sure that representing the trust would not be a conflict of interest for the lawyer.

In addition to drawing up and filing initial trust papers, the attorney may continue to serve the trust in land acquisition and management matters. The group should enumerate the scope of work involved and should establish payment for services on an "as needed" basis. The lawyer may be willing to work for a reduced fee.

B. The Paper Process

For reasons that will be discussed below, land trusts are generally organized as corporations. The land trust's legal existence begins when the incorporation papers are filed with the secretary of state. Shortly after, several other documents should be filed, the most important of which is the application for federal tax-exempt status, which is discussed elsewhere in this book. In addition, the trust should file either a registration or an exemption form concerning charitable solicitations and may wish to request exemption from the sales tax. (Although the discussion of the legal requirements in this section is not totally applicable in every state, the issues to consider will generally be similar.)

1. *Incorporation*

Most land trusts are actually not trusts at all in the legal sense, but are nonstock corporations organized for charitable purposes. A genuine trust is usually established by an individual transferring property to a trustee and is administered under conditions stated in a trust document. In contrast, the corporate form used by land trusts allows much greater flexibility in involving interested individuals, obtaining contributions, and managing holdings.

Corporations have a legal identity which is separate from that of individuals involved in their management. This legal structure protects individuals from liability for most suits involving corporate activities. Unincorporated associations do not provide such protection and are not appropriate for use in land preservation.

The following discussion is intended to assist the group forming the trust in preparing the necessary documents for incorporation. There is considerable flexibility in both format and text so long as the basic requirements are met. Procedural requirements vary from state to state.

The major issues to decide in creating a nonstock corporation are the corporate name, the size and manner of selection of the board of directors, whether to have members, and, if so, their authority. Once these decisions have been made, preparation of the corporate documents can proceed in a straightforward manner.

a. *Major issues*

i. *Corporate name.* Land trusts are often named after the town or region in which they plan to operate. Other names that provoke interest or identify the trust with the area may also be chosen. The only legal requirements are that the name be distinct from that of any other corporation and that it contain "corporation," "company," "incorporated," or an abbreviation of one of these terms.

ii. *Board of directors.* Crucial to the organization's success, the board is responsible for managing the property and affairs of the trust and for making the critical decisions. Considerable thought should be devoted to who should be on the board and how they should be selected.

From the legal perspective, there is great flexibility in organizing the board. In most states it must have a minimum number of directors.[1] Including a cross-section of interests such as community leaders, experts, and public officials on the board will help the trust qualify as a public charity for federal tax purposes. Major contributors may be on the board without endangering public charity status if they do not have a controlling interest.[2]

Directors should be able to assist in carrying out the goals of the trust: to obtain appropriate land and to manage it for the public good. Some of the key people discussed earlier may be asked to serve on the board. Other members may be individuals who have made or intend to make contributions to the trust, or those with relevant professional skills, such as a banker, a forester, a realtor, a public relations expert, or an attorney. Of course, the prime qualification for all directors is their willingness to spend time, money, and energy in making the trust a success.

The group forming the trust must decide how many directors there will be, how they will be selected, how long they will serve, and who will be on the initial board. The board should be large enough to represent the varied interests of the group, but not so large as to be unwieldy. A board with seven to fifteen members is most efficient, but a larger number may be helpful in generating interest in the trust.

The initial board is selected by those who sign the certificate of incorporation. Thereafter, if the trust has members, they will generally select some or all of the subsequent directors. The trust's bylaws should provide that persons occupying particular offices or positions, or who are chosen by related organizations, are automatically also directors. The directors can choose their own successors, but an organization with a wholly self-perpetuating board might have difficulty demonstrating public support to the Internal Revenue Service. It might also miss opportunities for involving other helpful people.

Directors serve for one-year terms unless a longer term is specified. Terms of two or three years with staggered selection dates usually mean greater continuity in operations.

iii. *Members.* Many land trusts have members who elect some or all of the directors at annual meetings and who may approve organizational changes such as amendments to the bylaws and the certificate of incorporation. Membership gives large numbers of people the opportunity to participate in the organization's affairs and, through dues, raises funds to help with trust expenses.[3]

If there are to be members, qualifications of membership must be established. Members may have to meet residency requirements and be approved by the board. There may be classes of membership—such as regular, organizational, sustaining, and lifetime—with different voting power or dues.

Membership authority to act upon fundamental changes such as amendments to the certificate of incorporation or merger with another organization is often a difficult issue. Some statutes provide that the affirmative vote of two-thirds of the entire membership (not just those at a particular meeting) is necessary for approval, unless the certificate of incorporation does not allow members to vote on such changes. Even though proxy votes may be permitted at membership meetings, this requirement may effectively prevent any changes, particularly if the membership is large. Bylaw changes are not considered fundamental and require only the approval of the majority of the members attending a meeting, unless the certificate of incorporation provides that members cannot vote on these issues.

b. *Necessary documents*

Once the decisions discussed above are made, the documents necessary for incorporation can be drafted and reviewed. In Connecticut the document that creates a corporation is called a certificate of incorporation. It must be filed with the secretary of state along with the statutory agent form discussed below.

The next step, which is often done simultaneously, is selecting the initial board of directors and officers and adopting the bylaws. The filing of the first biennial report form completes the process. Filing fees are modest. Copies of all documents should be kept by the trust with the minutes of corporate meetings.

i. *Certificate of incorporation.* Within the basic guidelines, the certificate should be kept as simple and flexible as possible. Detailed provisions are better placed in the bylaws, which are much easier to amend. Most statutes require the certificate to contain the name of the corporation, a statement of purpose, a statement that the corporation is nonprofit, and information about the rights of members.[4] In order to qualify for tax-exempt status under federal law, the trust must also include in the certificate limitations of the purposes according to the particular tax status sought, a statement limiting political activity, and a provision for disposition of assets upon dissolution of the corporation.

The statement of purpose should be broad enough to include all charitable activities in which the trust might engage. The trust should specifically limit its activities to those allowed under Sec. 501(c)(3) of the Internal Revenue Code.

Ordinarily, the certificate should not restrict activities to a particular geographic area even though such a restriction is intended, since situations may arise where the trust can assist another trust or fill a void by accepting property interests temporarily in another area.

If the land trust intends to qualify under the federal tax laws as a private operating foundation, the certificate must contain provisions requiring its income to be used for charitable purposes and prohibiting it from engaging in self-dealing, lobbying, and certain financial activities. Trusts intending to qualify only as public charities must include a statement that lobbying will not constitute a substantial part of their activities. All charitable organizations must avoid participation in political campaigns.

The certificate must indicate whether the corporation is to have members. If so, any designations of classes, the manner of election or appointment, and the qualifications and rights of members must be specified. Again, the provisions in the certificate should be general, leaving details to the bylaws. The principal rights to be covered should be whether the members can vote on fundamental changes and on bylaw amendments.

If the trust dissolves, it may give its assets to a specific charitable organization or governmental body or to any appropriate entity designated by the board of directors at the time of dissolution. If the certificate of incorporation names a specific organization, advance approval should be obtained as a matter of courtesy, and an alternative disposition of assets should be included in case the organization declines to accept some or all of the parcels.

The certificate is signed by one or more persons, who are known as the incorporators. One to three people should be designated to perform this task, which is ceremonial once the decisions have been made. A certified copy of the certificate should be requested from the secretary of state to be kept in the corporation's files.

ii. *Appointment of statutory agent for service of process.* This form, available from the secretary of state's office, merely designates a state resident to be served with any lawsuits or legal notices directed to the corporation. It must be filed with the certificate of incorporation.

iii. *Bylaws.* The bylaws should include the organizational structure and rules of procedure.

Several sections should be noted particularly. One way of coping with large boards of directors is to create an executive committee that can exercise part or all of the board's authority as specified. A general provision authorizing the board to receive and transfer land eliminates the need for specific authorization each time the situation arises. Similarly, a general provision allowing the board to employ staff or consultants should be included.

The bylaws are adopted, and directors and officers are elected by the incorporators at the organization meeting. In practice, the incorporators generally consent in writing to a set of minutes that indicate that the bylaws have been adopted and particular individuals have been elected as officers and directors.

iv. *First biennial report.* This report, with the names and addresses of officers, directors, and the statutory agent, usually must be filed within thirty days of the organization meeting. It may be filed with the certificate of incorporation if the organization meeting has already been held.

2. *Charitable solicitation act*

Some states have a charitable solicitation act. For instance, a Connecticut statute requires all charitable organizations, including land trusts, to file either an annual registration form or a form indicating why they are exempt from registering with the Department of Consumer Protection.[5] The purpose of the statute is to make public financial information about organizations that are soliciting charitable donations. There are special provisions for filing information if professional fundraising consultants are retained. All forms are available for public inspection.

Some trusts may be able to file the form exempting them from annual registration.[6] If members are able to vote or otherwise participate, membership dues are not considered to be a contribution. One provision exempts organizations with no paid staff that do not intend to receive, and do not receive, annual contributions worth more than $5,000 or from more than ten contributors. Other provisions exempt organizations which solicit funds only from their own membership, or which receive 80 percent of their contributions in number and dollar amount from their membership.

Organizations that must register are supposed to do so before beginning solicitation. At the end of the fifth month following the close of the fiscal year, registration expires and an annual financial report and new registration form must be filed. The registration fee is low—ten dollars in 1980.

Nonexempt organizations must file one of two categories of financial reports, depending on the amount of contributions received. Organizations that receive over $100,000 per year (including the value of any donated property) must file a report with a balance sheet and statement of income and expenses that have been audited by an independent public accountant. Organizations receiving less than $100,000 per year must file a statement of income and expenses, but it does not have to be audited.

3. *Sales tax exemption*

Charitable organizations such as land trusts are exempt from state sales tax on the purchase of equipment and supplies. In some states the tax department will issue an exemption permit upon receipt of a certified copy of the certificate of incorporation and an affidavit showing the sources and disposition of income and the nature and scope of proposed activities. If the trust has received a determination of federal tax-exempt status, it, too, should be submitted.

Notes

1. *See, e.g.,* Conn. Gen. Stat. §§33-448 (1981), requiring at least three directors.

2. An organization that intends to qualify under the Internal Revenue Code as a private operating foundation could have a nonrepresentative board composed solely of major contributors.

3. Thus, providing for membership helps meet public charity requirements under the Internal Revenue Code.

4. *See, e.g.,* Conn. Gen. Stat. §§33-427 (1981).

5. Conn. Gen. Stat. §§19-323k *et seq.* (1981).

6. Conn. Gen. Stat. §§19-323n (1981).

Becoming and Remaining a Tax-Exempt Organization

Marion R. Fremont-Smith
and Roger E. Koontz

To operate effectively, a land trust must clear two Internal Revenue Service hurdles. One establishes the trust's own tax-exempt status as a charitable organization; the other establishes the right of donors to the maximum allowable deduction for their contributions to the trust. Application for both of these determinations is made by means of a single document, IRS Form 1023. Although most land trusts should have no difficulty in qualifying as exempt organizations, maintaining that status depends on how the trust operates.

A. Obtaining a Federal
Tax Exemption
1. *Application*
Land trusts usually claim exemption as charitable organizations under Sec. 501(c)(3) of the Internal Revenue Code. A revenue ruling has held that the purposes of a typical land trust are "charitable."[1] The overriding issue is whether the organization has been formed for an allowable public purpose rather than to serve the private interests of particular individuals.

As soon as it is organized, a trust seeking tax exemption should file IRS Form 1023 at the district director's office. Certain materials must accompany the form, including the organizational charter, which would be either a certificate of incorporation or a trust indenture; a copy of the bylaws of incorporation; and a statement of receipts and expenditures and a balance sheet. For an organization that has not yet begun operations, a proposed budget for two full accounting periods and a current balance sheet showing assets and liabilities are acceptable. Many trusts are established with a minimum amount of assets (such as $10.00) and do not accept contributions until tax-exempt status is determined. In that case the trust must note that information on the application, and there is no need to fill out the balance sheet.

Form 1023 contains an extensive set of instructions. It should be filed within fifteen months from the end of the month when the organization was established. Materials should be sent together; otherwise, approval may be delayed, or the trust may have to resubmit the entire package.

The trust will receive a letter from the IRS acknowledging receipt of the appropriate form. It will then be assigned to an examining agent for review. In some cases the trust will receive a request for additional information and clarification. In most instances the trust will receive a ruling that it is an exempt organization as of the date of its creation. However, if the application is filed more than fifteen months after its creation, exempt status will be effective only as of the date of filing of the application. Contributions made prior to that date will not be deductible. Although public charity land trusts with normal annual gross receipts of less than $5,000 are not required to file for exemption, the ability to assure potential donors deductibility makes filing worthwhile.

2. *Appeal*
If exempt status is denied, the trust may file an administrative appeal within thirty days of the date of the adverse determination letter. Where the appeal is directed will depend on whether the determination was made at the district or national level. If the administrative appeals procedure results in an adverse "notice of final determination," the trust may seek a declaratory judgment in the United States Tax Court, United States Court of Claims, or United States District Court in the District of Columbia by filing a petition within ninety days of the IRS notice.

B. Obtaining Maximum Donor Deductions

Obtaining tax-exempt status for the land trust does not automatically give donors maximum federal income tax benefits. Donations to all tax-exempt organizations are deductible. However, cash donations to certain types of charitable organizations are deductible up to 50 percent of the donor's adjusted gross income, with amounts in excess of the limit carried forward through the next five years. Gifts of "capital gain property" (such as land held for more than a year) to these organizations are deductible up to 100 percent of the fair market value.[2] Gifts to other types of organizations are deductible up to only 20 percent of adjusted gross income, with no provision for carrying any excess forward and with a reduction in the value of donations of capital gain property.[3] For a donor who is considering a large gift, these are significant differences.

There are three ways in which a land trust can qualify for maximum donor deductions: as a publicly supported charity, as a private operating foundation, or as a supporting organization. These distinctions are a result of the Tax Reform Act of 1969 that reflected congressional concern about potential abuse by certain charitable organizations that are established and controlled by a few individuals, or that accumulate income in a way unrelated to their charitable purposes. These organizations, designated as "private foundations," are subject to an elaborate set of restrictions and reporting requirements, including the severe limits on the deductibility of large contributions just described. All charitable organizations are presumed to be private foundations unless they can demonstrate that they should be excluded from this status.[4]

"Public charities" that can show broad public support are not considered private foundations. "Private operating foundations" are a special form of private foundation. They are allowed maximum donor deductions because they spend most of their income directly for their charitable purposes, and meet other tests demonstrating that they are not primarily investment funds making grants to other organizations and individuals. "Supporting organizations" are formed to carry out the purposes of an existing public charity or governmental agency.

1. Public charity status

a. Application

Application for public charity status is made by completing Part VII of Form 1023. Under Part VII.A, land trusts ordinarily indicate that their basis for exclusion is No. 7, "normally receiving a substantial part of its support from a governmental unit or from the general public." (Some land trusts file under No. 8, but, as shown below, the requirements of No. 7 provide greater flexibility.) By checking No. 7, a trust is requesting exclusion under Sec. 509(a)(1) of the code as a "publicly supported organization." In order to receive this exclusion, it must show that it meets one of the following tests.

b. One-third support test

A land trust will be found to be a public charity under Sec. 509(a)(1) if it normally receives one-third of its support from the government and the general public.[5] "Normally" is defined as the aggregate support for the four years preceding the current year. General public support includes contributions from governmental units, other public charities, and individuals, except that only that portion of an individual contribution which is less than 2 percent of the organization's total support for the applicable period is counted as public support. This can be a problem for land trusts where support often comes mainly in the form of large pieces of land. An initial endowment may not prevent an advance ruling from issuing since future public support is expected. But the obligation to satisfy this requirement is a continuing one. This problem will be discussed in greater detail below.

c. Facts and circumstances test

If the trust fails to meet the one-third support test, it may still qualify under the facts and circumstances test.[6] This test can be used only by organizations applying under Sec. 509(a)(1), and is the major reason for a trust to seek exclusion under No. 7 rather than No. 8.[7] There are two primary requirements involved in this test:

(1) *10 percent of support.* This limitation operates in the same way and with the same qualifications and restrictions as the one-third support requirement. However, the lower percentage of public support required makes meeting the standard easier.

(2) *Attraction of public support.* To meet this requirement, the trust must show that it has a continuous and bona fide program of solicitation of funds from the public, government, or other charitable organizations. A trust seeking to meet this test may find it especially advantageous to have a large and broad membership.

In addition to these requirements, the following secondary factors will be considered as indications of public support. Not all of these factors need to be complied with, but weakness in one factor means the trust must be stronger in the others.

(1) *The percent of public support.* Obviously this figure will lie somewhere between 10 percent (the nonqualifying level) and 33⅓ percent (a level sufficient by itself for public charity status). The lower the percentage, the stronger the combination of remaining factors must be. If a large portion of income derives from endowment interest, the origin of the endowment will be considered.

(2) *Sources of support.* The trust should try to demonstrate broad support, a variety of potential donors, and significant governmental contributions.

(3) *Representative governing body.* A governing

body that includes a cross-section of interests such as public officials, experts, and community leaders will weigh more heavily in the trust's favor.

(4) *Public facilities or services.* Benefiting the public directly through programs or services is considered evidence of public support.

(5) *Miscellaneous factors.* Breadth of solicitation, restrictiveness of dues, and broad appeal of activities will also be considered.

d. *New organizations*

Since a final determination of public charity status cannot be made until the end of the first taxable year (at least eight months after the trust is founded), the trust should apply under Part IV.2 of Form 1023 for an advance ruling and an extended advance ruling in order to protect initial donors and to avoid the excise taxes on net investment income and undistributed income applicable to private foundations.[8] An advance ruling will be issued if the organization can reasonably be expected to meet one of the support tests during the first two taxable years, or three, if the first taxable year is less than eight months. The deductibility of contributors' donations will be protected during this period, even if the trust later fails to meet the tests.[9] However, if the trust is disqualified, its taxes are payable retroactively.

If the trust seeks an extended advance ruling, it must apply at the time of the initial application.[10] The advantage of the extended advance ruling is that the support tests are spread out over an aggregate five or six years, rather than two or three. This may give the trust time to acquire more broad-based support to balance whatever large grants were part of the initial endowment. Contributors' donations will be protected to the same extent as during the advance ruling period.

Once the organization has been determined to be a public charity, this status is effective for the period used as the basis for the determination and for the two tax years immediately following. No further applications are necessary, though the trust must demonstrate continued compliance on the annual returns.

2. *Private operating foundation status*

Private operating foundations are also entitled to maximum donor benefits for gifts of entire interests in land and of cash and securities, but they need not demonstrate broad public support. Operating foundations are subject to the reporting requirements and restrictions applicable to all private foundations, including prohibitions on self-dealing,[11] lobbying,[12] and certain financial transactions.[13] These restrictions must be included in the organization's certificate of incorporation or trust indenture.[14] In addition, a 2 percent excise tax is imposed on net investment income, if any exists.[15]

None of these restrictions should severely hamper a land trust's operations. Although only a few trusts are presently qualified as private operating foundations, this status should be seriously considered as it avoids the problem of demonstrating broad public support when the principal donations are a few substantial gifts of land. The major drawback is that they are not "qualified organizations" within the meaning of Sec. 170(h) and therefore are not eligible to receive deductible gifts of partial interests such as conservation easements. A trust wishing to change its status from "public charity" to "private operating foundation" should make sure that its certificate of incorporation or trust indenture includes the proper restrictions or that state law imposes them on the trust, and then file an application.

a. *Application*

Application for private operating foundation status is made by completing Part VIII of Form 1023. New organizations must also submit a "good faith determination" that the land trust will fulfill the requirements outlined below.[16] This statement should be in the form of an affidavit, signed by the organization's attorney and principal officer, that there is a reasonable basis in law and in fact that the organization is an operating foundation and that to the best of their belief the accompanying information is correct. The affidavit is necessary for an advance ruling; existing organizations, which cannot obtain such a ruling, need not file the affidavit.

b. *Requirements*

To qualify as a private operating foundation, the organization must spend directly for the conduct of actual activities constituting the purposes or function for which it was organized the lesser of (1) 85 percent of its adjusted net income, or (2) its minimum investment return.

Gifts of land (or other gifts, grants, or contributions) are *not* considered part of adjusted net income. A foundation's minimum investment return is 5 percent of the fair market value of all assets it holds for investment. The organization must also meet any one of three additional tests: assets, support, or endowment. A trust that cannot meet one of the public charity support tests will not be able to meet the private operating foundation support test; the endowment test is useful primarily to organizations operating largely on investment income. Land trusts, then, will want to look first to the assets test.

To meet the assets test, more than 65 percent of the organization's assets must be devoted directly to either the conduct of its exempt activity, to a functionally related business, or to a combination of the two. Real property that directly serves exempt purposes (not used for income-producing purposes) is a qualifying asset. Most property held by land trusts would therefore qualify. Endowment funds and other assets held for the purpose of producing income are not qualifying assets even if the income is used directly for the purposes of the exempt activity. Neither money set aside for future purposes nor a hotel or restaurant used to house employees is a qualifying asset. However, a building used to accommodate visitors to trust lands would be considered a functionally related business and would therefore qualify.

A new organization is treated as a private operating foundation if it files a satisfactory application and affidavit as described above. To maintain its status for the first three years, the organization must meet the financial tests by aggregating income and assets for all years completed. Thereafter, the organization must satisfy the income and assets requirements either for any three taxable years during a four-year period, consisting of the year in question and the three years immediately preceding, or for the entire four-year period on the basis of aggregate income and assets. Existing organizations wishing to be treated as private operating foundations must meet the same requirements for a four-year period before they can qualify.

3. *Supporting organization status*

A supporting organization is one formed and operated exclusively for the benefit of, to perform the function of, or carry out the purposes of a specified public charity or governmental agency.[17] The organization does not need to meet any public support test and can be quite flexible in its operations so long as the necessary relationship is demonstrated. It cannot be controlled by one or more substantial contributors.[18]

A land trust qualifying as a supporting organization must limit its functions in its founding documents to carrying out some or all of the purposes of one or more specified parent organizations. A second requirement—that it be operated, supervised, or controlled by or in connection with the parent—may be met in several ways. The easiest test is for the parent to appoint a majority of the trustees or board of directors. Under an alternate, the parent need appoint one or more directors but not a majority. However, in that case the parent must have a significant voice in the investment and operating policies of the trust, and it must meet still another requirement, called the "integral part test." This test also can be met in alternate ways. The trust must demonstrate either (1) that the activities it engages in for or on behalf of the parent are to perform the parent's functions or carry out its services, and, but for the trust, the parent would normally engage in these activities; or (2) the trust must pay substantially all of its income to the parent, and the amount of that support must be sufficient to assure that the parent will be "attentive" to the trust.

Application for supporting organization status is made by means of Form 1023. A permanent ruling may be obtained if the parent organization has permanent status as a public charity.

C. Maintaining Tax-Exempt Status

1. *Annual reports*

The Internal Revenue Service requires exempt organizations to file annual tax forms. These are due on or before the fifteenth day of the fifth month after the end of the organization's accounting period. The forms should be filed even if the application for exempt status is pending. The IRS makes all forms available for public inspection.

A public charity must submit Form 990 and Schedule A unless its gross receipts in each tax year do not average more than $25,000. Gross receipts include gifts, grants, and contributions, whether in the form of cash or property.

Private operating foundations submit Form 990-PF to the Internal Revenue Service and a copy of that form to the attorney general of the state in which the trust is organized or operates.

2. *Operational requirements*

The reporting forms filed by the land trust must continue to demonstrate compliance with the requirements for a charitable organization and the specific tests for public charity or private foundation status discussed above. Because compliance is generally assessed over a four-year period, one abnormal year does not necessarily disqualify the organization. The most frequent issue for a public charity, the receipt of a large grant, is discussed below.

a. *Changes in structure or operation*

If a land trust changes its legal status, such as from trust to corporation, a new exemption application must be submitted. If the charter or bylaws are amended, a letter containing the changes must be submitted to the district director of the IRS, either separately or with Forms 990 or 990-PF.

b. *Lobbying*

Charitable organizations are not allowed to support or oppose candidates for public office under the Internal Revenue Code, but they are allowed to engage in limited lobbying for or against proposed legislation if they are qualified as public charities.[19] Private operating foundations are prohibited from lobbying, except with respect to legislation affecting the organization's existence or status.[20] The penalty for violations by private operating foundations ranges from a tax to revocation of tax-exempt status.

Lobbying includes only attempts to influence legislation. Actions by executive, judicial, or administrative bodies such as the Department of Environmental Protection or zoning boards are not legislation; therefore, expenditures made to influence these bodies are not restricted or prohibited.

A public charity must demonstrate either that lobbying does not constitute a substantial portion of its activities, or, if it has filed an appropriate form, that the lobbying costs are less than a certain percentage of the organization's expenditures for charitable purposes. "Substantial" has never been precisely defined, although one case held that lobbying expenditures of less than 5 percent of the budget were not substantial.[21]

A charity that may engage in extensive lobbying should consider filing Form 5768, which will entitle it to devote up to 20 percent of its exempt purpose expenditures to lobbying activities.[22] Only 25 percent of these activities can be "grassroots lobbying," which is defined as urging members of the general public to support or oppose legislation. Form 5768 must be filed before the end of the taxable year in which it applies; it continues in effect until revoked.

3. *Change in support: the large grant*

Land trusts must be particularly aware of the potential effect of large grants on their public charity status. The basis for this status is a showing of relatively broad public support, rather than support by one individual or family. However, since a trust's principal revenue is large gifts of land, demonstrating compliance with this requirement may require careful planning and adjustments. The consequences of the failure to comply are severe: the trust becomes a private foundation with contributions deductible only up to 20 percent of the donor's income and no carry-forward of the undeducted balance.

a. *Determination of significance*

Both the one-third support test and the facts and circumstances test for public charity status refer to "normal support," which is defined as the aggregate support for the preceding four years. However, if in the current year there have been substantial and material changes in sources of support (apart from "unusual grants," to be discussed below), the current year is included in a new five-year aggregate.[23] Whether or not a large land grant would be considered a substantial and material change might depend on how much of the trust's past support came from such grants; however, "an unusually large contribution or bequest" is specifically mentioned as an example of such a change.

There are several possible ways of resolving the difficulty posed by large grants, the easiest and best of which is to cluster land grants.

b. *Unusual grant*

Another approach to the problem is to demonstrate to the Internal Revenue Service that the grant qualifies as an "unusual grant." If the IRS accepts this designation, the contribution is deducted both from total support and from qualifying support. The rule applies for the purpose of the one-third support test and the facts and circumstances test.

IRS regulations establish two sets of criteria for determining whether a gift qualifies as an unusual grant.[24] The IRS has issued guidelines for interpreting its regulations, describing certain kinds of gifts

that will be considered unusual grants.[25] A trust may request a ruling from the IRS before accepting a gift that would affect its public charity status.[26] Since a contributor who is responsible for a substantial and material change that disqualifies the trust as a public charity loses the benefits of the special deduction rules, the donor will also be concerned about this question.[27] The request for a ruling is filed with the IRS district director's office in the district in which the trust operates.

Finally, the large land gift would clearly upset the balance of public support, and if it would definitely not qualify as an unusual grant, the trust may want to seek reclassification as a private operating foundation.

c. *Record keeping and reporting*

It cannot be emphasized too strongly that merely obtaining a tax exemption ruling does not mean an end to government supervision or regulation. The Internal Revenue Code imposes a requirement that full records of all financial transactions must be kept. This includes a cumulative list of donors and the amounts of their contributions so that it can be determined whether they are substantial contributors.

The trust must also keep track of lobbying expenditures. Often one activity will encompass several aspects, such as research, writing, preparation of educational material for the general public, and the submission of information to legislators. It is advisable to keep sufficiently adequate records so that these components may be separated.

Finally, trust income derived from business activities that are unrelated to the exempt purposes of the trust may be subject to income tax even though other income of the trust remains tax exempt. Dividends, interest, annuities, rents, and royalties are generally exempt from all tax, as is income from any activity that can be determined to contribute importantly to the carrying out of a trust's exempt purposes. An accountant or attorney should be consulted before engaging in any business activity in order to ascertain whether or not the income it generates will be subject to tax.

The Internal Revenue Service conducts periodic audits of exempt organizations and has demonstrated particular interest in conservation groups. During an audit, an agent will want to see the minutes for the period in question, as well as all financial data. It is advisable to have him meet with someone from the trust (perhaps its accountant) who is familiar both with the organization and with the audit process.

There are also state and local filing requirements to be met, in some cases because the trust is a charitable organization and in others because it intends to solicit contributions from the general public and is required by state or local laws to obtain a certificate or license in order to do so. In most jurisdictions, exemption from real property tax is available only by meeting annual filing requirements. The trust may also be required to file state income tax forms. Finally, if there is a state sales tax, the trust may be eligible for exemption, but this will also require certain filings.

This article is intended as an educational guide; the trust should consult a tax attorney to ensure compliance with IRS rules and requirements.

Notes

1. Rev. Rul. 76-204, 1976-1 C.B. 152.
2. I.R.C. §§170(b)(1)(A), 170(d), 170(e).
3. I.R.C. §§170(b)(1)(B), 170(e).
4. I.R.C. §§508(b).
5. *See generally* 26 C.F.R. §§1.170A-9(e)(2), (6), (7). For purposes of this test, "support" does not include amounts received for an activity that is substantially related to the charitable purposes of the organization. Thus the proceeds from the sale of lumber from trees that had to be cleared would not be counted as support, while the proceeds from a bake sale would count as "support," but not as "public support."
6. *See generally* 26 C.F.R. §1.170A-9(e)(3).
7. Another reason is that gifts from "substantial contributors" and their families are wholly excluded from public support in computing the fraction under No. 8. Substantial contributors are those giving more than $5,000 to a trust if this amount is more than 2 percent of the total support received by that trust throughout its existence. Once an individual becomes a substantial contributor, he retains this status for all future years. I.R.C. §§509(a)(2), 4946, 507(d)(2).
8. I.R.C. §§4940, 4942.
9. Treas. Reg. §1.170A-9(e)(5). A contributor responsible for or aware of the act that caused disqualification will not be protected. Donors whose taxable-year contributions are less than 25 percent of total support from other sources over the past four years, or the number of years the organization has existed, whichever is less, are not deemed to be "responsible" for disqualification unless they are managers or directors. Rev. Proc. 81-6, 1981-1 C.B. 620.
10. Form 872-C, which is in the Form 1023 package, must be filled out by land trusts seeking an extended advance ruling as a waiver of the statute of limitations on tax liability.

11. "Self-dealing" refers to transactions such as leasing property between an organization and a disqualified person. A disqualified person includes a substantial contributor, officer, or director of a trust, or a member of the family of one of these individuals and other entities controlled by them. Disqualified persons are not barred from making contributions to the trust, however. I.R.C. §§4941, 4949. *See supra* note 7 for a discussion of substantial contributors.
12. See the discussion of lobbying in this article.
13. I.R.C. §4943 (excess business holding); I.R.C. §4944 (speculative investments); I.R.C. §4945 (expenditures for certain individual or organizational grants and noncharitable purposes).
14. I.R.C. §508(e).
15. I.R.C. §4940.
16. *See generally* Treas. Reg. §53.4942(b). Further information on private operating foundations is contained in IRS Publication 578.
17. I.R.C. §509(a)(3). *See* the regulations at I.R.C. §1.509(a)-4 for detailed guidance on many potential issues. Parent organizations may also include civic leagues, business leagues, and labor organizations that qualify as tax-exempt under I.R.C. §501(c)(4), (5), or (6), and that meet the further requirement of at least one-third support from the general public.
18. *See supra* note 7 for a discussion of substantial contributors. "Controlled" means that such contributors have a majority of the voting power on the board of directors.
19. I.R.C. §501(h).
20. I.R.C. §§508(e), 4945.
21. Seasongood v. Comm'r, 227 F.2d 907 (6th Cir. 1955).
22. I.R.C. §4911. For organizations spending over $500,000, the percentage limits are lower.
23. Treas. Reg. §1.170A-9(e)(4)(v).
24. Treas. Reg. §1.170A-9(e)(6)(ii). *See* Rev. Rul. 76-440, 1976-2 C.B. 58 for an example of the application of these regulations.
25. Rev. Proc. 81-8, 1981-1 C.B. 623.
26. Treas. Reg. §1.170A-9(e)(6)(iv).
27. Treas. Reg. §1.170A-9(e)(4)(v). Donors whose taxable-year contribution is less than 25 percent of total support from other sources over the past four years, or the number of years the organization has existed, whichever is less, are not deemed to be "responsible" for disqualification unless they are managers or directors. Rev. Proc. 81-6, 1981-1 C.B. 620.

Criteria for Acquisition and Management

Russell L. Brenneman

Quite commonly land conservation organizations originate out of a crisis—some particular piece of open space is about to be lost to development, or a historic site is on the verge of being demolished.

Samuel W. Morris
French & Pickering Creeks Conservation Trust[1]

People being the way they are, it is often not until something is about to be lost that they perceive its value, or, worse yet, do not appreciate its significance until it is gone.[2] A crisis over an anticipated loss or anger over some mindless act of destruction has provided the crucible within which many land-saving organizations and land-saving projects have been born. This response often emerges from deep and, in many instances, subjective needs brought consciously to light by a threat.[3] As Samuel W. Morris, a guiding spirit of the French & Pickering Creeks Conservation Trust (of Chester County, Pennsylvania), tells us, it was the threatened development of a 100-acre farm adjacent to French Creek (in the vicinity of the Valley Forge battleground) that caused conservation-minded citizens in that rural Pennsylvania neighborhood to organize themselves. Countless other organizations have similar stories. After that creational event, what comes next?

That is a very important question. Sophisticated large land conservation organizations, such as The Nature Conservancy and The Trust for Public Land, have spent many thousands of dollars and countless staff hours to define their goals and strategies. The smaller land-saving charity runs the risk of never (consciously) asking what its aims are and how they can be met. As a result, the entire land conservation movement—large organizations as well as small—may be jeopardized. All of its components are publicly perceived as part of the same charitable enterprise,

saving land, and, as such, must individually be able to explain their programs.

Consider the case of a land-saving organization that remains in a purely reactive mode. It is motivated not by its own policies but rather by the latest "brushfire," the importance of which may reflect the degree of public controversy it raises rather than its relevance to the larger and longer-lasting needs of the community. Or such an organization may be vulnerable to the influence of some valuable contributor, finding it all too easy to accept the ownership of land merely because it is offered. If the process is not brought to a halt, the organization may become the owner of a crazy quilt of small parcels having no relationship either to one another or to the management capabilities of the organization or, indeed, to any long-range goals of the organization or the community itself.

Danger lies in such apparent pragmatism. On the most superficial plane, resources may be stretched thin and the ability to keep track of, monitor, and defend the land acquired may become exhausted. On a more serious level, the general public, local officials, and other influential participants[4] may misperceive the organization's function and withdraw support or even actively oppose the organization. A local land trust whose program is perceived as acquiring property solely to "stop development" and for no discernible reason will scarcely find favor among those concerned with reconciling the need for conservation with the need for community growth.

Such an organization adrift risks losing the basic identity that brings to it a preferred legal and tax status—its identity as a charity. The "transcendent characteristic" shared by land-saving organizations is that they are "carrying on their work as charities, in the traditional sense . . . [and] are perceived to act in the general interest to further socially valuable objectives."[5] It is vital, in a philosophical sense, for a land-saving organization to keep this concept— acting for the public good—foremost in mind; and it is necessary, in the practical sense, for the organization to demonstrate that it does so in order to establish the authenticity and credibility of its programs.

The social aspects of a land-saving decision will not be neglected by an organization conscientious about its role as a charity, concerned about maintaining broad-based support, aware that the tax benefits it enjoys are the result of political decisions by legislatures, and desirous of being a responsible citizen. To speak plainly, a trust's decision to restrict the use of a parcel of land must be based on sound and carefully articulated reasons. It must have a solid reference to values expressed by the organization, which are within generally acceptable charitable purposes. The public benefit, even if long term and even if of a sort to which not all would subscribe, must be demonstrable. That means that it is essential for an organization to develop and adopt criteria that supply *intentionality* to its land acquisition and management programs.

This is not to say that all organizations will come up with the same answers. Indeed, the very creativity of the land-saving movement emerges from its diversity and responsiveness to local conditions. However, every land-saving effort must embody a process of reasoned discipline to establish land acquisition and management criteria. Guidelines are developed to tell an organization which gifts to accept and which to refuse, to determine how its resources should be invested, and to define both its limits and its possibilities. Without such criteria the organization is rudderless and cannot justify its actions. With them it can steer a clear course, attract public support around identified goals, and survive close scrutiny from those who question its purposes.

An intentional program, however, need not be mindlessly rigid. Property does not come to the marketplace at predictable times. Still less do land gifts come to organizations on any predetermined basis. An intentional program prepares the organization to deal with opportunities when they arise. It balances the need for intentionality and the need to be opportunistic. To have a reasoned plan of acquisition and management is not to say that an organization need forego opportunity. To be opportunistic, on the other hand, is not to say that an organization need not have a reasoned context within which opportunities are to be dealt with. As Mr. Morris observes: ". . . a conservation program must have form. But never let that form become hidebound. Keep in mind that it is the crises which bring the opportunities."[6] Just so, but it is the disciplined response to crises that confers authenticity upon a land-saving organization and justifies its special status as a charity.

Passing from this discussion of the need for land acquisition criteria, what are some things organizations should have in mind when developing useful standards? Certainly the first is a definition of the purpose of the organization. This may seem a simple task, but in many cases it may not

be. Land-saving organizations are often formed pursuant to legal documents that are intended to enable them to engage in the widest possible range of activities with the most extensive powers permitted by law while still assuring classification as exempt organizations under the Internal Revenue Code. Certificates of incorporation and bylaws prepared with such objectives in mind often do not provide the organization with clear guidance as to its specific role.

Not all organizations see ownership of land as a primary purpose. An organization may see its role as being primarily educational, whether through providing resources to the formal school system or through increasing public awareness of the necessity of conservation. It may perceive its function as enabling transactions through providing technical support to other organizations or receiving title to property and simultaneously passing it through to other permanent holders, whether private charities or governmental agencies. An organization may see its role as a contract manager for other charities or for private corporations or individuals, a managerial "expert." An organization may be primarily political in the sense that it acts as a coalition-builder among other organizations, groups, agencies, and individuals who can be marshaled together to serve a conservation end; or it may see itself as a mediator available to resolve conflicts among those having different perspectives on how a particular resource is to be used. Finally, and perhaps most conventionally, it may wish to carry out its land-saving mission by owning land, buildings, or interests in them.

Whatever the organization's view of itself, its target, in terms of land, may be very narrow—for example, the acquisition of rights in agricultural land, the conservation of wetlands, or even the protection of a particular historic building. In these instances, acquisition criteria may be quite straightforward. Land-saving purposes may also be quite broad—for example, the protection of "open space." What open space? A mountain range? A green belt? The environs of historic buildings? Here, organizations cannot fail to sharpen their own definitions of "open space" in developing acquisition criteria. Otherwise, they are vulnerable to acquiring properties that fall into no discernible pattern and to solicitations (and pressure) to accept unwanted property merely because it falls into the catch-all category "open space."

The science of definition may be complex and require research as well as thought. Baseline studies which are not resource or site specific may be a necessary predicate of a disciplined acquisition program. However, each organization need not necessarily finance and conduct such studies. The information may be available from governmental natural resource agencies, from educational institutions, or from other conservation organizations. Even so, an organization may choose to conduct a program to develop and deepen such information as an aid to its acquisition program.[7] Whatever specific course toward developing criteria is taken, the critical factor is that such an analysis is undertaken and used to inform the practices of the organization.

In addition to evaluating a category of land or a specific property against its own overall objectives, an organization must determine whether an acquisition serves a "long-term public benefit."[8] Unless such a benefit can be demonstrated, the organization must confront the prospect of investing its resources, perhaps in response to a local and temporary "brushfire," in an asset that will not produce an appropriate return in the conservation sense. For example, an organization may be engaged in protecting freshwater wetlands, but that is not to say that every wetland is suitable for protection.

A reference point to determine whether or not a public benefit exists will be found in the plans and programs of public agencies, at the local, county, state, and national levels: Is the acquisition consistent with relevant public plans and programs, or is there a conflict? For example, is the acquisition consistent with the locally adopted land-use plan because it is located in a conservation or green-belt zone, or is it in the middle of a plot slated for commercial or residential development? If there is a demonstrated long-term public benefit and consistency with public development plans and expectations, the acquisition may be supported through grants-in-aid from public agencies or it may be the beneficiary of technical support (in terms of planning, supervision, data-gathering, and monitoring) from such agencies.

Examination of the public benefit question also has critical tax consequences. Meeting the long-term public benefit test may mean that the acquisition will be eligible for beneficial tax treatment under local property law or under the Internal Revenue Code. If it fails this test, it may not be eligible for tax benefits, as in the case of open space easements that fail to meet the public benefit test under the Internal Revenue Code and thus are ineligible for a charitable contributions deduction by the donor.[9]

Acquisition decisions and criteria must also account for the response of the private sector. Does the community support the acquisition or does it not? What is the likelihood that the support will be expressed in donations or grants from individuals or corporations in the community? If it is necessary for the organization to launch a special fund drive in connection with a particular acquisition, what success can be predicted? Such questions must be answered if acquisitions, however worthy, are not to be fiscally ruinous. The relationship between these factors and the public benefit test may be substantial.

In developing acquisition criteria, organizations must also bear in mind the relationship between the acquisition of a parcel or category of properties and the related management costs. Whichever other tests the property may meet, if the cost of managing is to be incommensurate with its conservation value, an organization might be well advised to pass it up. For example, while few would quarrel with the general proposition that coastal wetlands should be preserved, should an organization accept a postage-stamp parcel in urban environs that must be aggressively managed against intruders, littering, and so on? The value of the objective must be weighed against the cost of attaining it, in this as in other cases. This may seem all too obvious, but learning to say no is a difficult task for most land-saving organizations.

Whichever types of land an organization seeks to protect, it must know a certain amount about a given parcel to evaluate its suitability. A wetland that is the habitat for a rare or endangered species obviously is in a different category from a wetland that is a recharge area for a city water supply or a wetland that is part of a historic farm. Knowing it is a wetland is important, but learning the particulars is also necessary. Here cooperation among organizations is required in order to assure efficient use of the available data. For example, a bird club may develop significant data on populations and feeding and migration patterns that can be used by a land acquisition organization to support acquisition and management decisions relative to wildlife areas. Thus an organization might well conclude that certain basic data must be in hand before it makes a judgment as to acquisition and that it have some policy as to how this data is to be developed (by the owner? by the organization? to what level of detail?).

Another acquisition criterion that might be adopted would be whether or not the property extends other holdings of the organization, provides a buffer for other holdings, or represents a toehold that can be extended through future acquisitions. That is, the property must be considered in relation to past and proposed holdings of the organization. Property of no particular distinction might be acquired purely to protect critical adjacent areas. In the case of property acquired for the purpose of generating funds for the organization through sale, economic values must obviously play the predominant role. If not acquired through gift, what is the cost of the property in relation to its probable market value now or at a later time when sale is contemplated?

Criteria for management both of the organization itself and of its holdings are perhaps even more neglected by land-saving organizations, particularly smaller ones, than are standards for acquiring property. Not to be forgotten is the fact that land ownership (even by charity!) requires the adoption of a coherent operating plan, which includes generating the necessary funds to carry it out. The management plan of an organization will vary according to its program. At the very least an acceptable property management plan must include three elements: identifying the resource that is to be managed, establishing a management goal and the methodology whereby that goal is to be achieved, and putting in place a system for auditing or monitoring performance on a regular basis. Each of these elements seems simpler than it is in fact.

Identifying the resource to be managed may be as simple as making sure that the location and boundaries of a parcel of land are well established. Does the organization know where the parcel is? Ten years hence will it know? Are boundaries known and acknowledged by all neighbors? Or the task may be so complex as to require a minute inventory of the flora and fauna in order to assure a baseline for the protection of a natural area. The point is that it cannot be assumed at the outset that enough is known about precisely what resource is to be managed. Just as the identification of the resource does much toward clarifying such questions as the type of ownership that should be acquired (if any), it also determines the appropriate operations plan that should be followed and the type of monitoring that is needed.

Once the resource has been identified, a sound management plan must express the purpose toward which the parcel is being managed. Once management goals have been articulated, such issues as the protection of the resource from unwanted intrusion and trespassers, marking boundaries, and, in some cases, fencing them can be rationally addressed. Where property is to be used by visitors, as for hiking or other forms of recreation, the plan should address the issue of risks to those visitors and insurance protection as may be required by local law. If the property is to be actively used by the organization, as for timber development or agriculture, the details of that arrangement should be established. If the property is to be severely restricted for scientific purposes, suitable precautions against unwarranted access must be taken.

Management goals will also give rise to ownership strategies. Will the organization contemplate long-term ownership or transfer to a public agency or another charity? When? Upon what terms? If the organization does not own the fee but instead is the holder of an easement or conservation restriction, how will it accomplish the periodic monitoring needed to make sure that the restrictions on the use of the property are observed? In determining the most appropriate form of ownership to pursue, the group should pay attention to the handling of disputes, since it is likely that disputes will eventually arise between the organization and someone affected by its ownership, particularly in the case of conservation and preservation easements.

Goals and strategies, however well formulated, are not self-realizing. Thus the management plan should address the issue of how resources to carry it out are to be assembled and organized, both economic resources and people resources. If significant economic resources are involved, consideration should be given to a special fund drive or the solicitation of a gift from the donor, if that is feasible. Depending upon the nature of the property, an organization may find it desirable to organize a policy committee for the management of a specific property (or category of properties) and perhaps, additionally, a technical committee to provide the scientific and other technical information that may be necessary for the policy committee to carry out its responsibilities. If management is to be carried out on an in-house basis, who specifically will do the job and how will the person be trained and supervised? If staff will not be utilized, how will management be achieved?

Last, a management plan must set out a monitoring system to see that its goals are in fact being met.

In conjunction with addressing the management of property, a plan must address the corporate and business management of the organization. The nature of the management requirement varies with the type of organization, the type of resource, and the type of ownership involved. An important choice is how an organization expresses its management—through professional (paid) staff or volunteers. If volunteers are relied upon, how are they to be organized, trained, supported, and supervised? If professionals are to be used, what financial resources are required and how are these resources to be attracted over the long term? Issues such as internal and external communications and the investment and handling of funds are often neglected as the organization puts all of its energy into its substantive work.

To conclude, it is clear that an organization safely can neglect neither criteria for acquisition nor criteria for management. Gordon Abbott, Jr., Director of the Trustees of Reservations (Massachusetts), has long maintained that "there are two steps involved in land conservation: first, the immediate step of acquiring or preserving, and, second, the too-often-neglected concern of providing the structure and mechanism to continue that preservation. We call that *management,* and we believe that it is every bit as important as protecting land in the first place."[10] (Emphasis added.)

Notes

1. Samuel W. Morris, "How Are Land-Saving Decisions Made? Establishing Criteria; Keeping Priorities," *Proceedings—1981 National Consultation Local Land Conservation Organizations,* Land Trust Exchange, Boston, Mass. (1981), at 107.

2. *See generally* C. Greiff, *Lost America* (Pyne, 1974).

3. The relationship between this response and "no-change constituencies" in "aesthetic" controversies is challengingly discussed in Costonis, *Law and Aesthetics: A Critique and a Reformulation of the Dilemmas,* 80 Mich. L. Rev. 355 (1982).

4. Such as the United States Congress and the Treasury Department, as the passage of the easement provisions of the Tax Treatment Extension Act of 1980, Pub. L. No. 96-541, 94 Stat. 3204, may attest.

5. Russell L. Brenneman, "What Is Open Space and How Should It Be Preserved?" *Proceedings, supra* note 1, at 35.

6. Morris, "How Are Land-Saving Decisions Made?" *Proceedings, supra* note 1, at 107, 108.

7. *See, e.g.,* A. Pesiri, "Sandplains of Connecticut" (The Nature Conservancy, Connecticut Chapter, 1982). Unpublished monograph.

8. Joan Vilms, "Land-Saving Decisions in Sonoma and Napa Valleys, California," *Proceedings, supra* note 1, at 113.

9. I.R.C. §170(h)(4)(A)(iii)(II).

10. Gordon Abbott, Jr., "Long-Term Management: Problems and Opportunities," *Proceedings, supra* note 1, at 134.

Criteria for Agricultural Land Protection

Jennie Gerard

Saving agricultural land has become a hot topic among local land trusts in the last few years. Over 100 trusts now mention this as a goal. Several of them identify saving agricultural land as their exclusive focus. For many land trusts, the conversion of farmland and rangeland to developed uses represents a loss of open space that is significant because of the views it affords and the animal habitats it provides. These are two of the usual public benefits mentioned by conservationists. For certain community land trusts and the new twist in conservation land trusts, the agricultural land trusts, protecting the land base for farm and ranch jobs and for food production is the overriding concern. To them this protection is the public benefit to strive for.

Regardless of the motivations, each land trust faces the knotty problems resulting from the fact that virtually no agricultural yield pays for the cost of buying the land today when it is located in the path of urban or recreational growth or over valuable mineral deposits. Few agrarians will buy agricultural land at developers' prices. Furthermore, many farming and ranching operations on such land cannot survive a transfer to younger generations of heirs without extraordinary estate-planning measures or outside incomes. Even with the currently increasing value of an estate that can transfer tax free, many land-extensive operations are too valuable to be fully exempt. Medium-size farms, valued today for development purposes at $3,000 or more per acre, with improvements, livestock, and machinery, can easily exceed the limit of $600,000 that will transfer tax free by 1987. It becomes apparent that the pressured farms and ranches represent a holding land-use pattern. Enter what Charles Little of the American Land Forum calls the "impermanence syndrome": Owner-operators make decisions about their operations based on the assumption that they will sell soon to development interests.

Nothing would work better to protect agricultural land than better prices for the harvests. While theories of improved marketing abound, the experience of The Trust for Public Land's training and technical assistance program for agricultural land trusts shows that lowered taxes and strong community support are as important to agricultural land protection as the transaction aimed at preserving a given piece of land.

Components of Agricultural Land Protection

Let's start with what it takes to preserve a piece of agricultural land. First, we must eliminate the pressure of conversion on the land so that it can stay in production. Preserving the land's food-producing capability requires removing the potential to develop the land for uses that would be incompatible with agricultural practices. It means barring subdivision of the land into uneconomically small agricultural parcels. It means tying the water rights to the land, where they are adjudicated, to assure sufficient irrigation for crops. Acquiring gifts and bargain sales of conservation easements over agricultural land is the most popular method for achieving these objectives. A handful of states have purchased the development rights over selected agricultural lands. A few municipalities have purchased fee title to the lands, then leased back the right to farm them. These site-specific efforts are like leading the proverbial horse to water. Eliminating the pressure of conversion on a specific piece of land may have preserved it but does not guarantee the continuing practice of agriculture. If this were as far as the effort went, we could have preserved the land only as open space. Agricultural land protection requires more than preservation of specific parcels. Its focus must be on the viability of the local agricultural economy.

Leadership by Agriculturists

The first prerequisite for protection of agricultural land is the presence of a local community of farmers or ranchers intent on keeping agricultural land in production. Their intent is a measure of the vitality of the agriculture economy. As a community, their presence represents the volume of business that the essential agriculturally related services need to stay close by. Their participation behind the wheel of the local land trust is its strongest selling point to other agriculturalists.

Community Support

A second valuable criterion to meet when determining whether a land trust transaction will result in protecting agricultural land is community support for the industry. Examples are numerous. Community support for dog leash laws has cut down on the death loss suffered annually by woolgrowers. Fence laws requiring all landowners, stockmen or not, to maintain half of their fences are standard in intermountain west states. Farmers' markets have formed around the country to improve sales from truck farms.

Surrounding Land Uses

Community support is vital in determining surrounding land uses. The uses of the land neighboring the preserved agricultural land are of vital concern. A single farming operation, no matter how well laid out and managed, faces tremendous odds without compatible neighbors. Nuisance ordinances outlawing livestock operations and restricting spraying emerge in communities where too many farms have turned into ranchettes and other homesites for city folk. Protecting one parcel of agricultural land requires consideration of the guarantees that ensure that the surrounding land uses will stay compatible. Otherwise, that parcel is likely to become the preserved open space for adjacent development. This is a tough judgment call.

Land-use regulation is the most effective means of gaining community support for reducing development pressure. Larger minimum lot sizes and exclusive agricultural zones are the usual types. Complex ordinances such as those permitting the transfer of development rights are attractive conceptually because they would harness the private market to the purchase and removal of development rights from "donor" agricultural lands. Ordinances encouraging planned unit developments can preserve agricultural land but will protect it only if the proposed configuration of development will not intrude on production. Clearly, livestock operations so vulnerable to dogs and orchards and crops with their customary spraying are hardly protected by neighboring residential development. Both types of ordinances have been adopted in jurisdictions where substantial land conversion to other uses already has occurred. Yet the urban tax base that supports such sophisticated land-use regulation diminishes the viability of agriculturally related businesses and the dependence of lending institutions on their farm and ranch accounts. In addition, the shortcoming of any of these regulations is that it takes only three votes and thirty days to change them.

Participation by agricultural landowners in programs offering preferential property tax treatment can be an indicator of commitment by neighbors. The strength of the commitment depends on the cost and degree of difficulty in dropping out of the program. These programs, too, are relatively short term in their impact. In essence, there is little long-term guarantee of surrounding land use.

Summary

What then are the criteria for agricultural land preservation? Any land trust contemplating a transaction, such as acquisition of a conservation easement for the purpose of saving agricultural land, has to consider what else will influence the use of the land for agricultural purposes. Local agricultural leadership is a vital indicator, as is community support for regulations that promote agriculture. Compatible surrounding land uses are all-important. These are the criteria that must be met.

Land trusts in their educational capacity can influence the presence of these factors. In their effort to protect agricultural land, their educational role may be as important as their specific transactions. One example of an event that land trusts could sponsor is a farm day. Several years ago, an environmental organization and the county farm bureau sponsored just such an activity in Marin County, California, to give urbanites a chance to learn something of the practice of agriculture. It was so well received, it is now an annual event. One board member of the newly formed land trust, who has attended every year, commented: "This is the way that folks who never grew up on a farm can learn how to be their good neighbors. In just five years, the audience here has come a long way in its understanding of this county's agricultural industry."

Criteria for Scenic Areas Preservation

Benjamin R. Emory
and Davis Hartwell

For centuries Americans have drawn strength and inspiration from the beauty of our country. It would be a neglectful generation indeed, indifferent alike to the judgment of history and the command of principle, which failed to preserve and extend such a heritage for its descendants.

President Lyndon B. Johnson[1]

The founding and evolution of Maine Coast Heritage Trust has sprung directly from a very strong commitment to preserve for coming generations the beauty of the Maine coast. Our descendants will need strength, inspiration, refuge, affirmation of man's place in nature, and pure aesthetic delight just as much as we do today—perhaps more so if new technologies and higher population densities separate man even more from the natural world. Yet the supply of natural landscape will certainly be less than it is today. If the world that our children, and their children, and their children inherit is to be worth inheriting, then we must do all we can to preserve beautiful landscapes.

In Maine we are blessed with one of the world's most scenic shorelines. Speaking at a symposium on the Maine coast back in 1966, Dr. Joseph L. Fisher, then president of Resources for the Future, Inc., commented, "The Maine coast, of course, is a matchless scenic and recreation resource. There are more than 3,000 miles of coastline, of rocky points, coves, inlets, sand beaches. In my opinion the Norwegian coast, the Dalmatian coast, Acapulco, the Inside Passage of Alaska, none of these surpass the Maine coast in the variety, the beauty, the excitement of its natural features."[2]

Scenery need not be spectacular to be worth preserving, however. An area may lack magnificent vistas, yet still possess a familiar beauty that residents cherish. A study in New Jersey determined that among the most popular landscapes in the state's Pinelands region are historic buildings along streambanks.[3]

Scenic preservation programs always face the question of what are the most important properties to preserve. The quality of a view is difficult to rank, for people's perceptions of beauty vary. At Maine Coast Heritage Trust we evaluate scenery on a purely subjective basis. Other programs have tried to develop objective ranking systems. The methodology and criteria that work in one area may not in another. Much depends on the particular landscape and the people conducting the program. The Maine Coast Heritage Trust experience is set forth here as just one example of an active, effective effort to preserve beautiful lands, and the trust's methodology is briefly contrasted with two other approaches to the evaluation of scenery.

In the late 1960s people who loved the Maine coast were becoming increasingly alarmed. Haphazard, unzoned, second-home development was sprouting along island and mainland shores; and industrial developers, attracted by the deep water close to shore, were proposing supertanker ports and oil refineries. The individuals who ultimately came together to establish Maine Coast Heritage Trust asked themselves how growth and development could be guided in ways that would best help the people of Maine and, at the same time, preserve the beauty and the ecological balance of the Maine coast.

Ninety-seven percent of the Maine coast was privately owned. What could private property owners do on their own initiative to help preserve the coast's natural integrity? The question was studied by a team of first-rate attorneys, who made this recommendation: Grant conservation easements on land of particular scenic and ecological importance. Since then, we at Maine Coast Heritage Trust have regarded conservation easements as the strongest way to legally establish permanent land-use guidelines for properties that will remain in private ownership.

Maine Coast Heritage Trust, a publicly supported, nonprofit organization, was founded in 1970 to promote the use of conservation easements. Although the trust today has experience in the whole array of land conservation techniques, the conservation easement program remains at the heart of trust efforts. Unusual among conservation easement programs around the nation, Maine Coast Heritage Trust until 1981 avoided holding conservation easements itself. Although the trust now will accept easements under certain circumstances, it prefers to limit its role to acquainting landowners with the conservation easement device and to making arrangements between landowners wishing to grant easements and the various government agencies and nonprofit organizations willing to accept them.

Scenic preservation remains one of Maine Coast Heritage Trust's highest priorities. The trust also actively works to preserve ecologically fragile and important areas, and the trust is very concerned with the well-being of the people and communities of the Maine coast. It is in scenic preservation, however, that leadership by the trust is most needed. Few other land conservation organizations are working aggressively to protect the Maine coast's beauty. In recent years The Nature Conservancy has drastically narrowed its criteria for conserving land, excluding scenic importance as a criterion in its decisionmaking. The Conservancy now concentrates its efforts wholly on protecting land of unusual biological significance, and scenic preservation is simply a byproduct. The National Audubon Society, also active on the Maine coast, is less rigid than The Nature Conservancy but, nonetheless, emphasizes ecological values in deciding whether or not to acquire land or a conservation easement. The U.S. Fish and Wildlife Service and the Maine Department of Inland Fisheries and Wildlife preserve wildlife habitat. Only Acadia National Park, operating on just one part of the Maine coast, and a handful of small, local land trusts join Maine Coast Heritage Trust in working actively to protect the coast's scenic resources.

In determining which Maine coast properties are scenically important enough for Maine Coast Heritage Trust to try to preserve, the trust makes its judgments based on familiarity with the coast. The board of directors and staff members know the coast exceedingly well. One of the great recreational pursuits along the Maine coast is cruising in pleasure boats, and fishing is a major commercial activity. Many of the board and staff have seen most of the coast—in some cases many times—from the decks of small vessels. We also have driven along the coast and poked up and down the back roads extensively. From this detailed knowledge of what the coast looks like we make judgments on where to concentrate our efforts.

Our subjective evaluation of scenic importance is now unavoidably affected by the Conference Report on the Tax Treatment Extension Act of 1980. This law and its accompanying committee report established standards that donated conservation easements must meet in order to have their appraised values deductible for federal tax purposes. A conservation easement may meet the standards if it "is for the scenic enjoyment of the general public. . . . [P]reservation of land may be for scenic enjoyment of the general public if development of the property would interfere with a scenic panorama that can be enjoyed from a park, nature preserve, road, waterbody, trail, historic structure or land area, and such area or transportation way is open to, or utilized by, the public."[4] In considering possible conservation easements we carefully review the "visual access" of the public—that is, the opportunity of the public to view the property, the actual amount of public viewing, and how much of the property can be seen from a public place, be it land or water.

We believe, however, that the opportunity for public viewing of a scenic vista is much more important than the number of people who actually see it. We agree very much with a sentiment expressed in a recent Jackson Hole, Wyoming, study on preservation priorities and feel it applies equally well to the Maine coast: "Jackson Hole is full of extraordinary views. Some are seen by millions of people; others by very few. A valid argument can be made that the solitary nature of these less popular views adds to their beauty; and whether or not they ever become popular . . . these views have public value."[5]

Although intimate familiarity with the Maine coast has provided Maine Coast Heritage Trust with an excellent basis for evaluating scenic priorities, there are times when some sort of step-by-step process for objectively ranking scenery may be helpful to a scenic preservation program. For example, Maine's State Planning Office has a Critical Areas Program, which is developing a register of critical natural areas. The declaration of purpose in the enabling legislation stated that "[a]reas of unusual natural, scenic, scientific or historical interest should be inventoried to facilitate their preservation for present and future generations."[6] Created in 1974, the Critical Areas Program has yet to tackle the job of inventorying scenic areas. It is much easier to identify rare plant stands, for example, or the nesting sites of endangered bird species. Judging scenery is more subjective, and scenic areas typically lack discrete boundaries. Often a scenic vista covers a large amount of land. The Critical Areas Program has not yet developed a system for identifying and ranking Maine's most important vistas.

Efforts to develop objective criteria for establishing scenic priorities have been made in other states. A noteworthy work in this field is the Pinelands Scenic Study conducted during the 1970s by the U.S. Department of the Interior, the New Jersey Pinelands Commission, and the New Jersey Department of Environmental Protection. The study tried to describe the variety of Pinelands scenery and to measure people's preferences for different kinds of landscapes and different places within New Jersey's Pinelands. The investigators divided Pinelands vistas into fifty-three categories under the general headings of natural landscapes, disturbed landscapes, and built landscapes. The public was then invited to meetings at which paired slides were shown, and each viewer was asked to mark on a questionnaire which scene of each pair he or she preferred.

In this way the study developed a ranking of what sorts of Pinelands vistas are most pleasing to most people.[7]

The previously mentioned Jackson Hole report provides another interesting way of trying to establish scenic priorities. The study rated the relative public value of Jackson Hole's various vistas. The ratings are based on so-called resource and human components. In the resource component the study ranked as most important the views that offer the greatest diversity of physical features, views in which the human use of the land is most compatible with the natural scenery, and views of which the boundaries are clearly defined by topography, vegetation, or a change in land use. For the human component, greatest importance was given to views that are likely to be seen by the greatest number of people—despite the acknowledged argument for the public value of more solitary views—and views seen by recreational sightseers, such as the people rafting on the Snake River. One product of the Jackson Hole study is a map showing the popular viewpoints and the general direction and breadth of the views from these points.[8]

In New Jersey, Wyoming, Maine, and many other states there are varied but active approaches to preserving the best of each area's scenery. Although each approach has its own advantages, the underlying strength of scenic pres-ervation programs comes from deep, emotional commit-ments to beloved landscapes. In closing his message on natural beauty President Johnson reminded America, "The beauty of our land is a natural resource. Its preservation is linked to the inner prosperity of the human spirit."[9]

Notes

1. President Johnson's Message to Congress, "Natural Beauty," 111 Cong. Rec. 2085 (1965).

2. J. Fisher, "Toward a Maine Coastal Park and Recreation System," *The Maine Coast: Prospects and Perspectives* 90 (1967) (Center for Resource Studies, Bowdoin College).

3. U.S. Dept. of the Interior, Heritage & Recreation Service, *The Pinelands Scenic Study: Summary Report* 6 (undated).

4. Senate Comm. on Finance—Temporary Tax Provisions—Extension, S. Rep. No. 96-1007, 96th Cong., 2d Sess. 11, *reprinted in* 1981 U.S. Code Cong. & Ad. News 11013, 11023.

5. Jackson Hole Project/Izaak Walton League of America, *Jackson Hole: Protecting Public Values on Private Lands* 34 (Aug. 1981).

6. Me. Rev. Stat. Ann. tit. 5, §3311 (West 1979).

7. U.S. Dept. of the Interior, *supra* note 3, at 7.

8. Jackson Hole Project/Izaak Walton League of America, *supra* note 5, at 33-37.

9. President Johnson, *supra* note 1, at 2085-89.

Criteria for Community Land Trusts

Charles Matthei

Community land trusts (CLTs) share a number of structural features with local land conservation organizations (LCOs) and utilize many of the same techniques for land acquisition and organizational development. Like the LCOs, CLTs are locally based, nonprofit corporations committed to the public interest. However, as the loosely descriptive term "community" in the name of a CLT is meant to suggest, there are several significant differences in the CLT's concepts and working definitions of the public interest and public benefit: (1) the CLT adopts a broader definition of the public interest and addresses a wider range of community needs—human needs as well as environmental, social goals as well as land preservation; (2) while *public* benefit is at the center of the CLT's purposes, it is tempered by a commitment to the *private* use of most trust lands, particularly by those segments of the public which are most often denied the benefits of property ownership; and (3) the CLT recognizes the need to integrate social and environmental objectives, and public and private interests. These unique commitments shape the acquisition and management criteria of the CLT.

Public Interest/Public Benefit

The CLT makes an effort to understand the full range of its community's needs for land and the relative urgency of the needs of various residents. Needs for recreation, housing, employment, commerce, public services, and environmental conservation are all considered. Land is then acquired and made available to individuals, families, businesses, and other organizations for a variety of uses.

Most CLTs have a particular concern for and commitment to meeting the needs of low-income people. They work to provide the access to land and decent, affordable housing that is often difficult—or virtually impossible—for low-income people to obtain, especially in periods of economic recession. They try to fulfill the desire for the benefits normally associated only with property owner-

ship and therefore unavailable to low-income tenants. CLTs offer an alternative to the traditional roles of owner or renter and bridge the gap between public and private ownership.

Indeed, CLTs address not only the issues of land use, but also rights of access, land value, and the allocation of equity. They reconsider traditional structures of ownership and attempt to strike a new and fair balance between the legitimate interests of individuals and the community as a whole. Individuals want lifetime security, to have a home and a livelihood and the confidence that they will not be taken away; they want fair equity for their investment of capital and labor; and they want a legacy for their descendants. These, in themselves, are legitimate interests and should be safeguarded. But the community also has legitimate interests. It has a responsibility to ensure that the right of access is widely and fairly available to all of its members; it has an interest in long-term land-use decisions, exercising control over its own evolution; and it has a right to the equity or land value created through public investment, cooperative or community-wide development activity, and larger economic forces. A reassessment of property rights and land tenure structures is a necessary counterpart to land-use planning and conservation efforts.

CLTs recognize the need to integrate these individual and community—private and public—interests when formulating social and environmental land-use goals. Conservation goals must be conceived, understood, and presented in this context in order to generate the necessary public understanding and support. Effective planning—and preservation—will require a fairly balanced plan for community development and land use.

Acquisition Criteria

Just as the CLT's organizational purposes reflect a mixture of social and environmental concerns, so its land acquisition criteria are also a mix. The acquisition process begins with an assessment of the community's needs and available resources, which includes: (1) an inventory of land and buildings (physical characteristics, current use, productive capacity and potential use, the pattern of land use and the oversupply or undersupply of land for specific purposes, and unique or endangered areas); (2) a demographic or social inventory (population, ethnic groups, income mix, occupations, skills, and employment needs); and (3) a study of ownership patterns and market conditions (absentee ownership, multiple property ownership, the percentage of owner-occupied and rental properties, vacancy rates, prevailing market prices, and rental costs). In each case, both present conditions and projected trends are considered.

Acquisition criteria will differ somewhat, of course, from community to community and from rural to urban areas, but the principal criteria will include the quality of the property and its potential usefulness, affordability, strategic value, and the capability of the CLT.

Quality and Usefulness

While the local LCO may seek only "wild" land or land with unique ecological features, the CLT will consider "any and all" land within the community, looking not only at its natural characteristics, but also at its productive capacity and its development potential. CLTs often acquire land with buildings on it; the condition, current use, and potential use of these structures must be evaluated. Factors such as location and proximity to services must be taken into account.

Evaluation of the usefulness of the land and buildings is accompanied by a consideration of the potential users. The acquisition must meet the broader needs of the community *and* suit the CLT's membership or the constituency it has chosen to serve: their needs, skills, and priorities.

Affordability

A major factor in the usefulness of any property to its prospective users is the cost in land lease fees and mortgage payments. (The CLT is a mixed ownership model, in which ownership of the land is retained by the CLT and made available by lease; however, lessees own the buildings and improvements on the land.) Most of the CLT's lands, productive and in use, are income-producing; the CLT will use lease fee payments to assist in land acquisition. But the members of most existing CLTs are low-income people, without personal access to credit or capital and limited by already-tight monthly budgets.

In calculating the financial requirements, the CLT must consider not only the purchase price, but also the cost of any site development, rehabilitation or construction, and maintenance or management necessary to make the property useful to the prospective lessees. In addition to costs related to any particular property, the CLT must consider —and perhaps include, in part, in its lease fee charges— its costs of management of open space and vacant lands awaiting lessees and its administrative overhead.

Strategic Value

The strategic value of each property may be a significant factor in establishing priorities for acquisition. "Strategic value" may refer to the community at large, particular individuals, the land itself, or the CLT's own momentum of development.

In some cases the CLT may want to acquire property near existing CLT holdings to serve as a buffer zone of environmental protection or to consolidate a larger tract for further development and efficiency of management. In other cases the CLT may adopt a "checkerboard strategy," acquiring scattered tracts throughout an area to block major development that would disrupt the community or to discourage speculation and gentrification through a kind of "reverse blockbusting," thus guaranteeing the continued presence of established residents.

The CLT may secure the position of indigenous leaders in the neighborhood by purchasing the rental properties that they currently occupy or by purchasing other properties suited to their needs. Their presence and their leadership may be crucial for the CLT's own future development, as well as for the strength of the neighborhood as a whole. In a related action one CLT purchased a property housing a vital neighborhood service center when the building was put up for sale, knowing the rent increase by any new owner would have exceeded the center's budgetary limit.

Individual needs may determine the acquisition priorities. One urban CLT grew out of the efforts of local clergy to meet the urgent needs of an eleven-member, low-income family facing eviction after their building was sold for luxury renovation. Another group moved first to acquire the home of a nineteen-year resident whose landlord left the area and placed the property on the market. In the same way a CLT may establish environmental priorities—targeting ecologically unique or endangered lands for early acquisition.

Young CLTs, especially when they are approaching their first acquisitions, should pay attention to the visibility— and visible significance—of the property and to the speed with which it can be put to the intended use. An early "success" will contribute to the CLT's community organizing effort, draw new members into the organization, and open access to new resources and support. For this reason some groups look first to occupied or occupiable properties to avoid the long delays for rehabilitation or construction.

In most cases these early acquisitions should relate directly to the CLT's principal goals, making a clear statement to the community of the organization's purposes and capability. Sometimes, however, this may be difficult, and another strategy may be appropriate. One urban CLT, whose principal goal was development of low-cost housing but that lacked both the technical and financial resources to undertake such a program, began by acquiring (through donation from the city government and long-term leasing from private owners) a number of vacant lots and establishing a highly successful community garden program. The gardens—for schoolchildren, elderly residents, and neighborhood families—gave the CLT a high visibility, a positive image, and a successful track record of community service—at very little cost—and drew new members into the group. Always the CLT must remain flexible, ready to adapt to the community's changing needs and circumstances, and to seize the unexpected opportunity.

Organizational Capability

The pace and timing of acquisitions is often a critical issue. Many CLTs are struggling to respond in communities where speculation, development, displacement, or environmental destruction has already begun; the clock is ticking, and there is limited time in which to achieve critical goals. Nevertheless, the CLT must be mindful of its own organizational resources and limitations. To move too quickly, to exceed its capabilities for acquisition and responsible management, is to risk its reputation, its base of support, and its prospects for future achievement. Any acquisition must be preceded by a careful and realistic assessment of the CLT's base of support in the community, its staff and volunteer resources, its management skills, and available financing.

Most CLT acquisitions are fee simple, but CLTs may also acquire partial interests or use conservation easements, as many LCOs have done, to stretch limited dollars over a greater number of acres and limit management responsibilities. In some instances, certainly, this can be an appropriate and effective strategy, but once again it is important to consider and foresee the social as well as environmental impact and benefits of the acquisition strategy.

In many areas conservation easements have significant limitations. They may protect farmland or forestland from development but may not thereby preserve its productive role or its contribution to the character and stability of a rural community. Even restricted land can command full market prices—as recent experiences in Montana, California, and New England suggest—prices too high for farmers or would-be farmers. Land preservation is an important environmental objective, but the corresponding economic and social objectives are equally important and very much related. Such a balance of social and environmental goals applies to urban as well as rural areas—to "historic" preservation as well as "farmland" preservation.

Whichever criteria shape a CLT's acquisition program, the *process* of locating acquisition properties is very important. The CLT should make a concerted effort to involve its own members and other community residents in preliminary research and identification and selection of properties for acquisition. Community involvement may well speed the acquisition process and increase its impact; it will certainly broaden the CLT's base of membership and support, identify indigenous leadership, educate neighborhood residents, and communicate the CLT's concern for its community.

In every transaction the CLT must consider the impact and benefits of its acquisition program for both the land itself and the local residents. Throughout the acquisition process—from preliminary assessment, through scouting and targeting, to acquisition and development—this mixture of social and environmental concerns must guide the CLT.

Management Criteria

With most of its landholdings leased for active use by individuals, families, community organizations, or businesses, the CLT needs a management structure that balances the public interest and its own responsibilities with the private interests and responsibilities of the lessees themselves. The CLT's management responsibility begins with the preliminary land-use planning before acquisition; then the more detailed analysis of the land's appropriate use and carrying capacities is undertaken after acquisition. Based on this analysis, the land is leased for appropriate uses to qualified users. The particular abilities of the prospective lessees to develop and manage the property may be significant criteria in their selection—or in the CLT's decision to acquire a property with existing tenants.

The mixed ownership model of the CLT—with lessees holding a lease interest in the land and title to the improvements—means a sharing of both the benefits and the liabilities inherent in ownership. The lease agreement is the legal mechanism by which these respective rights and responsibilities are delineated, striking a fair balance between the legitimate interests of the individual and the community as a whole. The lease is, in effect, the principal management tool of the CLT.

In the typical CLT lease, the individual's interests are secured by provisions for (1) the long term of the lease (lifetime, or renewable at the lessees' discretion), which will remain binding and unaffected in the event that ownership of the land should change for any reason; (2) general land-use guidelines that define broad categories of accepted use (for example, "for purposes of residence and agriculture") and give express permission for unrestricted use by the lessees within those parameters; (3) ownership by the lessees of all improvements, with equity for their own investment of capital and labor; (4) inheritance of the leasehold interest in the land by the lessees' heirs, if they choose to use it; and (5) arbitration of any serious disagreements between the CLT and the lessees regarding their respective obligations under the lease, with equal representation for each party on the arbitration panel.

The community's interests, represented by the CLT's stewardship of the land, are protected by provisions for (1) the same land-use guidelines, which may expressly prohibit specific land-use practices that would do serious environmental damage and will require lessees to seek permission for any activities that are doubtfully consistent with the terms of the lease; (2) the right to inspect the premises at any reasonable time; (3) control over subleasing, with the ability to prevent absentee ownership or control of the property; (4) the option to purchase the lessees' improvements, should they come up for sale, at a price that gives the lessees equity for their own investment but retains the appreciated value of the land for the CLT; (5) lease fees for the use of the land, which can be used for acquisition, administration and management, or other services; (6) equal representation in the arbitration process; and (7) the right of eviction should lessees substantially violate the terms of the lease agreement.

While delineating clearly the responsibilities and requirements of the lessees, the CLT also recognizes and accepts the need to offer them personal and practical support. This may be particularly true for low-income lessees, who have limited financial resources of their own to draw on.

Many CLTs establish ongoing support services, although much of the actual responsibility can be borne by the lessees and other CLT members helping one another. The CLT, bringing people together as it does to meet such basic needs as land and housing, is an appropriate foundation for the development of a range of cooperative activities and services. Useful or necessary support services may include (1) assistance in planning and financing of development, perhaps even assuming a "codeveloper" role; (2) homeowner/land-user training to introduce the lessees to the physical features and systems of the land and buildings, basic maintenance tasks, energy conservation, simple repairs, local tradespeople and services, and budgeting for taxes, utilities, maintenance, and other expenses; (3) a cooperative maintenance program, with lessees and other members assisting one another with repairs; (4) a joint contract for maintenance, management, and repair services; (5) an emergency loan fund—funded by lease fees, grants, or a sum added to the sale prices of the homes to the lessees—for use by lessees for major expenses and emergency repairs; and (6) personal services, such as employment counseling or child care.

Once land-use planning has been completed and the land leased, the CLT's management role is principally one of oversight and assistance. In some circumstances, however, the CLT must, as local LCOs more routinely do, assume direct and full management responsibility. This is true in relation to selected lands that are held out of use for preservation or conservation purposes, or any tract during the period of transition from one lessee to the next. The CLT may establish a management committee to play this role. It may also, where appropriate and possible, lease lands set aside for preservation to a local conservation organization or public agency.

In addition to withholding some lands from use entirely, some CLTs lease lands for residential, agricultural, or other uses but withhold the mineral or timber rights. In these cases lessees are usually given access to the natural resources on the leasehold for reasonable personal use but not for commercial exploitation. The lease will often provide for some process of consultation or negotiation between the CLT and lessees before the CLT would exercise its own rights to the resources, but the responsibility for long-term resource planning, management, and development rests with the CLT. Such an arrangement is particularly common for limited or nonrenewable resources—resources on which the entire community and, perhaps, many others ultimately depend.

Responsibility for both direct management and oversight of leased lands rests, of course, with the CLT's board of trustees. The board is structured to include representatives of the lessees, representatives of the general membership, and "public interest" representatives with expertise useful to the CLT or with a notable record of service to the community. Once again it is pointed out that this structure reflects the balance of personal and public interests in community land use.

CLTs have received assistance from a number of sources. Nevertheless, the lack of technical skills—along with limited access to acquisition and development capital—remains a major barrier to the rapid development of many CLTs. This problem may offer another important opportunity for cooperation between LCOs and CLTs. The local land conservation trust movement is an older and much larger movement; a number of the LCOs have acquired substantial experience and skill. An offer by LCOs to share technical and financial skills could greatly benefit the emerging CLT movement. CLTs, on the other hand, can offer LCOs a new base and breadth of public support.

The CLT's board may delegate some management responsibilities to various committees, or it may contract for specific services. Whichever formal delegation of management responsibilities the CLT adopts, however, it is critically important that it involve many of its members— and a cross-section of community residents—in its ongoing activities. "Management" for the CLT must be more than a stewardship of the land itself. It must reflect as well the CLT's commitment to the human community in this natural environment. CLT development is as much a process of community organizing, membership development, and public education as it is a process of careful land stewardship. Community residents must be interested and involved in the CLT, and CLT trustees and staff must be fully accountable to their membership. Throughout its program of activity, the CLT must strive to maintain that essential balance of individual and community interests and the integration of social and environmental objectives.

Criteria for Urban Land Trusts

Peter Stein

Land conservation has not been widely practiced in areas such as East Los Angeles, New York City's South Bronx, Newark, Detroit, Cleveland, or the Roxbury neighborhood in Boston. Yet the tools, techniques, and stewardship philosophy embodied in the mainstream of American land conservation have now been rooted in a multitude of inner-city locations through the establishment of urban land trusts.

In dozens of cities across the United States, residents of low-income neighborhoods have banded together to form local nonprofit land conservation organizations generally referred to as urban or neighborhood land trusts. Since 1975 The Trust for Public Land (TPL) has been instrumental in the incorporation of and the initial land transactions for trusts in eight major metropolitan areas. In addition, TPL staff members have assisted numerous community groups in more than twenty other cities with specific land transactions that meet a variety of open space and community development needs.

How did the techniques of the rural preservation community find their way to the central city? The answer can be found only if you analyze the reasons urban community groups cite for their interest and involvement in neighborhood land trusts. Local control, self-reliance, reduced dependence on government, protection of open space resources, mistrust of governmental programs, and lack of public agency resources are all recounted by numerous community groups as the reasons for their investment of time and energy in establishing a neighborhood land trust. The Barretto Street Park case study[1] illustrates the process of applying traditional land-saving techniques to urban problems.

The Barretto Street project is a good example of responsible management and demonstrates the successful application of many other land revitalization techniques. Starting with a core group of seven people, the organization expanded, incorporated, negotiated a donation of prop-erty, and designed and built a park. As its successes multiplied, it renovated the site and used the skills it acquired to tackle other land revitalization projects in the neighborhood. This model of neighborhood self-help became the keystone of the South Bronx Open Space Task Force, which was established to channel over one million dollars in funds and services to fourteen open space projects similar to Barretto Street in the South Bronx.

Barretto Street Park

In 1975 an abandoned building at 636 Barretto Street burned and left in its place a dangerous ruin and a lot filled with debris. Although abandonment and rubble are not unusual in places like the South Bronx, the residents of Barretto Street decided they would not sit back and allow their block to continue to deteriorate. Many families on the block had raised their children and grandchildren there.

In 1976 a group of seven people organized and agreed that something should be done. Together they convinced the Housing Preservation and Development Department of the City of New York to demolish what was left of the abandoned building. Even though what remained was a rubble-strewn lot, their success in getting the building demolished was important for the group's spirit because "people felt they could accomplish things" by working together.

Later a larger group was formed to help clean out the lot. It planned a carnival fundraising event to raise money for a crime prevention program; local merchants had requested assistance in preventing crime. For a local "block watch" scheme, the community needed walkie-talkies with which to patrol the neighborhood. It raised $1,800 from the carnival and felt a sense of pride in its accomplishment.

In the spring of 1976, a bulldozer cleared the rubble from the lot. Later the group learned that the owner intended to develop a parking lot for his oil trucks. Through collective action and a lot of yelling, the Barretto Street Block Association (as the group called itself) was successful in changing the zoning to prohibit a parking lot in this residential block.

During this time, a member of the block association suggested that the site (approximately 75 feet by 100 feet) be used for a community garden. When the other members in the group agreed that a garden was a good idea, they contacted the Bronx Frontier Development Corporation and the Cornell Cooperative Extension Service to assist them in site planning and collecting materials. The group divided up responsibilities. One member got involved in designing the site and coordinating the kids, while others were involved with general organizing and making some of the legal and financial arrangements. The site was first designed by a Harvard Design School student at Bronx Frontier Development Corporation. Development was started by local residents and CETA summer youth workers during the summer of 1977. This design included a vegetable garden, amphitheater and stage, cornucopia mural, and sitting area with trees.

One and one-half years after the project was initiated, the South Bronx Open Space Task Force was incorporated by the Bronx Frontier Development Corporation, People's Development Corporation, and Community School District 10 to assist in organizing and financing a total of fourteen open space projects like Barretto Street in the South Bronx. The task force was established to be the entity through which federal funding allocated by the Department of the Interior could be channeled through the state and city parks department to local groups involved in developing community and small-scale neighborhood open space projects. The grant of $1.1 million was to be matched by $1.1 million's worth of "sweat equity," donated compost, in-kind services, and approximately $100,000 in Community Development Block Grant funds provided by the City of New York.

The South Bronx Open Space Task Force has necessitated formalized, contractual relationships with Barretto Street and with outside technical assistance organizations that provide needed services (i.e., The Trust for Public Land and Bronx Frontier Development Corporation). The task force involves the government in the review of the open space plans for all fourteen sites. The community residents involved with all these projects, including the Barretto Street Block Association, are expected to assist in the construction and to perform all ongoing management and maintenance responsibilities. For the Barretto Street group, these responsibilities have not been a problem. To the South Bronx Open Space Task Force staff, the Barretto Street project is considered an example of their most successful efforts.

The Barretto Street site has now been renovated with both the support of the task force and local residents and has different functional areas, such as a vegetable garden, sitting area, amphitheater, and flower and shrub garden.

It is used primarily by local residents. The site has a fence, gate, and lock, and it is open only if someone from the block association is working in it. However, it is fairly easy to climb into the site if the gate is closed. Residents say the reason for the gate is more to demonstrate that the site is cared for than to keep people out.

With the assistance of The Trust for Public Land, donation of the land was negotiated, with the title of the site being conveyed to a newly incorporated nonprofit land trust formed by the community. Group members interviewed stated that ownership is important because it allows the site to become "theirs," and they feel "you take better care of something that you own." In addition, they feel they will no longer have to "worry that all efforts will be lost." As owners, they plan to improve the facilities further by adding a barbecue, fish pond, and garden furniture. By law, because of the use of federal dollars, the site has to remain as open space for at least the next ten years.

In addition to this project, the block association has other neighborhood projects already under way. It plans to sponsor several block cleanings, block parties, and activities for the local kids. Two lots on the same side of the street are currently being converted into parks—one will be a sand area for young children, the other a basketball court. Two other areas are also being considered: a sealed-up house for an indoor recreation facility and a tree nursery, which can give trees to other block associations in the Bronx that are involved in similar community beautification programs.

In urban areas faced with financial hardship and antiquated recreational and open space facilities, neighborhood land trusts provide the only mechanism whereby community residents can be empowered to provide their "own" amenities and the legal vehicle necessary to protect their investment. A case in point is the White Terrace Conservancy located in Newark, New Jersey.

In the wake of Newark's riots, the residents of White Terrace organized a block association to protect their block from becoming a "slum and a ghetto." Its first efforts focused on code enforcement home maintenance and sidewalk landscaping. Maud Carroll, the president of the White Terrace Block Association first heard of The Trust for Public Land while taking a community gardening course at Rutgers University. When a house at the end of her block was burned and abandoned, she called TPL. With that call White Terrace residents began the battle to reclaim a small portion of their neighborhood.

With support from neighbors, politicians, and a local foundation, the community was able to demolish the burned-out building and recycle the land, using "sweat equity" to create a neighborhood recreation space. Many hours of donated labor plus thousands of dollars of donated equipment from local corporations were instrumental to the development process. TPL incorporated the block association into the White Terrace Conservancy, a 501(c)(3) nonprofit organization, in order to provide the means to protect the community's investment. Because the land was owned by the City of Newark due to foreclosure for non-payment of real estate taxes, it was necessary for TPL to assist the White Terrace Conservancy in acquiring the property through a restricted auction from the City of Newark. The acquisition was successful, and the park is well used and well maintained by the neighborhood.

Urban land trusts as well as the application of private land conservation techniques do have some historical roots in the city, namely Gramercy Park in New York and Louisburg Square in Boston. Unfortunately the experience gained from these trusts was applied to America's rural communities, and little of that expertise was available to urban residents. The urban social disorders of the 1960s coupled with the disinvestment of the 1970s created a new frontier in America, characterized graphically by the burned-out buildings and rubble-strewn vacant lots that covered substantial portions of hundreds of neighborhoods across the United States. This neglected land base served to remind local residents of the despair and destitution of those who live at the margin of America's cities. Beginning spontaneously in a multitude of locations, community-based enterprises such as block associations, community development corporations, neighborhood improvement associations, and nonprofit housing groups began to creatively recycle some of this urban wasteland into food-producing community gardens and much-needed neighborhood recreation areas.

These neighborhood-initiated projects soon began to confront some of the same challenges that have traditionally faced rural conservation groups, namely, how permanent or long-term land protection can be assured, and how local residents can maintain a voice in the decisionmaking and management tasks related to such efforts. Some tentative solutions to these issues were attempted in the 1960s through a number of local park and recreation agencies that developed vest-pocket park programs. However, these did not solve the issues related to resident involvement and control, and for that reason and because of poor planning and design, most vest-pocket park programs failed.

In an attempt to share private land conservation techniques with inner-city residents, TPL began to incorporate land trusts in Oakland, California, in the fall of 1975. From 1975 until the present, TPL has used the urban land trust concept in a variety of land-use situations, ranging from the protection of community gardens to combining open space protection and low-income housing. We have found that it is not applicable to all community open space issues, but it works exceedingly well when community initiative can be maximized through direct participation in ownership or control. Following are two case studies that demonstrate the success TPL has had working with urban neighborhoods.

In some instances the site you want to acquire may consist of several individual parcels under multiple ownership. This was the case with Jungle Hill Park in Oakland,

California. As you read about that project, pay special attention to the timing of acquisition of different parcels and the importance of understanding the special needs and priorities of different types of landowners.

The El Sol Brillante case study[2] provides an interesting and complex view of community organizing on Manhattan's Lower East Side. A large community garden was developed on 12th Street to complement a housing rehabilitation project on 11th Street. The relationship between the two neighborhood groups involved was formalized by the incorporation of a separate land trust for the garden. The land trust's success in acquiring and developing four city lots as a garden has encouraged it to expand its revitalization efforts.

Jungle Hill Park

Residents in the Santa Rita neighborhood of Oakland, California, decided they wanted to do something about a steep, one-acre landslide area called "Jungle Hill," so named because it was a tangle of refuse, broken glass, abandoned auto parts, and high brush. The hill was not even staying in one place; every winter part of the hill would slide down to Harrington Street. So far, it had taken three single-family houses with it.

The site's neighbors had made countless calls to the City of Oakland to try to get the city to stabilize the hill and develop it into a park. The city was simply not interested in developing a park on land that kept sliding away. The neighbors decided they would have to do it on their own, but they faced several obstacles. First, they had to clear the rubble. Then, with very little money, they had to negotiate with several different owners to purchase the site. Eventually, some means had to be developed for stabilizing the slide area before development as a park could proceed.

Rather than trying to tackle everything at once, the group decided to proceed one step at a time, beginning with an investigation of ownership. Residents wanted to acquire the property and have ultimate control over developing and maintaining the site. The investigation showed that Jungle Hill had been divided into eight parcels and was currently owned by two savings and loan associations, two individuals, and the City of Oakland.

The Trust for Public Land was contacted to help neighbors develop a strategy to acquire the property. Together, TPL and the neighborhood group approached the landowners with a proposal to clear the hill and make it into a neighborhood park. The two savings and loan associations, which had acquired four parcels of the property through mortgage foreclosure, wholeheartedly supported the proposal and willingly donated the property to TPL. TPL became the temporary title holder until the neighborhood group incorporated and received nonprofit, tax-exempt status from the Internal Revenue Service. Private landowners liked the proposal, too, and agreed to sell their parcels at a very low price—a bargain sale—taking advantage of certain tax benefits. In fact, both the private landowners and the savings and loan associations received tax savings by donating or bargain selling their properties to the neighborhood group.

The final step was to approach the city, the last remaining owner of the land. Negotiating with the city was not as difficult as it might have been since the group was already owner of properties on either side of the city-held property and as such was able to acquire the parcels by participating in a sealed-bid sale. (Sealed-bid sales allow adjoining landowners first chance at acquiring properties from the city without fear of competition from outside bidders.) These parcels, added to the others, had been appraised at $25,000, but because the neighborhood had done such an effective job of selling its proposal to the various landowners, its total acquisition costs amounted to only $1,500.

Acquiring the land at such a modest price was a great triumph for the neighborhood, but local enthusiasm for the project did not end there. Next, the group turned its energy to developing the property. To do that, it had to search for resources in and around the neighborhood. Following are just a few of the creative solutions it came up with.

Clearly, one of the first tasks was to figure out why the hill was falling into the street. The group was able to get the California Society of Engineers to volunteer over 200 hours to help find a solution to this problem.

Santa Rita–Harrington neighbors were fully aware that no mere hand-shoveling expedition would solve the slide problem, so they approached the Navy Seabee Engineering Company and a local contractor, McGuire and Hester. Together, they studied the plans laid out by the engineers and donated fifteen days to excavate and restructure the hill.

The hill was stabilized at the beginning of California's rainy season. With spring planting several months away, neighbors decided to seed the hill with wild grasses to hold the soil. Within two weeks they had a velvety green hillside—a striking difference from the eyesore of months before.

Since the seeding, the group has received donations of money and services from local corporations and a nearby university and is proceeding to develop the community park it worked so hard for.

El Sol Brillante Community Garden

El Sol Brillante Community Garden is located on the Lower East Side of Manhattan, an area which from the early nineteenth century has never lost its identity as a major port of entry for poorer immigrants to America. There have been succeeding waves of Irish, German, Italian, Jewish, and Chinese immigrants; and the neighborhood today has become predominantly Hispanic, with some remnants of Russian, Ukranian, and Italian communities still living within the area. The neighborhood's residents remain overwhelmingly low income, and the housing stock consists primarily of very old tenements available for relatively inexpensive rents. The past few years have seen the onset of private owner disinvestment on the Lower East Side, with consequent deterioration, abandonment, city foreclosures for nonpayment of property taxes, vandalism, fires, and demolition of vacant buildings—creating many vacant lots.

In the fall of 1976, four buildings were demolished on East 12th Street. To replace the cleared lots, people from the 11th Street Movement, a group involved with housing on 11th Street, began organizing for the development of a community garden. The 11th Street Movement people were first involved in an "urban homesteading demonstration project" to rehabilitate a multifamily dwelling on East 11th Street behind the 12th Street lot, using a "sweat equity" development approach. Later, the group's efforts focused on solar heating and installing a wind generator for the building. As part of its 11th Street open space plan, a pocket park was constructed adjacent to the building on East 11th Street. The same year it initiated the 12th Street garden project, which became known as El Sol Brillante (The Bright Sun) Community Garden.

Assistance in organizing the project was requested from local 12th Street residents, an 11th Street architect, the Horticultural Society of New York (gardening advice), the Cornell Cooperative Extension Service (gardening advice), and the CETA Summer Youth Corps (labor on the site and jobs for local kids).

The 11th Street Movement members were primarily interested in neighborhood revitalization and community organizing. The initiation of the garden was intended by the group both to improve the quality of the environment and to provide an opportunity to organize people and identify local leadership. There were approximately forty people in the 12th Street group organized that summer to begin developing the El Sol Brillante garden. That group consisted of low-income Hispanic and white residents who had lived in the neighborhood for many years.

Early design plans were prepared by the architect member of the 11th Street movement, but the residents involved stated that most real decisions were made by negotiations with one another on the site itself. The initial design is almost totally preserved today, although a few elements have been rearranged. The garden is continually upgraded: wooden beds replaced by concrete, paths paved, and so forth.

Very little money was spent in developing this site. In a participant's own words, "a little went a long way." Members scrounged materials and depended to a large extent on local technical assistance organizations for providing what the group couldn't gather on its own.

In the fall of 1978, the 11th Street Movement and the El Sol Brillante Community Garden group together requested the assistance of The Trust for Public Land in attempting to acquire the four lots composing the garden site. Following The Trust for Public Land's suggestion, the group incorporated so that it could cooperatively own the property as a nonprofit land trust.

At about the same time research was begun by TPL to identify the owners of the lots. It was discovered that two lots were owned by the city while the other two were in the process of being foreclosed by the city for nonpayment of property taxes. Eventually, after a long series of complications and much research, a decision was made to prepare a "restricted auction package" in an effort to purchase the lots inexpensively for the group. In this process land is sold at public auction with a restriction placed on its eventual use. In this case the property was to be used only by a nonprofit community organization for a garden, park, or other open space activity. Such a restriction usually keeps the price at a reasonable level.

The process of acquiring the land was completed in March 1980, and now the battle by the El Sol group and TPL for property tax exemption (or reassessment) has begun. A total of $2,500 was needed for the purchase of the land, and an additional $1,000 was required to cover legal expenses.

What was once a rubble-filled lot is now a thriving vegetable garden with approximately forty raised beds. There is also a covered sitting area (where dominoes are often played), and a cluster of benches for chatting is in the middle of the site. Painted on the back wall, a mural of a sunset overlooking a vegetable farm immediately catches the eye. Everyone in the neighborhood is welcome to use the garden as a social place when someone from the group is there, which is most of the time. A gate, fence, and lock control access when no one is in the garden.

The El Sol Brillante gardening group plans to continue improving the site while maintaining its present character. The group has now converted a vacant lot across from this site into another garden for use by area residents and is contemplating the renovation of a dilapidated city park adjacent to the garden.

Notes

1. This case study is based on material published in *The Making of Neighborhood Open Spaces,* by L. Cashdan, M. Francis, and L. Paxson (New York: City University of New York, Center for Human Environments, 1981).
2. Ibid.

How To Manage Land Acquired by the Trust

Suzanne C. Wilkins

Too many trusts receive and hold land rather than maintaining and/or improving it. Land management is an essential component of the conservation ethic. Addressing potential problems when a parcel is acquired facilitates management of the land. This article discusses various considerations and tools a trust can use to manage its holdings.

A. Management Plan

The trust should draw up a management plan for each of its parcels, no matter how small. Of course, the amount of detail and the ambitiousness of the plan will depend on the particular parcel and the capabilities of the trust.

B. Access

How much access is desirable for each parcel depends on the use of the land; entrance must be permitted, but natural resources should be protected. The trust should make sure that access is clearly spelled out in the property deed, particularly if the parcel is landlocked.

If the parcel is not located along a public thoroughfare, the trust must establish an access route. The width of the access varies according to its use, but it is normally between ten and twenty feet wide. This size allows for entrance of a trust vehicle for property maintenance and emergency vehicles such as fire equipment and lessens trespassing on the property of abutting neighbors.

1. *Need for access*

Before it acquires a parcel, the trust will need to obtain access from the owner in order to inspect and maintain the parcel. Once the land belongs to the trust, access may be limited to such purposes as occasional inspection of wildlife preserves; or it may be general, allowing the public to enjoy the land. During the acquisition process, the trust should try to secure unrestricted access for its own use, so that it will have maximum flexibility for potential change in the use of the parcel.

Whether the access is owned entirely by the trust or whether it is a right-of-way (as contained in a perpetual easement on an adjacent property), its location should have clearly marked boundaries. Access should not involve trespassing on private property, nor should it create a negative impact on neighboring land.

2. *Difficulties*

Homeowners who are unaware of a nearby trust parcel with access adjacent to their property can become alarmed by supposed "trespassers." The trust should inform neighbors about its general activities and the specific use for the trust land in their area. The names of neighbors are on record in the tax assessor's office; individuals may be contacted by letter or in person. By establishing a strong ongoing relationship with parcel neighbors, the trust can help avoid problems and perhaps recruit new members of the parcel's stewardship committee.

In the case of a developmental setaside, the trust should make sure that the developer marks the access and completes the grading of any nearby road so that access is possible. Whether the land is accessible to the general public or only to the residents of the development may affect the parcel's tax deductibility.

3. *Physical deterrents*

Occasionally the trust will have to limit access, either to redirect persons to an appropriate entrance to the parcel or to discourage entry for improper use, such as illegal woodcutting or vehicular travel. In addition, physical deterrents can set off specified areas needing protection from grazing or human activities.

Physical deterrents may be composed of strategically planted bushes, such as multiflora rose or raspberry; well-placed logs or posts driven into the ground; barbed wire;

or fences. In choosing which form to use, the trust should consider what activity it wishes to curtail; whether or not the work involved is permanent or temporary; the extent of the work; and the availability and cost of materials and labor.

C. Boundary Marking

1. *Locating entrances*

In the case of a parcel designated for extensive public use, the trust should consider several factors as it determines the location of the entrance. Such points include the parcel location and its terrain; the location of fragile natural resources needing protection; the impact on neighbors; the surrounding land use, both present and future; and the availability of nearby parking space.

The entrance should be a focal point where parcel visitors would naturally come. The trust can set off the entrance by means of a sign, trail map, or a fence. Such designation will channel access, thus minimizing damage to neighboring properties and sensitive sections of the parcel itself.

2. *Boundary identification*

Each parcel should contain a permanent marker denoting its legal boundaries, based on work done by a competent surveyor. The most logical time to accomplish this task is when the trust obtains the parcel, since this information should also appear in the deed. The trust should have a competent surveyor complete the necessary work to eliminate potential future problems.

The surveyed boundary can be marked unobtrusively by painting brown rings on trees. This is a good activity for members. In areas where there is undergrowth, it is best done in early spring.

In the case of developmental setasides, the trust should have the developer's surveyors determine the boundaries of the setaside while they survey the rest of the development. The trust should insist not only that the developer absorb the surveyors' cost, but also that the developer provide permanent markers designating the setaside and/or access boundary. In this way the trust will not have to underwrite costly work at a later date.

3. *Signs*

a. *Pros and cons*

Signs advertise trust ownership of the land to the public. They may affect relations with neighbors, and they may provide good publicity for the trust. The trust should decide whether to use signs based on the surrounding land use, the designated use or the misuse of the property, the access, or natural resources.

b. *Permanent or temporary*

Assuming that signs are desirable, the trust must decide whether they should be permanent. Often soon after "permanent" signs are carefully constructed, they disappear or are vandalized. Some trusts find that aluminum and paper signs are less susceptible to vandalism and are cheap to replace. Other trusts use a secured permanent marker at the preserve entrance and temporary signs intermittently along the parcel's frontage.

Entrance signs are usually secured in the ground; boundary signs are often placed high in trees (about seven feet above the ground) to decrease vandalism. The trust should comply with any local ordinances governing signs and with any legal posting requirements, such as No Hunting signs.

c. *Sign information*

How a trust presents information about the preserve will influence the public's attitude; often the same information can be presented positively or negatively. The sign should contain the name of the property manager and which uses are and are not allowed.

d. *Special signs*

In addition to the entrance sign designating public use of the parcel and boundary markers, the trust may decide to post other notices. It may wish to call attention to minor hazards, such as poor trail footing, or major hazards, such as cliffs or poisonous snakes. If the trust does announce the existence of a hazard, it must continue to do so as long as the danger exists, or it may find itself with a liability problem.

In the case of a particularly sensitive natural area that should not be disturbed, the trust must decide whether to draw attention to the phenomenon. Factors such as the volume and type of traffic in the vicinity and the nearness of the area to the trail may help the trust make its decision.

Examples of Signs

> *CAUTION*
>
> *WATCH YOUR STEP!*
> *LOOSE ROCKS*
> *STEEP TRAIL SECTIONS*
>
> SMITHTOWN LAND TRUST

> **JAMES C. MILLER PRESERVE**
> TRAILS OPEN FOR PUBLIC USE
>
> *Please help us protect wildlife*
> *Keep on designated trails*
> *No fire building, camping, woodcutting*
> *No motorized vehicles*
> *Thank you*
>
> JONESVILLE LAND TRUST

D. Stewardship

1. *Responsibility*

The trust must determine who will oversee the preserve. Many trusts find that the most effective stewardship tool is a preserve committee composed of general members or preserve neighbors. Depending on the size and use of the parcel and the trust's capability, preserve maintenance can range from simply checking periodically for problems, eliminating litter, and reporting to the board to overseeing and restoring trail and natural areas and conducting tours.

2. *Various tasks*

The committee should draw on the information and resulting recommendations found in the management plan, as that determines which stewardship activities are necessary. One task is to collect data about the preserve. By establishing the status quo of the parcel, the trust can facilitate its overall management and guard against potential encroachment.

Another task is trail building and maintenance. The completed natural areas inventory will indicate where trails should be placed. In some preserves the trust can form a trail easily with uniformly spaced markers. In other instances, with steep terrain and surfaces that erode easily, the trust may have to build sections of the trail. A land trust located in Connecticut has employed an adopt-a-trail system by which certain persons are responsible for overseeing certain trails.

Other maintenance activities might include field mowing, sign and marker replacement, litter cleanup, fence or post repairs, selective tree harvesting, erosion control, brush clearing, and species maintenance. Even simple undertakings, whether done by trust members or outside persons, must be supervised so that unfortunate errors do not occur. If the trust hires someone to do the work, it may need coverage for workers' compensation.

If the committee is supervising an ambitious management plan to maintain a particular species, for example, it would do well to consult experts, who might be members of the preserve committee or the trust or residents of the community. The trust might want to obtain an outside consultant.

3. *Problems*

Trusts can minimize improper parcel use by selecting the most appropriate use for the parcel. Nonetheless, they are increasingly plagued by vandalism, littering, illegal woodcutting, and difficulties with structures on the land. Why these problems are more prevalent in certain areas is unclear. The possible reasons for these difficulties include traditional "misuse" of the parcel; increasing pressures on preserves because of urban sprawl; a decrease in recreational opportunities for local youths; insufficient education about the trust, its purposes, and its preserves; the location of the parcel, which may be too remote or allow too much access; and a lack of signs designating the ownership of the land.

Since each community, each trust, and each parcel is different, the trust should try to determine the most likely cause of the problem and the most likely solution to it, such as improving education, placing signs on the parcel, increasing patrol by trust members or police, or even hiring a warden.

a. *Vandalism*

Vandalism of trust property frequently takes the form of removal or defacing of signs, wanton destruction of natural resources (such as bark cutting or stripping, arson, or killing saplings or small game), or joyriding with dirt bikes or snowmobiles. If the damage appears to be caused by young persons, the trust should institute an education program in the local school to inform community youngsters about the trust's purpose. Placing signs higher on trees may discourage their disappearance. Posts, logs, or fencing in key locations may cut down on illegal vehicles.

b. *Littering*

Litter is a continuing problem for trusts. If the trouble is caused by neighbors who think that the property is not cared for, education and posting of signs may prove effective. If passersby are disposing of unwanted material along the property's frontage, posting signs or printing a story in the local paper might help. Teenagers hosting beer parties may be educated not to litter or kept off the land with surveillance by a warden, neighbor, trust member, or local police.

If the problem occurs in the interior portions of the parcel, the trust should place signs and/or deterrents to minimize foot and vehicular traffic. If the problem occurs on the perimeter, the trust should establish a "litter patrol" of members, and perhaps the public as well, to pick up the debris periodically. Since the presence of litter seems to encourage more litter, the sooner it is removed, the less of a problem it should be. Solving the litter problem may decrease vandalism as well.

c. *Wood theft*

The problem of unauthorized firewood cutting is becoming more common as more people turn to this alternate source of energy. The culprits are usually adults who think that because the land is unmarked and seemingly not cared for, they can go in and help themselves to wood. The problem can be minimized by posting signs, by education through the local newspaper, by decreasing access for vehicles, and by improved surveillance. For those persons who deliberately steal firewood, the trust should respond by reporting the theft to the police.

d. *Structures*

While most trusts are hesitant to accept land containing structures, sometimes they choose to do so. Historic structures, farm buildings, and dams are among the structures with which a trust may have to contend.

Before accepting land with a structure on it, the trust should consider the amount of repair and maintenance the structure requires; its effect on the trust's operational costs, including maintenance and insurance; whether it comes with an endowment if it is to be maintained; whether it can be sold, with the proceeds going toward future land acquisition; whether it can be demolished; whether it can be given to another organization for operation; and whether it can be eliminated from the transaction without adversely affecting the negotiations. The trust may be able to work out a cooperative agreement for maintenance with another organization, such as the local government or historic society.

e. *Other encroachments—adverse possession and prescription*

Occasionally a trust is confronted by serious encroachments on its land, such as roads, dumping, water diversion, or illegal construction. It should deal forthrightly with the situation. Failure to stop someone from using property for a period of fifteen years can, under certain conditions, result in the user's acquiring title to the property through "adverse possession" or acquiring an easement through "prescription."

Generally, to obtain adverse possession the person must maintain open, visible, and exclusive possession of the property under a claim of right without the permission of the owner.[1] One difficulty posed by this rule for land trusts is that the amount of use required to establish possession depends on the nature of the land. Property held as wilderness, for example, would require much less use than would residential property.

Nevertheless, the possession must be exclusive and the use must be sufficient to provide reasonable notice of the claim.

The requirements for creating an easement by prescription are similar; the use must be open, visible, continuous, and made under a claim of right.[2] A typical example would be a road used by an adjoining owner, without permission, for access to his property. Use of a path by unrelated groups of people does not establish an easement since in that case no particular individual is claiming a right.

To defeat claims of adverse possession or prescriptive easement, the trust should periodically monitor the use of all its property and should act whenever an unauthorized person is using a parcel. If a road is not a present nuisance, however, the trust could enter into an agreement with the user for a specific term, or create an agreement terminable at the trust's option. To prevent unauthorized use, the trust should take steps such as posting, fencing, contacting the police, or evicting squatters. Legal counsel should be obtained in difficult situations. Particular care should be taken with newly acquired property because a claim based on fifteen years of use is not usually affected by a transfer of title to the property.

Notes

1. Robinson v. Myers, 156 Conn. 510, 244 A.2d 385 (1968); Lucas v. Ferris, 95 Conn. 619, 112 Atl. 165 (1921); 7 Powell on Real Property, §§1012 *et seq.* (1979).

2. Zavisa v. Hastings, 143 Conn. 40, 118 A.2d 902 (1956); Great Hill Lake v. Coswell, 126 Conn. 364, 11 A.2d 396 (1940); 3 Powell on Real Property, §413 (1979).

Monitoring Protected Lands

Jan W. McClure

Introduction

New Hampshire is blessed with majestic and extensive forests—not just "wooded areas," but acres and acres of trees. Their scenic beauty and their productivity are the foundation of our state's economic and social prosperity. The quality of life shared and treasured by New Hampshire residents is inextricably linked to our forestland and rural landscapes.

The founders of the Society for the Protection of New Hampshire Forests recognized the forest's importance to life as they knew it in New Hampshire. The organization's early efforts established the White Mountain National Forest and moved on to provide progressive forestry legislation encouraging the conservation and wise use of the resource rather than its profitable demise. Today the Forest Society, as we are called, sponsors a multitude of educational activities and has become deeply involved in critical and timely state environmental issues, but protection and conservation of resource-producing land remain at the core of its programs.

Acquisitions, restricted sales, and conservation easements are the three primary land protection techniques that the Forest Society utilizes. We also "preacquire" properties, eventually transferring them, when funds become available, to other private organizations or the state or federal governments. We operate a revolving loan fund to assist the land protection activities of other groups and agencies. In this article I will focus on the Forest Society's criteria for direct and long-term involvement with a property and our stewardship and monitoring procedures.

Acquisitions

Typically, the Forest Society acquires land through an outright donation, a bequest, or a donation with reserved life estate. Occasionally we "bargain purchase" or exercise an option or right of first refusal. If we become aware of a bequest only after the death of the donor, there is little opportunity for evaluation. For the others, however, we have ample time for review and analysis, and this process provides an opportunity to develop a relationship with the landowner and to plan for our future stewardship of the property.

Our primary objective in the evaluation of a potential acquisition is to dovetail the donor's goals and objectives for the property with our organizational goals and objectives. We begin by learning about the property from the landowner—past management activities, vegetative and topographical characteristics, and areas of special importance to the landowner, such as the junction of two streams with a small waterfall, the old red pine plantation, the field corner where deer are often spotted, the trail to a rocky promontory, or the beaver swamp. We become familiar with the property through the landowner and develop a working relationship with him or her; most important, we acquire a sense of his or her long-term management objectives.

Concurrently, we discuss our society's land management philosophy and our management activities on other properties we own. Although tailored to the specific natural and resource characteristics of each property and to the specific guidelines, if any, of the donor, management of our approximately 14,000 acres concentrates on multiple-use forest management practices. We aim for a healthy forest that produces strong, healthy, economically valuable trees and to create optimum conditions and habitat for all species of wildlife as well as to provide aesthetic and recreational enjoyment opportunities for those who visit the land.

Since we pay property taxes on all our properties, sufficient income to cover taxes and maintenance expenses is an important consideration in our preacquisition evaluation. In some cases, of course, forest management and its income are not options, as when the property is valuable for reasons other than its forest. For example, it may be a unique natural area—a habitat for a rare orchid, a stand of rare Atlantic white cedar, or an important wetland or scenic ridgeline. An endowment or the income from other holdings can help support the carrying costs of these lands.

If the property is predominantly forest, however, our evaluation includes a forester's inventory of timber variety and quality, access, and terrain. Management and harvesting recommendations are made, and income is projected over a period of years. This analysis along with information concerning the property's location relative to other society or protected lands, unique natural features, suitability for demonstration and education purposes, proximity to other protected areas, vulnerability to development, and the owner's objectives are thoroughly described in a Lands Project Criteria Sheet. Our Lands Committee, a subcommittee of the board of trustees, reviews the material and recommends appropriate action concerning acquisition to the full board.

Restricted Sales

For potential restricted sales, our criteria are less concerned with unique features since these properties are less likely to have them. These are properties that either have been given to us with the expectation that we will sell them or have been evaluated by us as unsuitable for our long-term ownership. In some cases they may be properties we purchase in order to protect through resale with restrictions. In all these cases our analysis focuses on appropriate uses for the property.

If the land is capable of long-term resource management and in an area where local land-use regulations encourage such use, restrictions prohibiting development are imposed in the sale. Restrictions on cleared agricultural land, for example, may require that the land be kept open, and development, if permitted, may be restricted to a particular area of the property. These restrictions lower our sale price but make the transaction clearly consistent with our society's land-protection purposes. Since we do not retain a right of first refusal on these properties or in any other way interfere with its subsequent transfer, it is important for us to monitor them, as we do land under conservation easement, to ensure that the restrictions are upheld.

Easements

Our criteria for properties we seek to protect through easements are similar to those for properties we acquire in fee. Wherever possible and practical we like to involve directly a local conservation trust or the Town Conservation Commission as grantee. We want to encourage local stewardship, and a local grantee makes an effective monitor. (If a local group cannot serve as grantee, it can often assist as the local monitor.) When a local group assumes grantee responsibilities, our society often takes an executory interest in the easement, giving us the ability to intercede in the future by assuming the grantee role in the event the local grantee fails in its duties or ceases to exist. Our search for and reliance on the involvement of local groups in our easement work leads into our monitoring procedures.

Monitoring

Monitoring is, of course, a critical element to the success of our easement program, indeed to the success of the easement technique for the long term. From our society's standpoint the conservation easement is the most important tool for the protection of New Hampshire's forestland because it provides for private ownership *and* perpetual protection. The public benefit served by protected forestland is an economic, aesthetic, and cultural one. Our state's economy depends on the availability of forest products and so, in turn, on the health of our forest resource. A New Hampshirite's sense of place and the quality of life he cherishes also depend on the forests he lives among. Therefore, it is critical that we make the technique work for the long term; hence the importance of monitoring.

Our monitoring procedures vary depending on the property's location and size and whether we have a grantee or executory interest. For all easements, we prepare location maps of the property and abstracts of the easement restrictions. The abstract includes basic information such as the names and addresses of the grantor and grantee and the volume and page number of the recorded easement. Most important, the abstract outlines the specific land-use restrictions of the easement.

Each spring we send, by certified mail, the abstract along with a stamped, self-addressed postcard to the grantees of the easements in which we hold an executory interest. In our letter we remind the grantees of the easement, their responsibilities, and our executory interest; and we request that they fill out and return the postcard, confirming that they have monitored the property and that the ownership has not changed, or if it has, giving us the new owner's name and address.

As the backup to the grantee, we have a responsibility to ensure that the grantee is doing its job, and this procedure serves the purpose well. A yearly reminder to the grantee is particularly important at the local level where personnel changes are frequent. The local grantee has three months to return the postcard, time enough to do the monitoring if not done already. Finally, by sending the material by certified mail we are certain it is received, and it impresses upon the grantee the importance of annual monitoring, of the easement itself, and of the seriousness with which we view our executory role. Since we have instituted this procedure we have had a 100-percent response from grantees.

For easements in which we are the grantee and for properties we have sold with restrictions, monitoring is more direct. Besides preparing a map and abstract, we take aerial photographs of the property soon after the execution of the easement. These eight-by-ten-inch photographs serve as our documentation of the property's condition at the time the easement was granted. Each spring after the snow has melted, before leaf-out, we fly over the properties, checking what we see from the plane against our photographs. Primarily, we look for any signs of development, such as roads, excavation, substantial clearing, and new structures. By paying careful attention to the property's boundaries and road frontage when leaves do not interfere with our view of the ground, we can easily spot any activity of this sort from the air. For smaller parcels and properties not easily within our aerial route, we have local volunteer monitors from whom we receive reports annually.

After our flight, we write each landowner, informing him of our annual check and commenting on anything we noticed from the air, such as recent timber harvesting, blowdowns, or signs of disease or insect infestations. This yearly contact reminds the landowners that we are serious about our enforcement responsibilities, and it fortifies our relationship with them.

Our Conservation Easement Monitoring Fund helps defray the costs of our annual monitoring activities. Suggested annual contributions to the fund by grantors and landowners are voluntary and are based on the per-easement cost of the annual monitoring plus a small amount for possible future legal enforcement expenses, should there ever be a violation that cannot be rectified by other means.

The thoroughness of our annual monitoring procedures gives our easement program added credibility and strengthens our land-protection program. Open space in private ownership and, we hope, productive management can provide an even greater public benefit than publicly owned land. The private individual often has more time to devote to the land's maintenance, and income from management activities stimulates the local economy and provides wood products and energy for public consumption. The discrimination we exercise in selecting lands for permanent protection combined with the seriousness and thoroughness of our monitoring procedures make for long-term, effective, and productive land protection to everyone's benefit.

Government Monitoring Program for Partial Interest Projects

Warren Illi

An effective monitoring program is the most important part of any private or public land-preservation project. The lofty ideals and goals of the project and well-meaning intent of easement language are no more than words on paper. The real success or failure of the entire product lies in an effective monitoring program.

Government monitoring programs will vary with the objectives of the legislation or project plan being implemented. The National Wild and Scenic Rivers Act, various national recreation area acts, and national seashore acts are examples of legislation that initiated acquisition of partial interests (conservation easements or scenic easements) on private lands. The following discussion will deal with monitoring and managing these partial interests, not management of government fee lands. Monitoring partial interests in real estate involves joint land management between the underlying fee landowner and the government (easement holder).

Monitoring files consist of a master file, plus a separate tract file for each individual easement. The master file contains documents that pertain to the entire project. For government projects, this would include the legislation or directive that created the project, agency policy directives implementing that legislation, land-management plan for the project, land-acquisition plan, and the monitoring plan. Many of these documents may be combined into one comprehensive plan. Also included in the master file are all the subsequent policy and legal directives that affect easement language interpretation or monitoring policy. The overall purpose of the master file is to develop a single source file that provides a complete up-to-date project record.

The next step is to develop a tract file for each individual easement. A copy of the final executed easement forms the basic building block of this file. Since the final easement language may be subject to various legal interpretations, the "intent" of the language can be clarified for future administration and landowners by inclusion of draft easements and related papers in the tract file. Because some final easement provisions will have undergone several rewrites, the review of earlier drafts will help interpret the intent of the final easement language. The tract file should also include all notes, memos to the files, documentation of telephone calls, and letters that were developed during negotiations. Here again, these documents will help future administrators and landowners interpret the intent of the original parties.

It is readily accepted that difficulty in easement administration will probably increase with second- and third-generation landowners. The original landowner's file may be lost over time, so that subsequent landowners will have little evidence of intent except the recorded final easement. Therefore, the easement holder will need to maintain the project and tract records.

Besides having a full history of easement negotiations, the file should contain a complete property description as of the date of deeding. The property description section contains a written description of the property. This should include all physical features such as existing buildings, fences, irrigation systems, vegetation, crops, and so on. A complete inventory of physical features is needed. For easements where maintenance of a natural ecosystem is a project objective, a very complete inventory of the property's flora and fauna is key. Part of the property description should include a short written description of current and past property uses.

A sketched map of the property showing property boundaries, building locations, roads, forested areas, pastures and crop areas, improvements, and fences is a very useful tool. Photographs, if properly done, can be an invaluable part of the tract file. Photos can be indisputable evidence of what existed on the date of deeding. Photos can be taken from ground level, or they can be aerial or aerial-obliques taken from nearby vantage points. Aerial photos provide a bird's-eye view of the entire property, vegetation types, natural and man-made features, and land-use patterns.

It is very important that all written property descriptions and photographs be signed (author and photographer) and dated. Aerial photos usually have the date of photography on the photo margin.

The last section of the tract file is the monitoring section. It contains documentation of all contacts between the easement holder and property or property owner. It is a continuing chronology of how the easement area is being managed and various decisions and agreements between the easement holder and landowner. Over time, the intent of the original easement can be subtly changed by various "mini" agreements between the easement holder and landowner. Therefore, it is important for the easement holder to establish a clear line of authority for these kinds of decisions.

On-the-ground monitoring of the easement area should be both informal and scheduled. Informal monitoring consists of all unscheduled contacts with the property and property owner by various employees of the government agency. This may simply include a visual inspection of the property as someone drives past the property on other business. Care must be taken to avoid having the landowner develop a sense of being under constant surveillance. On the other hand, many absentee landowners like the idea of knowing some local folks are keeping an eye on their property. Informal monitoring is usually not documented in the tract file unless some problem is noted. When a possible problem is noted, the agency action plan is implemented. This usually means a prompt, formal, on-the-ground meeting with the landowner.

Scheduled monitoring consists of periodic, usually annual, on-the-ground meetings with the landowners. These formal meetings are usually most effective when each party's goals and objectives are clearly spelled out in advance. Also, decide whether field work will be included. This type of meeting should be conducted in a manner that develops a common bonding between the project objectives of the easement holder and desires of the landowner. This relationship can make or break the success of the entire project.

If both the landowner and easement holder think a formal on-the-ground meeting is unnecessary, the tract file should document this joint decision. It is important that the tract file display a continuous and active interest in maintaining the easement rights. Many states have laws that allow for abandonment of easement rights where there has been a long break in the exercise of easement rights. That is why annual contact between the easement holder and landowner is so important.

The first formal on-the-ground meeting should occur very soon after the easement conveyance if monitoring personnel and easement negotiators are not the same people. The easement negotiator has probably met on the

can therefore
nitoring per-
with a copy
ory. Each ease-
erpreted among
ring people. Any
and signed off by
letters, sometimes
signed by both the
epresentative. Letters of
ment joint land-manage-
val or consent of both parties. These ... nstrued as periodic interpretation and modificatio... easement language. Therefore, they must be developed with the same care and review as the original easement.

For a complicated easement on a property with intensive and varying land-management activities, an annual or multiyear management plan may be necessary. This kind of easement monitoring is expensive and time consuming.

The total cost (time and money) of an effective monitoring program must be considered at the time of project inception and easement language development. Monitoring must be continuous and is not inexpensive. Legal costs will be incurred to enforce intent of easement provisions. Well-documented easement monitoring files will minimize these costs.

Forestland Preserves

Preservation of forestland is frequently a goal of rural land-preservation projects. Forests are normally long lived, so natural changes are frequently subtle and not obvious to the casual or untrained observer. But like other natural communities, a forest is dynamic and ever changing. Plant and animal composition of a forest changes with time because of numerous physical and biological factors. Too many people view an existing forest environment as "wonderful," then set about to preserve that condition by shutting off all management by man. In the long term, that may not meet preservation objectives. Don't let the term *management* become confused with *forest management* as practiced on commercial forestland. Management on forest preserves is those deliberate actions or inactions necessary to meet the goals and objectives of the preserve.

The first step in preserving a desired forest environment is a complete inventory of its flora, fauna, and land types. Land types are a combination of topography, soil, aspect, water table, and so on. This inventory is necessary not only to tell us what currently exists, but to allow projections of what will occur or result from the use or lack of various forest management activities.

For all practical purposes, there are no natural forests remaining in the continental United States. Even the remaining vast wilderness areas of the western United States reflect the imprint of man. While these forests have been spared the impact of logging, all have been "protected" from the natural role of forest fires. Remnants of eastern "natural areas" also reflect man's activities. Consider the widespread impact of *introduced* diseases such as Chestnut Blight and White Pine Blister Rust. Acid rain may make significant future changes in the "natural" condition of eastern forests.

Both forest fire protection and new diseases are examples of how all existing forests have been influenced, and will continue to be influenced, by man. That's why all forestlands, even so-called natural preserves, need management.

Management is also necessary because forests are constantly undergoing a series of natural successional plant stages. Successional stages range from *pioneer* forests to *climax* forests. A pioneer forest usually consists of the initial, or first, trees and other forest vegetation that naturally occupy an area that has been disturbed. This disturbance may be man caused, such as logging or clearing for agriculture; or natural, such as fire, insect epidemic, or windstorm. A pioneer forest includes such common species as balsam-fir, birch, aspen, lodgepole pine, and red alder. These are generally short-lived tree species, which serve as a cover crop for long-lived, permanent tree species such as sugar maple, white oak, ponderosa pine, and hemlock, which occur in climax forests. At least in theory, climax forests are permanent and self-perpetuating. The pioneer forest may take from 50 to 300 years to evolve naturally into a climax forest, with intermediate stages occurring in between. In some parts of their natural ranges, pioneer species may also be in the climax forests.

Along with the major tree species, wildlife composition and numbers will change with the successional stages of a forest. White-tail deer, for example, are much more plentiful in a pioneer forest, while turkeys do better in the more mature climax forests. A forest inventory will establish at which stage the existing forest is in this natural successional process. The maximum number of wildlife species can usually be produced in a forest of mixed successional stages.

The forest inventory should be accomplished by professional foresters, botanists, biologists, and other natural scientists. When you order an inventory from a professional forester, he must be carefully advised on the type of complete biological inventory needed. This inventory should include a brief history of the tract, especially those historic man-caused activities that have tended to modify the natural forest environment.

With the inventory and history in hand, the forester can then predict what the long-term forest will look like under various forest-preservation management alternatives. Management alternatives may vary from doing nothing (letting nature take its course) to more intensive management that allows some timber cutting, especially if cutting is necessary to maintain a particular project goal (aesthetics, for example). A forest that has been ravaged by fire, disease, insects, or a storm may be natural, but certainly not beautiful.

Once the trust or government agency has reviewed the successional changes that will be likely to occur under various management alternatives, broad project goals and objectives can be established. The land-acquisition policies can then be developed, including appropriate easement language to meet these goals.

While some forest-preservation projects will use natural evolution and plant succession as its management tool, many larger preservation projects will have a primary objective of maintaining an aesthetically pleasing forest environment.

A well-managed forest can be a place of continuing beauty, and it can provide a sustained flow of tangible forest products and income. This is especially desirable when preserving larger tracts of forestland. Managing forests on the basis of a pathological rotation, rather than an economic rotation, is a way to reach this kind of objective.

Most commercial forests are managed to maximize income by harvesting timber when it is economically most prudent (economic rotation). Harvesting techniques or logging systems usually include methods that are most cost effective, not necessarily techniques that cause the least impact on other forest resources, which include scenic values. Harvesting on a pathological rotation permits harvesting when trees become old and decadent. At that stage the forest landscape may become less aesthetically pleasing in the absence of some action by man. Even more important, these less-healthy, less-vigorous forests are more susceptible to disease and insect epidemics, impacts which can leave a forest with a devastated appearance. Therefore, as individual trees or groups of trees in a mixed stand of timber reach their pathological maturity, selective timber harvest will ensure maintenance of a continuing healthy forest environment. Logging techniques that have minimal impact on the forest should be selected. In many areas of the country, logging with horses is becoming, as it once was, a common way to harvest timber in environmentally sensitive places.

Even when selective timber harvesting is chosen as an overall management technique, some smaller subunits may be managed as "natural" areas. Some amount of over-mature trees should always be left to maintain a continuous supply of hollow, or cavity, trees for animals such as squirrels, raccoons, wood ducks, and other animals that require tree cavities as part of their habitat.

The perpetuation and regeneration of some tree species require more exposure to sunlight than is commonly found in typical shaded forest settings. In order to maintain or regenerate these tree species, some openings in the forest are needed. These openings may be from one-fourth acre to several acres and can be created during timber harvesting by using the clearcutting timber harvest method. Clearcutting essentially removes all trees on a given area, allowing direct sunlight to reach the forest floor. This allows regeneration of trees and plants that need full sunlight for survival. Clearcutting on forest preserves should not be eliminated as a management tool simply because it has been misused and overused on some commercial forestlands. On forest preserves clearcutting can be used to reach a specific and desired forest condition.

Forest preserves can be maintained by trusts either through direct or fee landownership (total ownership) or through conservation easements (partial interests). The dollar value of conservation easements that preclude or severely restrict prudent production of commercial forest products may approach the fee value of the land. On the other hand, similar easement restrictions on forested lands near urban or recreational areas, where property value is not tied to commercial timber production, may not cause a significant loss in property value. In these kinds of areas, forestlands may be most valuable for "gentleman" estates that have management goals similar to those of land preserves.

Generally, easement provisions for forest preserves should identify and set the goals and objectives for the future forest environment, rather than attempt to identify specific forest management practices to be permitted or not permitted.

Easement provisions that identify easement goals such as maintaining species diversification, emphasizing pathological rotation, percent of crown cover retention, natural plant succession, scenic beauty, and so on will best meet the general long-term goal of maintaining a pleasing forest environment. It is usually difficult to ensure preservation objectives by attempting to specifically define permitted and prohibited cutting and management practices. Forest-management technology is changing so rapidly it is difficult to predict all future impacts on the forest. It is generally better to let future trust officers and landowners determine how the goals of the easements will be accomplished.

Protecting Agricultural Lands

Edward P. Thompson, Jr.

Agricultural Land Conversion and Its Implications

Few natural resource conservation issues have captured public attention as quickly as has agricultural land conservation. A 1981 study by the U.S. Department of Agriculture and the Council on Environmental Quality, National Agricultural Lands Study,[1] catapulted the issue to national prominence by revealing that between 1967 and 1975 approximately 23 million acres of agricultural land in the United States had been converted to nonagricultural uses. That represents the loss of 12 square miles per day and a total amount of land taken permanently out of production equivalent to the combined areas of Vermont, New Hampshire, Massachusetts, Rhode Island, Connecticut, Delaware, and New Jersey.

Land uses displacing agriculture on the urban fringes include residential subdivisions, commercial strip development, highways, and other growth-inducing infrastructure such as new sewerage systems. Outside metropolitan areas, agricultural land is consumed by energy and mineral

Farmland Losses by Region, 1967–1977
(*Millions of Acres*)

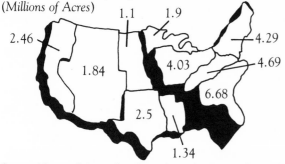

Source: National Agricultural Lands Study, Interim Report No. 2 (1980)

exploitation, impoundments, and recreational development. No region of the country has been immune from agricultural land conversion.

National Implications

If agricultural land conversion continues at present rates, the results are likely to be higher domestic food prices and a diminished national ability to earn foreign exchange through agricultural exports, which now are in excess of $40 billion annually. Land conversion, however, is only one of several phenomena that dovetail as causes of diminished agricultural production capacity. Soil erosion, estimated at 3.9 billion tons per year, causes a reduction of capacity equivalent to the conversion of more than a million acres of land annually.[2] Obtaining adequate water for irrigation in the semiarid West is becoming problematic as aquifers are drawn down and agricultural producers face intense competition from urban and energy consumers.[3] Rising energy prices have increased the cost of the fertilizer and agricultural chemicals that have been responsible for over half of the gain in crop yields during the past thirty years.[4] These and other trends have caused a leveling off of annual increases in crop yields, from 1.5 percent to roughly half that figure.[5]

Unless a dramatic breakthrough occurs in agricultural technology, within a decade or so the land itself will once again become—if it ever ceased to be—the most important factor in our nation's agricultural production equation. The United States now has roughly 413 million acres under cultivation and another 127 million in its cropland reserve. If crop yields continue to increase only at current rates, the USDA projects that to meet an anticipated 65 to 80 percent increase in demand for American farm products within the next twenty years, an additional 77 to 113 million acres of land will have to be brought under cultivation.[6] Viewed in this light, the prospect of *losing* 60 million acres over that period is significant. Statistically, that's almost half our reserve, but the resource implications would be even more serious than the numbers alone suggest.

Our so-called cropland reserve consists of marginal lands now used for pasturage, rangeland, and forestry because of thin soils, steep slopes, and lack of moisture. Cultivation of this land would undoubtedly increase erosion, exacerbate water competition, increase total food production costs, and, perhaps, reduce livestock and forest production. It could also result in the conversion of prairie wetlands and bottomland hardwood forests, included in the reserve despite their value as waterfowl and seafood nurseries, to intensive agricultural uses. As Secretary of Agriculture John Block once explained, "The chain of problems would be lengthy and expensive."[7]

Local and Regional Implications
If the nationwide implications of agricultural land conversion are just over the horizon, local and regional implications occupy the foreground of public concern. Nonfarmers are preoccupied with the disappearance of open space and the deterioration of air and water quality that often accompany conversion. Although this deterioration may be serious for localities that are attractive places to live because of scenic and environmental qualities, equally significant are the implications of the loss of open space for agricultural production.

Open space is as important as seed and fertilizer are to agricultural production. Modern agriculture relies on technology to sustain crop yields and tends to produce odors, noise, dust, chemical spray drift, and other spillover effects that cause problems for nearby residential areas.[8] Farmers often find that the conversion of adjacent land to nonagricultural uses leads to strict local governmental regulation of once-routine farming practices and sometimes to litigation over what their new neighbors consider nuisances. These pressures on agriculture increase production costs and downtime. In addition, retaliation in the form of farm thefts and vandalism can occur as the countryside becomes more crowded.

What is more, the loss of open space to suburban sprawl tends to increase property taxes because of higher community service costs. Higher taxes further reduce net farm income and hasten land conversion. As the number of farms in a region declines, agriculturally related businesses suffer; and if they fail, remaining farmers incur still higher production costs by virtue of uncertain supplies, reduced competition, and the need to travel farther to have equipment repaired. Ultimately, the level of agricultural activity may be so diminished that there no longer exists a critical mass. Long before all the agricultural land in a locality succumbs to conversion, agriculture as an economically sustainable enterprise may cease.

Whether agricultural land conversion is seen as a threat to amenities and the quality of life or to the continuation of the business of agriculture, it is an immediate cause for concern just about everywhere that nonagricultural land uses are encroaching into the rural countryside. Public policymakers have been attentive to the concerns of their rural constituents, farmers and nonfarmers alike. The result has been a recent flurry of policy legislation aimed at conserving agricultural lands.

The Role of Public Policy in Agricultural Land Conservation

Although this book is devoted to private-sector approaches to land conservation, no discussion of the subject in a distinctly agricultural context would be complete without acknowledging the important role of governmental programs and policies. For better or worse, public policy defines private opportunity in this context, not least by confining it largely to charitable ventures.

Private organizations have traditionally conserved land by relying almost exclusively on charity, purchasing interests in land with funds derived from tax-deductible charitable contributions and accepting tax-deductible charitable contributions of such interests in land as conservation easements. Because the amount of agricultural land threatened by conversion is so great and the relative value of agricultural land is so high, unless federal tax policy is changed to provide incentives to conservation that go beyond a stimulus to charitable instincts, private-sector agricultural land conservation must be content to remain a supplement to governmental conservation programs.[9] As we shall see, this observation by no means diminishes the important contribution that private organizations can make in the agricultural land conservation field.

Survey of Governmental Agricultural Land Conservation Programs
In order to work with them, private organizations should understand governmental agricultural land conservation programs. Over half the states and literally hundreds of local jurisdictions have adopted measures to conserve farm and ranchlands, and new variations and combinations of the basic techniques they use are being devised all the time. The following survey was adapted from a highly useful publication of the National Agricultural Lands Study, entitled *The Protection of Farmland: A Reference Guidebook for State and Local Governments.*[10]

Differential Taxation. All but two states have adopted some form of differential *ad valorem* taxation of agricultural land as a means of reducing financial pressure on farmers and forestalling premature land conversion. Sometimes called "current use value" taxation, such measures typically require that agricultural land be assessed at its lower agricultural production value—what a farmer can pay for land and still make a go of it—rather than at its "highest and best use," a formulation that often makes development a self-fulfilling prophecy. In some cases taxation is merely deferred or a penalty is imposed when the land is converted to nonagricultural use. However, in the absence of complementary land-use controls, preferential taxation can amount simply to a subsidy of land speculation.

An important variation of differential taxation is used by Wisconsin in conjunction with planning and zoning. In counties where agricultural zoning has been adopted, farmers qualify for a state income tax circuit breaker, in effect a tax credit that varies inversely with income and is based on property tax burden but does not reduce local revenues. In Wisconsin as well as in states like California, farmers may also qualify for preferential taxation by signing an agreement to forego development of their land for a stated period of time, in effect the voluntary equivalent of public land-use controls.

Agricultural Zoning. Modern agricultural zoning bears only superficial resemblance to traditional zoning that classified rural areas as residual land where almost any use was permissible. The most widely employed agricultural conservation technique, agricultural zoning, is generally adopted as part of a larger land-use control scheme based on a comprehensive plan that balances growth and resource conservation. New variations of agricultural zoning are continually evolving.

Large lot zoning is the most primitive conservation technique, forbidding subdivision of parcels smaller than a certain size, ranging from 10 to 160 acres depending on the minimum acreage required for successful farming. A criticism of this approach is that when a purchaser can afford a large residential lot, the amount of agricultural land taken out of production is much greater than necessary. To solve this problem, *fixed area allocation* zoning was developed, requiring a minimum parcel size but further requiring that houses be clustered on as few acres as possible within the larger tract. A further refinement is represented by *sliding scale* zoning, which reduces the density of permissible development as parcel sizes increase. Thus, five houses may be permitted on the first 100 acres of a farm, but only one additional house for each additional 100 acres. These approaches tend to produce strip development along roads.

Conditional use zoning permits nonagricultural development in rural areas only if it satisfies criteria related to soil classification, relationship to agricultural production units, and proximity to existing urban services. This approach concentrates development near established urban centers and minimizes land-use conflicts, while the former techniques can result in scattered subdivision. While all of the foregoing permit a limited amount of nonagricultural development in rural areas, primarily as an accommodation to landowners, *exclusive agricultural zoning* simply forbids all nonagricultural use of land within a delineated zone and encourages development within separate urban service boundaries. To be truly effective, all of the agricultural zoning techniques must be coordinated with state and local capital improvement programs so that, for example, water and sewerage are not extended into agricultural zones to frustrate the intent of their establishment.

Agricultural Districts. A popular agricultural land conservation technique used by states is agricultural districting, which generally allows farmland owners to agree not to develop their property for a period of years in exchange for certain benefits such as protection from condemnation and excessive regulation or, indeed, the tax preferences discussed above. This approach is the functional equivalent of agricultural zoning, but its coverage of the land is less comprehensive, usually producing a checkerboard pattern of conserved and unrestricted lands. The chief drawback of this technique is that, because it is voluntary, it tends not to result in the conservation of the agricultural lands that are most threatened by conversion because of their greater development potential. Nevertheless, districting is important and effective because it commits land to future agricultural use and, thus, combats the psychology of impermanence that often accompanies changing land-use patterns and hastens the demise of regional agriculture. In some states, such as New York, more than half of the agricultural land is conserved within districts.

Purchase of Development Rights (PDR). At the other end of the spectrum from agricultural zoning, which tends to be coercive and nonremunerative in its effect on landowners, is the purchase by state and local governments of the "development rights" to agricultural lands under voluntary agreements with landowners. Six states and a couple local jurisdictions have now adopted this technique; and, with further refinements that it is hoped will reduce its cost to the public treasury, it promises to become even more popular in the future.

Typically the price paid for development rights—the equivalent of a conservation easement restricting the use of land to agriculture—is the difference between its fair market value for development and its value for agricultural production purposes. The landowner, who is not always the farmer who cultivates the land—a very significant point—retains title to the land and is, of course, free to continue its farm use or to sell it to anyone who is willing to use it for agriculture. Jurisdictions that employ this technique are usually very selective about which land they target as priorities for PDR, basing their selections on soil fertility and strategic location of farms (see Selection Criteria below). A major question raised by the need to set priorities is whether agricultural land should be purchased only if it is under a threat of conversion, in which case the price is likely to be higher, but the substantive results are more tangible, than if land is purchased in areas where there is little development pressure.

The combination of PDR with other techniques such as agricultural districting and zoning can result in a very effective conservation program. In Maryland, for example, the purchase by the state of development rights to about 15,000 acres and the establishment of districts on another 70,000 (a prerequisite to PDR under state law) have served as political justification for local agricultural zoning that conserves some 800,000 acres of agricultural

States Using Farmland Protection Tools

State	TI*	AD	PDR	TDR	AZ	RFL	GEO	%**	State	TI*	AD	PDR	TDR	AZ	RFL	GEO	%**
AL	X					X		8	MT	X					X		23
AK	X							1	NB	X				X			1
AZ	X	X				X		19	NV	X							1
AR	X					X		2	NH	X		X			X		100
CA	X	X			X			15	NJ	X	X	X		X	X		9
CO	X				X	X		19	NM	X					X		44
CT	X		X	X		X		70	NY	X	X	X	X		X		16
DE	X					X	X	13	NC	X					X		17
FL	X					X		100	ND	X				X	X		2
GA	X					X	X	14	OH	X	X						9
HI	X	X			X			20	OK	X					X		1
ID	X	X			X	X		4	OR	X				X	X		9
IL	X	X			X	X	X	4	PA	X	X	X	X	X	X	X	21
IN	X				X	X		4	RI	X		X			X		100
IA	X	X			X			2	SC	X					X		20
KS					X			1	SD	X				X			8
KY	X	X				X	X	10	TN	X					X		9
LA	X							2	TX	X					X		5
ME	X				X	X		1	UT	X				X	X		35
MD	X	X	X	X	X	X	X	44	VT	X					X	X	43
MA	X		X	X		X	X	51	VA	X	X				X		24
MI	X				X	X		11	WA	X	X	X		X	X	X	23
MN	X	X			X		X	2	WV	X		X					73
MS	X					X		5	WI	X				X	X		1
MO	X					X		2	WY	X					X		1

*The seven basic protection tools are tax incentives, agricultural districting, purchase of development rights, transfer of development rights, enabling legislation for agricultural zoning, right to farm laws, and governors' executive orders.

**This column represents the percentage of farmland each state can expect to lose by the year 2000 if conversion continues at the 1967–1975 rate, as projected by the National Agricultural Lands Study.

land. The negative effects of land-use controls are mitigated by the prospect of eventual compensation of landowners.

An innovative but as yet experimental variation of PDR is the *transfer of development rights* approach used in a handful of localities. Farmers whose land has been downzoned are compensated not by government but by private developers who purchase development rights that entitle them to build at higher densities within designated receiving areas near existing urban centers. This technique relies not only on strict zoning but also on strong demand for growth to create a market for development rights.

Other Approaches. Of less importance to private conservation, but deserving of mention, are two additional agricultural land conservation approaches. The first is the adoption by forty-three states of "right to farm" laws designed to insulate farmers from nuisance liability.[11] This approach addresses only effects rather than the cause of land-use conflicts, namely, the conversion of agricultural land in the first place. Still, right to farm protection is important to farmers and can be a further incentive to other approaches.

The second approach is the execution by state governors of executive orders that call upon state governmental agencies to consider and mitigate the effects of their actions on agricultural land conversion.[12] These orders function in much the same way as the National Environmental Policy Act. At the federal level the Farmland Protection Policy Act of 1981 parallels the approach of the governors' executive orders but lacks an effective mechanism for enforcement.[13] This federal statute, as discussed below, is more important as the first explicit expression of national policy respecting agricultural land conservation.

Opportunities for Private Agricultural Land Conservation

As noted earlier, the opportunities for private-sector agricultural land conservation are largely defined by the governmental programs and policies that bear the principal burden of conservation in this context.

Targets of Opportunity. Land-use control programs such as agricultural zoning and, to some extent, agricultural districting create opportunities for private conservation by narrowing the field of agricultural lands that should be the targets of easement and fee title acquisition. Even if non-agricultural development is not entirely forbidden within a given area, the pace of development is generally regulated so that private conservation organizations can concentrate their attention on farms that successively come under the threat of conversion. Further, agricultural zoning may reduce the asking price of agricultural land by making the prospect of holding out for rezoning a risky proposition. An offer to purchase a conservation easement or the prospect of a tax deduction resulting from the donation of such an easement to a private organization may look significantly more attractive in this context.

As examples of how private conservation organizations can capitalize on the opportunities presented by land-use controls, consider the following. In lieu of selling off a number of building lots under a fixed area allocation zoning scheme, a landowner may find that the donation or bargain sale of a conservation easement on all or part of his land will yield just as great a return. Or prior to putting land into an agricultural district under contract with the state, a landowner may find it advantageous to donate an easement to a private organization and obtain an additional financial bonus. The latter approach would be especially attractive to a farmer who plans to retire before the term of the contractual agreement with the state expires.

Government Co-ops. Another opportunity presented to private conservation organizations in states and localities that have adopted PDR programs is, of course, the chance to preacquire agricultural land in anticipation of the later resale of development rights. This technique is often termed a *government co-op.* The American Farmland Trust (AFT), a national private organization committed exclusively to agricultural land conservation, is negotiating to purchase farms from landowners who are unwilling to deal directly with the government or whose need for cash is more immediate than the state's ability to close a PDR transaction. In the typical case the farm will be purchased in fee, the development rights will be sold to an authorized state agency, and the underlying land will be conveyed at less than half its fair market value to a young farm family who otherwise might not have the opportunity to own a farmstead of their own.

In such situations the opportunity also exists for a *bargain sale*, enabling the private organization to take advantage of the deductibility of charitable donations of interests in land to purchase agricultural land at less than its fair market value. Such transactions are considered by the IRS to be part donation and part sale, with the deduction equal to the value of the donation. This can, in turn, enable conservation organizations to increase the chances of reselling development rights to the government by offering to do so at a reduced price, often a consideration of state agricultural conservation agencies. Care should be taken, however, to make sure that private conservation organizations are in fact eligible sellers of development rights under the applicable state PDR program. Attention must also be paid to the quality and location of the agricultural land, since state PDR agencies generally establish purchase priorities under strict guidelines.

Another technique that can be used by private organizations to assure that highly productive and strategically located farms do not suddenly succumb to conversion is the negotiation of purchase *options* and *rights of first refusal* with farmers. The former enable private organizations to purchase interests in agricultural land at a specified price, whereas the latter entitle them to preempt any third-party purchase offer by matching it. The favorable tax consequences of a purchase at less than fair market value may give private conservation organizations additional leverage in negotiating a preemptive acquisition contract with flexible terms, including the possibility of matching an offer with different terms that yield the same net return.

A variation of the "government cooperative" approach to private land conservation, which has particular applicability in the agricultural context, is *limited development.* Whereas the development of a portion of a tract of critical wildlife habitat may defeat the purpose of its acquisition by a conservation organization, the subdivision of a few building lots from a larger farm may be entirely appropriate, provided that houses are located on the least productive soils and placed where they will present the least possibility of conflict with active farm operations. Moreover, the subdivision of one or more building lots may be the only way that a private conservation purchaser can break even on a transaction because of the relatively higher market value of agricultural land in contrast with most ecologically significant lands.

Agricultural Conservation Easements. One of the most important private conservation opportunities created by the existence of governmental agricultural conservation programs and policies—an opportunity that would be lacking but for such policies—is that of negotiating agricultural conservation easements that permanently restrict land to agricultural uses. If such easements meet the tests of the Internal Revenue Code, their donation to qualified private organizations can result in a tax deduction to the landowner. Section 170 of the Code is discussed generally elsewhere in this text, and the following discussion will focus on special considerations that apply specifically in the context of conserving the agricultural capacity of land, apart from whatever scenic or other values it may possess.

Section 170(h)(4)(A)(iii) of the Code provides that conservation easements qualify for tax deductions if they serve the conservation purpose of "the preservation of open space (including farmland and forestland) where such preservation is . . . pursuant to a clearly delineated Federal, State or local governmental conservation policy, *and* will yield a significant public benefit." (Emphasis added.) No Treasury regulations have as yet been issued to clarify this statutory provision, so interpretation is largely a matter for conjecture.[14] Nonetheless, the following is an attempt to suggest how the variety of existing agricultural conservation programs and policies adopted by state and local governments might be used to support the argument that an agricultural conservation easement donation qualifies for the federal tax deduction. The same argument would, of course, apply to donations of fee interests in agricultural land with a retained mineral interest, and to donations of remainder interests in such land.

The Code basically establishes two conditions for agricultural conservation easements. First, they must further a clearly delineated government conservation policy. The purpose of this requirement is apparently to discourage the "locking up" of any land that arguably could support agriculture when, in the judgment of local officials, it would be better suited to development. Second, the easement donation must yield a significant public benefit, the apparent rationale being that the public must expect to receive something of value in exchange for subsidizing conservation with tax dollars. These two conditions tend to merge to the extent that the existence of a governmental conservation policy can be said to be prima facie evidence that the agency which adopted it was of the official opinion that a public benefit would thereby result.[15]

On the question of which governmental agricultural conservation policies meet the "clearly delineated" test, the committee report on P.L. 96-541 notes that a single policy statement by a public official or a legislative body is insufficient.[16] The report does suggest, however, that something less than a conservation program backed up by an appropriation or other commitment of public funds may suffice. Programs that devote public funds to the purchase of agricultural land development rights would, therefore, almost certainly meet the policy test. Arguably, programs granting tax preferences that imply revenue foregone and those that merely involve administrative expenses, as in the case of zoning and districting, could also meet the test, provided, of course, that the conservation of agricultural land for agricultural purposes is an expressly stated purpose of the program.

The committee report further says that the governmental conservation policy must represent "a significant commitment with respect to the conservation project." This would seem to imply that the specific parcel of agricultural land on which an easement will be imposed must fall within the general class of lands sought to be conserved by the governmental policy. Thus, if a farm is located outside of an agricultural zone where zoning for agricultural conservation exists, or if it is located within an urban service boundary where development is officially encouraged, private conservation organizations should be reluctant to accept easement donations if the landowner expects a tax deduction. In contrast, it would not appear that the failure of a landowner to place his land within an agricultural district under an applicable state program would necessarily defeat a tax deduction for an easement donation, so long as the land arguably would qualify for inclusion within a district under state criteria. The report, in this regard, notes that a sufficient governmental program need not include a means of certifying specific parcels of agricultural land as within its conservation ambit. Thus, programs that do involve certification would seem to have an excellent chance of meeting this test. Zoning classification as well as districting, and even preferential taxation of agricultural land if strings are attached, arguably could be considered certification. The key point remains that the particular agricultural land in question must somehow be distinguished from "just any old land," and an official body must recognize the distinction.

In making the case for the validity of agricultural conservation easements, private conservation organizations would be well advised to "piggyback" governmental policies where, for example, both the state and the local jurisdiction in which the land is located have adopted them. The strengths of one may compensate for the weaknesses of others, so that the entire fabric of applicable public policy, viewed as a whole, can be seen to represent a commitment to agricultural land conservation. In this regard the federal Farmland Protection Policy Act may also be cited as a clearly delineated policy commitment to agricultural land conservation.

The purpose of the federal law is "to minimize the extent to which Federal programs contribute to the unnecessary and irreversible conversion of farmland to nonagricultural uses, and to assure that Federal programs are administered in a manner that, to the extent practicable, will be compatible with State, unit of local government, and *private* programs and policies to protect farmland."[17] (Emphasis added.) Scant legislative history supports it, but the reference to private programs was a deliberate attempt by the sponsors of the legislation to recognize the legitimacy and importance of private conservation easement donations as a means of conserving agricultural land. Among the congressional findings recited in the act are that "continued decrease in the Nation's farmland base may threaten the ability of the United States to produce food and fiber in sufficient quantities to meet domestic needs and the demands of our export markets," and that "the extensive use of farmland for nonagricultural purposes undermines the economic base of many rural areas." The statute requires the U.S. Department of Agriculture to devise guidelines to be used by its sister agencies in reducing agricultural land conversion in planning construction projects and administering public lands. Litigation to enforce the act is expressly forbidden.

There is little question that the Farmland Protection Policy Act represents a clear commitment by the federal government to the conservation of agricultural lands. Arguably, private conservation easement donors might rely exclusively on this governmental policy to support a tax deduction claim. The problem with this approach lies in referring the specific parcel of agricultural land in question to the object of the remote federal policy. The federal statute contains a definition of farmland, but it would be wise to refer the land in question to the class of lands that state or local policy seeks to protect, and then to piggyback the federal policy with its reference to state and local programs and policies.

One final suggestion with respect to meeting the clearly delineated policy test of the Internal Revenue Code would be to include specific references to applicable policies, quoting relevant portions thereof, in the prefatory text of all agricultural conservation easement instruments. For example, "WHEREAS, the Commonwealth of Massachusetts has adopted a clearly delineated agricultural conservation policy, providing that . . . (Statutory reference)."

The second condition for the validity of agricultural conservation easements is that they "yield a significant public benefit." Again, one might argue that the existence of a clearly delineated governmental conservation policy alone would necessarily imply that its sponsors held the belief that a significant public benefit would thus accrue. The general principle that governmental action must serve a legitimate public purpose bolsters this conclusion. The committee report states, however, that the public benefit of an easement donation should be evaluated on the basis of "all information germane to the contribution," and lists several relevant factors to be considered.

The "uniqueness of the property" is one such consideration. Again, we see the notion of distinguishing a specific parcel of agricultural land from other lands that may be capable of supporting farming or ranching. A conundrum is raised by the fact that agricultural land is more or less undifferentiated compared to habitat and scenic lands. True, there are various soil classifications (see Selection Criteria below), but Class IV soils, generally thin and steeply sloped, may be as important—because they can support high-value orchard crops—as Class I soils, the flattest, deepest, most fertile land. The approach to take in this regard would appear to be to show how the agricultural land in question fits within the class of lands that state or local officials have delineated as important to agricultural production pursuant to their conservation programs. It may be equally important to demonstrate that other lands have been excluded from this class because of their limited agricultural capability or because they are reserved for nonagricultural development. Improvements made by the farmer, such as investments in soil conservation, special equipment, and farm structures, may also be relevant to the uniqueness of the property. All other things being equal, an especially efficient and conscientious farm operation may single out a particular farm as deserving of conservation treatment.

Another factor that the committee says should be considered in evaluating public benefit is "the intensity of land development in the vicinity of the property (both existing development and foreseeable trends of development)." The theory behind this consideration seems to be that the greater the threat that a parcel of agricultural land will be converted to nonagricultural use, the greater public benefit can be said to obtain from its conservation. One might argue that this consideration serves little purpose since the value of an easement declines as development pressure and fair market value of agricultural land decrease, and thus the tradeoff between public benefit and loss of revenue to the Treasury would be self-regulating. Nonetheless, the best approach to take in demonstrating public benefit to be derived from the donation of an agricultural conservation easement would seem to be to document the conversion of agricultural land in the jurisdiction (preferably in the locality rather than statewide) and recent increases in land values (including the assessment of the agricultural land in question) as an indicator of future development trends. In areas where there is little or no development pressure, the consideration of this factor may weaken the case for an easement donation, but the inherent productivity of the land and investments in soil and water conservation or other improvements may be compensating factors. As noted earlier, some states purchase development rights to agricultural land whether or not it is in jeopardy of conversion, and the same principle applies to private transactions. Of course, if none of these factors is present and the purpose of an easement is really to preserve a scenic vista or environmental amenities in a remote area, reliance on those aspects of the tax code addressed to agricultural land conservation may simply be an ineffectual makeweight.

Finally, the committee report includes as criteria of public benefit "the consistency of the proposed open space use with public programs for conservation in the region, including programs for water supply protection, water quality maintenance or enhancement, flood prevention and control, erosion control, shoreline protection and protection of land areas included in, or related to, a government approved master plan or land management area." The nexus between the existence of a government conservation policy and public benefit, noted above, is reinforced by this language. Agricultural land conservation may serve purposes other than conserving agricultural production capacity, and it does no harm to recite these other benefits in easement instruments along with the policies intended to secure them. One caveat is that, because agriculture can have inimical effects on air and water quality if proper management practices are not employed, the conservation of the land for agriculture could arguably detract from other policy objectives and public well-being. The question of whether and to what extent certain agricultural practices should be restricted by the terms of a conservation easement, so as to avoid the frustration of other public purposes and possibly the validity of the easement's deductibility, is considered below.

The final point to make about the use of private agricultural conservation easements as a technique for agricultural conservation is that, since the state of the federal law is still in question, it may be advisable for conservation organizations to encourage farmers and other landowners to apply to the IRS for private letter rulings before executing easement documents. In so doing, it might be helpful to keep in mind that while private letter rulings may not be cited as legal precedent controlling in cases other than that of the taxpayer, structuring ruling requests to seek a ruling on the broadest possible grounds may, if the ruling is favorable, pave the way for successful easement negotiations on similar agricultural lands in the general area.

Special Considerations of Agricultural Conservation

The conservation of agricultural land for the purpose of protecting the business of agriculture and the nation's agricultural capacity is a different proposition from preserving open space for its scenic beauty or ecological significance. The most beautiful farm may not always be the one that deserves to be saved. And ecological purity usually takes a back seat to the practical considerations of farming when it comes to management of the land. Because of these differences, there are special considerations that private-sector conservation organizations must give to the selection of agricultural lands for conservation and to their management as a "working landscape."

Selection Criteria

As implied earlier, states and local governments generally establish their own criteria for selecting which agricultural lands within their jurisdiction should be conserved and which should be devoted to nonagricultural uses. If a private conservation organization hopes to cooperate with a governmental entity in purchasing a farm, or if it wishes to have the donation of an agricultural conservation easement qualify for a federal tax deduction, attention must be paid to the specific land selection criteria established by the governing jurisdiction. In general there are four basic criteria that are often used to determine the relative importance of agricultural land as a target for conservation.

Soil quality is obviously highly important because productive soil is fundamental to agriculture. The U.S. Soil Conservation Service (SCS), with offices in most counties in the nation, officially classifies soils into seven groups based on their depth, ease of tillage, moisture content, and slope. Flat, well-drained, deep soils with good tilth are designated Class I soils, the best that exist. Classes II and III rank just below the top and, along with Class I, are generally defined as *prime* agricultural land, although they may not be as deep, may have steeper slopes, or be wetter or drier. Farms that are composed of predominantly prime soils are the most important targets of conservation, all other considerations being equal. Class IV land often is highly suitable for orchard crops because its still-steeper slopes promote air drainage and reduce the risk of frost damage. Some Class IV lands, as well as those in better soil classifications, are termed *unique* agricultural land because their microclimate allows the production of specialty crops such as fruits, nuts, and vegetables. These, too, are important conservation targets. Soil information can be readily obtained from the local SCS office, where detailed county soil maps are available. SCS technicians can help interpret this information.

Location of agricultural land is important for a number of reasons. First, as explained above, many private approaches to conservation depend upon the existence of a governmental conservation policy that applies to the agricultural land in question. If the jurisdiction in which an important farm is located does not have a sufficient conservation policy, it will be necessary to encourage the adoption of one. The requirements of P.L. 96-541 should be kept in mind in devising such policies, and the approaches taken by other jurisdictions can serve as models.

Second, for purposes of allowing for balanced growth and development, farms should not be located in areas where future urban growth should logically occur. Although it smacks of triage, farms can be divided into three rough groupings by location: those so close to existing urban settlements that their development is appropriate, those so far away from development pressure that active measures to assure their conservation probably are not called for, and those in the middle that are productive enough to conserve but that are under significant development pressure. As a general proposition, private conservation should concentrate its attention on the third group in order to maximize its effectiveness.

Third, farms should be located within areas where agriculture is the predominant land use. An analogy can be drawn to agricultural zones and districts, the purpose of which is to conserve relatively large, contiguous agricultural areas so as to minimize the risk that farming will come into conflict with nonagricultural uses, and to assure that a critical mass of land continues to support the business of agriculture. The conservation of a "keystone" farm can spell the difference between the success or failure of surrounding farm operations.

The *size* of a farm parcel is another factor to consider in the selection of conservation priorities. Although there are no hard and fast rules, generally speaking, the most important targets of conservation are tracts of land that constitute an economic production unit or that can be added as logical extensions to other existing farm units. Because of the economics of farming, some parcels are simply too small to support the commercial production of the crops that can be grown in a given climate and with a certain amount of investment. If, however, a smaller parcel can be added to a larger neighboring farm, or if some agricultural use can be made of it, size becomes less of a consideration, except as it relates to price.

Finally, the *actual and potential use* of agricultural land should be considered. Farms on which landowners have practiced good soil and water conservation, in which buildings and other infrastructure have been kept up by adequate investment, and which hold the potential to be used to grow a variety of crops, are more attractive conservation targets than those that have been worn out or neglected. Adequate investment in farm operations is also a good indicator that the location of a farm makes it suitable for conservation, because if an area becomes too urbanized, farmers tend to neglect upkeep in anticipation of selling the land for nonagricultural use. Investment in soil conservation is especially important because it makes little sense to conserve the land if the soil is allowed to wash or blow away.

To these four physical criteria might be added the *price* of the land, obviously an important consideration if the private conservation organization intends to purchase the farm rather than to accept the donation of an easement. In this respect care should be taken not to pay more for a parcel of land than can be recouped by selling development rights and the underlying fee to a competent farmer. Again, farmers can pay only so much for land and still make a living from it, considering the specific crops and type of operation the climate and business environment permit.

Farm Management

Conserving a working landscape is different from conserving scenery or wildlife habitat because it necessarily implies manipulation of the environment, the very essence of agriculture. Private conservation organizations that hold easements on agricultural land have an obligation to assure that the purpose of the restrictions embodied therein is upheld. In exercising this responsibility, conservationists should take care not to impose restrictions on the land that could so limit the flexibility of the farm operator that as a practical business matter agriculture is no longer a possible use of the land. In actual practice, farm operators themselves will understand the nuances of this general proposition and will not be likely to agree to excessive restrictions if they themselves intend to remain on the land. Prospective operators should be consulted when farms are to be purchased outright and sold subject to easement.

Modern agriculture often involves removing wildlife cover, changing drainage patterns, the use of potentially harmful chemicals, and other practices that may offend ecological purists. In almost all cases, however, compromises are possible so that the production of food is compatible with the protection of the environment. The laws that govern environmental manipulation in the agricultural context tend to represent such compromises. It may be advisable and entirely justifiable to rely on these strictures alone to assure that farm management is consistent with other conservation objectives, rather than to impose additional constraints on farm operators through restrictive covenants.

Perhaps more than anything else, the selection of a competent, conscientious farm operator—one who "comes with" the farm or who expresses an interest in acquiring land conserved by purchase—is the key to assuring sensitive, businesslike farm management. After all, if our goal is to conserve the nation's agricultural capacity and the vitality of the local agriculture industry, we must save farmers as well as the land.

Notes

1. U.S. Dept. of Agriculture and Council on Environmental Quality, National Agricultural Lands Study, Final Report 35 (1981).

2. N. Sampson, Farmland or Wasteland: A Time to Choose 117 (1981).

3. *Id.* at 156.

4. 2 (2) Dupont Context 5 (1981).

5. National Agricultural Lands Study, Final Report, *supra* note 1, at 56.

6. *Id.* at 59.

7. Speech by John Block, Secretary of Agriculture, to the National Agricultural Lands Conference (Chicago, Feb. 10, 1981) *reprinted in* 2 (4) Aglands Exchange (Mar.–Apr. 1981).

8. *See* E. Thompson, Jr., *Case Studies in Suburban Agricultural Land Use Conflict,* 1982 Zoning and Planning Law Handbook (ed. F. Strom) 297 *passim.*

9. *See* Subcomm. on Public Lands and Reserved Water of the Senate Comm. on Energy and Natural Resources, 97th Cong., 2d Sess., Workshop on Land Protection and Management 556 (Comm. Print June 15, 1982) (testimony of Edward Thompson, Jr., Counsel, American Farmland Trust) (text available from AFT).

10. R. E. Coughlin, J. Keene, *et al.*, The Protection of Farmland: A Reference Guidebook for State and Local Governments *passim* (National Agricultural Lands Study, 1981).

11. *See* E. Thompson, Jr., *Defining and Protecting the Right to Farm,* 5 (1) Zoning & Plan. L. Rep. 57 (Sept. 1982).

12. *See Governors' Executive Orders,* 1 (1) Farmland: The Newsletter of the American Farmland Trust 3 (Aug. 1981).

13. 7 U.S.C. §§4201 *et seq.* (Supp. V 1981).

14. 43 Fed. Reg. 29,940 (1983) (to be codified at Treas. Reg. §1.170A-13) (proposed May 23, 1983). The proposed regulations will become final only after a sixty-day public comment period. The most interesting feature of the proposal is what Treasury terms a "sliding scale" approach to the application of the "clearly

delineated policy" and "significant public benefit" tests: "The more specific the governmental policy with respect to the particular site to be protected, the more likely the governmental (policy) decision, by itself, will tend to establish the significant public benefit associated with the donation." *See infra* text accompanying note 15. Further revision of the proposed regulations is likely before they are codified at Treas Reg. §1.170A-13.

15. This observation has been recognized in the proposed Treasury regulations, *supra* note 14.

16. S. Rep. No. 1007, 96th Cong., 2d Sess. 11 (1980); *see* H.R. Rep. No. 96-1278, 96th Cong., 2d Sess. 17 (1980); M. Schuster, *Charitable Contributions of Real Property Interests for Conservation Purposes*, Est., Gifts & Tr. J. 25 (Nov.-Dec. 1981).

17. Farmland Protection Policy Act of 1981, *supra* note 13, at §1540.

Protecting Forestlands

Charles Matthei

Interest is growing among local land conservation organizations (LCOs) in the protection and management of productive forestlands. Mounting pressures for development and increasing reliance on wood for fuel now pose a serious threat to forest resources. Environmentally sound management could double or triple production; but a large percentage of forestland remains unmanaged and unproductive, while other land is overcut, thus damaging its long-term capacity and jeopardizing the interests of future generations. Many local and state governments are concerned, but they have been frustrated by political and budgetary limitations. In the face of these problems, the new interest of LCOs is a natural extension of their traditional concerns.

Forestlands contribute greatly to the character and quality of life of many areas and hold tremendous potential for regional economic and energy futures. They can also be integrated into a broad program of land preservation and limited use for recreational purposes. They offer an important opportunity for LCOs to make a twofold contribution—both economic and environmental—to their communities and strengthen their base of public support in the process. In addition, the income derived from forest management may provide critical resources for organizational development, program operations, and further land acquisition at a time when many budgets are strained.

Several conservation groups have long been active in this field. Others have only recently acquired productive lands or begun to assess the potential of lands they already hold. All of these groups, however, realize that the pressures on resource lands are now so strong and widespread that a strategy of direct acquisition and management cannot, by itself, prevent serious loss or damage.

Any solution to these problems must include private landowners. Vast areas of forestland are fragmented into small, individually owned tracts. In New England, for example, 80 percent of the land is forested, but more than 500,000 people own forestland, and the average tract is less than fifty acres. Small tracts are not conducive to efficient, cost-effective management, and many landowners lack the time, skills, financial resources, or interest required to carry out sound management practices.

The particular problems of these private owners must be addressed; both incentives to sound management and practical assistance must be offered. LCOs can play an important role in the development and administration of new programs. An experiment in a new kind of public/private partnership is now under way in New Hampshire, where nonprofit organizations and individual landowners are engaged in a detailed study of a proposed "forestland trust."

A forestland trust (FLT) would bring together a number of landowners and forest tracts and utilize the resources, management skills, public interest perspectives, and tax-exempt status of local and regional organizations. Landowners within a fifteen-to-twenty-mile radius would pool their forest resources into a common management unit. (As originally conceived, this entity would be a limited partnership: each participating landowner would become a limited partner, and the value of each landowner's partnership share would be determined by the proportionate value of his forest in the FLT pool.) Landowners would retain title to their land, but conservation easements may be placed on the forest tracts involved to provide long-term protection to the forests and perhaps qualify the landowner for a charitable tax deduction.

The manager (or general partner) of the FLT would be a local community land trust or other nonprofit organization. A regional group might serve as comanager to represent the broader public interest. A consulting forester hired by the manager(s) would implement the forest management plan. Income to the FLT from harvesting of sawtimber, fuelwood, pulpwood, Christmas trees, maple syrup, or other sources would be divided proportionately each year among the participating landowners (after deducting the management fee paid to the nonprofit organizations). Income to landowners would thus be spread over a number of years, instead of the occasional larger payments from infrequent individual harvests.

The FLT model offers significant benefits to landowners, the managing organizations, and surrounding communities. The benefits to landowners include: integration of their forest into an ecologically sound, long-term management program, increasing its productive capacity and giving even small landowners the benefits of professional forestry skills and economies of scale; potential tax benefits in the form of income tax deductions, reduced income tax liabilities, estate tax reductions, and probable property tax reduction (changes pending in federal tax law may affect these benefits); annual income and the flexibility to take advantage of market fluctuations; and protection from development pressures and the opportunity to make a significant contribution to the environmental, social, and economic well-being of their communities.

The benefits to the managing organizations include: income to sustain their educational and charitable programs; and long-lasting success in fostering the responsible, democratic management of natural resources.

The benefits to local communities and the region include: increased supply and long-term protection of valuable wood resources for energy and other uses; facilitation of community-based economic development, with new forest-related industries and increased employment for local residents; increased revenues through expanded economic activity and energy savings; and the ability to preserve their distinctively rural character while strengthening the local economy.

The FLT concept was conceived by the Institute for Community Economics (ICE), which assists community land trusts in both rural and urban areas. In the fall of 1980, ICE contacted the Society for the Protection of New Hampshire Forests (Forest Society), an old, highly respected conservation organization that owns and manages more than 14,000 acres of forestland, and the Monadnock Community Land Trust, a young group formed by local residents in the Monadnock region of southwestern New Hampshire. Together, the three organizations approached individual and institutional landowners within a twenty-mile radius of Peterborough and proposed to conduct an FLT "demonstration project"—a detailed study involving a number of landowners and specific forest tracts.

Response was very good. The local newspaper published several articles about the project and an editorial noting its importance for the region; one local town conservation commission formally endorsed the effort; and twenty-one landowners committed 5,190 acres of land (in tracts ranging from 49 to 2,000 acres) to the study. The effort is being coordinated by the Forest Society, and a twenty-member steering committee has been assembled to provide direction and assistance.

The study began with an extensive timber inventory and management report for each tract of forestland involved. The inventories provided information on: forest stand history and structure; soil characteristics; access and other operational characteristics; outstanding ecological features; a summary of information by stand types, including the average number and size of trees, available veneer, sawtimber, pulp and cordwood, and growing stock; timber liquidation volumes and values by species; and silvicultural recommendations and harvesting schedules by stand.

Structural, economic, and market research are now in progress. The structural analysis will evaluate the relative advantages and applicability of limited partnerships, cooperatives, and other legal structures. The respective roles and responsibilities of the managing organizations and participating landowners will be described, a procedure for entrance and withdrawal outlined, a formula for calculation of the proportionate shares devised, and the necessary legal documents drafted.

The economic analysis will project cash flows over fifteen years of operation for each landowner and forest tract individually, and for the FLT as a single unit. It will analyze the potential tax benefits to participating landowners and project the rate of return and payback period for each of them. Benefits to landowners will be compared to the benefits they might derive from selling their land for development or entering into an individual management program. And the economic impact of an FLT on various towns and the region will also be considered, including changes in property tax revenues and projected positive effects on economic development.

The market analysis will explore potential forest product markets and investigate the price advantages of long-term supply contracts. It will analyze the impact of various marketing options on employment and economic development in the region. All of the results of the study will be presented to participating landowners, local officials, and the public. The information should enable landowners to make a thoughtful decision regarding their participation in a Monadnock FLT.

While the study now under way is limited to a particular area, it should serve as a useful model for other regions of the country as well. Inquiries have come to the sponsoring organizations from community groups, government agencies, and landowners in a number of other states. This interest from both public and private sectors reflects the FLT's ability to address their respective concerns.

Individual landowners are concerned about their equity and the return on their investment; they want to preserve ancestral ties to the land, and they are anxious to protect their residential environment and make use of the land for recreational and other purposes. The general public recognizes these traditional prerogatives of private ownership. At the same time, however, there is also an inherent public interest in the preservation, management, and development of natural resources. The changing market and rising prices for wood products reflect growing demand. In a world where wood is already a scarce resource in many areas and where population and demand for resources continue to grow, this public interest can only become more insistent.

As a result, there is a growing potential for conflict between public and private interests—clashes over planning and zoning, over measures that would limit or regulate the traditional rights of ownership. There is in most communities a characteristic resistance to government intrusion on the part of landowners. But as the needs for resources grow more pressing and issues of management and development more critical, government intervention will be inevitable if the public interests are ignored.

The challenge, once again, as with so many other land-related problems, will be to strike a balance between the legitimate private and public interests. The FLT model can do this—with economic, social, and environmental benefits for the landowner and the community alike, and protection for the forest resources and wildlife. The FLT can offer landowners sufficient incentives to recruit their participation and achieve important community conservation and planning goals without the need for additional governmental appropriations or new policy. It should be an effective, voluntary, community-based response to a growing dilemma.

One year later, the FLT project, as it was originally proposed and is described in this article, has itself changed shape due to the limited resources of the sponsoring organizations and the interests of some participating landowners. With the commencement of the timber inventories, the Forest Society assumed principal responsibility for the project. The inventories and resulting cash flow projections were very encouraging, demonstrating the potential viability of the FLT. However, several participating landowners with timber ready for harvest in the near future were reluctant to enter a pooled arrangement that would defer some of their projected income.

Although the FLT as a limited partnership or marketing cooperative was not feasible at the time, given the participating landowners' attitudes and objectives, and the full study originally planned was not published, the project was a success. It assembled and motivated local landowners, obtained complete timber inventories at low cost through a joint contract, identified qualified foresters, and offered a range of expert advice and assistance, all to the great benefit of participating landowners. The positive response of the participants has now led the Forest Society to explore the possibility of a limited-service co-op for forest landowners.

In such a co-op the Forest Society might organize groups of landowners in various parts of the state. The society would offer land protection and management assistance and could form a bridge between landowners and qualified professional foresters by arranging group contracts for inventories and management. In exchange for these services, the landowners might agree to consult with the society if and when they choose to sell their land and to explore the possibilities for long-term conservation through easements, creative development, donations, and other mechanisms. While the co-op concept now being pursued is less inclusive than the FLT, both can contribute substantially to the management of private forestlands in many areas of the country.

Enabling Technical Assistance

Jennie Gerard and Mary Lester

If you give a man a fish, you feed him
for a day.
If you teach a man to fish, you feed him
for a lifetime.

An old Chinese proverb

The proverb introduces two options for the relationship between someone with a need and someone who can help. The first option takes care of the need today but leaves the man hungry tomorrow, still depending on a provider for help. The second option, when independence and effective help are the goals, is the way to go. In the realm of providing communities with help, it is called *enabling technical assistance.*

This article is about the enabling relationship of communities of laymen who want to protect open land resources and The Trust for Public Land (TPL), one conservation organization committed to showing them how. The experience of TPL in assisting communities is the basis for the article. In ten years of operation we have helped sixty-five land trusts to form. During that time, we have evolved a relationship with community groups that is designed to enable them to acquire and manage significant lands for public benefit.

Local Land Trusts: Why?

When trying to understand why local land trusts are so important, some ask if long-standing national, state, and regional conservation organizations with their professional staffs are able to address local land-saving concerns. The answer is emphatically no! They haven't historically and they shouldn't even try. Here's why.

Land saving needs constituencies, and local land trusts build them. Land trust supporters are people who might never have given a second thought to habitat preservation or forestland protection or the saving of jewels of the living landscape had these issues not been raised in their own backyards. These constituencies represent potential voters for local as well as state and national land-use issues.

Local land trusts are tremendously effective because of their focus on the resources close to home. It's the concern for protecting the amenities important primarily to the immediate public that prompts busy people to invest their volunteer time in local land trusts. They are motivated by the prospect of community control, a fraternal twin of home rule. Organizations that operate on a larger scale cannot provide the community control, and consequently do not generate the tremendous volunteer efforts that distinguish local land trusts.

While larger-scale organizations offer professional staffs, local land trusts have at their command the most effective tool used yet for land conservation: peer pressure. Because most land transactions are not highly technical, volunteers can accomplish them by using peer pressure in concert with basic negotiating skills, attention to detail, and time. The proof of this lies in the successful track record of local organizations. According to the 1981 Land Trust Exchange survey, 450 such groups have already protected 670,000 acres of significant lands, and the potential for new groups is virtually limitless.

Training and Technical Assistance: Why?

When brand new land trusts are trying to get off the ground, they often seek reassurance for their vision from the wealth of cumulative experience developed by already established organizations. Historically conservationists have been very generous with their time and resources. Through an informal method of disseminating information, fledgling groups have benefited from the experience of these folks. But as the number of local organizations seeking help increases, particularly in areas outside New England, the Mid-Atlantic states, and northern California, where land trusts abound, these informal systems become inadequate. TPL was the first organization, although it is not the only one now, to recognize the potential value of a formal program of assistance that could encourage and nurture local involvement in land protection. In 1974 we developed the necessary training capabilities and began delivering technical assistance to rural and urban community groups.

TPL got into this backwards and learned an important lesson. Initially our approach, like that of others, was to acquire a significant resource in a community and then try to interest a local group in taking title and accepting the ongoing management responsibility for the land. Even if we found local residents interested in the project, they remained dependent on TPL's overextended staff for ongoing assistance. This early experience showed that these efforts would not result in effective, independent grassroots organizations focused on the goal of land stewardship. Nor would the approach allow us to assist great numbers of communities.

It quickly became clear that the best role for us, who are dedicated to building organizations to address local concerns, was to assist the community groups to achieve their own land-saving objectives. Thus emerged our approach to providing enabling technical assistance to land trusts.

Investing: Twenty to One

In this era of diminishing resources, it is important that conservationists get the biggest return on their investment. Consequently, TPL is most interested in working with groups who can succeed and in turn inspire others to try. Our standards are high because the demands on our time are great. Before we invest lots of energy, we want to know that a community group is willing to match each hour we put in with twenty productive hours of its own. Finding the groups who can do this is a trick. TPL applies criteria for assessing the likelihood of success before we make the investment of time and energy to develop a new land trust. These criteria focus on the group's capacity for functioning as an effective organization.

We look for a demonstration of strong leadership by the land trust proponents. Their land-saving vision must have gained broad community support, including that of local government. That support helps us determine the public value of the idea, but support for stopping development in and of itself is not sufficient justification for our involvement. We are encouraged by groups that have clearly stated objectives for local control of land use. By applying these criteria, we can determine whether a group will be able to attract the board members, supporters, and prospective donors that spell success.

If a group meets the criteria, we can demonstrate how to recruit a strong board of directors. We can then train that board to negotiate with landowners and to build a constituency to support their efforts. If they don't meet these criteria, our training will not help them nor will it

further our objective of peppering the American landscape with thriving local land trusts.

The Team Approach

Local groups starting with dynamic and energetic members, strong local support, and clear objectives have a good chance of succeeding. In all honesty, they probably could launch themselves without outside assistance. However, since the groups tend to form as a response to an impending threat, they may lose important opportunities if they have to start from scratch. A team composed of an established organization such as TPL and a newly forming land trust enables the new group to start quickly and on the right foot. Training and technical assistance help the novice organization avoid reinventing the wheel and taking unnecessary turns. Along with the above benefits, an experienced conservation organization lends credibility and clout to the efforts of the new group. The young organization, instead of being viewed as an inexperienced collection of well-intentioned neighbors, takes on the appearance of a promising problem solver of land-use issues.

Being able to tap the expertise of an experienced organization gives the new group more freedom when recruiting board members. There is less temptation to make the mistake of recruiting attorneys and C.P.A.s to get unlimited free legal and financial counsel.

Phases in Developing a Land Trust

Every community group goes through seven specific phases in establishing a viable land trust. Certain of these phases must be experienced by the group on its own, others with the assistance and guidance of experienced land conservationists. We currently see our role in helping a land trust as that of a midwife. Once the land trust concept has been conceived, we provide information, assistance, encouragement, and reassurance in bringing the organization to life. There are specific points at which it is appropriate for us to intervene and critical times when we should not.

We have closely examined the questions of when it is valuable to assist, when it is more valuable not to assist, and when it is most helpful for us to simply provide reassurance. What is presented here reflects our current thinking on the best methods for helping land trusts to develop and become self-sufficient.

Phase I: The Vision of Land Saved
The formation of a land trust must be initiated by the community. It typically begins with someone's vision of protecting locally significant land. Motivated by this concept, the individual contacts TPL, asking for assistance and ideas. We respond by validating that vision and encouraging the enthusiasm, largely by relating the experience of other groups. Nothing satisfies those hungry for

help more than case studies of successful land trusts. Not surprisingly, many of the written materials we mail out to explain the concept more fully are news articles describing the accomplishments of established land trusts.

Our main aim for this first contact is to spell out to the individual what steps the group must take. We make it clear at this point, as at every point, what we expect them to do and what we can do in turn.

Phase II: The Inspiration

Inspiration is essential, and fortunately can be infectious. The task of the original land trust contact is to spread this inspiration by talking up the idea with neighbors. For the land trust vision to flourish, the individual must project enthusiasm and create enough interest in the idea to bring a group together to learn more. Government employees, no matter how exemplary their public service, do not serve successfully as the catalyst for bringing a group together. Why? They lack credibility in promoting a nongovernmental solution.

In many cases we never hear from the community again, or at least not for a long time. We conclude that either the community support for the idea is not there, the contact is not catalytic, or the requisite commitment is missing. One in twenty-five requests for information results in an initial presentation.

When the contact succeeds in gathering together a group of twenty-five to seventy-five community members, we offer to make an initial presentation and evaluate the feasibility of the land trust. The purpose of the presentation is to inspire the participants. Eighty percent of the information imparted deals with the experiences of existing land trusts. The stories we tell help establish the credibility of the land trust concept as an effective land-saving tool. The successes of other groups plant seeds in people's minds for solutions to their own community's land-use problems. If a group does get together for a presentation, the chances of a land trust's evolving within six months are fifty-fifty.

During the presentation, the previously mentioned criteria for assessing the group's potential for setting up a successful land trust come into play. The people present must represent a broad range of community interests, including those of landowners. There must be evidence of broad community support for the land trust idea. Perhaps most important, there must be at least one individual who can act as the prime mover, someone who has lots of contacts and commands the respect necessary to move the group forward in the face of inevitable skepticism and competing demands on time. Groups that have no movers and shakers might take years to get anywhere or may get nowhere at all.

The desired result of this phase is that six to twelve individuals volunteer to be on a steering committee to explore further the land trust concept. Once a steering committee does form, we lay out the specifics of what the next steps are and how to make them. When, after further examination of the land trust concept, the steering committee decides to proceed, its next and most important task is to recruit a board of directors.

Phase III: The Buy-In

Next comes the actual recruitment of the board. This phase, the buy-in, or commitment, must be completed by the community on its own. We counsel regularly during this phase because the job is difficult. It normally takes the committee four to six months before all the members (ideally between seven and eleven) have agreed to serve and the board is in place.

It is crucial that the right people be recruited for the board of directors. The people the committee should seek out as board members must be willing to make the land trust their major priority after family and job. Because land trusts typically do not employ staff, at least not initially, the commitment of time and effort of the board members is paramount.

Board members need to have community contacts and collectively represent a broad range of local interests. If there are not enough gray hairs or longtime community residents represented, the board is in trouble. The committee also needs to know which people to avoid, for example, more than one or two who belong to the "old boys' club," or those who join boards for the sake of being on a board. Poison to a board are "environmental screamers," that is, people with too high an environmental activist profile.

Board members must be able to talk with landowners. Recently, two women who wanted to form an agricultural land trust to protect dairyland asked for our help. One was a rancher's wife and the other, along with the majority of their supporters, was a blue-ribbon conservationist. We told them that they needed the support of the ranching community before we would work with them further. They went home and got the support of the county farm bureau. That land trust now has a board of eleven, appropriately dominated by owner-operators. They have an up-and-coming agricultural land trust working on sophisticated land transactions to protect farm ground.

During this period of board selection, the committee needs reassurance. Often prospective board members ask them tough questions about land trusts. We provide the committee members with the answers so that they can be convincing and effective.

TPL then counsels the steering committee and emerging board on the procedures for setting up a corporation. The committee drafts articles of incorporation and bylaws using sample documents that we provide. We review the papers and show how to complete the application to the IRS for public charity status. We also help them respond to the inevitable questions the IRS will have on their statements of intent, purposes, and financial sources.

The next step in this phase is board training. TPL instructs the newly formed board on its role, its legal and managerial responsibilities. We show members how to present their land trust to landowners, how to assess a landowner's situation, and how to begin negotiations. We train them in how to use the organization's preferred tax status to solicit donations. We discuss in detail various kinds of real estate interests to which the trust might take title.

At this point new board members are weighing whether they want to make the commitment to the land trust. Meanwhile, we are helping them to identify with the land trust and to speak in terms of "we, the land trust" rather than "it" or "they."

Phase IV: Planning

Young groups tend to overlook initially the importance of this phase, opting rather to accomplish it later. Typically it takes a few years before the resources (that is, staff time and funding) and interest in doing long-range organizational planning come together. Ideally, what should happen now in the development of the land trust organization is the identification of targets, the refinement of goals, and the adoption of criteria for judging potential projects.

The criteria for accepting and rejecting projects are painstaking for a land trust to develop, yet very important. In the first years, land trusts are eager to take on projects that justify their existence and give them a track record. It is the role of TPL to begin teaching the members how to discern good projects from those that are poorly conceived. We assist the land trust in evaluating each project as it is proposed. In this way the board begins to establish a valid set of criteria appropriate for the evolving goals.

It usually takes two years to establish the credibility, find a worthy project, and consummate the transaction. This is a tough time for a new organization. One eager group proposed negotiating a conservation easement over land that was to be partially developed with many homes. Had it not been for our guidance, the board members would have tied up their energy on a project with too little conservation significance for the tremendous monitoring responsibility it entailed. Learning to say no is a difficult task for a young land trust.

Phase V: The Approval

Selecting a first project is like running a rapid: there's only so much preparation the river allows. While the land trust board members may carefully decide what to take on and how to proceed, unexpected opportunities may arise that deserve the priority.

In areas where land-use plans exist, this approval stage is often a great deal easier when the plans represent a community consensus about local land use. The Humboldt North Coast Land Trust (California), the Jackson Hole Land Trust (Wyoming), and the Yakima River Greenway Foundation (Washington) all have benefited from such plans. An excellent example, prepared privately, is the planning completed in 1981 for protecting the public values of Jackson Hole—wildlife habitat, recreation opportuni-

ties, the appearance and products of a traditional ranching community, and the spectacular setting—by identifying where they occur on private land.

A good example of the consensus developed by public planning occurred in Yakima County, Washington. Early efforts on the part of local citizens to develop a riverine greenway not only targeted specific lands but generated remarkable civic interest from eighty community organizations and clubs. When the land trust began, it already had a tremendous base of support and clearly defined goals. Saying yes to the first offers of donations came easy; the land trust knew which acquisitions the community would support.

Eventually there emerges a first project. If a land trust wants our help and the project meets our criteria, that is when the land trust and we set down our relationship in writing. The purpose of the contract between the land trust and TPL is to lay out the roles and expectations of both organizations. The contract specifies the responsibilities, tasks, and dates so we each know the project will not slip through the cracks. This contractual relationship gives both organizations a tool for measuring each other's fulfillment of the obligations.

Phase VI: The Implementation

Now all is in readiness for the implementation of the first project. TPL guides the land trust through this demonstration transaction, providing continuous assistance and advice. Our organizational experience in land transactions (both simple and highly technical) comes heavily into play at this point. The major objectives of this phase are that TPL demonstrates how to do it, and the board members demonstrate that they can do it. The board members' main role in the landowner/land trust negotiations is to establish the credibility of the land trust as a qualified recipient. We rely on one member of the board to develop and maintain a cooperative relationship with the landowner, the one who can bring the most peer pressure to bear.

Another role of the board is to raise project funds, if necessary. In the early years we urge land trusts to avoid transactions that require much money. We do this to demonstrate that land trusts can frequently achieve important land-saving objectives with a minimum of cash.

TPL's role is to coach and advise the land trust so that the members obtain the maximum educational benefit from the transaction and thus learn how to perform their responsibilities professionally. TPL helps the land trust to structure the transaction and develop a negotiating strategy. Our technical help at this juncture may include the preparation of a tax analysis for the land trust's use in showing the landowner the after-tax cash consequences of being generous. TPL may draft the conveyance agreements as the details are worked out. The land trust completes the transaction with our coaching on opening an escrow account and obtaining title information. The land trust then records the appropriate documents.

In some instances TPL's role extends beyond the one described thus far. On occasion we take title to land before an organization actually has formed. We do this when we have an agreement with community leaders that they intend to establish a land trust and take responsibility for the land at the appropriate time. In other cases we have taken title to parcels on behalf of trusts that haven't yet received their public charity status from the IRS. In either case the land trust assumes the title from us as soon as they are able. In Colorado a land trust may not take a conservation easement within its first two years of existence. Consequently, we have agreed to take and hold conservation easements over 9,000 acres on behalf of four local land trusts until they come of age.

Phase VII: Follow-Through

With the first transaction accomplished, the land trust is fully under way. The members now take the initiative and begin to fulfill the obligations of the organization. Management of the property or the monitoring of easements becomes the task at hand. Our direct involvement tapers off here as the land trust's requests for help drop off.

TPL's own follow-through includes providing general advice, assistance, and reassurance in three specific ways. The first is the regular publication of technical bulletins on a wide range of topics, which have recently included risk management and liability insurance, federal tax law revisions, land trust accomplishments, and many others. The topics for the bulletins arise from questions asked us by land trust members.

The second is the coordination of regional land trust workshops. These sessions foster the exchange of information among similar organizations and assist trust members in making valuable contacts. Through the workshops we help build regional networks that can soon function on their own to provide members with information and reassurance. The best example of this is the Northern California Land Trust Council, which emerged after three years of our taking the initiative to bring it together. Now ten local land trust representatives meet quarterly.

The third way is consultation on complex and highly technical transactions in which a land trust may become interested. In these instances we may conduct the negotiations and structure the transaction.

Results

Once a land trust has completed these phases and established a track record, TPL has accomplished its goal. We have transferred nonprofit land acquisition skills to the land trust in order to create local stewards to protect significant resources. The board members have demonstrated their ability to use the tools and to continue on their own. They are ready to take on future projects with little or no assistance from us.

Much like the players in a basketball game, the board members call their own shots and take credit for their own baskets. The coach can take pride in having trained the team well. The measure of the coach's success is the number of games won by the team. In coaching and assisting these groups, TPL is clearly making the most effective use of the expertise built up over the last ten years. In this way we are developing new teams and expanding the ability of the whole league to meet the increasing demands of our country.

PART III
CONSERVATION
TRANSACTIONS

The formal protection of land involves the disposition of the legal rights of a particular parcel and most often requires a transaction of some sort between a landowner and a protection agency. Part III considers in detail the conveyance of easements and restrictions, or partial interests in land, in order to protect specific parcels for specific purposes. There also is an article on limited development as a protection device and one that summarizes the forms of land acquisition available to a charity and the tax consequences of each form. This section does not include a separate treatment of the transfer of the entire bundle of rights, the so-called fee simple, to a land-saving organization. Although such a transfer offers complete protection, it is such a straightforward and common transaction—whether by gift, deed, or devise—that it needs no elaboration here.

The opening article in Part III, "Environmental Conservation and Historic Preservation Through Recorded Land-Use Agreements," presents a detailed analysis of the history of and potential for partial interests as protection devices. These interests, which represent only a portion of the entire bundle of property rights, can be used effectively to achieve desired conservation ends without the added cost and responsibility of incorporating the entire fee simple within a conservation scheme. As such, then, partial interests offer a range of flexibility and practicality that has made them the cornerstone of voluntary land conservation efforts. This article examines the past and present use of partial interests and indicates their increasing value as the demands upon our nation's open land become ever more complex and intense.

The second article is a republication of the Uniform Conservation Easement Act. This act is one in a series of model laws drafted by the National Conference of Commissioners on Uniform State Laws to provide uniformity in a variety of statutory contexts. The Uniform Conservation Easement Act is intended to standardize the treatment of partial interests by the states and to remove the uncertainties attendant upon the common law treatment of these interests when there is little or no statutory reference. It is presented here for the legislative encouragement of the use of partial interests in the conservation context.

The third article is an actual recorded agreement, filed to protect the land and buildings of a historic property in Connecticut. It is included as a practical example of the complicated set of goals that can be accommodated by carefully drafted easements. Here, both land and buildings are covered, thereby achieving conservation and historic preservation goals at once—an alliance often neglected by practitioners in one area or the other. Also, continued family use of the property was contemplated in addition to the stewardship by a conservation organization, a situation requiring careful negotiation of the roles of the respective parties.

The last article in Part III that deals with easements themselves considers their significance in protecting archaeological sites. While this is not a typical concern of the land-saving community, it is a prominent issue in some parts of the country and one that involves substantial areas of land. "An Introduction to Conservation Easements for Colorado Archaeologists" examines easements in quite a special context, once again illustrating their adaptability.

Another major topic in Part III is the role of private development as a protection device. "Private Purchase and Limited Development as a Means of Achieving Land Conservation Goals" presents three case studies wherein private development achieved conservation goals that otherwise would have remained impossible. These transactions occurred in a setting foreign to many in the land-saving community—one containing commercial as well as conservation elements. Since many parcels worthy of protection require

the funds and community support that are earned through limited development, this technique, although now relatively unfamiliar, is a vital component of a successful private conservation program.

The final article on conservation transactions is "A Summary of Forms and Tax Consequences of Land Acquisition by a Charity." In some sense the article goes beyond the confines of this section by incorporating tax consequences in its discussion of types of transactions. However, sacrificing a degree of analytical nicety to achieve a level of practical assistance appeared worthwhile. This summary provides a concise overview of the types of transfers that are available to land-saving organizations and their respective tax ramifications.

Environmental Conservation and Historic Preservation Through Recorded Land-Use Agreements

Ross D. Netherton

I. Property Law Strategies for Environmental Protection

The decade of the 1970s generally is identified with the beginning of Americans' active recognition that environmental constraints must be accommodated in planning for future growth, both domestically and worldwide. In var-ious ways the interrelationship of nature and the interdependence of the man-made and natural worlds are continually being documented; and the central idea of applying an ecological viewpoint to proposals for land development is becoming more widely accepted.[1] A popular axiom in the doctrine that has grown up around this viewpoint states that there are "no free lunches" in modern society's choice of strategies for guiding land-use and community development. Every apparent right or privilege connected with land, water, or natural resources can be exercised only by paying costs deducted from another facet of the community's store of resources or growth potential.

This viewpoint and its implementation are mandated by the Environmental Policy Act[2] and related statutes dealing with specific public works and pollution control programs, historic preservation, and conservation of natural resources. Most of these environmental laws require the making of impact assessments and rely on them to facilitate reconciliation of conflicting interests in the planning process. Some go further to introduce the necessity of negotiating mutually agreeable solutions to these conflicts. The record of the Advisory Council on Historic Preservation in using its "right to comment" on proposals that are felt to injure historically significant sites and structures is impressive because it emphasizes the policy of seeking alternatives that provide for peaceful coexistence rather than forcing decisions that result in one agency's program prevailing over another's.[3] However they are formalized, legal and administrative mechanisms through which negotiation is facilitated seem likely to become increasingly more important as sensible alternatives to litigation over environmental issues.

These trends have various implications for the future evolution of property law. One which seems to emerge from the emphasis on negotiatory processes is the need for property law rules to offer more options to the negotiators. Restrictive rules which no longer serve the interests that originally justified them should be realigned with the main streams of the national community.

Common law rules relating to less than fee interests in land illustrate this point. Historically, where such interests were held in gross, common law and equity rules discouraged their assignability and enforceability among successive generations of holders. As a consequence, the potential for developing innovative arrangements for protection of environmental resources through less than fee interests held by charitable corporations or trusts or public agencies never has been reached, or even seriously approached. In the great majority of cases, efforts to design arrangements for conservation or preservation are limited to what it is feasible to regulate through the police power, or to acquire in fee. Where less than fee interests have been acquired, they have tended to be perpetual negative easements aimed at prohibiting certain specified activities, usually bordering on the character of nuisances.

The history of American conservation and preservation movements up to the 1950s is a reminder of these constraints. The nation's first step toward protecting its heritage of natural wonders was taken by establishing the national parks on land either already part of the public domain or purchased in fee by the United States.[4] Its first major step toward preserving its historic heritage was taken when a private charitable organization purchased George Washington's Mt. Vernon in fee. The feeling that full ownership of the land or water in question is the only basis for effective conservation or preservation has prevailed with only a few notable exceptions. The Great River Road, envisioning a scenic and recreational corridor on both banks along the full length of the Mississippi River, is perhaps the most ambitious plan relying on easements and similar agreements. Today several hundred miles of the river's banks are covered by the terms of easements. The same technique has been used for other major scenic parkways, such as the Blue Ridge Parkway and Natchez Trace Parkway. Use of easements as buffers or transition zones between incompatible land uses has occurred in many cases where protection of small individual sites or features is an objective. But in the total picture the use that has been made of less than fee acquisitions remains relatively small.

In the long run, however, there are clear limits to how much land or water the nation can afford to buy.[5] When the same space is sought by several competing users, the price is bound to be high. Turning the matter around, there are also clear limits on how much land and water the nation can afford to own. Publicly owned property is off the tax rolls; generally it is not put to its full potential of multiple use; and often it is not as well cared for or maintained as it would be in private ownership. Similarly, there are clear limits to the extent that conservation and preservation goals can be achieved through exercise of police-power regulation of land-use development. The police power seldom can guarantee the long-run stability of social and economic conditions that good land development planning needs for success. Its constitutional limitations are spelled out in a mass of case-by-case determinations from which differing advocates can draw differing inferences and applications. When exercised, it is a power that often leaves "winners" and "losers," with the latter unreconciled and waiting for an opportunity to reopen the contest. In highly urbanized areas the time and cost required to process zoning applications are factors that contribute to slowing down urban growth, or to extending the time required to obtain protective action against adverse environmental impacts.

The case for reconsidering common law restraints on the establishment, assignability, and enforceability of less than fee interests for conservation and preservation purposes is not based entirely on reaching points where the police power and the power to purchase property become unacceptable. In their own right less than fee interests represent the opportunity to develop a new dimension of real property law capable of accommodating the wide range of competing demands upon land, water, and natural resources much more fully and effectively than in the past.[6]

II. Historical Perspective

A. Roman Roots and English Branches

Anglo-American common law and equity have provided three types of less than fee interests for achieving conservation and preservation objectives. They are easements, covenants running with the land, and equitable servitudes.

English common law borrowed from Roman law in developing these concepts. In Bracton's day, however, the distinctions between them had not emerged, and the literature spoke generally of the "rights" pertaining to dominant estates and the "servitudes" pertaining to the burdened estates. In this respect common law judges seem to have been influenced by the Roman praedial servitude.

In its rural setting this servitude concerned uses of the surface and subsoil in their natural state and included rights-of-way and the severance and removal of soil or minerals. In urban settings it related to structures and is illustrated by the right to adjacent support of a building wall or to have light or view over adjacent land.[7] Praedial servitudes had to be appurtenant and were not recognized in gross—with one significant exception, no affirmative duties were required of the servient landowner. This exception contemplated support of structures on the dominant land by structures on the servient parcel that the servient owner was obliged to keep in repair.

Such a duty was clearly affirmative; and Roman law held that it was not solely personal to the original obligor, but passed with the ownership of the servient estate.[8] In this feature some have seen the beginnings of the notion that affirmative duties can attach to and run with the land.[9] From other features of the praedial servitudes, English courts developed their concepts of easements and profits and found precedents for initially refusing to recognize easements in gross.[10]

Roman law placed no limit on the affirmative or negative obligations that make up the praedial servitude, and thus it provided a potential flexibility for extension to novel situations that arose with intensified land use. In the hands of the early English judges, however, this potential was largely lost in the rigid formalities required for the running of real covenants and the general conservatism regarding obligations that adversely affected the transferability of titles or burdened land with restrictions on use.

These predispositions against the running of easements and real covenants were part of the common law baggage that British colonists brought to America in the seventeenth and eighteenth centuries, and they were reflected in the warnings of nineteenth-century English judges that "it must not be supposed that incidents of a novel kind can be devised and attached to property at the fancy or caprice of any owner."[11] But they never were applied literally to bar the running of all such agreements. The position of the common law in the nineteenth century seems to have been that covenants relating to land, expressly made for the benefit of the land conveyed and expressly enforceable by any succeeding owner, ran with the land as against the grantor, though not incident to any privity between the parties. On the other hand, covenants that placed a burden on land did not run in such cases, except in the instances of easements for light, air, support of buildings, and the flow of artificial streams.[12]

From these distinctions came the classification of easements as either positive or negative. Positive easements enabled the holder to enter the servient estate and do affirmative acts which, but for the easement, would have been unauthorized—for example, to have a right-of-way across neighboring land. Negative easements gave their owners only veto powers to prevent a servient owner from doing acts on his property that ordinarily he would be privileged to do and that would adversely affect the dominant property.[13]

Another method of classification distinguishes between easements appurtenant and easements in gross. An appurtenant easement is created for the benefit of a particular dominant estate through the possessor's use of his land. An easement in gross belongs to its owner independent of his ownership or possession of other (dominant) land that is benefited by this interest in the servient estate. This distinction is important because historically English common law courts favored easements appurtenant over easements in gross. So, for example, the benefits of an easement appurtenant have been freely assignable by its owner, while considerable uncertainty has prevailed regarding the extent to which an easement in gross may be assigned.

Historical and economic factors explain some of the difference in rules. Prior to England's industrialization, easements almost always were employed among neighboring owners of farms, grazing land, or streams. The law did not hesitate to enforce these easements or allow their burdens and benefits to run because it was felt that they fostered orderly development of the types of land use on which the economy of the times depended. Easements in gross appeared as the economic uses of land became more diversified and common law rules for assuring that a dominant estate would be benefited proved too rigid for some of the types of arrangements that were desired.

B. American Adaptation of Common Law Principles

By the beginning of the nineteenth century, English and American courts began to grow in different directions. British judges permitted creation of easements in gross where the dominant owner's rights were accompanied by a profit, such as a right to enter upon the servient estate and remove soil or minerals for personal or commercial use.[14] This reflected the prevailing belief that increased commercial use of land and natural resources stimulated and sustained national growth. Easements in gross *without* a profit could not readily be justified on these same grounds for they appeared to merely benefit the owner personally while burdening the use and marketability of the servient estate. Hence, the English common law persisted in the view that easements in gross are not recognized or enforced unless accompanied by a profit.

Nineteenth-century American courts responded to their own circumstances. Like the British judges, Americans regularly permitted the creation of easements in gross when accompanied by a profit, but beyond this point a broad diversity of decisions developed regarding the assignability and inheritability of easements in gross.[15] The extent to which an interest or benefit was of a commercial nature often was cited as the decisive factor. But the issue remained unclear well into the twentieth century when Simes became the prime mover in working for a change in the rules of American common law to recognize noncommercial easements in gross as assignable interests. As a result, the *Restatement of Property* adopted the position that such interests are alienable, if made so by the terms of their creation.[16]

III. Contemporary Common Law Rules Regarding Less Than Fee Interests

A. Easements

As the *Restatement* describes American property law, easements appurtenant may be enforced among the original parties, their burdens may run with the land, and their benefits may be assigned with relative ease.[17] Easements in gross may be enforced between the original holder and the original owner of the servient estate. Beyond these parties the burden of an easement in gross runs to successive holders of the servient estate for the benefit of the original holder for as long as the successive holders retain the same estate or interest held by the promisor at the time the easement was created.[18]

The *Restatement* has more difficulty with the question of assignability and attempts to apply the commercial/noncommercial distinction to easements in gross.[19] Notwithstanding this, the cases continue to show no clear preponderance of view. In twelve states easements in gross are not assignable; in four more dictum favors nonassignability.[20] In five states the cases clearly sustain assignability, and in six others assignability is based on statutes.[21] In nine states the holdings are in conflict.[22]

There is general agreement that such diversity perpetuates a confusing and unsatisfactory situation.[23] To improve the state of the law, some have argued that noncommercial easements in gross should be assignable wherever the requisite intent is present and the consequences do not create an undue encumbrance on the servient estate. Others have urged legislatures to preempt the issue and lay down the limits of assignability by statute. As to the urgency of commencing movement in either direction, many feel that the economics of modern land use and the trends in real property taxation have now shortened substantially the lead time available for lawmakers to act. In 1975 Richard Powell expressed a widely held view of the prospects of less than fee property interests when he wrote as follows:

> Over the past several decades . . . the case law [concerning easements] has been marking time, in that the same topics have been litigated for generations. In the coming decades, however, substantial legal questions remain to be answered and new techniques fashioned. . . . The coming of age of cluster housing developments, with their maximization of open lands, as well as the condemnation of scenic easements by public authorities, will also prove a fertile source of new approaches. Esthetic considerations will certainly move to the forefront. Finally, questions concerning easements . . . will continue to challenge the ingenuity of the judiciary, as an attempt is made to achieve sensible land use within the confines of not overly flexible rules of traditional property law. In summary, it may be anticipated that the next decade will witness long overdue progress in the field of easements, perhaps by way of federal, state, and local legislation.[24]

B. Restrictive Covenants at Law

Common law covenants specifying permissible and unpermissible uses of land may be one of two types—those that are enforceable at law and those that are enforceable in equity. In order to run with the land, a common law covenant must satisfy rigid requirements of form, intent, "privity," and "touching and concerning."[25] Even where these requirements are met, however, the party in whose favor it runs may feel poorly protected since pecuniary damage is the only remedy available in law for breach of such covenant.

When either type of covenant is held in gross, problems arise regarding its assignability and running. Historically, English courts refused to allow the burden of a covenant in gross to run, and in this respect their position was consistent with their rule against recognition of easements in gross.[26] A majority of American courts also deny enforcement of covenants at law where the benefit is in gross (that is, where the covenant does not benefit a dominant estate);[27] but they cannot claim that in so doing they merely extend their rules regarding easements, for American decisions recognize several situations in which easements in gross are enforceable.[28] In its view of the law, the *Restatement of Property* takes the position that a burden will not run where there is no corresponding benefit to other land; and thus, as in the case of an easement in gross, the benefit of a covenant in gross is not assignable and will die with the original covenantee.[29]

A few cases may be found supporting the view that the burden of a covenant in gross should run with the land.[30] However, it is rare to find a covenant with the benefit held in gross. The impossibility of possessing privity of estate, or of "touching and concerning" dominant and servient estates, plus the inconvenience of being able to recover only money damages, and the majority rule against assignability, all have combined to discourage the use of common law covenants in gross for environmental protection efforts.[31] As a result, arguments against this hostile climate of the common law regarding covenants in gross have not been as persistent or heated as those offered in favor of increasing the assignability of easements in gross.[32]

C. Equitable Servitudes

Covenants enforced in equity, generally known as "equitable servitudes," were developed to circumvent the common law's traditional hostility toward "novel" easements and covenants restricting the use or marketability of land, as it had been expressed in Keppell v. Bailey in 1834.[33] Fourteen years after Keppell v. Bailey, the English judges were given an opportunity to reconsider this position against the background of growing intensity of land use and industrialization. The opportunity was provided in Tulk v. Moxhay,[34] where a subsequent owner of a servient estate attempted to build on his land despite the fact that he had purchased with notice of his predecessor's promise limiting use of the land for anything other than a vacant pleasure ground. The court enjoined the servient owner from building and stated the doctrine of equitable servitudes in this way:

> A covenant between vendor and purchaser, on the sale of land, that the purchaser and his assigns shall use or abstain from using the land in a particular way, will be enforced in equity against all subsequent purchasers with notice, independently of the question whether it be one which runs with the land so as to be binding upon subsequent purchasers at law.[35]

American courts appear to have moved more quickly than British courts in this matter; and an American decision applying this principle occurred in Hills v. Miller in 1832,[36] where an agreement not to build on a parcel of land was enforced in equity against a purchaser with notice.

The court reasoned that he who takes land with notice of a restriction upon it will not in equity and good conscience be permitted to act in violation of the terms of those restrictions. As this decision was followed in later years, the presence of notice and the prospect of injustice if relief was denied became the decisive elements of the rationale of relief.

Where an agreement met the criteria of relief, it was enforced substantially as a servitude or as an easement. The reported cases espouse both theories, with what has been called a "drift" in the direction of treating enforceable agreements as interests in the nature of equitable easements.[37] Frequently the two theories lead to the same results, and pragmatic considerations determine which one will be emphasized in explaining a holding.[38]

The choice of theories may, however, be significant in cases involving successors of the original parties to an agreement. In theory, privity of estate between promisor and promisee is not required to enforce a servitude in equity.[39] So, a restrictive agreement may be enforced by strangers to each other's titles, provided the benefit of the servitude "touches and concerns" the land.[40] As a practical matter, this latter requirement presents a fundamental obstacle to enforcement of servitudes in gross.[41] The majority of the states take a position that the burden of an equitable servitude will not run when the benefit is in gross.[42] A minority hold the view that the burden of an equitable servitude runs whether or not the benefit is in gross, and this view has enjoyed support in some legal literature.

Regarding the assignability of servitudes in gross, the number of cases dealing with these questions is small; yet they agree that the benefit of an equitable servitude cannot be assigned.[43]

IV. A Contemporary Rationale for the Common Law

A. Policy Favoring Free Use and Alienability of Land

The foregoing summary, relating to the rules for recognizing and enforcing easements, covenants, and servitudes, shows the capacity of the common law and equity to evolve accommodations between competing demands of society. It documents this evolution in regard to interests appurtenant to burdened land but has more difficulty in accommodating desires to transfer and enforce interests in gross. For the most part American courts in the present century have continued to oppose the assignability and running of covenants, easements, and servitudes when they are held in gross. Where American law has favored the use of rights or interests in gross, it generally has been the result of legislation rather than judicial innovation.

The rationale for stopping the common law's evolution short of recognizing the assignability and running of rights or interests in gross often is drawn from the dictum of Keppell v. Bailey that "incidents of a novel kind [cannot] be devised and attached to property at the fancy or caprice of any owner." This declaration has the sound of common sense that appeals to judges' instinctive caution. But in fact it has not been an excessive novelty or capriciousness in proposed agreements that has seemed to threaten the system of property. Most proposed restrictions of land use through creation of interests in gross have reflected reasonable land-use proposals. At closer range it appears that the instinctive opposition of the common law is based on the fear that such an arrangement has the tendency to unduly burden the title to land. Commenting on this "counsel of caution," Clark has observed:

> It expresses an ingrained view that land interests should be made freely available for commercial development, that "encumbrances upon title" should be generally frowned upon, and that the long tying up of realty and consequent removal of it from the market should be prevented.[44]

Upon this rationale the common law courts' consistent objections to the assignability and running of easements, covenants, or servitudes in gross are understandable. When the issue hinged on an encumbrance of title, and titles typically were passed by transfer of muniments, and reliance was placed on the examination of these instruments to validate an owner's title, courts could readily accept and sympathize with the argument that rights or interests in gross might become lost or forgotten by successors in title, only to be discovered years later after the original holder had died or moved away. In contrast, an appurtenant easement or servitude, benefiting adjacent or nearby land, was less easily overlooked, and its holder usually could be ascertained with little difficulty.

These reasons still apply to a large part of the land in England (except for interests requiring notice in the "charge indexes" since 1925). For most of the nineteenth century they also applied in the United States. Here it was not until the 1840s that indexes of the public records were required by statute, and it was not until the 1870s that abstracting from public land records became common. In the twentieth century reliance on record searches became so universal that the chances of overlooking interests held in gross were greatly minimized. At the same time the technology of record systems experienced a period of expansion and improvement that made title search procedures surer and more expeditious, further cutting away the danger of recorded agreements remaining hidden from successors in interest to the original parties.

B. Balancing Land-Use Needs

The twentieth century has witnessed other developments in the concept of property and the techniques of land-use regulation that have a bearing on the contemporary rationale of American common law rules regarding the running of less than fee interests in land. At midcentury, however, the *Restatement of Property* reflected the values that traditionally had shaped the American view of property and its economic role in the past. Succinctly it declared:

> There is a social interest in the utilization of land. That social interest is adversely affected by burdens placed on the ownership of land.[45]

And, specifically as to interests held in gross, it said:

> Unless a burden has some compensatory advantage which prevents it from being on the whole a deterrent to land use and development, the running of the promise by which it was created is not permitted. The requirement of such a compensatory advantage is commonly expressed by saying that the promise must "touch and concern" the land with which it runs [that is, it must operate to benefit some person in the use of his land].[46]

Whether a new restatement of this law, looking to the end of the century, would be as insistent on demonstrating social interest by a requirement that a land-use restriction must "touch and concern" the land with which it runs is the real question. There is much to suggest that the area of justifiable restriction has widened significantly in the past twenty-five years. In this respect events have validated the forecast of Clark, who, also at midcentury, wrote as follows:

> Traditionally we argue in favor of unencumbered titles, and title-searchers and real-estate men who desire free exchange of realty are in accord with such a view of policy. Yet apparently we are coming to see that in many ways permanency of development of land is desirable. Witness the prevalence of equitable restrictions, and the tendency toward zoning laws and . . . building-line restrictions. A covenant such as one to repair or to pay certain assessments for land improvement may be of great service so far as concerns the actual value of the premises. In view of all the encumbrances which are being upheld, it is certainly questionable whether there is any unanimity of feeling in favor of a policy against upholding such covenants. . . .
> . . . To a generation familiar with many forms of encumbrances, such burdens on titles would seem not improper.[47]

If the recent national debates over land-use planning legislation and the increasing refinement of national and state environmental impact and pollution control programs correctly reveal contemporary thinking about land use, the present generation clearly recognizes that some situations call for putting a higher priority on *management* than on *development* of land. With allowance for his bias as a sponsor of proposed federal land-use policy legislation, Senator Henry Jackson came close to summing up the contemporary view of the land-use regulation issue in the following statement:

> The crucial question is whether we are to allow rapid development, the irretrievable dedication of our land, to be done in accordance with the tenets of our traditional pioneer land ethic or whether we are prepared to demand that our land be managed and used to best meet our Nation's environmental and social requirements.[48]

Sound management and use of land resources call for balancing the freedom of choice in selecting land uses and stability in the resulting patterns of land use. Real property law rules affect both of these factors and, through them, affect the success of both public and private landowners in achieving their goals, including the conservation of resources and environmental values and the preservation of historical and cultural landmarks.

Emphasis on making the legal tools of land-use restriction more easily available to public agencies and private landowners for use in land management is not to be misconstrued as calling for a "no-growth" policy in the law. Rather, it calls for a new growth policy in the law—one that places in parity the needs for land development and for the conservation of the resources of our natural and man-made environment. It calls for preventing irreversible depletion and destruction of resources that are finite in quantity and must be shared with future generations. It calls for recognizing that ownership of land in contemporary America is heavily conditioned by the economics of the prevailing urban industrial society. What was an excessive encumbrance and burden to landowners a century ago may now be an essential facet of the system of land-use regulation that stabilizes the value of sites where development capital is committed for substantial periods of time. Finally, it calls for recognizing that where public agencies are made responsible for conservation and preservation programs, their traditional options have been to acquire fee title through purchase or condemnation or to invoke police-power controls of land use. Freeing interests in gross to be assignable and to run with the land adds a third—and a middle—way for public agencies to carry out their programs; and it is a way that permits public-private sector cooperative activity on a scale not possible with other options.

C. The Role of Recording

When carefully considered, the bias of the common law and equity courts against interests in gross seems to be based on a fear of excessive encumbrance of land titles. Excessive encumbrance, however, is a relative standard. Landowners in the twentieth century accept a wide range of land-use limitations that would have seemed outrageous to their predecessors a century earlier; and it is likely that in areas where population, commerce, and industry are concentrated landowners in the future will accept even more limitations on land use; hence, the necessary chore of noting or clearing encumbrances in the certification of marketable title.

What courts and landowners cannot permit to proliferate are encumbrances that are hidden, or discoverable only by chance. Thus, whether an encumbrance in gross is permitted to run with the land may depend upon how easily it can be discovered and cleared if the parties desire it.

Current recording systems therefore provide an answer

to a major part of the common law's concern to protect landowners from surprise and the difficulty of finding parties from whom releases can be obtained. As refinement of land data systems generally increases, the particular problems of compiling and maintaining special records of land-use agreements have been identified and are being addressed. Where modernization of land data systems is progressing, conversion of traditional descriptions is being supplanted by new uniform systems of parcel identifiers capable of being utilized in automated data processing for easier access and retrieval of title information.[49]

Additional assurance that agreements for conservation and preservation purposes will not go unnoticed or become lost to successive parties is provided in some states by mandatory procedures for review and approval of such agreements by public bodies prior to their recording. A variety of reviewing bodies is used. Montana law requires that conservation easements are subject to review by the local planning authority of the county in which the burdened area is located.[50] In this case the review is advisory and mainly to prevent conflicts with local land-use plans. In Arkansas proposed preservation restrictions must be accompanied by a certificate of approval from the state's Commemorative Commission when submitted for recording.[51] South Carolina's Heritage Trust Program requires that when areas are dedicated as heritage preserves, a land management plan must be prepared for them and all interested parties, public or private, shall have input into the plan.[52] The Massachusetts statute is unique in establishing a "public restriction tract index," and conservation or preservation agreements registered therein need not be re-recorded within the thirty-year period required by the state's marketable title act in order to retain their validity.[53] A prerequisite to registration of a land restriction in this index is approval by Commissioner of Natural Resources (in the case of conservation restrictions) or the Massachusetts Historical Commission (in the case of preservation restrictions). Colorado is typical of several other states in which the protection of the state's law freezing conservation easements in gross from their common law limitations extends only to properties that are listed in the state's inventory of recognized resource areas and historical or cultural landmarks.[54]

These provisions, which illustrate current practice in the scrutiny and screening of proposed land management arrangements for conservation and preservation purposes, strengthen the role that recordation plays in meeting the traditional common law objection to the assignability and running of interests in gross. At the present time the states with these procedures are acknowledged leaders and innovators. Further experience may well lead to modifications in current procedures. In any event the results will be welcome, for they contribute to perfecting a contemporary rationale for the common law that will be responsive to both the needs and the conscience of American society in the management of its land resources.

V. Assignability and Enforcement Among Successors in Title

A. Modification of Common Law Rules

When parties desire to create rights or interests in gross for the promotion of conservation or preservation objectives, they are well advised to become familiar with applicable rules governing the assignability and enforcement of such interests among their successors in these interests. Since the requirements of privity and appurtenance cannot be met, common law precedents may oppose the running of the burden of the agreement to successors in interest. A similar result may occur where an assignee of the original holder of a right or interest in gross attempts to enforce it on the theory that its benefit ran to him. The present state of the common law regarding easements, restrictive covenants in gross, and equitable servitudes has been noted earlier.

The possibility that this state of the law may be changing is suggested by a handful of cases in which enforcement of recorded interests in gross has been upheld.[55] Chief among these is United States v. Albrecht,[56] sustaining the right to enforce a restriction in gross pursuant to public policies of the Migratory Bird Conservation Act.[57] The interest acquired by the federal government was in the form of a recorded agreement for environmental protection, and its enforcement was alleged to be barred by a hostile state law. The federal court ruled, however, that the government's interest was a reasonable property right that "effectuates an important national concern, the acquisition of necessary land for waterfowl production areas, and should not be defeated by possible North Dakota law barring the conveyance of this property right."[58]

The decision in United States v. Albrecht may point the way to a liberalization of the rules of assignability and enforceability, at least in cases where the holder of an interest in gross is a public agency. Being immortal and locally fixed, such agencies do not die or move away as natural persons do, and so their interests present no unusual complications to the task of documenting the marketability of the burdened property.[59] To a great extent charitable corporations and trusts share these characteristics, and thus may claim to be covered by the rationale of enforcement.

Currently forty states have enacted statutes dealing with the creation, transfer, and enforcement of less than fee interests for conservation or preservation purposes. (See Tables 1 and 2.) In twenty-two states these laws include provisions to facilitate the assignment and enforcement of rights or interests in gross. They are:[60] Arkansas, California, Colorado, Connecticut, Delaware, Florida, Georgia, Illinois, Indiana, Louisiana, Maine, Maryland, Massachusetts, Michigan, Minnesota, Montana, New Hampshire, New York, Rhode Island, South Carolina, South Dakota, and Utah. In all but three of these states, it is provided specifically that recorded agreements of the type covered by the statute shall be assignable whether or not they benefit a dominant estate or the parties have privity of contract or estate, and that they shall not be unenforceable on account of failure to meet these common law requirements.

In the three states not utilizing this direct approach—California, Michigan, and South Dakota—the statutory authority for creation of conservation easements or restrictions specifies that the instruments of the agreement shall contain covenants running with the land.

B. Contingency Provisions to Assure Enforcement

A special, but important, facet of the subject of assignability and enforceability involves substituting holders of conservation and preservation interests when proposed or actual holders are incapable or unwilling to carry out the terms of an agreement. Maryland's law resolves this problem by transferring the right or interest to the state's principal preservation agencies—the Maryland Historical Trust or the Maryland Environmental Trust.[61]

The primary purpose of this provision of the Maryland law is to prevent courts from declaring a conservation or preservation interest to be extinguished or unenforceable on the grounds of changed conditions or frustration of purpose. The language of the statute leaves the duty of enforcement to be implied from other provisions. It has been recommended, therefore, that legislation on this subject specifically provide that in the event a specified holder for any reason is or becomes incapable of taking or holding the interest, it will be construed to pass to a designated organization with appropriate authority and responsibilities for enforcement of the interest.[62]

VI. Affirmative Obligations in Recorded Agreements

A. The Affirmative/Negative Distinction

Exploratory discussion of the use of less than fee interests for conservation and preservation objectives invariably encounters the question of whether such interests entitle the holders to actively use the land of the servient estate or oblige the servient owner to perform positive acts of land management to promote the objective of the agreement. This question may arise in the course of applying the affirmative/negative classification of interests or because of a persistent expression of the need for positive obligations by public agencies or private trusts working with these legal tools.

In literature on easements it is accepted that an affirmative easement entitles its holder to enter upon the servient estate to perform acts for the benefit of the dominant estate, which, except for the easement, he would not be privileged to perform.[63] A negative easement entitles its holder to prevent the owner of the servient estate from acting or using that estate in particular ways which, except for the easement, the servient owner would be privileged to choose.[64]

The possibilities for both types of arrangements are extensive. Affirmative agreements may include rights of passage across servient land or rights to enter servient land and take water from a stream thereon or rights to use various facilities located on the servient tract and belonging to its owner. In contrast, easements utilized in the protection of scenic highways illustrate negative easements and typically restrict the servient holder in permitting the use of his land for outdoor advertising, junkyards, or trash dumps, or for the cutting of timber or erection of new structures without advance approval of the easement holder. Conservation easements typically call for perpetuating the servient land in its natural state, with specific restrictions on cutting timber, excavating soil or rock, and building structures.

Negative easements may include incidental affirmative rights, such as a limited right of entry onto the servient estate to inspect or to correct conditions not taken care of by the servient owner's management of his land. Judicial interpretation of easement instruments may be required to say whether such incidental rights of entry are implied from the establishment of the negative obligations or specified in the instrument's language.

A more subtle form of affirmative interests is suggested by a dictum of the Wisconsin Supreme Court in Kamrowski v. State, which speaks of the public as acquiring a "visual occupancy" of roadside land through condemnation of a scenic easement.[65]

Ultimately, however, the significance of these concepts of affirmative/negative rights and interests depends on whether the law treats the two classes differently. General observations have been made that negative easements appear to be less favored than affirmative ones.[66] In terms of assignability and running with the land, however, the affirmative/negative classification appears to be much less important than whether an interest is appurtenant or in gross. Easements appurtenant are assignable regardless of whether they are affirmative or negative in their nature, while a variety of easements in gross have been held nonassignable.

Various forms of recorded agreements may be used to provide for affirmative acts, but an initial difference must be noted in the character of the action contemplated. When presented in the form of easements, the affirmative features *allow the promisee* to perform positive acts on the servient land; when cast in the form of equitable servitudes, the affirmative features *obligate the promisor* to perform positive acts on his own (servient) estate.

B. Enforcement of Affirmative Obligations

Traditionally English courts of equity enforced only negative restrictions, taking the position that enforcement of affirmative agreements by mandatory injunction was too difficult to supervise, and that such agreements imposed additional burdens on the land.[67] Some American courts, notably New York's, followed the English rule for a time; but more recently they have tended to permit affirmative obligations to be enforced where their burden is "reasonable, customary, and necessary."[68] This trend is in accord with the view of a number of commentators who argue for enforcement of both affirmative and negative obligations where the equitable remedy is the only adequate one.[69] Many instances are reported where an affirmative agreement was enforced on a purchaser from a promisor with notice of the agreement.[70] Although the purchaser may not be personally liable for its nonperformance, he takes the land subject to the chance that a court of equity will enforce its performance by decree.[71] The cases upholding enforcement insist, however, that such affirmative agreements must "touch and concern" the promisor's land, just as in the case of any other enforceable servitude. In these instances affirmative agreements in gross have required the assistance of enabling legislation in order to run with the land.

Affirmative agreements that impose positive duties on the servient landowner may take a variety of forms. They are illustrated by the obligation of the owner of a historic building to maintain it in repair or a particular state of restoration. In the case of easements, the common law discouraged the imposition upon servient owners of duties to perform positive acts and refused to allow the burden of such easements to run to subsequent owners.[72] Similarly, equity was cautious in enforcing servitudes that imposed positive obligations on landowners. Where mandatory injunction was the requested remedy, the strongest proof of injustice was required.[73]

Legislators apparently have not felt the same constraints that judges have concerning the imposition of positive duties upon servient owners, and in some instances they specifically mentioned them in enabling statutes. Thus, New Hampshire's conservation restriction is defined by statute as "a right to prohibit or require, a limitation upon, or an obligation to perform, acts on or with respect to, or uses of, a land or water area. . . ."[74] A preservation restriction is also described as "a right to prohibit or require, a limitation upon, or an obligation to perform. . . ."[75] Utah's statute states that a preservation easement may "entitle its owner to take certain action, to require certain action to be taken by the owner of the burdened land, or require that certain action not be taken by the owner of the burdened land, and under any such circumstances may be either appurtenant or in gross."[76] Statutes authorizing Rhode Island's conservation restrictions and Colorado's conservation easements employ essentially the same language as New Hampshire does in dealing with duties of servient landowners.[77] In Canada provincial legislation establishing the Ontario Heritage Foundation authorizes that body to acquire and enforce positive as well as negative easements and covenants.[78]

Statutes in California, Connecticut, and Michigan authorizing establishment of agricultural preserves or restrictions may present particular problems of defining affirmative obligations since the central purpose of these restrictions is to preserve prime agricultural land in farming or other compatible uses.[79] Determinations of what constitutes allowable or compatible uses for land covered by agricultural restrictions require the approval of a public planning or supervisory body, which may also be authorized to impose certain affirmative duties in connection with the land uses that are designated.[80]

These statutes present a contrast to those that are concerned solely with negative limitations on landowners,[81] as well as those that leave the servient landowner's options hazily defined by stating merely that the objective of the restriction is to retain specified land or water areas "predominately in a natural, scenic or open condition . . . or in other use consistent with the protection of its environmental quality."[82] The disadvantages of these latter methods of drafting are evident, just as it is clear that the more specific treatment of affirmative obligations must depend heavily upon skillful administration for their success. Nevertheless, observers who have studied the experience with these laws are persuaded that the ability of the holder to require affirmative acts by the servient landowner can be a valuable feature of conservation and preservation agreements and recommend provision for such features in enabling legislation.[83] This view is understandable, particularly against the background of emphasis on *management* of land and water for conservation and preservation objectives. Passive preservation, sought solely through prohibition of acts that are damaging to the status quo, is neither fully responsive to the issue of accommodating environmental objectives along with development pressure, nor fully sensitive to the potential of affirmative arrangements in this field.

Where affirmative obligations are imposed on a servient landowner, various collateral questions may be encountered. For example, who should be liable for injuries sustained by an invitee using the facilities to which the affirmative obligation pertains? If the obligation calls for maintaining a right-of-way for visitors, does the distinction between ordinary and gross negligence apply to this duty? Should a landowner-obligator owe the same degree of care to members of the public as to agents of the obligee who enter the land for inspection purposes? Should a landowner who donated a right of access to his land and maintains the land in a condition conducive to public use and enjoyment be partially relieved of the usual burden of tort liability? These are questions that the common law cases have not answered at the present time. Generally the statutes also are silent on these matters, with the exception of California's law relating to agricultural preserves. That law provides that where a landowner agrees to permit the use of his land for free public recreation, the county board or municipal council that establishes the preserve may agree to indemnify the owner against claims arising from such use.[84]

VII. Formalities of Conveyance and Recordation

A. Common Law Conveyancing

Given the predisposition of common law judges to limit the running of rights and interests in gross, it is not surprising to see them insist on strict compliance with the formalities applying to conveyance of real property, even where the running or assignability of an agreement is not in issue and there is no question about the agreement touching and concerning a dominant parcel of land. The insistence on compliance with conveyancing formalities seems based, rather, on the practical need to be certain that courts can later determine whether the parties' action creates a covenant or other interest running with the land, or merely a restriction in a deed that does not affect the estates that the parties hold.

The basic formalities for conveyance of property interests have remained essentially unchanged over the years. Property must be described accurately; consideration must be recited; words of grant must be used; intention to bind heirs, assigns, and successors must be clear; an habendum clause must be included; and seals and acknowledgments must be shown. In determining the legal effect of an instrument that speaks of limiting the use of land or its development potential, courts are guided by the intent of the parties as drawn from the specific words used or gleaned from careful examination of the entire instrument.[85] Determination of whether the instrument creates a property interest in land or a personal obligation between the parties also affects the range of remedies available for enforcement.

B. Recordation Requirements

Covenants and other interests running with the land are perpetuated through the recording system, the purpose of which is to preserve the "muniments," or evidences of title, and give public notice of all changes in the ownership of property and the circumstances accompanying such changes. Anyone dealing with land is presumed to know of the substance and effect of every properly recorded instrument.[86] Recordation of instruments creating conservation and preservation agreements must be carried out in compliance with the general statutory procedures prescribed for the applicable recording system.

In some instances, however, statutory requirements for recording are linked to the basic questions of assignability or enforceability of the rights or interests created. Colorado's legislature is specific on this point, stating: "Instruments creating, assigning, or otherwise transferring conservation easements in gross must be recorded upon the public records affecting the ownership of real property in order to be valid and shall be subject in all respects to the laws relating to such recordation."[87] Enabling laws in other states specify features of the recording requirement that must also be considered as affecting the enforceability of conservation and preservation agreements. Most relate to the location of the record of the transaction (generally the county where the burdened land is situated) and the office of record (generally the county registrar of deeds).[88] In some instances, also, recording statutes include directions regarding the manner of describing the restrictions and the restricted lands.[89]

As the problem of assuring that recorded instruments will be readily accessible to the public has been considered, several states have established special facilities and procedures for records of conservation and preservation agreements. These laws have provided two types of features: special sets of records,[90] and special notice to other governmental offices having an interest in the subject.[91]

Related to these special procedures for recording is another series of rules for screening proposed agreements or acquisitions. These procedures generally call for action by a third party, in most cases the state land-use planning agency or natural resource department, or a special commission to review and, sometimes, approve the protective rights or interests. Review of proposed agreements by these agencies may include public hearings or other procedures for giving public notice and obtaining public comment, and thus supplement the recording system in providing wide notice of the condition of the title of the property affected.[92]

VIII. Conclusion

Within the past decade a national commitment has been made to expand and intensify conservation of the nation's land and natural resources and to preserve the landmarks that serve as symbols of the identity, experience, and goals that Americans share through their history. This commitment is expressed in a wide range of action programs at federal, state, and local levels. It also is reflected in growth of the use of charitable corporations and trusts to hold land for conservation or preservation purposes. In most of these activities a key feature is the establishment of special arrangements regarding the use of land.

Not all of these arrangements can or should be made by recourse to eminent domain or the police power. Real property law is being asked to provide authority for the creation, transfer, and enforcement of less than fee rights and interests in land and landmarks having conservation or preservation significance. Increasingly there are calls to have these interests held or enforced by public or quasi-public agencies or by charitable corporations or trusts operating programs of national, statewide, or regional scope. In many instances the rights and interests held for conservation or preservation purposes are held in gross and are not appurtenant to the land burdened by them.

Nineteenth-century precedents in common law regularly denied the assignability and running with the land of interests held in gross; and equitable servitudes that were not found to "touch and concern" a dominant parcel of land had small chance of being treated as anything but a personal obligation of the original parties to the agreement. The rationale of these rules has been criticized for being out of step with present-day priorities and land economics. Additionally, modern recording systems have minimized the risk that purchasers of land will be surprised by undisclosed encumbrances on their titles. Yet a majority of states that still rely on common law rules in such matters do not recognize or enforce interests held in gross.

The evident need for greater use of less than fee interests in managing land use has prompted more than thirty states to enact legislation for this purpose. After studying this body of law, Russell Brenneman made the following observation: "There is obviously a very active awareness in the state legislatures of the usefulness of less-than-fee controls for conservation and preservation purposes. However, this interest has taken various forms. Some states appear to have focused primarily on authorizing acquisition programs by existing or new units of state and local government without attempting to clarify whatever difficulties may be presented with regard to assignability, enforcement by and against remote parties. . . . Others have made major efforts to clear up these common law problems. . . .

"The legislatures have acted with the diversity and ingenuity which are a hallmark of the federal system. Of the . . . state statutes, none is precisely like any other; each has strengths and weaknesses peculiar to itself. . . . It appears desirable to develop at this time . . . legislation which clears away common law impediments to the use of easements for conservation and preservation purposes."[93]

This observation seems both correct and timely. The United States is ten years into an era of new commitment to responsible management of its land and water areas. Conservation and preservation programs have come into being, and better inventories of natural and man-made resources are being made. The next critical need is to provide legal tools capable of use in both the public and private sectors to accommodate the demands of development with the conservation/preservation imperative. Recent state legislation offers a number of possible prototypes for the development of uniform state laws to guide the evolution of these needed tools.

Table 1
Purposes, Interests, and Parties Involved in
Conservation and Preservation Agreements

State and citation	Authorized purpose	Interests or rights involved	Parties eligible to hold interests or rights
Alabama Code (1979) 41-10-20 – 41-10-34	Restoration, construction, operation, acquisition, or disposal of land, buildings, or facilities listed on the National Register of Historic Places.	Fee and less than fee interests.	Public corporations, called Historical Preservation Authorities.
Arizona Rev. Stat. (Supp. 1974) 9-464; 9-464.1; 11-935.01	Preservation of open space land.	General less than fee interests.	Any governmental unit.
Arkansas Stat. Ann. (Supp. 1978) 50-1201– 50-1206; 9-1409; 9-1411; 9-141	Preservation of structures, sites, or open space historically significant for their architecture or archaeology.	Preservation restrictions.	Any governmental body; any charitable corporation or trust authorized to hold land.
76-2520; 76-2521	Preservation of roadside areas.	Scenic easements.	State governmental agencies.

State and citation	Authorized purpose	Interests or rights involved	Parties eligible to hold interests or rights
California Gov't Code (West Supp. 1978) 51050–51065; 51070–51097; 6950–6954; 7000–7001	Preservation of open space land.	Conservation easements; scenic easements; development rights; term easements; resale or leasebacks; general less than fee interests.	Any governmental unit.
51230–51239	Assurance of compatible use and development of agricultural preserves, wildlife habitats, salt-ponds, managed wetland areas, and submerged areas.	Recorded contractual restrictions limiting use to compatible activities during the contract period.	County and municipal governments.
50280–50290	Preservation of qualified property in historic zones.	Recorded contractual restrictions limiting use to compatible activities during the contract period.	County and municipal governments.
Colorado Rev. Stat. (Supp. 1976) 38-30.5-101–38-30.5-110	Retention of land, water, or air space predominantly in natural, scenic, or open condition for wildlife habitat or other use "consistent with wholesome environmental quality or life-sustaining ecological diversity" or preservation of structure or site with historical, architectural, archaeological, or cultural value.	Conservation easements in gross.	Any governmental unit; any charitable organization exempt under I.R.C. §503(c)(3) and at least two years old.
Connecticut Gen. Stat. Rev. (Supp. 1978) 47-42a–47-42c; 7-131b–7-131c	Control of future land use to retain areas in natural, scenic, agricultural, or open space. Preservation of structures, sites, or open space of historic value.	Conservation restrictions; preservation restrictions.	Any governmental unit; any charitable corporation or trust authorized to hold land.
P.L. 78-232	Conservation of certain arable agricultural land and adjacent pastures, woods, natural drainage areas, and open spaces.	Development rights.	State Department of Agriculture.

State and citation	Authorized purpose	Interests or rights involved	Parties eligible to hold interests or rights
Delaware Code (Supp. 1979) 6811–6815	Retention of land or water areas predominantly in natural, scenic, recreational, or open condition, or in agricultural, farming, forest, or open space use. Preservation of structures or sites historically significant for their architecture, archaeology, or associations.	Conservation and preservation easements.	Any governmental body; any charitable corporation or trust whose purposes include conservation of land or preservation of historic sites or buildings.
Florida Stat. Ann. (Supp. 1979) 704.06	Retention of land or water areas predominantly in their natural, scenic, open, or wooded condition; retention of habitats for fish, plants, or wildlife; preservation of buildings or sites of historic or cultural significance.	Conservation easements.	Any governmental body; any charitable corporation or trust whose purposes include conservation of land or water areas or preservation of buildings or sites of historical or cultural significance.
Georgia Code Ann. (Supp. 1978) 29-301	Preservation of open space land.	General less than fee interests; scenic easements.	State governmental units.
43-2301–43-2307	Preservation of land with unique natural features, historic significance, or recreation value.	General less than fee interests.	State Department of Natural Resources for "Heritage Trust Program."
85-1407–85-1410	Preservation of historically or architecturally significant structures or sites in designated historic districts. Preservation of land or water areas predominantly in natural, scenic, landscape, or open condition, or in agricultural, farming, forest, or open space use; or return of land or water to such condition.	Facade easements; conservation easements.	Any governmental body; any charitable or educational corporation, trust, or organization that has the power to acquire interests in land.
Idaho Code (Supp. 1978) 67-46-1; 67-4613	Preservation of the historical, architectural, archaeological, and cultural heritage of the state.	"Historic easements," including easements, restrictions, covenants, or conditions running with the land.	Any county or city.
Illinois Ann. Stat. (Supp. 1978) c.85, §§2101–2111	Preservation of open space land.	Conservation restrictions.	Any governmental unit.

State and citation	Authorized purpose	Interests or rights involved	Parties eligible to hold interests or rights
c.24, §§11-48.2-2 – 11-48.2-7	Preservation of sites and structures of historical, architectural, or cultural value.	Development rights; preservation restrictions.	Local governmental units.
Indiana Burns Stat. Ann. (1978) §14-4-5.5-1	Preservation of open space land; preservation of sites and structures of historical, architectural, or cultural value.	Conservation easements; preservation easements.	Any governmental unit.
Iowa Code Ann. (Supp. 1974) 111D.1-5	Preservation of open space land.	Conservation easements; term easements.	Any governmental unit.
Kentucky Rev. Stat. (Supp. 1978) 65.420	Park development and restoration or preservation of scenic beauty, areas of historical interest, community development, and similar public purposes.	Scenic and recreation easements.	Local legislative bodies.
Louisiana Rev. Stat. (Supp. 1979) Civil Code 1424	Furtherance of educational, charitable, or historical purposes.	Servitude of immovable property, including but not limited to the facade, exterior, roof, or front of any improvements.	Any nonprofit corporation chartered for the furtherance of educational, charitable, or historical purposes.
Maine Rev. Stat. Ann. (Supp. 1978) 33-667; 33-668; 36-701-A	Preservation of open space land.	Conservation restrictions.	Any governmental body authorized to acquire interests in land, whose purposes include conservation of land and water areas.
(Supp. 1979) 29-1551–29-1555	Preservation or restoration of historic property.	Preservation interest.	Governmental body or nonprofit preservation or historical organization whose purposes include preservation of historic property.
Maryland Ann. Code (1975) RP 2-118; Art. 81, §§12E–12E-1	Protection of designated land and water areas from specifically designated activities. Preservation of sites and structures of historical, architectural, and cultural value.	Conservation restrictions; preservation restrictions; architectural facade and historic easements.	Any governmental unit; any charitable corporation or trust.

State and citation	Authorized purpose	Interests or rights involved	Parties eligible to hold interests or rights
Massachusetts Gen. Laws Ann. (Supp. 1978) c. 184, §§31–33	Retention of land or water areas predominantly in natural, scenic, or open condition, or in agricultural, farm, or forest use. Preservation of sites and structures historically significant for architecture, archaeology, or associations.	Conservation restrictions; preservation restrictions.	Any governmental unit; any charitable corporation or trust authorized to preserve buildings or sites of historical significance or to conserve open space.
c.132A, §§11A–11D	Retention of land or water areas predominantly in their agricultural, farming, or forest use; forbidding or limiting construction of buildings (other than for farming or landowner's residence), and excavation, dredging, or removal of materials in a manner adversely affecting future agriculture or other uses detrimental to agriculture.	Agricultural preservation restrictions.	Any governmental unit; any charitable corporation or trust whose purposes include conservation of land or water areas or preservation of buildings or sites of historical significance.
Michigan Stat. Ann. (Supp. 1978) 26.1287(5); 26.1287(6)	Preservation of open space land.	Conservation easements; development rights agreements.	Any governmental unit.
(Supp. 1979) 15.1816(1)	Acquisition and maintenance of historic sites.	Land and rights in land.	Secretary of State.
Minnesota Stat. (Supp. 1978) 86.64–86.65	Retention of land or water areas predominantly in natural, scenic, open, or wooded condition, or suitable habitats for fish and wildlife.	Conservation restrictions.	State Department of Natural Resources.
Missouri Ann. Stat. (Supp. 1978) 67.870–67.910	Preservation of open space land.	Conservation easements.	Any governmental unit; any charitable corporation or trust.
Montana Rev. Code (1978) 76-6-201–76-6-211	Preservation of significant open space land, and native plants or animals or biotic communities, or geological or geographical formations of scientific, aesthetic, or educational value. Preservation of buildings and sites of historical significance.	Conservation restrictions; conservation easements.	"Public bodies" and "certain qualifying private organizations."

State and citation	Authorized purpose	Interests or rights involved	Parties eligible to hold interests or rights
New Hampshire Rev. Stat. Ann. (Supp. 1978) 477:45–477:47; 79-A:1; 79-A:5; 79-A:15– 79-A:21	Retention of land or water areas predominantly in their natural, scenic, or open condition, or in agricultural, farm, or forest use. Preservation of structures or sites historically significant for architecture, archaeology, or associations.	Conservation restrictions; preservation restrictions.	Any governmental unit; any charitable corporation or trust.
New Jersey Stat. Ann. (Supp. 1978) 13:8A-30; 13:8A-46	Establishment of areas for recreation and conservation.	Conservation easement.	Commissioner of Environmental Protection; any local government unit receiving state assistance for conservation or recreation.
13:8-29	Protection of the Appalachian Trail.	Easements; "controlled-use agreements."	
13:8-32	Establishment of natural and scenic areas along state trail system.	Scenic easement.	Commissioner of Environmental Protection.
New Mexico Stat. (Supp. 1977) 83-22-4	Preservation, protection, or enhancement of historic areas, or areas of special architectural or visual interest.	"Any interest."	Any county or municipality.
New York Gen. Mun. Law (Supp. 1978) 247	Protection of open space and natural scenic beauty; enhancement and conservation of natural and scenic resources.	Fee or any lesser interest, development right, easement, covenant, or other contractual right necessary to achieve the purpose of this chapter.	Any local government.
North Carolina Gen. Stat. (Supp. 1978) 113A-90	Conservation and appreciation of significant scenic, natural, historic, ecological, geological, or cultural areas (North Carolina Trails System).	Scenic easements; cooperative agreements; easements of access running with the land; leases; less than fee interests.	State Department of Natural and Economic Resources.
160A-407	Preservation of open space and areas for public use and enjoyment through limitation of future use.	"Fee or any lesser interest or right in real property."	Any local government.

State and citation	Authorized purpose	Interests or rights involved	Parties eligible to hold interests or rights
121-35	Preservation of structure or site historically significant for its architecture, archaeology, or historical associations. Retention of land or water areas predominantly in their natural, scenic, or open condition, or in agricultural, horticultural, farming, or forest use.	Preservation agreements. Conservation agreements.	Any public body of the state, or public corporation; any nonprofit corporation or trust or private corporation or business entity whose purposes include preservation and conservation purposes of this act.
(1979 Cum. Supp.) 121-9	Protection and preservation of property of historical, architectural, archaeological, or other cultural importance to the people of North Carolina.	Fee simple, but when a lesser interest, including development right, negative or affirmative easement in gross or appurtenant, covenant, lease, or other contractual right of or to real property is deemed to be most practical and economical method of protecting and preserving historic property, the lesser interest may be acquired.	Department of Cultural Resources.
Ohio Page's Rev. Code Ann. (Supp. 1979) 149.30	Promotion of knowledge of history and archaeology.	Easements on historic or archaeological sites, or on property adjacent or contiguous to these sites to control land use for the purpose of preserving or restoring the historic, archaeological, or educational value of the sites.	Ohio Historical Society.
Oregon Rev. Stat. (1976) 271.740	Preservation of existing state of recreational, cultural, scenic, historic, or other appropriate space of public significance.	Conservation or scenic easements.	Any state agency, local government, park or recreation district, public corporation, political subdivision, or nonprofit corporation having the purpose of protecting, preserving, or enhancing historic sites, scenic or important ecological areas.

State and citation	Authorized purpose	Interests or rights involved	Parties eligible to hold interests or rights
Pennsylvania Stat. Ann. (Supp. 1979) Tit. 16, 11941–43	Conservation of natural or scenic resources; enhancement of value of neighborhood lands and public recreation opportunities; preservation of sites of historic, geologic, or botanic value and open space; promotion of orderly growth.	Covenant for farm, forest, water supply, or open space use.	Any county government.
Tit. 22, 5001.5	Preservation of open space in and near urban areas; meeting needs for recreation, amenity, and conservation.	Any interest in real property.	State Department of Forests and Waters.
Tit. 32, 82101–82104	Protection of outstanding aesthetic and recreational values of state's scenic rivers.	Scenic easements and access easements.	State Department of Environmental Resources.
Tit. 64, 801–805	Establishment, protection, and maintenance of walking trail right-of-way for Appalachian Trail.	General fee interest; rights-of-way and easements.	State Department of Environmental Resources.
Rhode Island Gen. Laws (1976) 34-39-1– 34-39-6	Protection and preservation of real property predominantly in its natural, scenic, or open condition, or farm, open space, forest, wildlife, or other use consistent with environmental quality.	Conservation restriction; preservation restriction.	Any governmental body; any charitable corporation or trust, or other entity whose purposes include conservation of land or water areas or preservation of structures or sites of historical significance.
South Carolina Code (1976) 27-9-10–27-9-20	Retention of land or water areas predominantly in their natural, scenic, wooded, or open condition.	Conservation restrictions.	Any governmental body; The Nature Conservancy.
51-17-80	Protection and preservation of the natural and cultural character of an area or feature.	Fee simple or lesser interest under a "dedication agreement."	South Carolina Wildlife and Marine Resource Commission for the South Carolina Heritage Trust.
South Dakota Comp. Laws (Supp. 1978) 1-19A-11; 1-19B-16	Preservation of historical, archaeological, architectural, and cultural heritage of the state.	Historic easement, including any easement, restriction, covenant, or condition running with the land; development rights.	Any county or municipality.

State and citation	Authorized purpose	Interests or rights involved	Parties eligible to hold interests or rights
Tennessee Code (Supp. 1976) 11-1801–11-1808	Protection and preservation of state's historic, architectural, archaeological, and cultural resources listed in national or state registry, and state's publicly owned natural areas.	Interests and rights in real property adjacent to or with visual, audible, or atmospheric effects on state's historic, architectural, archaeological, or cultural resources or natural areas; scenic easements; protective easements.	"Public bodies" including state, counties, municipalities, metropolitan governments, and historic commissions of such governmental units, and park and recreation authorities.
Texas Rev. Civ. Stat. (Supp. 1979) 7150	Promotion of park and recreation use of land including development of historical, archaeological, scenic, and scientific sites.	Restriction instrument limiting use of land for a term of years.	State governmental agency.
Code Ann. Natural Resources (Supp. 1979) 181.054–181.103	Conservation of natural, scenic, historical, scientific, educational, inspirational, wildlife, and recreational resources for future generations of Americans.	Easements or other rights for preservation, conservation, protection, or enhancement by and for the public.	Texas Conservation Foundation.
Utah Code Ann. 63-18A-1–63-18A-6	Preservation and restoration of historically significant sites and structures listed on State Register.	Preservation agreement.	Any governmental unit or charitable corporation or trust.
Vermont Stat. Ann. (Supp. 1978) Tit. 10, 6301–6308	Maintenance of present use of farm-, forest-, and undeveloped land; preservation of scenic natural areas; strengthening recreation industry.	Any right or interest in real property.	Any municipality or State Department of Highways, Forests, and Parks, Fish and Game, and Water Resources.
Virginia Code (Supp. 1976) 10-152–10-158	Preservation or provision for permanent open space land.	Easement in gross; any interest or right in real property.	Any public body.
Washington Rev. Code Ann. (Supp. 1978) 84.34.200–84.34.220	Preservation of open space land.	Development rights; "conservation futures."	Any county, city, town, metropolitan, or municipal corporation.
West Virginia Code 20-1-7(11)	Promotion of forestry; protection of watersheds; promotion of public recreation; preservation of scenic, cultural, archaeological, and historic values and natural resources.	Any interest in real property.	State Natural Resources Commission.

State and citation	Authorized purpose	Interests or rights involved	Parties eligible to hold interests or rights
Wisconsin Stat. Ann. (Supp. 1977) 61.34; 63.22	Promotion of parks, libraries, historic places, recreation, beautification, and public improvements.	Property rights in land and water, including rights of access and use, negative or positive easements, restrictive covenants, covenants running with the land, scenic easements, or any other right that may be acquired for public purposes.	Any village or city.
(Supp. 1979–1980) 23.09(10)	Establishment of adequate and flexible system for protection, development, and use of forests, fish, and game, lakes, streams, plant life, flowers, and other outdoor resources of the state.	Conservation easements, including negative easements, restrictive covenants running with the land, and all rights for use of property of any nature whatsoever.	Department of Natural Resources.

Table 2
Major Elements of Conservation/Preservation Agreement Laws

State	Authority for acquisition by eminent domain	Assessed value of property affected by agreement	Recordation of agreement required by law	Assignability and running with the land authorized	Provision for modification or termination	Authority for enforcement
Alabama		P				P
Arizona	C(1)					
Arkansas			P	P	P	P
California	C/P	C	C	P	C/P	C
Colorado		C/P	C/P	C/P	C/P	C/P
Connecticut		C/P	C	C/P	C	C/P
Delaware			C/P	C/P		C/P
Florida			C/P	C/P	C/P	C/P
Georgia	C/P(2)	P	C/P	P	C/P	P
Idaho		P				
Illinois	P	P(3)		P		
Indiana	C	C	C		C	C
Iowa			C		C	
Kentucky		C/P	C/P		C/P	C/P
Louisiana			P	P	P	P
Maine	P	C	C/P	C/P	C/P	C/P
Maryland	C	C		C/P	C/P	C/P
Massachusetts		C/P	C/P	C/P	C/P	C/P
Michigan		C	C	C	C	C

State	Authority for acquisition by eminent domain	Assessed value of property affected by agreement	Recordation of agreement required by law	Assignability and running with the land authorized	Provision for modification or termination	Authority for enforcement
Minnesota		C	C	C	C	C
Missouri	C/P	C/P				
Montana		C/P	C/P	C/P	C/P	C/P
New Hampshire	C	C/P	C/P	C/P	C/P	C/P
New Jersey	C				C	
New Mexico	P	P(4)				
New York		C	C	C		C
North Carolina	P(5)	C/P	P	P	P	P
Oregon		C/P				
Pennsylvania		C/P	C/P		C/P	C/P
Rhode Island			C/P	C/P		C/P
South Carolina	C/P		C/P	C		C/P
South Dakota	P	P(6)		P(7)		
Tennessee		C/P				
Texas		C/P	C/P		C/P	C/P
Utah		P(8)		P		P
Vermont		C				
Virginia		C/P				
Washington		C				
West Virginia		C/P				
Wisconsin		C/P(9)				

Notes

(1) *Ariz. Rev. Stat. Ann.* §§9-464, 9-464.1, and 11-935.01 are limited to declaring that open space land acquisition is a public purpose and authorizing use of public funds for such acquisition.

(2) *Ga. Code Ann.* §43-2305 implicitly includes condemnation by authorizing acquisition of heritage areas "in the name of the State of Georgia as otherwise provided by law." Also, §43-2306 requires recording in the form of filing the written recommendation and governor's approval of heritage preserves in the office of the clerk of the superior court of the county where the preserve is located.

(3) *Ill. Ann. Stat.* ch. 24, §1148.2-2 implies valuation change will be reflected in subsequent transfer of development rights and in financing acquisition of historic buildings subject to restriction of development rights.

(4) *N.M. Stat.* §3-22-4 implies that valuation change will be reflected in resale to private owner of preservation restriction interest acquired by local authority.

(5) *N.C. Gen. Stat.* §160A-399.8 authorizes acquisition of historic property by use of general powers granted to counties and municipalities. §121-9 authorizes condemnation after a finding by the State Department of Cultural Resources that destruction or serious impairment of a specific property is imminent, and with the approval of the governor and council.

(6) *S.D. Comp. Laws* (Supp. 1978), §1-19A-20 provides a five-year moratorium on taxation of real estate listed on the state register and rehabilitated or restored with state or federal funds, or individually funded with approval of the Board of Cultural Preservation.

(7) *S.D. Comp. Laws* (Supp. 1978), §1-19A-21 requires that a restrictive covenant running with the land to provide for maintenance of restored portions of property must be executed in order for such property to qualify for the benefits of the statute.

(8) *Utah Code Ann.* (Supp. 1975), §63.18A-6 provides that donation of a preservation easement may be deemed a charitable contribution for tax purposes.

(9) *Wis. Stat. Ann.* (Supp. 1977), §62.22(1m) authorizes acquisition of easements and limited property interests, and §62.22(2) authorizes donation, conveyance, sale, and lease of property owned by municipalities to nonprofit private corporations for public purposes.

Notes

*This paper was prepared by members of the Committee on Historic Preservation and Easements as background for consideration of possible uniform state legislation to facilitate use of less than fee interests in conservation and preservation activities. Research on the historical and case law aspects of this paper was performed in 1976–77 under the supervision of the Conservation Law Foundation of New England in a study sponsored by the Real Property Law Division. Other portions of the paper were researched by the author with advice and assistance of members of the Committee. The author gratefully acknowledges the significant contributions of Morris McClintock and Charles Goetsch, of the Conservation Law Foundation of New England, and of Albert B. Wolfe and Barlow Burke, members of the Committee on Historic Preservation and Easements, and Thomas A. Coughlin III, Bradford Carver, and Burton Klimon of the legal staff of the National Trust for Historic Preservation.

1. *See, e.g.,* W. K. Reilly, Conservation, Community and Personal Responsibility, Bicentennial Morrison Memorial Lecture, delivered at Annual Congress of the National League of Cities, Miami, Florida, Nov. 30, 1975; Hartke, *Toward a National Growth Policy,* 22 Catholic U.L. Rev. 231 (1973). *See also* reports on "environmental indicators," Council on Environmental Quality, Environmental Quality—1976, the Seventh Annual Report of the Council on Environmental Quality, Sept. 1976, 286-332.

2. Act of Jan. 1, 1970, Pub. L. 91-190, 42 U.S.C. 4341-4347.

3. Act of Oct. 15, 1966, Pub. L. 89-665, 16 U.S.C. 470(h), (i), (l-m). *See also,* Fowler, *Federal Historic Preservation Law: National Historic Preservation Act, Executive Order 11593, and Other Recent Developments in Federal Law,* 12 Wake Forest L. Rev. 31-47 (1976).

4. Council on Environmental Quality, Environmental Quality: The Third Annual Report of the Council on Environmental Quality, Aug. 1972, 311-337.

5. Reilly (ed.), The Use of Land: A Citizen's Policy Guide to Urban Growth, 145-175 (1973); Bosselman, *et al.,* The Taking Issue, prepared for the Council on Environmental Quality, 236-328 (1973).

6. Brenneman, Should Easements Be Used to Protect National Historic Landmarks? A Study for the National Park Service (1975).

7. Radin, Roman Law 373 (1927).

8. *See* Buckland, A Manual of Roman Private Law 158 (1930); Radin, Roman Law 375 (1927).

9. Reno, *The Enforcement of Equitable Servitudes in Land,* 28 Va. L. Rev. 951, 953-56 (1942).

10. *Id.,* at 957.

11. Keppell v. Bailey, 2 Myl. & K 517, 39 Eng. Rep. 1042 (Ch. 1834).

12. Gale, Easements 31 (11th ed. 1932).

13. *See* 3 Powell, Real Property §405 (1975) and Restatement of Property §§451, 452 (1944).

14. *See* 3 Holdsworth, History of English Law 153-157 (1903) and 3 Powell, Real Property §405 (1975).

15. 3 Powell, Real Property §405 (1975).

16. Restatement of Property §§491, 492 (1944), and 3 Powell, Real Property §§405, 419 (1975).

17. As to the common law's preference for finding easements to be appurtenant rather than in gross, even under factual situations in which it was difficult to find a dominant estate adjacent to the servient land, *see* 3 Powell, Real Property §405, ns. 31, 32, 33 (1975).

18. *See, e.g., Illinois:* Willoughby v. Lawrence, 116 Ill. 11, 4 N.E. 356 (1923); *Iowa:* Cusack Co. v. Myers, 189 Iowa 190, 178 N.W. 401 (1920); *Kentucky:* Levy v. Louisville Gunning System, 121 Ky. 510, 89 S.W. 528 (1905); *Massachusetts:* Baseball Pub. Co. v. Bruton, 302 Mass. 54, 18 N.E.2d 362 (1938); *Michigan:* Smith v. Dennedy, 224 Mich. 378, 194 N.W. 998 (1923); *New York:* Borough Bill Posting Co. v. Levy, 144 App. Div. 784, 129 N.Y. Supp. 740 (1911).

The decision in Baseball Pub. Co. v. Bruton is noted in 19 Calif. L. Rev. 201 (1931); 17 Cornell L. Rev. 683 (1932); 19 Cornell L. Rev. 138 (1934); 23 Minn. L. Rev. 966 (1939); 17 Texas L. Rev. 490 (1939); 17 Notre Dame Law, 158 (1942); and 42 Mich. L. Rev. 128 (1943). Easements in gross have been awarded in eminent domain cases. Brooklyn Eastern Dist. Terminal v. City of New York, 139 F.2d 1007 (C.C.A.2d, 1944) and Hartford National Bank v. Redevelopment Agency, 164 Conn. 337, 321 A.2d 469 (1973). *See, generally,* Clark, Real Covenants and Other Interests Which Run with the Land, 69-70 (2d ed. 1947); 2 Am. Law Prop. §9.33 (1952, Supp. 1962); and Restatement of Prop. §§530-534, 537 (1944).

19. Noncommercial easements are those "in which the use authorized inures primarily to the personal satisfaction of the owners." Restatement of Property §491 (1944). It may include either physical or spiritual satisfaction. Commercial easements contribute to the owner's economic benefit or financial well-being.

20. The following cases illustrate the general rule that in the absence of something in the instrument creating the easement indicating a contrary intention, an easement in gross is a right personal to the one to whom it is granted and cannot be assigned or otherwise transmitted by him to another.

Arkansas: Field v. Morris, 88 Ark. 148, 114 S.W. 206 (1908)—right to use land; assignability fails despite intent to make it inalienable because no use of "heirs and assigns" [dictum]. Ft. Smith Gas Co. v. Gean, 186 Ark. 573, 55 S.W.2d 63 (1932)—right-of-way. Rose Lawn Cemetery Ass'n. v. Scott, 229 Ark. 639, 317 S.W.2d. 265 (1958)—right-of-way held in gross cannot descend.

Connecticut: Hall v. Armstrong, 53 Conn. 554, 4 A. 113 (1886)—right-of-way made personal by terms of its creation [dictum]. Graham v. Walker, 78 Conn. 130, 61 A. 98 (1905)—an easement in gross is personal despite use of words "heirs and assigns" [dictum]. Lynch v. White, 85 Conn. 545, 84 A. 326 (1912)—intention that a right-of-way is personal clear from the instrument.

Idaho: West v. Smith, 95 Idaho 550, 511 P.2d 1326 (1973)—right-of-way.

Illinois: Garrison v. Rudd, 19 Ill. 558 (1958)—right-of-way. Koelle v. Knecht, 99 Ill. 396 (1881)—right-of-way made personal by terms of creation. Louisville & N.R. Co. v. Koelle, 104 Ill. 455 (1882)—right-of-way [dictum]. Kuecken v. Voltz, 110 Ill. 264 (1884)—right-of-way. Waller v. Hildebrecht, 295 Ill. 116, 128 N.E. 807 (1920)—right-of-way; alley for which no real necessity; takes broad view that easements in gross are not assignable; interpreted circumstances surrounding the interest in determining it to be personal. Messenger v. Ritz, 345 Ill. 433, 178 N.E. 38 (1931)—right-of-way. Traylor v. Parkinson, 355 Ill. 476, 189 N.E. 307 (1934)—right-of-way. *But see* McWhirter v. Newell, 200 Ill. 583, 66 N.E. 345 (1903)—burial rights; alienability intended at time of creation.

Indiana: Moore v. Crose, 43 Ind. 30 (1873)—right-of-way [dictum]. Hoosier Stone Co. v. Malott, 130 Ind. 21, 29 N.E. 412 (1891)—right-of-way [dictum]. Lucas v. Rhodes, 48 Ind. App. 211, 94 N.E. 914 (1911)—right-of-way [dictum].

Maine: Wadsworth v. Smith, 11 Me. 278, 26 Am. Dec. 525 (1834)—right-of-way; interest made personal by terms of creation. Davis v. Briggs, 117 Me. 536, 105 A. 128 (1918)—right to water and water-pipe connection.

Maryland: Raso v. McGee, 98 Md. 389, 56 A. 1128 (1904)—reservation of right to water from spring on land made personal by the terms of its creation.

Michigan: Stockdale v. Yerden, 220 Mich. 444, 190 N.W. 225 (1922)—right-of-way; private way of which no formal assignment to plaintiff. *But see* Hall v. Ionia, 38 Mich. 493 (1878)—easement to take water assignable [dictum].

Minnesota: Winston v. Johnson, 42 Minn. 398, 45 N.W. 958 (1890) [dictum].

Missouri: Wooldridge v. Smith, 243 Mo. 190, 147 S.W. 1019 (1912)—in gross easement in family burying ground cannot descend. Williams v. Diederich, 359 Mo. 683, 223 S.W.2d 402 (1949)—absence of words "heirs and assigns" evidence fishing right was intended only for the individual who reserved it. Kansas City Area Transp. Authority v. Ashley, 485 S.W.2d 641 (Mo. App. 1973).

Montana: Osnes Livestock Co. v. Warren, 103 Mont. 284, 62 P.2d 206 (1936)—but holding otherwise with reference to water rights.

North Carolina: Council v. Sanderlin, 183 N.C. 253, 111 S.E. 365 (1922). Davis v. Robinson, 189 N.C. 589, 127 S.E. 697 (1925). Shingleton v. State, 260 N.C. 451, 133 S.E.2d 183 (1963)—easement in gross mere personal interest and the failure to use "heirs and assigns" not controlling of interpretation.

Ohio: Boatman v. Lasley, 23 Ohio St. 614 (1873)—right-of-way held merely personal and thus nonassignable. Metzger & Co. v. Holwick, 17 Ohio C.C. 605, 6 Ohio C.D. 794, *aff'd without opinion* 57 Ohio St. 654, 50 N.E. 1131 (1897)—right-of-way, driveway for which no real necessity.

Rhode Island: Cadwalader v. Bailey, 17 R.I. 495, 23 A. 20 (1891). Chase v. Cram, 39 R.I. 83, 97 A. 481 (1916). *But see* Gardner v. Swan Point Cemetery, 20 R.I. 646, 40 A. 871 (1898)—burial lot easement inheritable [dictum].

South Carolina: Whaley v. Stevens, 27 S.C. 549, 4 S.E. 145 (1887)—right-of-way [dictum]. Fisher v. Fair, 34 S.C. 203, 13 S.E. 470 (1891)—right-of-way, private alley for which no real necessity, personal despite use of "heirs and assigns." McDaniel v. Walker, 46 S.C. 43, 24 S.E. 378 (1896). Kershaw v. Burns, 91 S.C. 129, 74 S.E. 378 (1912) [dictum]. Safety Bldg. & I. Co. v. Lyles, 131 S.C. 542, 128 S.E. 724 (1925)—right-of-way, driveway for which no real necessity. Brasington v. Williams, 143 S.C. 223, 141 S.E. 375 (1927)—right-of-way. Richards v. Trezvant, 185 S.C. 489, 194 S.E. 326 (1937). Steele v. Williams, 204 S.C. 124, 28 S.E.2d 644 (1944)—private alley for which no real necessity. Sandy Island Corp. v. Ragsdale, 246 S.C. 414, 143 S.E.2d 803 (1965)—rights-of-way which are in gross and personal are not assignable [dictum]. *But see* Columbia Water Power Co. v. Columbia Electric Co., 43 S.C. 154, 20 S.E. 1002 (1895)—a water right-of-way may be assigned.

Utah: Ernst v. Allen, 55 Utah 272, 184 P. 827 (1919) [dictum].

21. *Iowa:* Baker v. Kenney, 145 Iowa 638, 124 N.W. 901 (1910)—easements in gross may be made assignable by express language in creating instrument.

Massachusetts: Bates v. Sparrell, 10 Mass. 330 (1813)—pew rights, alienability intended. White v. Crawford, 10 Mass. 187 (1813)—ways, alienability intended. Kimball v. Second Congregational Parish, 24 Pick. (Mass.) 347 (1834)—in the absence of restrictive provisions, pew rights are assignable. Goodrich v. Burbank, 94 Mass. 459 (1866)—water from spring, alienability intended at time of creation. French v. Morris, 101 Mass. 68 (1869)—water from spring, alienability intended at time of creation. Owen v. Field, 102 Mass. 90 (1869)—water from spring, alienability intended. Amidon v. Harris, 113 Mass. 59 (1873)—water from spring, alienability intended.

Vermont: Barnard v. Whipple, 29 Vt. 401 (1857)—pew rights, alienability intended at time of creation. Lawrie v. Silsby, 76 Vt. 240, 56 A. 1106 (1904)—an easement to use water may be assignable. Percival v. Williams, 82 Vt. 531, 74 A. 321 (1909)—a water right may be assignable [dictum].

Virginia: City of Richmond v. Richmond Sand and Gravel Co., 123 Va. 1, 96 S.E. 204 (1918)—easements in gross may be assigned since they are an interest in property and all interests in property are alienable. *But see* Schultz v. Carter, 153 Va. 730, 151 S.E. 130 (1930)—interest made personal by the terms of its creation.

Wisconsin: Poull v. Mockley, 33 Wis. 482 (1873)—water right case, alienability intended at time of creation. Pinkum v. Eau Claire, 81 Wis. 301, 51 N.W. 550 (1892)—use of words "successors and assigns" sufficient to make in gross easement assignable.

22. *California:* PRO: Fudickar v. East Riverside Irrigation Dist., 109 Cal. 29, 41 P. 1024 (1895)—assignable unless expressly made personal as required by statute. PRO: Callahan v. Martin, 3 Cal. 2d 110, 43 P.2d 788 (1935)—assignable unless made personal to the individual as per statute. PRO: Collier v. Oelke, 202 Cal. App. 2d 843, 21 Cal. Rptr. 140 (1962)—easement for drainage pipeline; alienability intended at time of creation. PRO: Myers v. Berven, 166 Cal. 484, 137 P. 260 (1913)—right-of-way not benefiting any dominant land assignable.

CONTRA: Wagner v. Hanna, 38 Cal. 111, 99 Am. Dec. 354 (1869)—right-of-way; but probably overruled by *Fudickar supra* declaring easements in gross assignable. CONTRA: Gordon v. Corina Co., 164 Cal. 88, 127 P. 646 (1912). CONTRA: Eastman v. Piper, 68 Cal. App. 554, 229 P. 1002 (1924). CONTRA: Ocean Shore R. Co. v. Spring Valley Water Co., 87 Cal. App. 188, 262 P. 53 (1927) [dictum]. CONTRA: Elliott v. McCombs, 100 P.2d 499 (Cal. App. 1940).

Georgia: PRO: Ainslee v. Eason & Waters, 107 Ga. 747, 33 S.E. 711 (1899)—a license acted on created an easement in gross that was held assignable. PRO: Wright v. Hollywood Cemetery, 112 Ga. 884, 38 S.E. 94 (1900)—burial lot easement in gross inheritable. PRO: Bosworth v. Nelson, 170 Ga. 279, 152 S.E. 575 (1930)—descent of exclusive boating and fishing right allowed.

CONTRA: Stovell v. Coggins Granite Co., 116 Ga. 376, 42 S.E. 723 (1902)—right-of-way made personal by terms of creation. CONTRA: Mallet v. McCord, 127 Ga. 761, 56 S.E. 1015 (1907).

Kentucky: PRO: Hook v. Joyce, 94 Ky. 450, 22 S.W. 651 (1893)—burial rights, alienability intended at time of creation.

CONTRA: Thomas v. Brooks, 188 Ky. 253, 221 S.W. 542 (1920)—right-of-way, lays down broad rule that easements in gross are not assignable [dictum].

New Hampshire: PRO: Cross v. Berlin Mills Co., 79 N.H. 116, 105 A. 411 (1918)—use of words "heirs and assigns" clear evidence that interest intended to be assignable. CONTRA: Wilder v. Wheeler, 60 N.H. 351 (1880)—interest made personal by terms of creation. CONTRA: Beach v. Morgan, 67 N.H. 529, 41 A. 349 (1893).

New Jersey: PRO: Shreve v. Mathis, 63 N.J. Eq. 170, 52 A. 234 (1902)—a private way in gross is assignable. PRO: Standard Oil Co. v. Buchi, 72 N.J. Eq. 492, 66 A. 427 (1907)—a right-of-way for pipeline assignable. PRO: Goldman v. Beach Front Realty Co., 83 N.J.L. 97, 83 A. 777 (1912).
CONTRA: Joachim v. Belfus, 108 N.J.Eq. 622, 156 A. 121 (1931)—noted in 17 Iowa L. Rev. 235 (1932).

New York: PRO: McNabb v. Pond, 4 Brad 1 (N.Y. 1856)—pew rights, alienability intended at time of creation. PRO: Coatsworth v. Haywood, 78 Misc. Rep. 194, 139 N.Y. Supp. 331 (1912)—an easement in gross may pass with an appropriate deed [dictum]. PRO: Gould v. Wilson, 115 N.Y.S.2d 177 (1953)—if intent is shown in the instrument, an easement in gross is assignable and inheritable.
CONTRA: Huntington v. Asher, 26 Hun. 496 (1882) *rev.* 96 N.Y. 604, 48 Am. Rep. 652 (1884). CONTRA: Metcalf v. The Crystal Brook Park Assoc., 63 N.Y. App. Div. 445, 71 N.Y. Supp. 537 (1901)—intent of interest to be personal clear from the instrument. CONTRA: Matthews Slate Co. v. Advance Industrial Supply Co., 185 App. Div. 74, 172 N.Y. Supp. 830 (1918) [dictum]. CONTRA: Saratoga State Waters Corp. v. Pratt, 227 N.Y. 429, 125 N.E. 834 (1920) [dictum]. CONTRA: Moore v. Day, 199 App. Div. 76, 191 N.Y. Supp. 731 (1921)—lays down broad rule that easements in gross nonassignable. CONTRA: Atlantic Mills of Rhode Island v. New York Cent. R. Co., 221 App. Div. 386, 223 N.Y. Supp. 206 (1927), *aff'd* 248 N.Y. 535, 162 N.E. 514 (1928). CONTRA: Weigold v. Bates, 144 Misc. 395, 258 N.Y. Supp. 695 (1932). CONTRA: Antonopulos v. Postal Telegraph Cable Co., 261 App. Div. 564, 26 N.Y.S.2d 403 (1941), *aff'd without opinion* 287 N.Y. 712, 39 N.E.2d 931 (1942) [dictum]. CONTRA: Banach v. Home Gas Co., 23 Misc. 2d 556, 199 N.Y.S.2d 858, *aff'd,* 12 App. Div. 2d 373, 211 N.Y.S.2d 443 (ed dep't 1961), *motion for leave to appeal den.,* 10 N.Y.2d 708, 178 N.E.2d 191 (1961)—noncommercial easements in gross are inalienable.

Oregon: PRO: Salene v. Isherwood, 55 Ore. 263, 106 P. 18 (1910)—exclusive hunting right created by language using words of inheritance assignable. PRO: Talbot v. Joseph, 79 Ore. 308, 155 P. 184 (1916)—water rights may be assigned.
CONTRA: Houston v. Zahn, 44 Ore. 610, 76 P. 641 (1904).

Pennsylvania: PRO: Tinicum Fishing Co. v. Carter, 61 Pa. 21 (1869)—fishing right is assignable and inheritable. PRO: Jacobs v. Union Cemetery, 1 Pa. Super. 156 (1896)—burial right, alienability intended at creation. PRO: Tide Water Pipe Co. v. Bell, 280 Pa. 104, 124 A. 351 (1924)—intention of parties that the interest should be assignable, use of words "heirs and assigns." PRO: Miller v. Lutheran Conference & Camp Ass'n, 331 Pa. 241, 200 A. 646 (1938)—boating and fishing rights, showing that alienability intended at time of creation. PRO: Dalton Street Railway Co. v. Scranton, 326 Pa. 6, 191 A. 133 (1937)—intent that the interest should be assignable evident. PRO: Rusciolelli v. Smith, 195 Pa. Super. 562, 171 A.2d 802 (1961)—easements in gross generally personal and nonassignable unless made assignable by creating instrument.
CONTRA: Lindenmuth v. Safe Harbor Water Power Corp.,

309 Pa. 58, 163 A. 159 (1932).

Texas: PRO: Thew v. Lower Colorado River Authority, 259 S.W.2d 939 (Tex. Civ. App. 1953)—easement of water flowage assignable as provided by creating instrument.
CONTRA: Alley v. Carleton, 29 Tex 74, 94 Am. Dec. 260 (1867)—right-of-way [dictum]. CONTRA: Drye v. Eagle Rock Ranch, Inc. 364 S.W.2d 196 (Tex. 1963)—that ordinarily easements in gross are not assignable [dictum].

23. See, e.g., Gray, Restraints on Alienation 2 (2d ed. 1895), urging that all property interests should be alienable unless strong contrary policy reasons exist; Vance, *Assignability of Easements in Gross,* 32 Yale L.J. 813 (1923), stressing the difference between easements in gross and appurtenant in terms of surcharging property if rule remains diverse; Simes, *The Assignability of Easements in Gross in American Law,* 22 Mich. L. Rev. 521 (1924) urging full assignability of easements in gross accompanied by safeguards against surcharges; Kloek, *Assignability and Divisibility of Easements in Gross,* 22 Chi-Kent L. Rev. 239 (1944); and Welsh, *Assignability of Easements in Gross,* 12 U. Chi. L. Rev. 276 (1945), agreeing with Simes. See also, Restatement of Property §491 (1944) and 3 Powell, Real Property §419 (1975).

24. 3 Powell, Real Property §404 [2] (1975).

25. 5 Powell, Real Property §§672-75 (1975).

26. Formby v. Barker, 2 Ch. 539 (1903); London County Council v. Allen, 3 K.B. 642 (1914); Hill v. Tupper, 2 H. & C. 121, 159 Eng. Rep. 51 (Ex. 1863).

27. 2 Amer. Law of Property §9.13 (1952).

28. Restatement of Property §454, comment (a) (1944); Clark, Real Covenants and Other Interests Which Run with the Land, 106-111 (2d ed. 1947), stating, at 110: "In view of the general social policy which very clearly upholds restrictions on the use of property, it would seem proper that such agreements should be enforced without regard to the accident of the plaintiff's ownership of property in the vicinity."
See, e.g., Federal: Los Angeles University v. Swarth, 107 F. 798 (9th Cir. 1901); California: Bramwell v. Kuhle, 183 Cal. App. 2d 767, 6 Cal. Rptr. 839 (1960); Kent v. Koch, 166 Cal. App. 2d 579, 333 P.2d 411 (1958); Berryman v. Hotel Savoy Co., 160 Cal. 559, 117 P. 677 (1911); Georgia: Muscogee Mfg. Co. v. Eagle & P. Mills, 126 Ga. 210, 54 S.E. 1028 (1906); Maryland: Peabody Heights Co. v. Willson, 82 Md. 186, 32 A. 386 (1895); Massachusetts: Orenberg v. Johnston, 269 Mass. 312, 168 N.E. 794 (1929); Lincoln v. Burrage, 177 Mass. 378, 59 N.E. 67 (1901); Walsh v. Packard, 165 Mass. 189, 42 N.E. 577 (1896); Dana v. Wentworth, 111 Mass. 291 (1873); New Jersey: Caullett v. Stanley Stilwell & Sons, Inc., 67 N.J. Super. 111, 170 A.2d 52 (1961); Jennings v. Baroff, 104 N.J. Eq. 132, 144 A. 717 (1929); Welitoff v. Kohn, 105 N.J. Eq. 181, 147 A. 390 (1929); New York: Wilmurt v. McGrane, 16 App. Div. 412, 45 N.Y.Supp. 32 (1897); Oregon: Grussi v. Eighth Church of Christ Scientist, 116 Ore. 336, 241 P. 66 (1925).

29. Restatement of Property §§534, 537 (1944).

30. Federal: Empire Natural Gas Co. v. Southwest Pipe Line Co., 25 F.2d 742 (N.D. Okla. 1928), *aff'd* Southwest Pipe Line Co. v. Empire Natural Gas Co., 33 F.2d 248 (C.C.A. 8th 1929); Georgia: Smith v. Gulf Refining Co., 162 Ga. 191, 134 S.E. 446 (1926); Illinois: Van Sant v. Rose, 260 Ill. 401, 103 N.E. 194 (1913); Gibson v. Holden, 115 Ill. 199, 3 N.E. 282 (1885); Indiana: Conduitt v. Ross, 102 Ind. 166, 26 N.E. 198 (1885); Massachusetts: Inhabitants of Middlefield v. Church Mills Knitting Co., 160 Mass. 267, 35 N.E. 780 (1894); Pennsylvania: Bald

Eagle Valley R.R. v. Nittany Valley R.R. Co., 171 Pa. 284, 33 A. 239 (1895); *Texas:* Missouri, K. & T. Ry. Co. of Texas v. State, 275 S.W. 673 (Tex. Civ. App. 1925).

31. Clark, Real Covenants and Other Interests Which Run with the Land, 107-111 (2d ed. 1947).

32. Brenneman, *Techniques for Controlling the Surroundings of Historic Sites,* 36 Law & Contemp. Prob. 416, 419 (1971).

33. 2 Myl. & K. 517, 39 Eng. Rep. 1042 (Ch. 1834).

34. 2 Phil. 774, 41 Eng. Rep. 1143 (Ch. 1848).

35. *Id.* at 1143.

36. 3 Paige 254 (N.Y. 1832).

37. Reno, *op. cit., supra* note 9 at 1067. *See also,* Brenneman, Private Approaches to the Preservation of Open Land 56 (1967), stating: "[T]he drift of modern authority seems clearly in the direction of treating servitudes enforceable in equity as interests in the nature of equitable easements."

38. *See* Clark, *op. cit., supra* note 18 at 172-184 and 2 Am. Law of Property §§9.25-9.29 (1952).

39. *Id.,* at §9.26, stating: "[I]n equity no privity of estate, other than that arising from the covenant or agreement itself, need exist between the original promisor and promisee in order for the agreement to be enforceable as an equitable servitude against subsequent possessors of the burdened land."

40. Clark, *op. cit., supra* note 18 at 172.

41. *Federal:* Los Angeles University v. Swarth, 107 F. 798 (9th Cir., 1901).

Arizona: O'Malley v. Central Methodist Church, 67 Ariz. 245, 194 P.2d 444 (1948).

California: Bramwell v. Kuhle, 183 Cal. App. 2d 767, 6 Cal. Rptr. 839 (1960); Chandler v. Smith, 170 Cal. App. 2d 118, 338 P.2d 522 (1959); Kent v. Koch, 166 Cal. App. 2d 579, 333 P.2d 411 (1958); Townsend v. Allen, 114 Cal. App. 2d 291, 250 P.2d 292 (1953); Young v. Cramer, 38 Cal. App. 2d 64, 100 P.2d 523 (1940).

Connecticut: Pulver v. Mascolo, 155 Conn. 644, 237 A.2d 97 (1967); Rossini v. Freeman, 136 Conn. 321, 71 A.2d 98 (1949).

Indiana: American Cannel Coal Co. v. Indiana Cotton Mills, 78 Ind. App. 115, 134 N.E. 891 (1922).

Louisiana: Lillard v. Jet Homes, Inc., 129 So.2d 109 (1961).

Maine: Robinson v. Fred B. Higgins Co., 126 Me. 55, 135 A. 901 (1927).

Maryland: Boyd v. Park Realty Corp., 137 Md. 36, 111 A. 129 (1920); Forman v. Safe Deposit & Trust Co., 114 Md. 574, 80 A. 298 (1911).

Massachusetts: Petrone v. Falcone, 345 Mass. 659, 189 N.E.2d 228 (1963); Orenberg v. Horan Johnson, 269 Mass. 312, 168 N.E. 794 (1929); Dana v. Wentworth, 111 Mass. 291 (1873).

Michigan: Kotesky v. Davis, 355 Mich. 536, 94 N.W.2d 796 (1959).

New Jersey: Auerbacher v. Smith, 22 N.J. Super. 568, 92 A.2d 492 (1952); Welitoff v. Kohl, 105 N.J. Eq. 181, 147 A. 390 (1928); Genung v. Harvey, 79 N.J. Eq. 57, 80 A. 955 (1911).

New York: City of New York v. Turnpike Development Corp., 36 Misc. 2d 704, 233 N.Y. Supp. 2d 887 (1962); Wolff v. Green, 199 Misc. 758, 99 N.Y. Supp. 2d 495 (1950); St. Stephan's Church v. Church of Transfiguration, 201 N.Y. 1, 94 N.E. 191 (1911); Wilmurt v. McGrane, 16 App. Div. 412, 45 N.Y. Supp. 32 (1897); Graves v. Deterling, 120 N.Y. 447, 24 N.E. 655 (1890); Trustees of Columbia College v. Lynch, 70 N.Y. 440 (1877).

North Carolina: Stegall v. Housing Authority, 278 N.C. 95, 178 S.E.2d 824 (1971); Craven County v. First-Citizens Bank & Trust Co., 237 N.C. 502, 75 S.E.2d 620 (1953).

Ohio: Taylor v. Summit Post No. 19 American Legion, Inc., 60 Ohio App. 201, 20 N.E.2d 267 (1938).

Oregon: Grussi v. Eighth Church of Christ, Scientist, 116 Ore. 336, 241 P. 66 (1925).

Tennessee: Gaston v. Price, 12 Tenn. App. 543 (1931).

Texas: Aull v. Kraft, 286 S.W.2d 460 (Tex. Civ. App. 1956).

42. *Georgia:* Smith v. Gulf Refining Co., 162 Ga. 191, 134 S.E. 446 (1962).

Illinois: Van Sant v. Rose, 260 Ill. 401, 103 N.E. 194 (1913).

Massachusetts: Storey v. Brush, 256 Mass. 101, 152 N.E. 225 (1926); Riverbank Improvement Co. v. Bancroft, 209 Mass. 217, 95 N.E. 216 (1911).

New Hampshire: Pratte v. Balatsos, 99 N.H. 430, 113 A.2d 492 (1955).

Ohio: Huber v. Guglielmi, 29 Ohio App. 290, 163 N.E. 571 (1928).

43. Brenneman, *op. cit., supra* note 37 at 58-59.

44. Clark, *op. cit., supra* note 18 at 72.

45. Restatement of Property §537, comment (a) (1944).

46. *Id.*

47. Clark, *op. cit., supra* note 18 at 134.

48. Staff of Senate Comm. on Interior and Insular Affairs, 92d Cong., 2d Sess., National Land Use Policy 6 (Comm. Print, April 1972).

49. North American Conference on Modernization of Land Data Systems, Proceedings, Washington, D.C., April 14-17, 1975.

50. Mont. Rev. Code §76-6-209 (1978).

51. Ark. Stat. Ann. §9-1411 (Supp. 1976).

52. S.C. Code Ann. §27-9-10 (1976).

53. Mass. Gen. L. Ann. ch. 184, §27 (Supp. 1975).

54. Colo. Rev. Stat. §38-30.5-104 (Supp. 1976).

55. *See* Comment, *Conservation Restrictions: A Survey,* 8 Conn. L. Rev. 383 at 399-402 (1976).

56. 364 F. Supp. 1349 (D.N.D. 1973), *aff'd,* 496 F.2d 906 (8th Cir. 1974).

57. 45 Stat. 1222, 28 U.S.C. §1345.

58. 364 F. Supp. 1349, 1350 (D.N.D. 1973).

59. Inhabitants of Middlefield v. Church Mills Knitting Co., 160 Mass. 267, 272, 35 N.E. 780, 782 (1894).

60. Ark. Stat. Ann. §9-1409 (Supp. 1976); Cal. Gov't Code §50281(5) (West Supp. 1978); Colo. Rev. Stat. §§38-30.5-101 to -110 (Supp. 1976); Conn. Gen. Stat. Ann. §47-42b (1975); Del. Code §§6811-6815 (Supp. 1979); Fla. Stat. Ann. §604.06 (Supp. 1979); Ga. Code Ann. §85-1408 (Supp. 1978); Ill. Stat. Ann. ch. 24, §11-48.2-1A (Smith Hurd 1974); Ind. Stat. Ann. §35-5-2-1 (Burns 1973); La. Rev. Stat., Civil Code §1252 (Supp. 1979); Me. Rev. Stat. Ann. tit. 33, §668 (Supp. 1974); Md. Ann. Code RP §2-118 (1974); Mass. Gen. Laws ch. 184, §32 (Supp. 1975); Mich. Stat. Ann. §26.1287(2) (Supp. 1975); Minn. Stat. §84.65 (1975); Mont. Rev. Code §§76-6-206 to -209 (1978); N.H. Rev. Stat. Ann. §477.46 (Supp. 1973); N.Y. Gen. Mun. Law §247 (1978); R.I. Gen. Laws §§34-39-1 to -6 (Supp. 1978); S.C. Code Ann. §27-9-10 (1976); S.D. Comp. Laws §11-19A-16 (Supp. 1978); Utah Code Ann. §36.18a-5 (Supp. 1978).

61. Md. Ann. Code RP §2-118(d) (1974).

62. Brenneman, *Historic Preservation Restrictions: A Sampling of State Statutes,* 8 Conn. L. Rev. 231, 246 (1976).

63. Clark, *op. cit., supra* note 18 at 72.

64. *See* Pulver v. Mascolo, 155 Conn. 644, 237 A.2d 97 (1967) and Patrone v. Falcone, 345 Mass. 659, 189 N.E.2d 228 (1963). *See also,* Tondro, *An Historic Preservation Approach to Municipal Rehabilitation of Older Neighborhoods,* 8 Conn. L. Rev. 248, 281-284 (1976). *But see* Inhabitants of Middlefield v. Church Mills Knitting Co., 160 Mass. 267, 35 N.E. 780 (1894).

65. 31 Wis. 2d 256, 142 N.W. 793 (1966).

66. Brenneman, *op. cit., supra* note 37 at 24 (1967) and Reno, *op. cit., supra* note 9 at 959 (1942).

67. Clark, *op. cit., supra* note 18 at 179, n.35; 3 Tiffany, Real Property §859, n.29 (1939); 2 Am. Law of Property §9.36 (1952).

68. Note, *A New Phase in the Development of Affirmative Equitable Servitudes,* 51 Harv. L. Rev. 320 (1937) and 2 Am. Law of Property §9.36, n.6 (1952). *See also,* Nicholson v. 300 Broadway Realty Corp., 7 N.Y.2d 240, 164 N.E.2d 832 (1959).

69. Clark, *op. cit., supra* note 18 at 179-180, n.37.

70. Murphy v. Kerr, 5 F.2d 908 (8th Cir. 1925); Nordin v. May, 188 F.2d 411 (8th Cir. 1951); Frumkes v. Boyer, 101 S.2d 387 (Fla. 1958); Fitzstephen v. Watson, 218 Ore. 185, 344 P.2d 221 (1959). *See also,* Lloyd, *Enforcement of Affirmative Agreements Respecting the Use of Land,* 14 Va. L. Rev. 419 (1928); Note, *Affirmative Duties Running with the Land,* 35 N.Y.U. L. Rev. 1344 (1960); Note, 68 A.L.R.2d 1022 (1959).

71. Tiffany, Real Property §859 (1939).

72. Reno, *op. cit., supra* note 9 at 970.

73. 5 Powell, *op. cit., supra* note 13 at 671, n.11 (1975).

74. N.H. Rev. Stat. Ann. §447:45 (Supp. 1973).

75. *Id.*

76. Utah Code Ann. §63-18a-4-5 (Supp. 1975).

77. R.I. Gen. Laws §34-39-2 (Supp. 1976); Colo. Rev. Stat. §38-30.5-102 (Supp. 1976); Tenn. Code t.10, §6303 (Supp. 1976).

78. Bill 176, 29th Legislature, 4th Sess., Ontario (1974).

79. Cal. Gov't Code §§51230, 51231, 51238 (West Supp. 1979); Conn. Public Act. No. 78-232 (June 1, 1978); Mich. Stat. Ann. §§26.1287(5), 26.1287(6) (Cum. Supp. 1976).

80. For example, under California's Agricultural Preserves Law, Cal. Gov't Code §51238.5 (West Supp. 1979), a county may require a minimum capital outlay for the creation of an agricultural preserve, may designate the kinds of agricultural land desired within the preserve, and may specify the level of agricultural production for the preserve. Cal., 56 Ops. Atty. Gen. 160 (April 20, 1973).

81. Del. Laws 1978, ch. 476; Mass. Gen. Laws, ch. 132, §§11A-11B; ch. 184, §§31-32 (Supp. 1979); Minn. Stat. §84-64 (Supp. 1975).

82. N.H. Rev. Stat. Ann. §447:45 (Supp. 1973).

83. Brenneman, *op. cit., supra* note 62 at 246.

84. Cal. Gov't Code §51238.5 (West Supp. 1979).

85. Cook, Legal Drafting 323 (rev. ed. 1951).

86. Johnson v. Hess, 126 Ind. 298, 25 N.E. 445 (1890).

87. Colo. Rev. Stat. §38-30.5-106 (Supp. 1976).

88. Ark. Laws 1975, ch. 882; Colo. Rev. Stat. 38-30.5-106 (Supp. 1976); Conn. Public Act. No. 78-232, §3(b); Me. Rev. Stat. Ann. tit. 33, §668 (Supp. 1973); Minn. Stat. Ann. §84.65 (Supp. 1974); Mont. Rev. Codes §76-6-207 (1978); R.I., Gen. Laws §43-39-4 (Supp. 1976); S.C. Code §27-9-10 (1976).

89. Me. Rev. Stat. Ann. tit. 33, §668 (Supp. 1974); S.C. Code Ann. §27-9-10 (1876).

90. Mass. Gen. Laws Ann.,ch. 186, §33 (Supp. 1975), public restriction tract index; Mont. Rev. Code §76-6-207 (1978), separate file.

91. *E.g.,* Ga. Code Ann. §43-2306 (Supp. 1973), heritage trust property dedications filed in office of Secretary of State with copy of governor's approval filed in superior court of county where property is located; Mich. Stat. Ann. §26.1287(8) (Supp. 1975), state land-use agency approval filed with local government body where land is located; Mont. Rev. Code §776-6-207 (1978), copies of easement filed with county clerk and state department of revenue.

92. Cal. Gov't Code §§51232-51237.5 (West Supp. 1979); Conn. Public Act No. 78-232; Del. Code §6814 (Supp. 1979); Mich. Stat. Ann. §§26.1287(5)-26.1287(6) (Cum. Supp. 1976); Mass. Gen. Laws Ann., ch. 132A, §11B (Supp. 1979); Mont. Rev. Code §76-6-206 (1978).

93. Brenneman, *op. cit., supra* note 6 at 59-60.

Uniform Conservation Easement Act

National Conference of Commissioners on Uniform State Laws

Historical Note

The Uniform Conservation Easement Act was approved by the National Conference of Commissioners on Uniform State Laws in 1981. The complete text of the act, the prefatory note, and comments are set forth here.

Commissioners' Prefatory Note

The Act enables durable restrictions and affirmative obligations to be attached to real property to protect natural and historic resources. Under the conditions spelled out in the Act, the restrictions and obligations are immune from certain common law impediments which might otherwise be raised. The Act maximizes the freedom of the creators of the transaction to impose restrictions on the use of land and improvements in order to protect them, and it allows a similar latitude to impose affirmative duties for the same purposes. In each instance, if the requirements of the Act are satisfied, the restrictions or affirmative duties are binding upon the successors and assigns of the original parties.

The Act thus makes it possible for Owner to transfer a restriction upon the use of Blackacre to Conservation, Inc., which will be enforceable by Conservation and its successors whether or not Conservation has an interest in land benefited by the restriction, which is assignable although unattached to any such interest in fact, and which has not arisen under circumstances where the traditional conditions of privity of estate and "touch and concern" applicable to covenants real are present. So, also, the Act enables the Owner of Heritage Home to obligate himself and future owners of Heritage to maintain certain aspects of the house and to have that obligation enforceable by Preservation, Inc., even though Preservation has no interest in property benefited by the obligation. Further, Preservation may obligate itself to take certain affirmative

actions to preserve the property. In each case, under the Act, the restrictions and obligations bind successors. The Act does not itself impose restrictions or affirmative duties. It merely allows the parties to do so within a consensual arrangement freed from common law impediments, if the conditions of the Act are complied with.

These conditions are designed to assure that protected transactions serve defined protective purposes (Section 1(1)) and that the protected interest is in a "holder" which is either a governmental body or a charitable organization having an interest in the subject matter (Section 1(2)). The interest may be created in the same manner as other easements in land (Section 2(a)). The Act also enables the parties to establish a right in a third party to enforce the terms of the transaction (Section 3(a)(3)) if the possessor of that right is also a governmental unit or charity (Section 1(3)).

The interests protected by the Act are termed "easements." The terminology reflects a rejection of two alternatives suggested in existing state acts dealing with nonpossessory conservation and preservation interests. The first removes the common law disabilities associated with covenants real and equitable servitudes in addition to those associated with easements. As statutorily modified, these three common law interests retain their separate existence as instruments employable for conservation and preservation ends. The second approach seeks to create a novel additional interest which, although unknown to the common law, is, in some ill-defined sense, a statutorily modified amalgam of the three traditional common law interests.

The easement alternative is favored in the Act for three reasons. First, lawyers and courts are most comfortable with easements and easement doctrine, less so with restrictive covenants and equitable servitudes, and can be expected to experience severe confusion if the Act opts for a hybrid fourth interest. Second, the easement is the basic less-than-fee interest at common law; the restrictive covenant and the equitable servitude appeared only because of then-current, but now outdated, limitations of easement doctrine. Finally, nonpossessory interests satisfying the requirements of covenant real or equitable servitude doctrine will invariably meet the Act's less demanding requirements as "easements." Hence, the Act's easement orientation should not prove prejudicial to instruments drafted as real covenants or equitable servitudes, although the converse would not be true.

In assimilating these easements to conventional easements, the Act allows great latitude to the parties to the former to arrange their relationship as they see fit. The Act differs in this respect from some existing statutes, such as that in effect in Massachusetts, under which interests of this nature are subject to public planning agency review.

There are both practical and philosophical reasons for not subjecting conservation easements to a public ordering system. The Act has the relatively narrow purpose of sweeping away certain common law impediments which might otherwise undermine the easements' validity, particularly those held in gross. If it is the intention to facilitate private grants that serve the ends of land conservation and historic preservation, moreover, the requirement of public agency approval adds a layer of complexity which may discourage private actions. Organizations and property owners may be reluctant to become involved in the bureaucratic, and sometimes political, process which public agency participation entails. Placing such a requirement in the Act may dissuade a state from enacting it for the reason that the state does not wish to accept the administrative and fiscal responsibilities of such a program.

In addition, controls in the Act and in other state and federal legislation afford further assurance that the Act will serve the public interest. To begin with, the very adoption of the Act by a state legislature facilitates the enforcement of conservation easements serving the public interest. Other types of easements, real covenants, and equitable servitudes are enforceable, even though their myriad purposes have seldom been expressly scrutinized by state legislative bodies. Moreover, Section 1(2) of the Act restricts the entities that may hold conservation and preservation easements to governmental agencies and charitable organizations, neither of which is likely to accept them on an indiscriminate basis. Governmental programs that extend benefits to private donors of these easements provide additional controls against potential abuses. Federal tax statutes and regulations, for example, rigorously define the circumstances under which easement donations qualify for favorable tax treatment. Controls relating to real estate assessment and taxation of restricted properties have been, or can be, imposed by state legislatures to prevent easement abuses or to limit potential loss of local property tax revenues resulting from unduly favorable assessment and taxation of these properties. Finally, the

American legal system generally regards private ordering of property relationships as sound public policy. Absent conflict with constitutional or statutory requirements, conveyances of fee or nonpossessory interests by and among private entities are the norm, rather than the exception, in the United States. By eliminating certain outmoded easement impediments which are largely attributable to the absence of a land-title recordation system in England centuries earlier, the Act advances the values implicit in this norm.

The Act does not address a number of issues which, though of conceded importance, are considered extraneous to its primary objective of enabling private parties to enter into consensual arrangements with charitable organizations or governmental bodies to protect land and buildings without the encumbrance of certain potential common law impediments (Section 4). For example, with the exception of the requirement of Section 2(b) that the acceptance of the holder be recorded, the formalities and effects of recordation are left to the state's registry system; an adopting state may wish to establish special indices for these interests, as has been done in Massachusetts.

Similarly unaddressed are the potential impacts of a state's marketable title laws upon the duration of conservation easements. The Act provides that conservation easements have an unlimited duration unless the instruments creating them provide otherwise (Section 2(c)). The relationship between this provision and the marketable title act or other statutes addressing restrictions on real property of unlimited duration should be considered by the adopting state.

The relationship between the Act and the local real property assessment and taxation practices is not dealt with; for example, the effect of an easement upon the valuation of burdened real property presents issues which are left to the state and local taxation system. The Act enables the structuring of transactions so as to achieve tax benefits which may be available under the Internal Revenue Code, but parties intending to attain them must be mindful of the specific provisions of the income, estate, and gift tax laws which are applicable. Finally, the Act neither limits nor enlarges the power of eminent domain; such matters as the scope of that power and the entitlement of property owners to compensation upon its exercise are determined not by this Act but by the adopting state's eminent domain code and related statutes.

Uniform Conservation Easement Act, 1981 Act

An Act to be known as the Uniform Conservation Easement Act, relating to (here insert the subject matter requirements of the various states).

    Sec. 1. Definitions.
    Sec. 2. Creation, Conveyance, Acceptance, and Duration.

§1. [Definitions]

As used in this Act, unless the context otherwise requires:

(1) "Conservation easement" means a nonpossessory interest of a holder in real property imposing limitations or affirmative obligations, the purposes of which include retaining or protecting natural, scenic, or open-space values of real property, assuring its availability for agricultural, forest, recreational, or open-space use, protecting natural resources, maintaining or enhancing air or water quality, or preserving the historical, architectural, archaeological, or cultural aspects of real property.

(2) "Holder" means:

(i) a governmental body empowered to hold an interest in real property under the laws of this State or the United States; or

(ii) a charitable corporation, charitable association, or charitable trust, the purposes or powers of which include retaining or protecting the natural, scenic, or open-space values of real property, assuring the availability of real property for agricultural, forest, recreational, or open-space use, protecting natural resources, maintaining or enhancing air or water quality, or preserving the historical, architectural, archaeological, or cultural aspects of real property.

(3) "Third-party right of enforcement" means a right provided in a conservation easement to enforce any of its terms granted to a governmental body, charitable corporation, charitable association, or charitable trust, which, although eligible to be a holder, is not a holder.

Commissioners' Comment

Section 1 defines three central elements: What is meant by a conservation easement; who can be a holder; and who can possess a "third-party right of enforcement." Only those interests held by a "holder," as defined by the Act, fall within the definitions of protected easements. Such easements are defined as interests in real property. Even if so held, the easement must serve one or more of the following purposes: protection of natural or open-space resources; protection of air or water quality; preservation of the historical aspects of property; or other similar objectives spelled out in subsection (1).

A "holder" may be a governmental unit having specified powers (subsection (2)(i)) or certain types of charitable corporations, associations, and trusts, provided that the purposes of the holder include those same purposes for which the conservation easement could have been created in the first place (subsection (2)(ii). The word "charitable," in subsections 1(2) and (3), describes organizations that are charities according to the common law definition regardless of their status as exempt organizations under any tax law.

Recognition of a "third-party right of enforcement" enables the parties to structure into the transaction a party that is not an easement "holder," but which, nonetheless, has the right to enforce the terms of the easement (Sections 1(3), 3(a)(3)). But the possessor of the third-party enforcement right must be a governmental body or a charitable corporation, association, or trust. Thus, if Owner transfers a conservation easement on Blackacre to Conservation, Inc., he could grant to Preservation, Inc., a charitable corporation, the right to enforce the terms of the easement, even though Preservation was not the holder, and Preservation would be free of the common law impediments eliminated by the Act (Section 4). Under this Act, however, Owner could not grant a similar right to Neighbor, a private person. But whether such a grant might be valid under other applicable law of the adopting state is left to the law of that state (Section 5(c)).

Library References

Health and Environment ☜25.5(4).
C.J.S. Health and Environment §§91 et seq., 130, 132.

§2. [Creation, Conveyance, Acceptance, and Duration]

(a) Except as otherwise provided in this Act, a conservation easement may be created, conveyed, recorded, assigned, released, modified, terminated, or otherwise altered or affected in the same manner as other easements.

(b) No right or duty in favor of or against a holder and no right in favor of a person having a third-party right of enforcement arises under a conservation easement before its acceptance by the holder and a recordation of the acceptance.

(c) Except as provided in Section 3(b), a conservation easement is unlimited in duration unless the instrument creating it otherwise provides.

(d) An interest in real property in existence at the time a conservation easement is created is not impaired by it unless the owner of the interest is a party to the conservation easement or consents to it.

Commissioners' Comment

Section 2(a) provides that, except to the extent otherwise indicated in the Act, conservation easements are indistinguishable from easements recognized under the pre-Act law of the state in terms of their creation, conveyance, recordation, assignment, release, modification, termination, or alteration. In this regard, subsection (a) reflects the Act's overall philosophy of bringing less-than-fee conservation interests under the formal easement rubric and of extending that rubric to the extent necessary to effectuate the Act's purposes given the adopting state's existing common law and statutory framework. For example, the state's requirements concerning release of conventional easements apply as well to conservation easements because nothing in the Act provides otherwise. On the other hand, if the state's existing law does not permit easements in gross to be assigned, it will not be applicable to conservation easements because Section 4(2) effectively authorizes their assignment.

Conservation and preservation organizations using easement programs have indicated a concern that instruments purporting to impose affirmative obligations on the holder may be unilaterally executed by grantors and recorded without notice to or acceptance by the holder ostensibly responsible for the performance of the affirmative obligations. Subsection (b) makes clear that neither a holder nor a person having a third-party enforcement right has any rights or duties under the easement prior to the recordation of the holder's acceptance of it.

The Act enables parties to create a conservation easement of unlimited duration subject to the power of a court to modify or terminate it in states whose case or statute law accords their courts that power in the case of easement. See Section 3(b). The latitude given the parties is consistent with the philosophical premise of the Act. However, there are additional safeguards; for example, easements may be created only for certain purposes and may be held only by certain "holders." These limitations find their place comfortably within similar limitations applicable to charitable trusts, whose duration may also have no limit. Allowing the parties to create such easements also enables them to fit within federal tax law requirements that the interest be "in perpetuity" if certain tax benefits are to be derived.

Obviously, an easement cannot impair prior rights of owners of interests in the burdened property existing when the easement comes into being unless those owners join in the easement or consent to it. The easement property thus would be subject to existing liens, encumbrances and other property rights (such as subsurface mineral rights) which pre-exist the easement, unless the owners of those rights release them or subordinate them to the easement. (Section 2(d).)

Library References

Health and Environment ☞25.5(4).
C.J.S. Health and Environment §§91 et seq., 130, 132.

§3. [Judicial Actions]

(a) An action affecting a conservation easement may be brought by:

(1) an owner of an interest in the real property burdened by the easement;

(2) a holder of the easement;

(3) a person having a third-party right of enforcement; or

(4) a person authorized by other law.

(b) This Act does not affect the power of a court to modify or terminate a conservation easement in accordance with the principles of law and equity.

Commissioners' Comment

Section 3 identifies four categories of persons who may bring actions to enforce, modify, or terminate conservation easements, quiet title to parcels burdened by conservation easements, or otherwise affect conservation easements. Owners of interests in real property burdened by easements might wish to sue in cases where the easements also impose duties upon holders and these duties are breached by the holders. Holders and persons having third-party rights of enforcement might obviously wish to bring suit to enforce restrictions on the owners' use of the burdened properties. In addition to these three categories of persons who derive their standing from the explicit terms of the easement itself, the Act also recognizes that the state's other applicable law may create standing in other persons. For example, independently of the Act, the attorney general could have standing in his capacity as supervisor of charitable trusts, either by statute or at common law.

A restriction burdening real property in perpetuity or for long periods can fail of its purposes because of changed conditions affecting the property or its environs, because the holder of the conservation easement may cease to exist, or for other reasons not anticipated at the time of its creation. A variety of doctrines, including the doctrines of changed conditions and cy pres, have been judicially developed and, in many states, legislatively sanctioned as a basis for responding to these vagaries. Under the changed conditions doctrine, privately created restrictions on land use may be terminated or modified if they no longer substantially achieve their purpose due to the changed conditions. Under the statute or case law of some states, the court's order limiting or terminating the restriction may include such terms and conditions, including monetary adjustments, as it deems necessary to protect the public interest and to assure an equitable resolution of the problem. The doctrine is applicable to real covenants and equitable servitudes in all states, but its application to easements is problematic in many states.

Under the doctrine of cy pres, if the purposes of a charitable trust cannot be carried out because circumstances have changed after the trust came into being or, for any other reason, the settlor's charitable intentions cannot be effectuated, courts under their equitable powers may prescribe terms and conditions that may best enable the general charitable objective to be achieved while altering specific provisions of the trust. So, also, in cases where a charitable trustee ceases to exist or cannot carry out its responsibilities, the court will appoint a substitute trustee upon proper application and will not allow the trust to fail.

The Act leaves intact the existing case and statute law

of adopting states as it relates to the modification and termination of easements and the enforcement of charitable trusts.

Library References

Health and Environment ⚭ 25.5(4).
C.J.S. Health and Environment §§91 *et seq.*, 130, 132.

§4. [Validity]

A conservation easement is valid even though:

(1) it is not appurtenant to an interest in real property;

(2) it can be or has been assigned to another holder;

(3) it is not of a character that has been recognized traditionally at common law;

(4) it imposes a negative burden;

(5) it imposes affirmative obligations upon the owner of an interest in the burdened property or upon the holder;

(6) the benefit does not touch or concern real property; or (7) there is no privity of estate or of contract.

Commissioners' Comment

One of the Act's basic goals is to remove outmoded common law defenses that could impede the use of easements for conservation or preservation ends. Section 4 addresses this goal by comprehensively identifying these defenses and negating their use in actions to enforce conservation or preservation easements.

Subsection (1) indicates that easements, the benefit of which is held in gross, may be enforced against the grantor or his successors or assigns. By stating that the easement need not be appurtenant to an interest in real property, it eliminates the requirement in force in some states that the holder of the easement must own an interest in real property (the "dominant estate") benefited by the easement.

Subsection (2) also clarifies common law by providing that an easement may be enforced by an assignee of the holder.

Subsection (3) addresses the problem posed by the common law's recognition of easements that served only a limited number of purposes and its reluctance to approve so-called "novel incidents." Easements serving the conservation and preservation ends enumerated in Section 1(1) might fail of enforcement under this restrictive view. Accordingly, subsection (3) establishes that conservation or preservation easements are not enforceable solely because they do not serve purposes or fall within the categories of easements traditionally recognized at common law.

Subsection (4) deals with a variant of the foregoing problem. The common law recognized only a limited number of "negative easements"—those preventing the owner of the burdened land from performing acts on his land that he would be privileged to perform absent the easement. Because a far wider range of negative burdens than those recognized at common law might be imposed by conservation or preservation easements, subsection (4) modifies the common law by eliminating the defense that a conservation or preservation easement imposes a "novel" negative burden.

Subsection (5) addresses the opposite problem—the unenforceability at common law of an easement that imposes affirmative obligations upon either the owner of the burdened property or upon the holder. Neither of those interests was viewed by the common law as true easements at all. The first, in fact, was labeled a "spurious" easement because it obligated the owner of the burdened property to perform affirmative acts. (The spurious easement was distinguished from an affirmative easement, illustrated by a right-of-way, which empowered the easement's holder to perform acts on the burdened property that the holder would not have been privileged to perform absent the easement.)

Achievement of conservation or preservation goals may require that affirmative obligations be incurred by the burdened property owner or by the easement holder or both. For example, the donor of a facade easement, one type of preservation easement, may agree to restore the facade to its original state; conversely, the holder of a facade easement may agree to undertake restoration. In either case, the preservation easement would impose affirmative obligations. Subsection (5) treats both interests as easements and establishes that neither would be unenforceable solely because it is affirmative in nature.

Subsections (6) and (7) preclude the touch and concern and privity of estate or contract defenses, respectively. Strictly speaking, they do not belong in the Act because they have traditionally been asserted as defenses against the enforcement not of easements but of real covenants and of equitable servitudes. The case law dealing with these three classes of interests, however, had become so confused and arcane over the centuries that defenses appropriate to one of these classes may incorrectly be deemed applicable to another. The inclusion of the touch and concern and privity defenses in Section 4 is a cautionary measure, intended to safeguard conservation and preservation easements from invalidation by courts that might inadvertently confuse them with real covenants or equitable servitudes.

Library References

Health and Environment ⚭ 25.5(4).
C.J.S. Health and Environment §§91 *et seq.*, 130, 132.

§5. [Applicability]

(a) This Act applies to any interest created after its effective date which complies with this Act, whether designated as a conservation easement or as a covenant, equitable servitude, restriction, easement, or otherwise.

(b) This Act applies to any interest created before its effective date if it would have been enforceable had it been created after its effective date unless retroactive application contravenes the constitution or laws of this state or the United States.

(c) This Act does not invalidate any interest, whether designated as a conservation or preservation easement or as a covenant, equitable servitude, restriction, easement, or otherwise, that is enforceable under other law of this state.

Commissioners' Comment

There are four classes of interest to which the Act might be made applicable: (1) those created after its passage which comply with it in form and purpose; (2) those created before the Act's passage which comply with the Act and which would not have been invalid under the pertinent pre-Act statutory or case law either because the latter explicitly validated interests of the kind recognized by the Act or, at least, was silent on the issue; (3) those created either before or after the Act which do not comply with the Act but which are valid under the state's statute or case law; and (4) those created before the Act's passage which comply with the Act but which would have been invalid under the pertinent pre-Act statutory or case law.

It is the purpose of Section 5 to establish or confirm the validity of the first three classes of interests. Subsection (a) establishes the validity of the first class of interests, whether or not they are designated as conservation or preservation easements. Subsection (b) establishes the validity under the Act of the second class. Subsection (c) confirms the validity of the third class independently of

the Act by disavowing the intent to invalidate any interest that does comply with other applicable law.

Constitutional difficulties could arise, however, if the Act sought retroactively to confer blanket validity upon the fourth class of interests. The owner of the land ostensibly burdened by the formerly invalid interest might well succeed in arguing that his property would be "taken" without just compensation were that interest subsequently validated by the Act. Subsection (b) addresses this difficulty by precluding retroactive application of the Act if such application "contravenes the constitution or laws of this state or the United States." That determination, of course, would have to made by a court.

Library References

Health and Environment ⟳ 25.5(4).
C.J.S. Health and Environment §§91 *et seq.*, 130, 132.

§6. [Uniformity of Application and Construction]

This Act shall be applied and construed to effectuate its general purpose to make uniform the laws with respect to the subject of the Act among states enacting it.

Library References

Health and Environment ⟳ 25.5(2).
C.J.S. Health and Environment §§61 *et seq.*, 91 *et seq.*, 106 *et seq.*, 115 *et seq.*, 125 *et seq.*, 133 *et seq.*

A Historic Preservation Restriction Agreement Used by the Society for the Preservation of New England Antiquities

William F. Morrill

Introduction

Mr. and Mrs. John A. Blum's gift of a Conservation and Historic Preservation Restriction Agreement to the Society for the Preservation of New England Antiquities (SPNEA) was extraordinary in many ways. In a real sense it was a gift to share in a family heritage. The Phelps family has held this property in Colebrook, Connecticut, for over two centuries. One of the present owners, Nancy Phelps Blum, is a direct descendant of Josiah Phelps, an original proprietor of the town. The land and buildings provide a living historical record of the Phelps family, from the original clearing of the land in the 1760s to the construction of the A. Phelps Inn in 1787, the General Phelps house in 1832, and the Yellow House cottage in 1862.

The family has long been conscious of their relationship to this land and its buildings, and they have taken a series of steps to preserve their history. In 1963, shortly after passage of the Connecticut law authorizing the establishment of historic districts, 1961 Conn. Pub. Acts 430, Conn. Gen. Stat. §§7-147a to 7-147k (1981), the Blums led the effort to create Colebrook Historic District No. 2, encompassing all of the Phelps Farms buildings. In 1971 the A. Phelps Inn was placed on the National Register of Historic Places. Also during the 1970s the Blums gave a 394-acre tract of woodland just west of the buildings to The Nature Conservancy to become the Phelps Research Area.

In 1979 the family applied to the Connecticut Historic Commission for National Register Certification of Colebrook Historic District No. 2 and the fields that provide the setting for the A. Phelps Inn. This application is still in process.

Finally, in early 1980, the Blums contacted SPNEA to explore the possibility of a historic easement on the build-

ings to reinforce their prior efforts. After 2½ years of negotiations and redrafts, the Preservation and Conservation Restriction Agreement with SPNEA was executed on September 27, 1982.

Several factors contributed to the complexity of the agreement, which is reprinted along with these comments.

1. The agreement covers not just one but a complex of seven buildings and applies not only to the exterior of the structures but covers the interior of some buildings as well.

2. The agreement embodies conservation purposes as well as historic preservation purposes. The thirty-three acres of land serve as an important scenic backdrop for the buildings and have intrinsic natural value as farmland and open space as well.

3. The owners intend to keep the property in the family. Their children, now adults, made a considerable effort to anticipate future contingencies and potential uses in the restrictions consistent with the intent of the agreement. This factor resulted in a negotiation and review process within the family as well as between the owners and SPNEA.

An important legal concern was to assure that the restriction agreement qualified for an income tax deduction under the Internal Revenue Code as modified by 1980 amendments affecting gifts of conservation easements. To help establish the qualification for a tax deduction, the preliminary statement in the agreement summarized the historic and conservation importance of the property and the governmental policies that are furthered by the agreement. The detailed provisions in the restrictions themselves provide further explanation of the intent of the parties in the agreement.

The agreement was recorded with the Colebrook Town Clerk together with a metes and bounds description of the property, a survey map, diagrams of each of the buildings, and fifty-three photographs of the historically important features of the buildings. The recording of the photographs in Connecticut is not a common practice but is a useful tool in preserving evidence of the architectural characteristics addressed by the agreement. The photographs will serve as base-line data for SPNEA and for future owners in evaluating compliance with the agreement. Each photograph was dated and initialed by both the owners and SPNEA and should be useful as documentary evidence in any enforcement action under the agreement.

In Connecticut the Town Clerk accepts original documents for recording, photocopies the originals, and returns them to the party. The photocopy is placed in the deed book in the land records. The Town Clerk was very helpful in making special arrangements to get high-quality reproductions of the photographs by the firm that photocopies documents for the land records.

Although this agreement involved protracted and detailed negotiations, the process went quite smoothly because of the goodwill, diligence, and common purpose of the owners and SPNEA.

Preservation and Conservation Restriction Agreement—Society for the Preservation of New England Antiquities

The Parties to this Preservation and Conservation Restriction Agreement ("this Agreement") are the Society for the Preservation of New England Antiquities, a Massachusetts charitable corporation having an address at Harrison Gray Otis House, 141 Cambridge Street, Boston, Massachusetts 02114 ("SPNEA"), and John A. and Nancy Phelps Blum, having an address at Phelps Corners, North Colebrook, Connecticut 06021 (herein together with their heirs, successors, or assigns called "Owner").

Preliminary Statement
Owner is the owner of property known as the Phelps Farms, which includes certain premises ("the Premises") consisting of 33.262 acres with buildings thereon, located at Route 183 in Colebrook, Connecticut, being more particularly described in Exhibit A attached hereto and being shown as parcels 1, 2, and 3 on a plan entitled "Map Showing Land of John A. and Nancy Phelps Blum, Route 183, Colebrook, Connecticut, scale 1″ equals 100′, August 1980, by John F. Whynott" ("the Plan"). Said Plan is filed in the Land Records of the Town of Colebrook in Case B, Row F-9. The Premises are also shown in the photographs and diagrams recorded herewith.[1]

Buildings on the Premises are located in the Colebrook Historic District number 2. The Premises have been continuously owned by the Phelps family since the original settlement of the Town of Colebrook in 1765. A present owner, Nancy Phelps Blum, is a direct descendant of Josiah Phelps, an original proprietor of the town. Each of the

parcels 1, 2, and 3 and the buildings located thereon are historically significant and are worthy of preservation. The open space on the Premises consisting of farm fields and forestland bordering Connecticut Route 183 on both sides and providing the setting for the historic buildings is worthy of preservation for the scenic enjoyment of the general public and as prime farmland.

The scenic setting of the Premises is enhanced by the 394-acre Phelps Research Area of The Nature Conservancy, which borders the Premises on the west. The land in parcels 1, 2, and 3 has been identified by the U.S. Department of Agriculture, Soil Conservation Service, as prime farmland of statewide importance.

This Preservation and Conservation Restriction Agreement is in furtherance of long-established and clearly delineated state governmental policies. In 1963 the Connecticut General Assembly declared "that it is in the public interest to encourage the preservation of farm land, forest land and open space land in order to maintain a readily available source of food and farm products close to the metropolitan areas of the state, to conserve the state's natural resources and to provide for the welfare and happiness of the inhabitants of the state" (P.A. 490, §1; C.G.S. §12-107a).

In 1971 the Connecticut General Assembly passed Public Act 1973 (C.G.S. §§47-42a to -42c), which authorizes the creation and enforcement of (1) conservation restrictions "whose purpose is to retain land or water areas predominantly in their natural, scenic or open condition or in agricultural farming, forest or open space use," and (2) preservation restrictions "whose purpose is to preserve historically significant structures or sites." It is the purpose of this Preservation and Conservation Restriction Agreement to fulfill both the conservation and historic preservation purposes of C.G.S. §47-42a.

Parcel 1 as shown on the Plan and the A. Phelps Inn built in 1787 located thereon are hereinafter referred to as the "Inn Parcel." The A. Phelps Inn is listed on the National Register of Historic Places. Parcel 2 as shown on the Plan and the 1862 cottage located thereon are hereinafter referred to as the "Yellow House Parcel." Parcel 3 as shown on the Plan and the 1832 General Phelps House and the other buildings located thereon are hereinafter referred to as the "General Phelps House Parcel."

SPNEA is a charitable corporation dedicated to the preservation and maintenance of structures or sites historically significant for their architecture, archaeology, or associations. Owner and SPNEA wish to ensure the preservation of the historically, agriculturally, and scenically significant characteristics of the Inn Parcel, the Yellow House Parcel, and the General Phelps House Parcel by means of preservation and conservation restrictions as those terms are defined in C.G.S. §§47-42a to -42c.

NOW, THEREFORE, for good and valuable consideration, SPNEA imposes, and Owner accepts the preservation and conservation restrictions listed below, which are intended to preserve the Inn Parcel, the Yellow House Parcel, and the General Phelps House Parcel.

1. **Restrictions on the Inn Parcel.** Owner agrees that none of the following alterations or additions shall be made to the buildings or land comprising the Inn Parcel:

(a) No alterations shall be made to the following exterior portions of the A. Phelps Inn located on the Inn Parcel (hereinafter referred to as the "Inn") as shown on the diagram attached hereto as Exhibit B:

(i) The Inn's northwest (facing the road) facade (numbered 1 on Exhibit B and shown in the photographs attached hereto as Exhibits C1 and C2); the southwest facade (numbered 2 on Exhibit B and shown in Exhibits C3–C5), the northeast facade, including surviving portions of the leanto (numbered 10 and 9 on Exhibit B and shown in Exhibits C6 and C7); and the southeast facade of the leanto (numbered 8 on Exhibit B and shown in Exhibit C8) (the terms "facade" and "elevations" shall include but not be limited to doors, door frames and decoration, window sash and window frames, original stone foundations and steps);

(ii) The southwest, northeast, and southeast facades of the ell attached to the southeast side of the Inn (numbered 3, 4, 5, 6, and 7 on Exhibit B); however, the ell being of recent construction, permission for minor alterations shall not be withheld or delayed if, in the reasonable opinion of SPNEA, said alterations are compatible with the historic character of the Inn;

(iii) The roof profile (including the ell);

(iv) The chimneys of the Inn and the ell chimney;

(v) The existing stone color exterior paint scheme. No sandblasting of the exterior shall be permitted.

(b) No alterations shall be made to the following interior, original, restored portions of the Inn as shown in the photographs attached hereto as Exhibits C9–C25:

(i) Woodwork, including but not limited to dadoes, cornices, mantelpieces, paneling, stairs, doors and door casings, and window and window casings;

(ii) Structural members, interior beams, and framing;

(iii) The built-in cage bar located in the southeastern taproom (Exhibit C14);

(iv) The built-in cage bar and the woodwork in the southeastern taproom is to remain unpainted;

(v) Woodwork and arrangement of partitions, upper entry;

(vi) Woodwork, including paneling, of the ballroom;

(vii) Floors (and this provision expressly prohibits sanding of floors);

(viii) The paint color scheme of the two front parlors and entry way in the Inn.

(c) The only restriction on alterations to the interior of the newly constructed (1965) wing at the rear of the Inn as shown on Exhibit B shall be that all unpainted woodwork shall remain unpainted. This restriction shall not prohibit the removal of all or any portion of such woodwork in the course of building alterations or redecoration.

(d) No portion of the Inn or ell shall be moved from its present location unless such moving is required by a taking by eminent domain;

(e) There shall be no exterior additions to the Inn or ell;

(f) Signage for any use of the Inn Parcel shall require the prior written permission of SPNEA, which permission shall not be unreasonably withheld, except that such prior permission shall not be required for the installation of an attractive and suitable historical marker;

(g) The Inn Parcel shall not be subdivided for resale or lease, provided that this clause shall not be deemed to prohibit the leasing of existing buildings on the Inn Parcel for uses permitted by this Agreement;

(h) No building, road, sign, billboard, or other advertising display, mobile home, utility pole, antenna, tower, conduit, or line or other temporary or permanent structure shall be constructed, placed, or permitted to be placed or to remain on, above, or under the Inn Parcel; provided, however, that with the prior written approval of SPNEA, not to be unreasonably withheld or delayed, as to design, location, size, and quantity, Owner may erect architecturally harmonious outbuildings, alterations, and amenities appurtenant to the residential use of the Inn, alterations utilizing renewable energy sources, and television and radio receiving antennas for residential service;

(i) No soil, loam, rock, or mineral resource or natural deposit shall be excavated, dredged, or removed from the Inn Parcel; and no soil, refuse, trash, vehicle bodies or parts, rubbish, debris, junk, waste, or other substance or material whatsoever shall be placed, filled, stored, or dumped thereon, provided that this clause shall not be deemed to restrict activities necessary and desirable to the residential use of the Inn, to the maintenance of the lawn and gardens, or to the conducting of a family farming operation;

(j) No trees, grasses, or other vegetation shall be cut, removed, or otherwise destroyed, except for the clearing of shrubbery, trees, and other vegetation for the purposes of beautification and maintenance of vistas, the maintenance of lawns and gardens around the Inn, and the carrying on of a family farming operation or construction of outbuildings, alterations, or amenities permitted under Section 1(g) above;

(k) The front fence, extending to and including the upright granite posts leading into the driveway northeast of the Inn shall not be altered or removed;

(l) The mounting block in the foreyard of the Inn shall not be altered or removed except to return it to its original position at the front gate, as shown in early photographs;

(m) No use or activity shall be permitted which might alter the open, natural, agricultural, and scenic character of the fields in the southerly portion of the Inn Parcel, which is more particularly shown on the recorded map attached hereto.

2. **Restrictions on the Yellow House Parcel.** Owner agrees that none of the following alterations or additions shall be made to the buildings or land comprising the Yellow House Parcel:

(a) No alterations shall be made to the following exterior portions of the Yellow House located on the Yellow House Parcel (hereinafter referred to as the "Yellow House") as shown on the diagram attached hereto as Exhibit D:

(i) The Yellow House's southeast and southwest (facing the road) facades with veranda (numbered 1, 2, 3, and 4 on Exhibit D and shown in the photographs attached hereto as Exhibits E1 and E2), the northeast facade and the northwest facade (numbered 5 and 6 on Exhibit D and shown in Exhibits E3 and E4) (the terms "facade" and "elevations" shall include but not be limited to doors, door frames and decoration, window sash and window frames, original stone foundations and steps);

(ii) The roof profile;

(iii) The chimneys;

(iv) The existing yellow exterior paint color schemes. No sandblasting of the exterior shall be permitted.

(b) No portion of the Yellow House shall be moved from its present location unless such moving is required by a taking by eminent domain;

(c) There shall be no additions attached to the Yellow House;

(d) Signage for any use of the Yellow House Parcel shall require the prior written permission of SPNEA, which permission shall not be unreasonably withheld or delayed, except that such prior permission shall not be required for the installation of an attractive and suitable historical marker;

(e) The Yellow House Parcel shall not be subdivided for resale or lease, provided that this clause shall not be deemed to prohibit the leasing of existing buildings on the Yellow House Parcel for uses permitted by this Agreement;

(f) No building, road, sign, billboard, or other advertising display, mobile home, utility pole, antenna, tower, conduit, or line or other temporary or permanent structure will be constructed, placed, or permitted to be placed or to remain on, above, or under the Yellow House Parcel; provided, however, that with the prior written approval of SPNEA, not to be unreasonably withheld or delayed, as to design, location, size, and quantity, Owner may erect architecturally harmonious outbuildings, alterations, and amenities appurtenant to the residential use of the Yellow House, alterations utilizing renewable energy sources, and television and radio receiving antennas for residential service;

(g) No soil, loam, rock, or mineral resource or natural deposit shall be excavated, dredged, or removed from the Yellow House Parcel; and no soil, refuse, trash, vehicle bodies or parts, rubbish, debris, junk, waste, or other substance or material whatsoever shall be placed, filled, stored, or dumped thereon, provided that this clause shall not be deemed to restrict activities necessary and desirable to the residential use of the Yellow House, to the maintenance of the lawns and gardens, or to the conducting of a family farming operation;

(h) No trees, grasses, or other vegetation shall be cut, removed, or otherwise destroyed, except for the clearing of shrubbery, trees, or other vegetation for the purposes of beautification and maintenance of vistas and the maintenance of lawns and gardens around the Yellow House and the carrying on of a family farming operation or construction of outbuildings, alterations, or amenities permitted under Section 2(f) above.

3. **Restrictions on the General Phelps House Parcel.** Owner agrees that none of the following alterations or additions shall be made to the buildings or land comprising the General Phelps House Parcel:

(a) No alterations shall be made to the following exterior portions of the General Phelps House located on the General Phelps House Parcel (hereinafter referred to as the "General Phelps House") as shown on the diagram attached hereto as Exhibit F:

(i) The General Phelps House's east (facing the road) facade (numbered 1 on Exhibit F and shown in the photographs attached hereto as Exhibits G1 and G2), the north facade (numbered 11 on Exhibit F and shown in Exhibit G3), and the south facade (numbered 2 on Exhibit F and shown in Exhibit G4), although replacement along the south facade of that portion of the veranda now missing which appears in early photographs is permissible (the terms "facade" and "elevations" shall include but not be limited to doors, door frames and decoration, window sash and window frames, original stone foundations and steps);

(ii) The east, south, and west facades of the ell attached to the south side of the General Phelps House (numbered 3, 4, and 5 on Exhibit F and shown in Exhibits G4 and G5); however, replacement of Victorian ornaments of the veranda which appear in early photographs is permissible, and permission for reasonable modifications in fenestration on walls numbered 5 and 6 shall not be withheld or delayed if, in the reasonable opinion of SPNEA, said modifications are compatible with the historic character of the General Phelps House;

(iii) The south facade of the rear ell of the General Phelps House, including the recessed portico with plaster ceiling (numbered 6 on Exhibit F and shown in Exhibit G6), and the west facade of the rear ell (numbered 7 on Exhibit F and shown in Exhibit G7), although SPNEA will permit a modest and reasonable enlargement of the present projecting kitchen in the rear ell, the exterior finish of said extension to copy in all respects the exterior finish of the existing extension;

(iv) The east, north, and west facades of the ell attached to the north side of the General Phelps House (numbered 10, 9, and 8 on Exhibit F and shown in Exhibits G3 and G8), although permission for reasonable modification in fenestration in the east, north, and west facades shall not be withheld or delayed if, in the reasonable opinion of SPNEA, said modification is compatible with the historic character of the General Phelps House;

(v) The roof profile (including the ells);

(vi) The chimneys of the General Phelps House and the ell chimneys;

(vii) The existing exterior paint color scheme of the General Phelps House and its ells. No sandblasting of the exterior shall be permitted;

(viii) Removal or retention of the existing exterior window shutters with movable slats (or replicas of them) is optional.

(b) No alterations shall be made to the following interior portions of the General Phelps House, south ell, rear ell, or north ell:

(i) The front parlor of the General Phelps House, including all woodwork, wallpaper, the Franklin stove, and the floors (and this provision expressly prohibits the sanding of floors) as shown in the photographs attached as Exhibits G9–G12;

(ii) The shelving and other built-in accessories of the buttery or pantry at the southwest corner of the General Phelps House as shown in the photographs attached as Exhibits G13–G15;

(iii) Structural members, interior beams, and framing;

(iv) Woodwork, including but not limited to dadoes, cornices, mantelpieces (see Exhibit G16), paneling, and stairs;

(v) The fireplace and exposed chimney in the rear, or "summer" kitchen (originally furnished with a set cauldron which may be restored);

(vi) All floors except the modern matched-board floor in the dining room (the original kitchen). This provision expressly prohibits the sanding of floors.

(c) No alterations shall be made to the front fence of the foreyard as shown in the photograph attached as Exhibit G17;

(d) No portion of the General Phelps House or ells shall be moved from its present location unless such moving is required by a taking by eminent domain;

(e) There shall be no exterior additions attached to the General Phelps House or ells, except as provided under paragraph 3(a)(iii) above;

(f) The southeast and northeast (facing the road) facades of the "Chimney House" (formerly called the "Creamery"), located on the General Phelps House Parcel behind the General Phelps House (shown in the photograph attached as Exhibit H), shall not be altered;

(g) The southeast (facing the road) and southwest facades of the "OH House" (so-called), formerly the pigpen, located on the General Phelps House Parcel north of the "Chimney House" (shown in the photographs attached as Exhibits J1 and J2), shall not be altered, although permission for modification of the fenestration of the southwest facade shall not be unreasonably withheld or delayed;

(h) The east (facing the road), south, and north facades of the old Barn, known as the "Coach House," at the north end of the General Phelps House Parcel adjacent to Route 183 (shown in the photographs attached as Exhibits K1–K3) shall not be altered;

(i) The exterior of the modern garage to the south of the General Phelps House (shown in the photograph attached as Exhibit L) shall not be altered, although permission to enlarge this structure along its south flank will not be unreasonably withheld or delayed;

(j) Signage for any use of the General Phelps House Parcel shall require the prior written permission of SPNEA, which permission shall not be unreasonably withheld or delayed, except that such prior permission shall not be required for the installation of an attractive and suitable historical marker;

(k) The General Phelps House Parcel shall not be subdivided for resale or lease, provided that this clause shall not be deemed to prohibit the leasing of existing buildings on the General Phelps House Parcel for uses permitted by this Agreement. (It is understood that a portion of the General Phelps House Parcel, consisting of approximately one-third of an acre and containing the OH House and the Coach House, is a separate lot under different ownership from the balance of the General Phelps House Parcel. This lot with buildings may be separately leased, but shall in all other respects be subject to the restrictions in this Agreement.);

(l) No building, road, sign, billboard, or other advertising display, mobile home, utility pole, antenna, tower, conduit, or line or other temporary or permanent structure will be constructed, placed, or permitted to be placed or to remain on, above, or under the General Phelps House Parcel; provided, however, that with the prior written approval of SPNEA, not to be unreasonably withheld or delayed, as to design, location, size, and quantity, Owner may erect architecturally harmonious outbuildings, alterations, and amenities appurtenant to the residential use of the General Phelps House, alterations utilizing renewable energy sources and television and radio receiving antennas for residential service;

(m) No soil, loam, rock, or mineral resource or natural deposit shall be excavated, dredged, or removed from the General Phelps House Parcel; and no soil, refuse, trash, vehicle bodies or parts, rubbish, debris, junk, waste, or other substance or material whatsoever shall be placed, filled, stored, or dumped thereon provided that this clause shall not be deemed to restrict activities necessary and desirable to the residential use of the General Phelps House, to the maintenance of the lawns and gardens, or to the conducting of a family farming operation;

(n) No trees, grasses, or other vegetation shall be cut, removed, or otherwise destroyed, except for the clearing of shrubbery, trees, and other vegetation for the purposes of beautification and maintenance of vistas, the maintenance of lawns and gardens around the General Phelps House, and the carrying on of a family farming operation or construction of outbuildings, alterations, or amenities permitted under Section 3(1) above;

(o) No use or activity shall be permitted which might alter the open, natural, agricultural, and scenic character of the fields in the southerly portion of the General Phelps House Parcel, which is more particularly shown on the Plan attached hereto.

4. **Use of Premises.** Owner agrees that no use shall be made of the Premises or any portion thereof and no activity shall be permitted thereon which, in the reasonable opinion of SPNEA, is or may become inconsistent with the intent of this restriction agreement, being the preservation of the Premises in their rural, natural, and scenic condition; the protection of environmental systems, prime farmland, and scenic enjoyment; and the preservation of historically significant architecture. Specifically, and without limiting the generality of the foregoing, Owner agrees that the Premises may be used solely for residential, agricultural, and certain limited commercial purposes consistent with the intent of this Agreement. The term "limited commercial purposes" shall be deemed to specifically exclude, without limitation, restaurants, gas stations, motels, liquor stores, bars, lounges, grocery stores, new and used car dealerships, the sale of automotive parts and accessories, trailer parks, farm implement sales, convenience stores, video game rooms, pool halls, bowling alleys, and theaters, and any use or activity not permitted under applicable law. This listing is not intended to be exclusive or exhaustive, but is intended only to provide a limited list of those uses which are clearly *not* consistent with the intent of this Agreement and are therefore not permitted.

5. **Written Permission.** SPNEA may grant permission for any alteration, addition, removal, or any other use or activity by Owner which is restricted by any provision of this Agreement. Written permission by SPNEA for any alteration, addition, or removal shall not be unreasonably withheld or delayed and shall be in recordable form executed and acknowledged by any one or more of the President, the Treasurer, or the Executive Director or such officer or officers who may succeed to their responsibilities

under other titles. The failure by SPNEA to act within 120 days of its receipt of any written request for SPNEA permission required under this Agreement shall be deemed to be approval of the entire request. In such event SPNEA shall issue a certificate of approval in recordable form as described above upon Owner's request. Permission as to one alteration or addition, or group of alterations or additions, shall under no circumstances be construed to waive the requirement for permission for subsequent alterations or additions.

6. **Definitions.**

(a) *Alteration.* For purposes of paragraphs 1, 2, and 3 of this Agreement the term "alteration" shall not be construed to mean the replacement of any element of the exterior by an item identical in design, or the reconstruction of any exterior element in an identical manner. Neither shall the term "alteration" be construed to include the following redecorating or refurbishing work:

(i) interior painting, except as otherwise provided in paragraphs 1(b)(iv), 1(b)(vi), and 1(c);

(ii) wallpapering, provided the paper does not cover woodwork, except as otherwise provided in paragraph 3(b)(i);

(iii) plastering, provided the plaster does not cover the woodwork;

(iv) rewiring, provided no electrical fixtures are placed in the woodwork;

(v) replacement of plumbing;

(vi) replacement of glass;

(vii) installation of window and door screens and storm windows and doors and porch screens on facade number 6 of the General Phelps House provided that SPNEA approves the color and design of same prior to installation, which approval shall not be unreasonably withheld or delayed;

(viii) installation of insulation, provided no blown-in foam insulation is introduced into side walls of the Inn, the Yellow House, the General Phelps House, or any of the ells.

(b) *Appurtenant Outbuildings and Amenities.* For purposes of paragraphs 1, 2, and 3 of this Agreement the term "appurtenant outbuildings and amenities" shall mean the pleasurable features and facilities of a residential estate including, but not limited to, gardens, plantings, shrubs, trees, fences, in-ground swimming pools, tennis courts, pool houses, playhouses, and other recreational facilities.

7. **Condemnation and Casualty.**

(a) If the Premises or any one or more of the three Parcels or any building or any substantial portion of any of the three Parcels shall be completely taken by eminent domain or be completely destroyed by fire or other casualty, there shall be no requirement to restore or rebuild the Premises or Parcel so taken or destroyed. If Owner elects to build, rebuild, or restore, he may use other materials and design provided that such other materials and design are architecturally harmonious and consistent with the remaining buildings located on the Premises and Colebrook Historic District No. 2, provided that any such buildings shall be used solely for the uses permitted by this Agreement and provided that he obtain the prior written approval of SPNEA with respect to the design, location, and size of any such buildings.

(b) If the Premises or any one or more of the three Parcels or any substantial portion of any of the three Parcels shall be so substantially damaged by a taking or casualty that preservation of the natural condition of the Parcels or the rebuilding or restoring of the Inn, the Yellow House, or the General Phelps House (using the same materials or same design) would in the opinion of SPNEA be infeasible or be unreasonably expensive after application of awarded damages or collected insurance proceeds, then the Owner in such cases may either decline to rebuild or restore the Inn, the Yellow House, or the General Phelps House, as the case may be, or if he elects to rebuild or restore, may use other materials and design, provided that such other materials and design are architecturally harmonious and consistent with the remaining buildings located on the Premises and Colebrook Historic District No. 2, provided that any such rebuilt or restored buildings shall be used solely for the uses permitted by this Agreement and provided that he obtain the prior written approval of SPNEA with respect to the design, location, and size of any such buildings.

(c) In the case of any taking or casualty which does not render restoration of the Premises infeasible or unreasonably expensive in SPNEA's opinion, Owner shall restore the Premises using identical materials and design.

(d) All provisions of this Agreement which are not rendered impossible of performance by a taking, fire, or other casualty shall remain in full force and effect after any such taking or casualty unless and until this Agreement is terminated by SPNEA.

8. **Taxes and Insurance.** Owner shall pay, before they become overdue, all real estate taxes assessed on the Premises, and shall carry reasonably adequate fire insurance coverage thereon, in accordance with insurance industry coverage standards as they may change from time to time.

9. **Maintenance of Premises.** Owner agrees to assume the total cost of continued maintenance, repair, and administration of the Premises so as to preserve the historically significant characteristics of the features, materials, appearance, workmanship, and environment thereof in a manner satisfactory to SPNEA. Nothing herein shall prohibit Owner from seeking financial assistance for the foregoing purposes from any sources available to him.

10. **Inspection.** SPNEA shall inspect the Premises at least annually, to ensure that Owner is in compliance with the restrictions hereby imposed. Owner agrees to grant SPNEA free access to all areas of the Premises upon which preservation restrictions are placed. Such inspections shall be made at reasonable hours and only after prior notice to Owner. This right of inspection shall be assignable by SPNEA to any governmental body or any entity whose purposes include preservation of structures or sites of historic significance. The failure of SPNEA to exercise this right of inspection for any period of time, however, shall under no circumstances be construed as a waiver of such right.

11. **Enforcement.** In the event that SPNEA, upon inspection of the Premises, finds a violation of the duty to maintain and preserve the Premises, SPNEA shall in writing notify the Owner of such violation, together with a recommendation as to how the violation may be cured. Such notice shall also inform the Owner as to the time period in which such violation must be cured, which time period must be such as to afford a reasonable time to cure. Such notice shall be recorded in the land records. In the event Owner contests either the existence of a violation or the length of time in which to remedy it, he shall notify SPNEA in writing, and if the parties cannot agree, either party shall have the right to submit the matter to arbitration within thirty (30) days by sending written notice to the other party within said thirty-day period naming an arbiter and requesting the other party to name an arbiter. The other party shall have thirty (30) days from the receipt of such notice to name a second arbiter; if he shall fail to name a second arbiter within such thirty-day period, the first party shall be entitled to name the second arbiter. A third arbiter shall be selected by the other two arbiters within thirty (30) days after the naming of the second arbiter. The three arbiters shall conclude the arbitration within 120 days of the date on which the third arbiter is named. A decision by a majority of the arbiters shall control. Arbitration shall be the sole and exclusive remedy of the parties.

In the event Owner does not comply with SPNEA's or the arbiters' recommendations within the stated period, SPNEA shall send a formal notice of default and record such notice in the land records. After such recording, SPNEA may enter the Premises and effect the repairs, replacements, or other work necessary to cure the violation. SPNEA shall perform only such repairs, replacement, or other work as is reasonably necessary to preserve the historically significant characteristics of the Premises and shall use its best efforts to have any such work done at a reasonable cost. Upon completion of repairs or other work, SPNEA shall notify the Owner in writing of the amount due and shall record such notice in the land records. If Owner does not pay SPNEA within thirty (30) days after the date of such notice, SPNEA may, forty-five (45) days after the date of such notice, record a notice of lien on the Premises in the land records. This lien, to which Owner hereby agrees in advance to be subject, shall be for the unpaid amount of the cost of repairs or other work plus interest at an annual rate on the unpaid balance equal to the prime rate of interest charged from time to time by The First National Bank of Boston and the costs of enforcement including, without limitation, any reasonable attorneys' fees incurred by SPNEA in connection with any actions taken by SPNEA pursuant to this paragraph 11. Owner hereby waives any right he may have to contest the amount of such lien. SPNEA shall have all the rights of a mortgagee to secure payment of such unpaid amounts plus interest, including, but not limited to, the right to foreclose.

Any lien which may arise pursuant to this paragraph shall be subject and subordinate to an existing first mortgage of record held by a bank, savings and loan association, trust company, credit union, insurance company, or other institutional lender to the extent of the principal amount stated in such mortgage as being secured by it.

Owner acknowledges that SPNEA is under no obligation to undertake repairs, nor to enforce this Agreement, and that any decision to enforce this Agreement shall be at SPNEA's sole discretion, provided, however, that SPNEA agrees to use all reasonable efforts to enforce this Agreement according to the intent of the parties hereto.

12. **Notices.** All notices, requests, demands, consents, waivers, and other communications given under any of the provisions of this Agreement shall be in writing and shall be mailed, postage prepaid, registered or certified mail, return receipt requested, addressed to the parties at the addresses set forth above or at such other address as the addressee may have specified in a notice duly given to the sender.

13. **Miscellaneous.** With respect to matters not covered by this Agreement, Owner shall have the right to operate and use the Premises in such manner as he determines provided that such operation and use is not inconsistent with the intent of this Agreement.

14. **Written Acceptance.** Before taking legal possession of the Premises, or any portion thereof, each new Owner of the Premises shall indicate his acceptance of this Agreement by a letter to SPNEA. Such acceptance shall include a promise to maintain at all times and in good condition the significant historical, architectural, scenic, environmental, and agricultural characteristics of the Premises covered by this Agreement.

15. **Restrictions Run with Land.** Notwithstanding anything to the contrary contained in paragraph 14 above, the burden of the preservation restrictions contained in this Agreement shall run with the land in perpetuity.

16. **Assignment.** All of the rights and restrictions enforceable by SPNEA pursuant to this Agreement shall be assignable by SPNEA for preservation purposes only and without consideration to any governmental body or any entity described in Section 170(b)(1)(A) of the Internal Revenue Code of 1954 as amended whose purposes include preservation of structures or sites of historic or architectural significance.

IN WITNESS WHEREOF, the parties hereto have executed this Agreement under seal this 27th day of September, 1982.

Witnesses:

Society for the Preservation of New England Antiquities

_____
Nancy R. Coolidge

By _____
Executive Director

Owners:

_____
Mary Ann Blum

By _____
John A. Blum

_____
Jonathan D. Blum

By _____
Nancy Phelps Blum

State of Connecticut) SS.: Colebrook
County of Litchfield) Sept. 27, 1982
)

Then personally appeared the above-named Abbott L. Cummings, Executive Director of Society for the Preservation of New England Antiquities, and acknowledged the foregoing instrument to be his free act and deed and the free act and deed of Society for the Preservation of New England Antiquities.

Before me,

_____
Commissioner of Superior Court

My commission expires:

_____

State of Connecticut) SS.: Colebrook
County of Litchfield) Sept. 27, 1982
)

Then personally appeared the above-named John A. Blum and Nancy Phelps Blum and acknowledged the foregoing instrument to be their free act and deed.

Before me,

_____
Commissioner of Superior Court

My commission expires:

_____

Exhibit A

To Preservation and Conservation Restriction Agreement between Society for the Preservation of New England Antiquities and John A. Blum and Nancy Phelps Blum.

Those three certain parcels of land with buildings thereon standing situated on both sides of Connecticut Route 183, Town of Colebrook, Litchfield County, Connecticut, containing a total of 33.262 acres as shown on a survey map entitled "Map Showing Land of John A. and Nancy Phelps Blum, Route 183, Colebrook, Connecticut, scale 1" equals 100', August 1980, by John F. Whynott, R.L.S. #8178, Colebrook, Connecticut," being more particularly bounded and described as follows:

Parcel 1:

Beginning at a Connecticut Highway Department monument in the southerly line of Prock Hill Road approximately 120 feet east of the intersection of Prock Hill Road with Route 183, thence following the southerly line of Prock Hill Road the following two courses and distances: (1) N. 26° 28' 55" E. 59.68 feet to a point and (2) N. 20° 33' 10" E. 69.67 feet along a stone wall to a point on the westerly side of a barway across a wood road; thence across other lands of John A. Blum the following nine courses and distances: (1) S. 61° 56' 00" E. 139.52 feet to a point, (2) S. 26° 00' 00" W. 43.00 feet to a point at the intersection of another stone wall, (3) S. 37° 51' 10" E. 145.45 feet to a point, (4) S. 50° 27' 35" E. 57.68 feet to a point, (5) S. 67° 36' 30" E. 31.69 feet, (6) S. 79° 01' 45" E. 86.67 feet to a set three-quarter-inch iron pin, (7) S. 16° 11' 55" E. 451.68 feet to a set three-quarter-inch iron pin, (8) S. 35° 39' 15" E. 532.50 feet to a set three-quarter-inch iron pin, and (9) S. 40° 02' 00" E. 434.21 feet to a set three-quarter-inch iron pin in the northerly line of Sandy Brook; thence across other lands of John A. Blum and following the center line of Sandy Brook westerly to where it crosses the eastern line of Route 183, which point is the following five courses and distances from the last mentioned three-quarter-inch iron pin: (1) S. 48° 14' 45" W. 278.91 feet to a set stake in the southerly bank of Sandy Brook, (2) N. 72° 01' 35" W. 234.75 feet to a set three-quarter-inch iron pin in the southerly bank of Sandy Brook, (3) S. 44° 42' 10" W. 168.80 feet to a set three-quarter-inch iron pin in the bed of Sandy Brook, (4) N. 62° 33' 00" W. 284.70 feet to a set three-eighth-inch drill hole in the bed of Sandy Brook, and (5) N. 74° 36' 50" W. 50.54 feet to the aforementioned point in the easterly line of Route 183; thence along the easterly line of Route 183 the following four courses and distances: (1) N. 15° 19' 00" W. 263.15 feet to a point, (2) along a curve to the right with radius of 5714.91 feet and arc of 402.47 feet to a point, (3) N. 11° 16' 55" W. 566.41 feet to a point, and (4) N. 17° 18' 05" W. 150.53 feet to a point at the intersection of Route 183 with Prock Hill Road; thence along the southerly line of Prock Hill Road N. 24° 41' 25" E.

119.64 feet to the Connecticut Highway Department monument marking the point and place of beginning; said Parcel 1 contains 20.253 acres and the two-story frame house known as the A. Phelps Inn.

Being a portion of the premises described in a Warranty Deed from Phelps Farms, Inc., to John A. Blum, dated August 3, 1956, and recorded in Colebrook Land Records at Volume 34, pages 272–275.

Parcel 2:

Beginning at a set three-quarter-inch iron pin in the northerly line of Prock Hill Road; thence along the northerly line of Prock Hill Road the following two courses and distances: (1) S. 10° 48' 45" W. 90.57 feet to a point and (2) S. 23° 20' W. 104.50 feet to a point in the easterly line of Route 183 right-of-way; thence along said easterly line of Route 183 N. 33° 49' 35" W. 240.23 feet to a point in the northerly bank of Sandy Brook; thence across other lands of John A. Blum the following two courses and distances: (1) N. 77° 25' 10" E. 65.29 feet to a set three-quarter-inch drill hole in the bed of said Brook and (2) S. 77° 19' 40" E. 131.59 feet to the set three-quarter-inch iron pin marking the point and place of beginning; said Parcel 2 contains 0.483 acres and the two-story frame house known as the Yellow House.

Being the same premises described in a Certificate of Distribution from the Estate of Marion P. Phelps to Nancy Phelps Blum, dated March 6, 1961, and recorded in the Colebrook Land Records at Volume 35, page 529.

Parcel 3:

Beginning at a Connecticut Highway Department monument in the westerly line of Route 183 at the intersection of Route 183 with Prock Hill Road; thence along the westerly line of Route 183 the following five courses and distances: (1) S. 06° 43' 45" E. 237.49 feet to a Connecticut Highway Department monument, (2) S. 15° 20' 25" E. 376.28 feet in part along a stone wall to a point, (3) again in part along a stone wall S. 13° 18' 45" E. 444.93 feet to a point, (4) S. 15° 11' 45" E. 212.83 feet to a point, and (5) S. 15° 22' 20" E. 2.55 feet to a point in the center line of Sandy Brook and in line of lands of The Nature Conservancy of Connecticut, Inc.; thence following the center line of Sandy Brook along line of lands of said Nature Conservancy to a set three-quarter-inch drill hole at the confluence of Brummagen Brook and Sandy Brook, which set three-quarter-inch drill hole is the following four courses and distances from the last-mentioned point where the center line of Sandy Brook crosses the easterly line of Connecticut Route 183: (1) N. 74° 36' 50" W. 195.22 feet to a set three-quarter-inch drill hole, (2) N. 33° 47' 10" W. 252.76 feet to a set three-quarter-inch drill hole, (3) N. 34° 38' 00" W. 289.98 feet to a set three-quarter-inch drill hole, and (4) N. 47° 37' 55" W. 213.22 feet to the aforementioned set three-quarter-inch drill hole at the confluence of Brummagen Brook and Sandy Brook;

thence continuing along line of lands of said Nature Conservancy the following nine courses and distances in part along a stone wall: (1) N. 26° 11′ 25″ W. 473.96 feet to a set three-quarter-inch iron pin, (2) N. 64° 11′ 00″ E. 118.86 feet to a set three-quarter-inch iron pin, (3) N. 57° 37′ 35″ E. 130.54 feet to a point, (4) N. 64° 36′ 10″ E. 48.06 feet to a point, (5) N. 54° 13′ 35″ E. 26.39 feet to a point, (5) N. 43° 30′ 30″ E. 99.15 feet to a point, (6) N. 39° 30′ 00″ E. 76.22 feet to a point, (7) N. 63° 40′ 35″ W. 55.00 feet to a pile of stones set with a stake, (8) N. 21° 33′ 10″ W. 120.00 feet crossing a wood road to a set three-quarter-inch iron pin, and (9) N. 60° 40′ 00″ E. 175.00 feet to a point in the westerly line of Route 183; thence following the westerly line of Route 183 the following three courses and distances: (1) S. 12° 51′ 25″ E. 80.39 feet to a point, (2) S. 26° 47′ 15″ E. 215.14 feet crossing Sandy Brook to a point at the northeasterly corner of a frame barn, and (3) S. 0° 57′ 15″ E. 69.63 feet to the Connecticut Highway Department monument marking the point and place of beginning. Said parcel 3 contains 12.526 acres and the five buildings known as the General Phelps House, the Chimney House (formerly the Creamery), the OH House, the Coach House, and the General Phelps garage.

Being a portion of the premises described in a Warranty Deed from Phelps Farms, Inc., to John A. Blum, dated August 3, 1956, and recorded in the Colebrook Land Records at Volume 34, pages 272–275, and also the premises described in two Quit Claim Deeds from John A. Blum to Nancy Phelps Blum, one dated August 3, 1947, and recorded in the Colebrook Land Records at Volume 32, page 64, and the other dated March 21, 1948, and recorded in the Colebrook Land Records at Volume 32, page 100.

Exhibit B

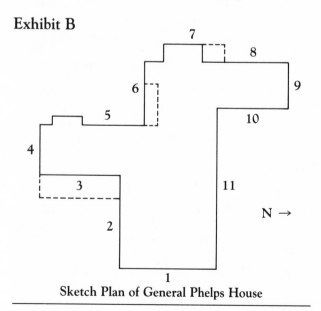

Sketch Plan of General Phelps House

Road

Exhibit C

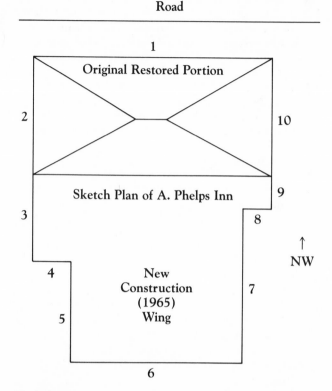

Sketch Plan of A. Phelps Inn

Exhibit D

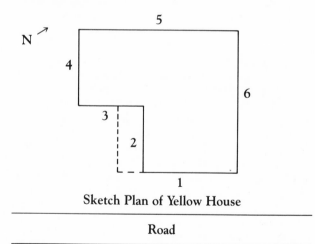

Sketch Plan of Yellow House

Road

Note

1. For the purposes of this book, only four exhibits have been included: the property description and three sketch plans, one for the A. Phelps Inn, the Yellow House, and the General Phelps House. If the reader wishes to see exhibits not included in this article, he or she is directed to volume 44, page 788, in the Colebrook Land Records. Further information can be obtained from the Town Clerk, P.O. Box 5, Colebrook, Conn. 06021.

An Introduction to Conservation Easements for Colorado Archaeologists

Glenn F. Tiedt

A few years ago I attended a meeting of the National Conference of State Historic Preservation Officers in Wilmington, Delaware. I was a stranger to the field of historic preservation, in the odd position of being an outdoor recreation planner at a gathering of historic preservation professionals. The Heritage Conservation and Recreation Service had only recently been created, and as a former employee of the Bureau of Outdoor Recreation, I was at the meeting because a number of people felt my detailed knowledge of conservation easements and federal income tax law could be applied to the historic preservation effort.

Our Delaware hosts had planned a number of special activities for their out-of-state guests, among which was a tour of the conservation workshops at Winterthur. I was personally pleased at the prospect of this tour because I had had a lot of experience in the field of conservation. Historic preservation was interesting enough, but it was going to be nice to spend a little time on familiar ground.

On the day of the tour, we were taken to Winterthur, broken up into small groups, and assigned guides. Our guide promptly led us to a room filled with woodworking equipment in the basement of the museum and began to describe all the things that could be done there to restore old furniture. After about ten minutes of this, I whispered to one of my companions, "I thought we were going to tour the conservation workshop." He replied, "This is it!"

The experience at Winterthur added a new dimension to my understanding of conservation and caused me to wonder whether others had as narrow a view of conservation as I did. I had always associated conservation with preservation of the natural environment, and I had only recently learned conservation could also be associated with preservation of the built environment. Now I was being told conservation was the restoration of old furniture. If every group had its own understanding of conservation,

did every group also have an understanding of how conservation easements could be used to meet its needs? I soon discovered that archaeologists seemed to know a lot about conservation and very little about conservation easements.

Nonacquisition Techniques

There are many ways to protect archaeological sites.[1] Notification of the existence of the site will sometimes prevent a landowner from inadvertently destroying it. Listing it on a federal, state, or local register will give him public recognition and additional incentive to protect it. Zoning, historic district ordinances, and local antiquities ordinances may deter the unwilling landowner from wreaking havoc with a site, but regulations and ordinances are effective only until someone gets them changed. Similarly, state environmental protection acts and farm, forest, and open space programs may provide protection, but such protection is assured only until the next legislature meets. Voluntary programs rely on the interest and goodwill of the landowner; involuntary programs place an uncompensated burden on him. In other words, all nonacquisition programs are at best only temporary.

Fee Simple Absolute

The traditional way to provide permanent protection to an archaeological site seems to be full "fee simple absolute" acquisition.[2] Fee simple absolute is a legal term that means the owner has acquired unconditional control of all interests in the property, and this is what most people consider to be ownership. If you own your own home, your deed will show you have a fee simple absolute interest. Such ownership has the advantage of giving the owner the right to permit or prohibit any and every activity on the land; it has the disadvantage of giving him the duty to do just that—to maintain the land in a manner consistent with its location; to protect it from fire, trespass, and vandalism; and to manage it in a way so that it does not become a nuisance to its neighbors.

Even if there were enough money to buy every archaeological site in Colorado—and there is not—there would not be enough money to take care of them. And money is not the only problem, either. Competing social and economic demands for natural resources prevent the dedication of every archaeological site in the country solely to the protection of its ancient treasures. Both the state and the nation need land for grazing, timber, and minerals as well as for cultural study of the past.

Recent experience in the San Juan Basin of Colorado and New Mexico has demonstrated that mineral exploration and development can be undertaken in a manner consistent with preservation of critical archaeological resources. The ruins of the Chaco culture are scattered over 50,000 square miles of Southwest geography—the same 50,000 square miles that contain one-sixth of the world's known uranium supply and one-fourth of our nation's near-surface coal reserves. A few of the most significant sites are protected by National Park Service ownership in the Chaco Culture National Historical Park, and a few others are under consideration for addition to this unit. But it is obvious that not every important archaeological resource in the San Juan Basin can be subjected to single-purpose management. Energy development will take place, and the energy companies already have been working closely with the public agencies in exploiting the minerals while protecting the archaeology.[3]

The major problem today is preserving archaeological resources in private ownership, and the basic question is how can multiple-use management concepts be permanently applied to private property? The simple answer—at least in Colorado—is by acquiring conservation easements.

The Conservation Easement Alternative

To say that conservation easement is a nonpossessory, partial interest in land is a legal way of saying that the owner of the easement has less than a fee simple absolute interest in the property and that possession is not one of his rights. The Colorado statute defines a conservation easement as: "a right in the owner of the easement to prohibit or require, a limitation upon, or an obligation to perform, acts on or with respect to a land or water area or air space above the land or water owned by the grantor appropriate to the retaining or maintaining of such land, water, or air space, including improvements, predominantly in a natural, scenic, or open condition, or for wildlife habitat, or for agricultural, horticultural, recreational, forest, or other use or condition consistent with the protection of open land hav-

ing wholesome environmental quality or life-sustaining ecological diversity, or appropriate to the conservation and preservation of buildings, sites, or structures having historical, architectural, or cultural interest or value."[4]

A conservation easement in gross is one that does not benefit any other property; a conservation easement appurtenant is one that does. A negative easement allows the owner of the easement to prevent the owner of the fee simple absolute from doing specified things on his property that he otherwise would have the right to do. An affirmative easement allows the owner of the easement to do specified things on the property that the owner of the fee simple absolute otherwise would have the right to prevent him from doing. There are a number of other refinements of the conservation easement concept, but knowledge of the complex legal details is not essential to an understanding of the potentially broad application of this tool to archaeological preservation. A detailed examination of the Colorado law may be found in an article I wrote soon after the statute was passed,[5] and a more scholarly study of conservation easement laws in general may be found in a later article written by the chairman of the American Bar Association's Committee on Historic Preservation and Easements.[6]

Conservation Easement Protection

A few specialists know conservation easements can be used to protect the facades of historic buildings, but probably the most commonly understood uses for conservation easements are open space preservation, natural area protection, and public outdoor recreation access. Easements have been described that preserve agricultural lands and provide for limited forms of public outdoor recreation use,[7] and a single property may be subject to more than one easement. A cattle ranch, for example, may be restricted by one conservation easement protecting its open space values, another providing public access for hunting, and still another providing public access for fishing.[8] Each of these easements of course could be owned by a different party, but each party must be qualified under Colorado law. The Colorado statute has some special limitations on conservation easement ownership.[9]

The first step in developing a conservation easement for an archaeological site is to determine whether the site itself qualifies under Colorado law. The statute provides: "Conservation easements relating to historical, architectural, or cultural significance may only be applied to buildings, sites, or structures when the state historical society of Colorado certifies that such a building, site, or structure is listed in the national register of historic places or the state register of historic properties or has been designated as a landmark by a local government or landmarks commission under the provisions of the ordinances of the locality involved."[10]

If the site does not qualify, steps should be initiated to

meet the requirements. Even if the site cannot meet the requirements of this provision, however, it still may receive substantial protection from a conservation easement. Another easement for another purpose may prohibit the very activities that would destroy the cultural resources. Archaeologists should work closely with other disciplines on any easement on any property containing archaeological resources to assure that cultural protection is an element of the restrictions.

Conservation easements for archaeological purposes most likely will be patterned after open space easements. The basic things that threaten open space, such as subdivision, alteration of the surface topography, and intensive commercial development, also tend to threaten archaeological resources.

When considering whether a conservation easement can provide adequate protection for a particular site, the professional archaeologist first needs to decide whether current uses constitute a threat. If they do, it is unlikely a conservation easement will work because the landowner probably will be unwilling to change his ways merely to accommodate cultural resource-protection needs. The most probable choice will be to purchase a fee simple absolute interest in the site, or forget about the whole thing.

But if the current uses do not constitute a threat, the professional archaeologist next needs to decide what would be the potential uses of the site. For each such use an attorney will need to draft a clause prohibiting it. Of course, if the property is already subject to a conservation easement, he will need to review that easement first to determine whether the restrictions already in place are adequate. Only if they are not will he need to draft additional restrictions.

A very important point to keep in mind here is that not all prohibitions need to be absolute. The mineral development in the San Juan Basin is an excellent example of how exploitation of natural resources can be undertaken in a manner consistent with preservation of cultural resources. Although conservation easements were not involved in this effort, conservation easements could have been drafted to impose the same limitations on development activities on cultural sites as were actually implemented by the companies. Other examples of activities that may be acceptable with appropriate limitations are subdivision, if critical sites are kept intact and excluded from development, and farming. If plowing is restricted to a shallow zone on the surface, erosion is not a problem and the cultural component is buried. In other words, each restriction and each conservation easement must be custom-tailored to meet the needs of the resource and the needs of the landowner.

Once the easement has been drafted, the next step will be to obtain an appraisal. If plans call for purchase of the easement, the potential purchaser should pay for it. If plans call for a donation, for tax reasons the potential donor should pay for it.

The final step, of course, is the conveyance. If the conservation easement is being purchased, money will change hands. If it is not—if it is being donated—the donee's money can be used for other purposes. Since there is never enough money for archaeology, archaeologists should *always* ask for a gift.

The Qualified Conservation Contribution

There are many reasons a landowner may be willing to make a gift of a conservation easement. He may take special pride in the cultural resource; he may feel he is making a unique contribution to man's knowledge; or he may want his property recognized as a valuable link with man's past. No matter what his other reasons are for making a gift, however, he will always be interested in the federal income tax benefits for charitable contributions.

Charitable contributions of conservation easements have been recognized as deductible under the Internal Revenue Code for nearly twenty years. The early Code provisions were relatively broad, but recently Congress has been making these provisions increasingly narrow and more explicit. The most recent amendment is the Tax Treatment Extention Act of 1980.[11] It replaces all prior law on the subject and introduces the new statutory concept of the qualified conservation contribution.

Although the new provision is quite complex and the regulations have not been issued yet, for the purposes of this article it is only necessary to know that a qualified conservation contribution includes gifts of conservation easements to protect historically important land areas, properties individually listed in the National Register of Historic Places, and properties located in registered historic districts that are certified by the Secretary of the Interior as being of historic significance to their districts. Remember that the provisions of the Colorado statute and the federal income tax law are somewhat different, and it would be possible for a conservation easement to meet the requirements of one law without meeting the requirements of the other. It is therefore essential that an attorney be retained to assure that all legal requirements of both are met.

A full discussion of the application of the federal income tax law to charitable contributions of archaeological resources may be found in my article "Easements and Artifacts: An Archaeological Investigation of the Internal Revenue Code."[12]

Conclusion

Conservation easements are a potentially powerful tool to protect archaeological sites in Colorado. As an alternative to fee simple absolute, conservation easements offer an opportunity to acquire some of the benefits of complete ownership without acquiring some of the burdens. A bull in a pasture protected by a conservation easement will do

130   PART III: CONSERVATION TRANSACTIONS

far more to discourage pothunters than the strongest fence around a vacant field protected by a fee simple absolute interest. The discerning Colorado archaeologist will select the protection tool most appropriate for the particular site and will work closely with other disciplines to assure that cultural protection is given consideration in the development of every conservation easement granted in this state. The archaeologist will also have enough knowledge of the federal income tax law to be able to encourage every grantor to also be a donor to the field of archaeology.

Notes

1. Gyrisco, Geoffrey M., "Legal Tools to Preserve Archaeological Sites," Heritage Conservation and Recreation Service, *11593 Special Issue* (Fall 1980).

2. Barnes, Mark R., "Preservation of Archaeological Sites Through Acquisition," *American Antiquity* 46 (1981): 610–618.

3. Kaplan, Howard M., "Can We Save This Mystery?" *Empire* (supplement to the *Sunday Denver Post*) 32(43) (1981): 12–25.

4. Colo. Rev. Stat. §38-30.5-102 (1973).

5. Tiedt, Glenn F., "Conservation Easements in Colorado," *Colorado Lawyer* 5 (1976): 1265–1272.

6. Netherton, Ross D., "Environmental Conservation and Historic Preservation Through Recorded Land-Use Agreements," *Real Property, Probate and Trust Journal* 14(3) (1979): 540–580.

7. Arnolds, David and Woods, Lucius, "The Conservation Easement," *Colorado Outdoors* 27(6) (1979): 18–22.

8. *Ibid.*, p. 20.

9. Colo. Rev. Stat. §38-30.5-104[2] (1973).

10. Colo. Rev. Stat. §38-30.5-104[4] (1973).

11. Tax Treatment Extension Act of 1980, Pub. L. No. 96-541, 94 Stat. 3204 (1980).

12. Tiedt, Glenn F., "Easements and Artifacts: An Archaeological Investigation of the Internal Revenue Code," *American Antiquity* 47(2) (1982): 376–381.

Private Purchase and Limited Development as a Means of Achieving Land Conservation Goals

Richard W. Carbin

The Problems

Problem 1
A private boarding school faces bankruptcy. To pay its debts the school's trustees decide to sell its 330-acre campus located on a former dairy farm on the outskirts of a historic hamlet. Asking price: $1,200,000. Community residents fear loss of scenic open space and productive farmland to development.

Problem 2
An owner of a small ski resort in a remote area of a rural town has permits to build 115 homes on 700 acres of land. Rather than develop the property himself, he puts it up for sale, marketing it on the premise that all permits are in hand. Asking price: $1,850,000. An out-of-state developer is negotiating a purchase. Neighbors want to limit development.

Problem 3
An owner of a 1,700-acre farm located in a rapidly growing region needs to retire his debts within a year or lose the property to the banks. The land has been owned by the same family since the 1880s. Stewardship of the farm has characterized this ownership. The current owner wants to find a way to meet his debts without opening up the farmland to development. The farm's estimated value is $3,000,000.

Each of these problems describes a real situation. The Ottauquechee Regional Land Trust (ORLT) resolved them through a combination of private purchase and limited development. In the process almost 2,500 acres of farm- and forestland have been conserved. A detailed discussion of each of these cases reveals the potential range and effectiveness of this approach in achieving land conservation goals.

Problem 1: The Woodstock Country School Project

In the spring of 1980 the trustees of the Woodstock Country School, a private secondary boarding school, in order to avoid bankruptcy, decided to close the school and sell its property. The 330-acre campus was located on a former dairy farm just outside the historic hamlet of South Woodstock, Vermont. The landscape had changed little since its prosperous agricultural days. Residents of South Woodstock became concerned that a sale of the school could lead to drastic changes in their community. They approached the ORLT for advice.

The ORLT suggested that through effective land-use planning, it should be possible to find a way to meet the school's financial needs while protecting the open space on the property. To accomplish this, however, would take time, and the Country School could not afford to take the property off the market while such work was going on. In order to deal with this situation, the ORLT negotiated a right of first refusal with the Woodstock Country School. This agreement would at least provide some ability to respond if a purchaser came along before the planning process was completed.

In July 1980, almost immediately after the signing of the right of first refusal, two potential purchasers came forward. One was a developer; the other was an owner of adjacent property in South Woodstock who was concerned about the future of the school's property.

The ORLT discussed plans for the school campus with

both possible buyers. It was impossible to get a handle on the developer's objective, except that the maximum permissible amount of development would occur if he gained control of the property. The neighbor was interested in reestablishing a working farm on the land, hoping to reduce the cost of purchase by reselling the school's buildings and some land not essential to the agricultural activities.

Finally, however, the developer made an offer beyond the reach of the neighbor to purchase the campus. The Country School, desperate to meet its financial obligations, had to accept. The agreed-to sales price was $1,065,000. In accordance with its right of first refusal, the ORLT had thirty days to match the developer's purchase price or forego the opportunity to protect the property. The ORLT board, in response to broad community concern, decided to try to find a way to buy the school.

It was clear that in order to exercise the right of first refusal within the thirty-day period, it would not be possible to raise the necessary funds through contributions. Instead, the ORLT proposed to the South Woodstock community to borrow the money with their backing. At this time a business partnership offered to purchase the main school buildings for use as office space if the ORLT became owner. This reduced the financing needed to approximately $600,000. This amount was broken down into $6,000 units. Residents of South Woodstock were asked to sign up with their credit or cash contributions for one or more units. Over fifty individuals and several community organizations committed themselves to the project, representing an entire cross section of the community. A master agreement between the ORLT and its credit backers was developed, detailing the arrangement and what would occur if the full purchase price of the property could not be recovered through resale after careful planning. In such an event the credit put up by the community would have been converted to cash contributions in the amount needed to cover all costs and in proportion to the amount of credit committed by each individual backer.

With the master agreement in hand, along with financial statements from each supporter and a comprehensive analysis of the property's worth, the ORLT approached the three local banks. A loan for the amount needed to purchase the school was arranged. With only a few days to spare the ORLT exercised its right of first refusal on August 11, 1980. Closing on the property took place in early October. A month after the closing, with zoning approvals received, the ORLT sold the main school buildings to the business partnership, enabling planning efforts to be concentrated on the remaining 315 acres.

As part of the master agreement between the ORLT and the South Woodstock community, a formal planning process was established. Ballots were distributed to residents of South Woodstock, who elected three people to a planning committee. The committee was rounded out with the ORLT executive director as chairman, an ORLT board member, and a representative from the town and regional planning commissions. Technical assistance was provided to the committee by ORLT staff, the regional planning commission, the county agricultural agent, the county forester, and a consulting architect and engineer. Minutes of the planning committee's meetings were distributed to the South Woodstock community so that the process would be as open as possible.

The planning committee quickly came to agreement over its goals. The planning process should endeavor to conserve the productive agricultural and forestry resources on the property, to make the best use of existing buildings (there were several buildings on the property: former residences for the Country School faculty, a fine historic building that once was the main house of the farm, and two dormitory buildings), and to allow for some limited development if this were necessary to meet financial obligations.

The technical team then went to work on an extensive land-use and facility analysis. The land-use study looked at soils, slopes, development potential, and potential of the land to support agricultural and forestry activities. The existing buildings were studied for possible adaptive uses. Costs related to each of these aspects were also analyzed.

As a result of this effort, the planning committee was able, in mid-December 1980, to make a series of recommendations with regard to the ultimate use of the Country School property. At an opening meeting in South Woodstock, these recommendations were presented. It would be possible, the committee felt, to resell the property to cover all costs and guarantee the protection of open space. The former faculty residences could be sold as single-family houses. One of the dormitories could be easily converted into four housing units (the committee recommended tearing down the other dormitory). The agricultural and forestry analysis showed that it would be economically possible to reestablish a working farm on most of the land and that, finally, the remaining land could reasonably be developed into a maximum of twelve house sites. The community supported the committee's recommendations.

With this support the committee went to the adjacent landowner who had initially expressed interest in purchasing the property. Learning how he could end up with the farmland at a reasonable cost through a combination of sale of existing buildings, limited development, and a tax-deductible gift back to the ORLT of conservation restrictions on the open land, the landowner agreed to purchase the property at the ORLT's costs. The sale took place on December 31, 1980. Shortly thereafter the new owner donated conservation restrictions to the ORLT, protecting 217 acres from development. A working farm is now operating on this open land.

Problem 2: The Sonnenberg Project

In the early 1970s the owner of the Sonnenberg Ski Resort in East Barnard, Vermont, revealed plans to develop 700 acres of farm- and forestland adjacent to the ski area. Initial plans called for the development of nearly 200 housing units. After lengthy and often controversial discussions in the local planning commission, approval was finally granted to allow the development of 115 house sites on lots ranging in size from 2 acres to 30 acres. State approvals through Vermont's environmental review process were also granted, despite objections from the regional planning commission that the development was not in conformance with the lower density requirements called for in the duly adopted regional land-use plan.

Several years went by and no development occurred. Neighbors in the area began to feel that it never would happen. In early 1981, however, the owner of the ski area decided to sell the property, appealing to potential buyers on the basis that all development permits were in hand. A number of East Barnard residents, upon hearing that an out-of-state developer was negotiating a purchase of the property, became alarmed and began looking for ways to limit development of the land. A public meeting was held with the ORLT to explore any alternatives available to the community to accomplish this.

Since neither the landowner nor the developer was willing to limit potential development voluntarily and since all public regulatory approvals had been received, there was little that could be done except to compete with the developer and try to buy the land. The ORLT contacted the owner. Although negotiations with the developer were ongoing, no final agreement had been reached. If the community was interested in trying to meet the sale terms, the owner said, the opportunity was still there for an alternative purchaser to step forward. It all depended on who was willing to place a deposit on the property. The owner indicated that further negotiation of the details of any sale was still possible after the deposit was made. The owner sent a telegram to both the interested developer and members of the East Barnard community stating his position. Twenty-four hours later six individuals from East Barnard borrowed the necessary funds to place a $25,000 deposit on the property.

To conclude an acceptable purchase and sales agreement for both the owner of the Sonnenberg property and the community participants, two major activities had to take place simultaneously: extensive negotiations over the terms of purchase and a workable land-use and financial plan for the supporters of the purchase.

The initial asking price for the property was $1,850,000. That included not only all of the undeveloped land surrounding the ski area, but the ski area and other resort amenities as well. The East Barnard residents were not really interested in taking over the operation of a ski resort. Their primary concern was to limit the amount of future development of the open space. If the ski area itself could be eliminated as part of the sale, the cost of a purchase of the open land could be considerably reduced. Also, the previous owners of the property held second mortgages on

the property with low interest rates. If any new purchaser could assume those mortgages and possibly arrange attractive financing with the owner himself, the cost of purchase would become more reasonable. Elimination of the ski area as part of the purchase and creative financing became the two principal issues in the negotiations.

Meanwhile, a workable land-use and financial plan had to be developed for the community purchase. In discussions with the East Barnard residents it became apparent that it would not be possible to raise any substantial amounts through cash contributions. However, as in the Woodstock Country School project, the borrowing capacity among enough concerned people did exist. A number of residents were prepared to borrow funds, but not without reasonable assurance that they would not lose money in the end.

The ORLT therefore undertook an extensive land-use study and analyzed financial alternatives. The results of this effort showed that a combination of tax-deductible gifts of conservation restrictions on the productive farm- and forestland linked with limited development of no more than forty house sites would more than cover a purchase of the open land at a cost of $1,500,000, assuming that the ski area was excluded from the package and that favorable financing could be achieved.

At this point two residents of East Barnard, having reviewed the ORLT plans and recommendations, indicated that if negotiations with the owner of Sonnenberg changed the assumptions of the plan into reality, they would be willing to purchase the property and implement the plan. This occurred in October 1981. The two East Barnard residents purchased the open land and are currently moving forward with the plan.

Problem 3: The Shelburne Farms Project

Shelburne Farms is one of the most unique properties in Vermont. Located in the heart of the state's fastest-growing region, the greater Burlington area, along the shores of Lake Champlain, it represents a resource under tremendous pressure.

The farm was established in 1886 by William Seward Webb and Lila Vanderbilt Webb. The original 3,800-acre estate demonstrated the state-of-the-art in agricultural technology, with landscaping done by Frederick Law Olmstead and a forest planned by Gifford Pinchot. The property was divided early in this century. The current owner, Derick Webb, inherited the remaining 1,700 acres in the 1940s. Stewardship of the land has continued to be the predominate characteristic of the Webb family's ownership. Ten years ago, for example, Shelburne Farms Resources (SFR) was established as a nonprofit corporation. Using the farm as its base, SFR is trying to create a model community of successful small businesses using Vermont-grown produce. Also, it carries on a wide variety of educational and cultural activities. In 1976 Derick Webb conveyed the three principal nineteenth-century buildings on the property—the Queen Anne–style farm barn, Shelburne House, and the coach barn—to SFR.

In 1981 Derick Webb decided that he wanted to retire the existing mortgage on the property and to make long-range plans for the preservation of Shelburne Farms after his ownership. After consulting with The Nature Conservancy, the American Farmland Trust, and the Ottauquechee Regional Land Trust, he decided to sell 600 acres that were on the periphery of the property and not essential to the farming operation. Because this land is adjacent to the farm and therefore highly visible, he asked the Ottauquechee Trust to help find a buyer whose plans for the property would be consistent with the setting of Shelburne Farms.

The ORLT conducted an extensive search for such a buyer, interviewing more than sixty individuals who expressed interest. After a hectic three months, an agreement was signed with five partners in December 1981 and closed in March 1982. The buyers plan to construct a limited number of year-round and vacation dwellings on part of the property and to convey permanent conservation restrictions to the Ottauquechee Trust on most of the remaining land. The restricted land can then be resold for agricultural use to one or more farmers, who could not otherwise afford Shelburne farmland.

Future tax savings from the charitable gift of conservation restrictions and the sale of land for agriculture and limited development allowed the buyers to pay a higher initial price for the 600 acres than a conventional developer could justify. This, in turn, has given Shelburne Farms more capital with which to continue its operations.

A new corporation, Shelburne Farms, Inc., owns the remaining 1,100 acres, buildings, cattle, and farm equipment. Over the next seven years, Derick Webb plans to transfer the stock in this corporation to the Ottauquechee Trust. The first gift of stock, valued at $300,000, took place in October 1982. Shelburne Farms Resources will have access to the property to continue its educational and cultural programs through a long-term lease agreement.

Many issues must still be resolved. The farm will need additional operating capital as it expands and improves its agricultural operations. SFR is planning an extensive fundraising campaign to carry out needed renovations to the buildings and establish a permanent endowment fund for its programs. Also, because of federal tax laws, it will be many years before both Derick Webb and the buyers can fully implement their plans.

Despite these uncertainties, the prospects for Shelburne Farms look brighter than they did a short time ago. Through imaginative use of land-planning concepts and income and estate tax planning, the Ottauquechee Trust helped find a solution that meets the needs of the seller, the objectives of the buyers, and the concerns of the public.

As a result of these three experiences, the ORLT is convinced that land conservation efforts can be effectively achieved through the use of private purchase and limited development techniques. The situations described do not in any way exhaust the possibilities. The variations that can come into play are literally endless.

There is a need for caution, however. Land conservation needs are so great that it would be easy to overburden an organization. The ORLT, for example, asks itself the following questions before deciding to become involved in a purchase and development project:

1. Would protection of the land be consistent with community goals as expressed in local and regional plans or other expressions of public policy?

2. Is there general community support (not necessarily financial) in having the land protected?

3. Is the land under imminent threat of sale or development?

4. Is the landowner unable or unwilling to protect the land voluntarily through donation of the property or donation of conservation restrictions?

5. Is the landowner willing to negotiate a sale to a conservation organization?

6. Is the price asked for the land a realistic one?

7. Is there a financially feasible way to purchase the property and cover all costs?

8. Could some of the land be reasonably developed without disrupting the land that should be protected?

9. Is the technical ability available to conduct the necessary planning for the use of the property?

10. Will taking on the project guarantee the permanent protection of the important natural resources of the property?

Although it is not necessary to answer all of these questions affirmatively, any "no" answers should serve as a signal to search for compensating factors before attempting a direct purchase of land. Unfortunately, time and space do not permit a detailed discussion of each of these points. However, within such a framework, after being thoughtfully considered, private purchase and limited development can enhance any land conservation organization's ability to achieve its goals. It can be done.

A Summary of Forms and Tax Consequences of Land Acquisition by a Charity

Russell K. Osgood
and Roger E. Koontz

This article describes property interests that a charity may acquire and discusses the consequences of each kind of transfer for both a charitable donee and the landowner. The protection of a parcel of land can be accomplished in a variety of ways. The charity and the owner will view the transaction from different perspectives, but their interests coincide on the most important point—they both wish to protect the land. In determining the best method to do so, the key is to define as precisely as possible the needs and wishes of the parties.

Several factors should be considered:

The land. Is it worthy of being protected? If so, what degree of protection is needed? Should it be protected indefinitely or for a limited term?

Stewardship. What are the management responsibilities and costs? Must the land be protected from trespassers? What insurance is needed?

The owner. Does he wish to continue to own or occupy the land? For how long? What financial return does he expect?

Taxes. What are the estate, income, gift, and property tax consequences of various transfer options for the donor and his family?

The charity. What resources does the charity have to manage or monitor the land? What resources does the charity have for acquisition? How does this land relate to the charity's priorities? Is the gift so large that the charity's federal tax status may be affected?

Public ownership. Is public ownership feasible? Are there advantages to public ownership, such as the availability of funds for acquisition and maintenance? What are the disadvantages?

Transaction costs. What costs for appraisal, title search, and closing are involved? Who will pay them?

1. Gifts without restrictions

The gifts described in this section are unrestricted in the sense that all property interests are transferred. The first two subsections deal with transfers made during the landowner's lifetime. Transfers by will, or devises, are discussed in the third subsection.

a. *Land to be preserved*

People give land to a charity for two primary reasons: because they want it protected or because they wish to receive some other benefit. Often both motives are present.

i. *Preservation.* The donor may wonder about the security and permanence of preserving land under the charity's ownership. The principal security is in the nature of the organization, which is specifically designed to provide protection. The law requires all charitable assets to be devoted to the charitable purposes for which the charity was formed.

Thus, although land donated to a charity without restrictions may be sold, the law and public relations pressures generally limit sales to situations where circumstances have changed dramatically.[1] A donor who feels strongly about forever preserving his parcel of land may give the parcel subject to a restriction, or a reverter, to be enforced by another charitable organization. However, since a fee simple gift[2] gives the charity more flexibility, the charity should try to convince the donor that unencumbered transfer is preferable.

ii. *Tax advantages.* The financial advantages to the donor come from various kinds of tax benefits, including

135

relief from property tax; avoidance of capital gains, conveyance, estate, and gift taxes; and the ability to take appropriate income tax deductions. When providing information about these benefits, a charity's representatives should emphasize that a charity cannot guarantee any particular tax result and that donors should consult their own attorneys or accountants.

(1) *Property taxes.* When the land has been transferred to a charity, the donor is no longer subject to the corresponding property taxes.

(2) *Taxes on transfer of property.* The donor avoids capital gains,[3] conveyance,[4] and transfer taxes, which would be imposed if he sold the property. A gift to a qualifying charity is subject to neither the federal gift tax nor the state transfer tax.[5] The donation of land will reduce the assets subject to death taxes when the donor dies.

(3) *Income tax deduction.*[6] The donor is entitled to a charitable contribution deduction in computing his income for federal tax purposes. The value of a parcel of land for the purposes of a charitable deduction is based on its fair market value, as determined by an appraiser.

A donor who has owned the land for at least one year may deduct up to 30 percent of the value of the gift from his or her adjusted gross income. Any undeducted balance is carried forward and may be deducted in each of the five succeeding years after the year of donation.[7] Alternatively, the donor may elect to reduce the total deduction by 40 percent of the amount that would have been long-term capital gain, and take a deduction of up to 50 percent of adjusted gross income with any residue being carried forward for five years.[8]

The gift of a piece of land may convert a nonliquid, nonincome-producing, and possibly burdensome asset—land—into cash, in the form of saved taxes, for other investment. This can be a great benefit to a high-bracket taxpayer.

Example: A donor with an annual income of $100,000, in the 50 percent tax bracket, gives land purchased for $80,000 and now worth $120,000. The donor may deduct $30,000 (30 percent of $100,000) each year for four years, eventually deducting $120,000. Or the donor may reduce the value of his or her contribution by $16,000 (40 percent of $40,000) and deduct $50,000 per year for the first two years and $4,000 in the third year, for a total deduction of $104,000 ($120,000 less $16,000).[9] Thus, the total tax savings or cash generated by this transaction is either $60,000 (50 percent of $120,000) spread over four years or $52,000 (50 percent of $104,000) spread over three years.

iii. *Impact on the charity.* In most instances a fee simple gift is the best kind of acquisition for a charity. However, there are two major potential drawbacks:

(1) If the charity is not financially and organizationally equipped to assume the stewardship responsibilities for the land, it should consider the other forms of acquisition discussed below or methods of raising the necessary funds to manage the property.

(2) If the charity is classified for tax purposes as a public charity, the gift might be so large that acceptance would endanger that status.

b. **Asset land**

"Asset land," or "trade land," is property given to a charity to sell, with the receipts used for charitable purposes, or to exchange for parcels that the charity wishes to preserve. In accepting such property, the charity should make clear to the donor and the community that it is an "asset" to be sold.

i. *Impact on donor.* The donor will receive all of the tax advantages that a donor of land for preservation would receive as discussed above. For developed land, the capital gains savings may be greater because of increased appreciation. The savings on real estate taxes may also be higher, but if the charity intends to sell the developed land and not use it for its charitable purposes, it may not qualify for abatements of real estate taxes. By donating appreciated property such as land, the donor will be able to make a larger contribution than if he sold the property, paid the appropriate taxes, and contributed the balance.

Example: A donor with an annual income of $100,000, who is in the 50 percent bracket, gives land purchased for $12,000 and now worth $60,000. Selling the property would mean the donor would be taxed on the capital gain of $48,000 ($60,000 less $12,000). If he contributed the balance, the charity would receive only $50,400, instead of $60,000, and the donor's savings from income tax deductions would be reduced by $4,800. The two transactions may be compared as follows:

	Sale of property and contribution of cash	Contribution of property
Sale price	$60,000	
Less capital gains tax[10] (20 percent of $48,000)	9,600	0
Net contribution	$50,400	$60,000
Income tax savings (50 percent of contribution)	$25,200	$30,000

This example excludes closing costs and real estate sales commissions, which would further reduce the donor's contribution and tax savings if the property were sold rather than given to the charity.

ii. *Impact on the charity.* A gift of asset land should be similar to a gift of securities that the charity can convert to cash to provide necessary funding. The marketability of the parcel should be closely examined: the land is not a real asset if it cannot be sold. Maintenance responsibilities should be considered, particularly if there are buildings or special hazards, but these possible difficulties can be avoided if a resale sale is arranged before the land is accepted. Maintenance responsibilities can be shifted by renting the property while the charity locates a buyer, but again it is pointed out that this will probably mean that the charity will not qualify for real estate tax abatements in the interim.

c. *Devises*

Devises are gifts of land made in the will of a property owner.[11]

i. *Impact on donor.* A donor who chooses to make a gift through his will has the benefits and burdens of ownership while he remains alive. The landowner controls the property but must pay property taxes and gets no income tax deduction. The donor also runs the risk that the charity may refuse the gift because of changed circumstances at the time of his death. A conditional devise, which designates alternate recipients if the first choice declines the gift, is a sensible protection against this contingency.

The value of land donated to qualified charitable organizations is not subject to either the federal estate tax or state transfer taxes.[12] The reduction in the taxable estate can be useful if the estate would otherwise have to sell property in order to pay the taxes. Giving a parcel to a charitable organization may accomplish the same purpose by taking it out of the taxable estate.

ii. *Impact on the charity.* A charity will rarely prefer a devise to a gift made during the donor's lifetime. In the former case the date of acquisition is uncertain, the charity has no control over the land while the donor is alive, and the donor may change his will at any time. The will may contain unusual restrictions that the charity must accept if it wishes to acquire the property. Both parties usually prefer a gift, with or without a life estate, made while the donor is living to a devise. If a donor wishes to devise property for preservation or otherwise, the charity should be permitted to review the terms of the devise at the time the will is drafted.

2. Purchases without restrictions

All the procedures discussed in this section involve the acquisition of land without any restrictions on its use or disposition. Except for the first subsection, all of the methods are compromises with a seller interested in land preservation, or devices for minimizing the charity's costs.

a. *Purchase at fair market value*

The fact that a charity is the purchaser in a sale of property at fair market value does not affect the tax consequences for the seller, who must pay capital gains taxes

and who receives no charitable deduction. The problem is that most charities are unable or unwilling to pay full price for land.

b. *Bargain sale*

This is a sale at less than fair market value. The difference between the sale price and the fair market value may be treated by the seller as a charitable contribution. The fact that the sale is a bargain sale should be explicitly stated in the sales contract, and the seller should have the land appraised by a qualified professional before the sale.

i. *Impact on seller.* The major advantage to the seller, aside from the protection of the land, is the combination of tax savings and return of capital invested. In addition to the charitable deduction, the seller's capital gains tax is reduced. Although appreciation in value of the property may still be taxable, some of the capital gain will be assigned to the gift portion of the conveyance.

The following example shows how this works. Assume that the fair market value of the land is $100,000 and that its adjusted basis is $56,000.[13] Thus the owner's potential capital gain is $44,000 if the land is sold at fair market value. Assume also that the seller is in the 50 percent tax bracket, which means that capital gains are taxed at 20 percent and that charitable deductions are worth 50 percent of the value of gifts.

(1) Seller's net at fair market value: $91,200.

Purchase price	$100,000
Less capital gains tax (20 percent of $44,000)	8,800
	$ 91,200

(2) Seller's net from bargain sale at $60,000: $74,720.

Purchase price	$ 60,000
Plus value of charitable deduction	20,000
	$ 80,000
Less capital gains tax (20 percent of $26,400,* the capital gains on the bargain sale)	5,280
	$ 74,720

*Capital gains on the bargain sale is figured: $60,000 minus $33,600 (60% of $56,000) = $26,400. Amount realized less pro rata share of basis = gain.

In this example a gift worth $40,000 costs the donor $16,480 ($91,200 less $74,720) in foregone cash. The sale at fair market value would probably include a real estate commission, which would shrink the difference. Thus a bargain sale is a compromise arrangement where a potential donor is able to make a gift, reduce income taxes, eliminate his property taxes, and still receive the minimal financial return he feels is essential.

c. *Sale-resale or sale-leaseback*

These are procedures whereby a charity buys an unrestricted parcel, places a restriction on it, then resells it or leases it. The commonest type of restriction in this sort of transaction is a conservation easement restricting development, although various other kinds of easements can also be applied. One possible use of this device is for the protection of a stretch of road or shoreline. A charity can buy a parcel, put on a conservation restriction, resell the land, and use the money from the resale as part of the purchase price for another parcel. Of course, the greater the decrease in the market value of the property due to the restriction, the lower the amount of proceeds upon a resale.

i. *Impact on seller.* The original seller is not likely to repurchase land bought for this purpose, since the same preservation result could be achieved if the seller himself put the conservation restriction on the land. However, the seller will receive a tax deduction and avoid capital gains tax from the sale if he restricts it himself.

ii. *Impact on new owner or lessee.* A new owner pays a lower price, since the restriction will decrease the market value of the land, without disadvantage if his intended use is consistent with the restrictions. The new owner will be subject to property taxes, though often at a lower assessment. A lessee would have to pay the fair market value rent, which may not be affected by the transaction.

iii. *Impact on the charity.* To effect a purchase-resale or purchase-leaseback, the charity must, of course, have sufficient funds. If a new owner or lessee can be found before the charity buys the land, purchase money can be borrowed or allocated more readily. Even so, the resale price will almost certainly be lower than the purchase price, so the charity pays for the restriction. The potential tax problems with leased land are discussed below.

These forms of land transfer are not particularly attractive because of the capital requirement and administrative expenses involved. In most situations a charity should encourage the seller to use instead one of the kinds of restricted transfers discussed below.

d. *Installment purchase*

There are three kinds of installment purchase: (1) buying the parcel outright and paying for it over a period of years; (2) buying the parcel in sections; and (3) buying fractionalized interests in the entire property.

In most instances, unless the charity is uncertain about future income or considers one part of the land more valuable than the rest, the first option is preferable. The transaction is complete. The seller cannot renege, and should he die, the remaining payments will be made to his estate or heirs. The parcel remains unified, whereas under the other options its management and control must be shared by the charity and the landowner or his estate or heirs.

Buying property in sections is useful when the preservation value of one part of a parcel exceeds that of the rest and the charity can purchase the more important part first. Buying undivided portions in the whole property may be useful if the charity's funding is uncertain and if the land is an ecological unity. However, the purchase of a conservation restriction might be a better alternative in this case since problems of use, responsibility, and management would be avoided.

If parts of, or interests in, a parcel are bought in installments, the charity should attempt to convince the donor to leave any untransferred interest to the charity in his will. If the charity is making installment payments, the donor could consider forgiving the debt in his will.

i. *Impact on seller.* Installment sales allow the seller to spread capital gains over more than one year, while still receiving full value for the property.[14] Any portion of the sale price may be received in any year, so the seller can, for example, split the capital gains between two years by receiving half of the price in December and half in January. The use of a mortgage back to the seller, or other security for payment, does not prevent the seller from having a qualifying installment sale.

The drawbacks are minor. The seller postpones receipt of some money and will continue to pay property taxes on untransferred portions of the land unless the charity undertakes to assume that obligation. (No property taxes would be due under the first option if the property itself is wholly transferred at the time of the sale and is used for charitable purposes.)

ii. *Impact on the charity.* Installment purchases are advantageous for a charity with modest but steady sources of income. The benefits depend on the terms of the contract with the seller.

e. *Strategic buying*

If a large area of significant land or wetland is threatened with development and the charity cannot afford to buy the whole parcel, it may be able to buy a strategically placed piece or pieces of the parcel.

i. *Impact on seller.* This technique presumes a conservation-motivated seller, since if the location of the charity's acquisition is strategic enough to benefit the charity, it will be particularly valuable.

ii. *Impact on the charity.* This device can maximize the use of scarce funds. However, it may cause a negative public reaction if the proposed development is regarded as socially desirable.

f. *Options to purchase*

If a charity is willing to buy a particular parcel but does not have the necessary funds, it may acquire an option to purchase it. This is an agreement granting the charity the exclusive right to buy the parcel at a specified price within a specified time limit. An alternative arrangement called a "right of first refusal" provides that before the landowner may sell the property to a third party, the charity has the right to buy the parcel at the offered price. In either case the landowner usually is paid something for limiting his freedom to sell. An option or first refusal agreement contract should be recorded with other land records and deeds.

3. Transfers of restricted interests in land

Ownership of property constitutes many separate rights and responsibilities. This section discusses ways in which some of these interests may be transferred to a charity. For our purposes the most important of these methods of transferring restricted interests are a reserved life estate and a conservation easement. A third device, the reverter, may be effective for ensuring that specified conditions are met—usually, according to state law, for only a limited period, such as fifty years. The remaining methods are either less common or less effective, but they may prove useful in particular situations. Where the transfers discussed in this section are by gift, the general discussion of charitable contribution deductions above is also applicable.

a. *Reserved life estates and remainders*

A donor may give or sell land to a charity, reserving a lifetime right to use the property.[15] The donor's interest in the property is called a reserved life estate and the charity's interest is called a remainder.

The remainder must be irrevocably given to a qualified charity in order for the donor to deduct its value for federal tax purposes.[16] The gift of a remainder to a charity is deductible only if the property is a residence or farm.[17] A residence must be a personal residence, but it does not have to be the primary residence; vacation homes are eligible.[18] A farm does not have to be lived on, but it must be farmed by the owner or his or her tenant.

i. *Impact on donor.* The major advantage of a reserved life estate for the donor is that he may continue to enjoy the property while obtaining many of the tax advantages of the donation. The donor receives a charitable deduction for the value of the land minus the value of the life estate (determined under Treasury Department actuarial tables) and minus depreciation or depletion.[19] As long as the land passes to the trust at the donor's death, it will not be subject to estate tax.

During the donor's lifetime, he is subject to restrictions against "waste" (failure to maintain the property in good condition).[20] In most cases the donor will wish to restrict or forbid public access to and use of the land during his lifetime, but he should permit inspections of the land. The donor usually must continue to pay the real estate taxes on the property.[21]

ii. *Impact on the charity.* The reserved life estate is an attractive alternative to the devise since it gives the charity a more secure hold on the land. Wills can be changed or may be lost.

A major disadvantage of gifts of remainder interests, that the charity has little present control over the land, is not a serious one particularly if there is a clear understanding on stewardship. Even without a specific provision, a charity may sue the donor for waste in a formal

court action. However, an owner who wants the land protected by a charity is not likely to be negligent.

b. *Conservation restrictions (easements)*

A conservation restriction limits what an owner can do with his property, and/or enables others to use it for specific purposes. State law defines such restrictions. For instance, in Connecticut a conservation restriction is any limitation on property ownership for conservation purposes "in the form of a restriction, easement, covenant, or condition."[22] The owner can still use the land and can sell it. However, if the land is sold, it remains subject to the restriction.

Conservation easements are more flexible than other forms of conservation dedication. They may be drafted to conform to almost any situation, such as: restriction against development; restriction against cutting down trees; restriction against altering land within a certain distance of a stream, coast, or road; restriction against putting up a structure that would block a view; granting a right-of-way to allow access to other property; granting a right-of-way for hikers or horseback riders; granting access to a beach or a stream; granting access for education or scientific study.

In most instances the monetary value of the restriction is equal to the reduction in the value of the donor's land. In traditional property law, if an easement was for the benefit of an adjacent piece of land (such as allowing access to that land), the value was the difference in the value of the benefited land with and without the easement. However, in the case of conservation easements there often is no benefited land. Thus the value of the restricted property before and after the restriction is the standard for measuring the value of the federal charitable contribution deduction that arises as a result of a qualifying restriction.[23]

Valuation is difficult. There are no set formulae. Highly developable land may lose as much as 90 percent of its value as a result of an antidevelopment restriction. In other cases the difference may be negligible.

i. *Federal tax requirements.* Recent amendments to the federal Internal Revenue Code have limited the availability of deductions for conservation restrictions *and* complicated the task of determining whether a particular restriction is in a qualifying form.[24] The tax law allows a deduction only for the donation of a "qualified conservation contribution." Such a contribution is a gift of a "qualified real property interest" to a "qualified organization" which is "exclusively for conservation purposes." A qualified real property interest is defined to include "a restriction (granted in perpetuity) on the use which may be made of the real property."

An eligible restriction must serve a "conservation purpose." Under Internal Revenue Code §170(A)(4)(A) a restriction on land must be for one of the following purposes:

(i) the preservation of land areas for outdoor recreation by, or the education of, the general public,

(ii) the protection of a relatively natural habitat of fish, wildlife, or plants, or similar ecosystem,

(iii) the preservation of open space (including farmland and forest land) where such preservation is—

(I) for the scenic enjoyment of the general public, or

(II) pursuant to a clearly delineated Federal, State, or local governmental conservation policy, and will yield a significant public benefit, or

(iv) the preservation of an historically important land area or a certified historic structure.

An eligible restriction must by its terms last forever. The gift of a restriction that does not meet all of the foregoing criteria will not be eligible for a federal charitable contribution deduction.

Although the Treasury Department has not yet adopted regulations concerning these provisions, a 1980 report of the Senate Finance Committee gives some insight into their meaning.[25] Open space restrictions that provide "visual access" only would meet the "scenic enjoyment" portion of the test. In order to meet the alternative test of preserving open space "pursuant to a clearly delineated" government policy, a taxpayer must demonstrate a "significant" commitment on the government's part, and not simply a "broad declaration by a single official." On the other hand, a particular property need not be specifically identified by the government.

Open space contributions must also meet a "public benefit" test. Compliance will be determined on a case-by-case basis, according to the report. Factors that may be considered are the "uniqueness" of the property, the "intensity of land development" in its vicinity, the "opportunity for the general public to enjoy the use of the property or to appreciate its scenic values," and the consistency of the proposed open space used with public programs "including programs for water supply protection, water quality maintenance or enhancement, flood prevention and control, erosion control, shoreline protection, and protection of land areas included in, or related to, a government approved master plan or land management area."

The above rules apply to donations made after December 17, 1980; gifts not completed by that date, including those contained in previously executed wills, should be reviewed carefully for compliance with these new rules. Of course, restrictions purchased by a charity or those whose value is not intended to be deducted for federal tax purposes are not subject to the Internal Revenue Code provisions.

ii. *Drafting an easement.* The following factors should be considered in drafting a restriction in the form of an easement.

(1) Since courts tend to assume that what was not mentioned in the provisions of an easement was not intended, the language should be detailed and precise. Which features are to be protected? Under which conditions may hikers pass through the land?

(2) If access is permitted, the kind and amount must be stated in the easement. Owners often will not accept public access, but the charity must be able to ensure that the terms of the easement are being fulfilled. Any provision for access should be carefully drawn to protect both parties from problems and misunderstandings.

(3) If an easement is not used for a long period of time, a court may rule that it has been terminated. However, some conservation easements may contemplate no use; therefore, a clause should be included stating that nonuse does not constitute an abandonment or other termination.

(4) An easement may be accompanied by a reverter clause; a reversion to the original owner will forfeit any tax deduction. One common practice is to give the land itself to a town or charity, and then give both a conservation easement and a reverter to a separate charity. If the new owner violates the restrictions in the easement, the land will pass to the organization holding the reverter. This has a deterrent effect. In addition, if the land belonged wholly to the town, with no reverters, and were condemned, compensation would go to the town. Although in most states the town has to use the compensation for the same purposes as the land,[26] it may not apply the money in the best way for conservation. If the easement and reverter are held by a charity and the land is condemned, the money passes to the trust.

In a similar fashion, an easement-reverter combination can be used to enforce restrictions on land that remains in private ownership. The owner can grant appropriate interests to a charity that monitors use by future owners. Should the charity go out of business, it may assign its reversionary interest to another organization.

iii. *Impact on donor.* If the restriction qualifies under the Internal Revenue Code provisions, the major advantage to the donor is a tax deduction for a diminution in the value of the property. Professional tax advice should be obtained on any proposed donation. If the donation fails to qualify, the donor may have to pay federal gift taxes.[27] The gift or sale of a conservation restriction on land held for more than one year will usually affect the owner's basis in property for tax purposes.

The restriction should provide other tax benefits also. The value of the land may be lowered for property tax purposes, but unless the easement is given to a municipality, the tax will not be lowered until time for the regular revaluation.[28] The restriction will also reduce the value of the donor's estate, whether it is transferred while the donor is living or by will.

Of course, a conservation restriction usually reduces the sale value of land. This loss may be partially or wholly offset by the tax benefits described above. A restriction may enhance the attractiveness of the land for recreational or residential purposes if neighboring properties are subject to similar restrictions.

iv. *Impact on the charity.* The conservation restriction can offer the charity a benefit for little money. A landowner who does not want to give land away may be willing to give a restriction. Restrictions can be used to create attractive roads and waterfronts. Rather than having to buy up all abutting property, the charity may acquire an easement of appropriate size. Even if the owner refuses to make a gift of the easement, the price in most instances would not approach the cost of purchase of either the land itself or of a nondevelopment easement covering the entire property.

When a charity accepts a restriction, it also accepts the accompanying management responsibilities. These may include periodic inspections of the property and other activities to see that the restriction is enforced. The charity should assess the condition of the property at the time of transfer in order to be able to identify any subsequent changes. Aerial photos are useful in this regard.

In short, the charity can use restrictions as an alternative method of preserving unique resources when a landowner does not want to completely give up his land.

c. *Reverters*

A donor may want to make a gift of land subject to a reverter. This means that if the charity ceases to preserve the land or destroys some element of the land (such as cutting down a particular stand of trees), the land will be taken away from it and given to someone else. A reverter ensures that a donor's wishes as to the future of the property will be respected.

There are two problems the donor will want to avoid. First, if the reversion is to the donor or his heirs, the value of the gift is not deductible.[29] However, if title is granted to one exempt organization and the reverter is assigned to another, the value of the land is fully deductible from income tax as a gift of the entire interest. Other possibilities are to have the land revert to a town or a state. Whichever entity is chosen, it should be notified in advance so the donor is certain that the gift will be accepted.

The second problem is a technical one. The way in which the reverter clause is written can determine whether the reversion is automatic or whether the person or organization with the reversionary interest must take active steps to obtain the land. Therefore, the reversionary clause (indeed, the entire contract and deed) should be prepared by an attorney experienced in land transfers.

If title and the reverter are both held by charitable organizations, the restrictions are valid indefinitely. Otherwise the event which triggers the reverter must take place within some period, thirty or fifty years, from the date the charity acquires the land.[30]

i. *Impact on donor.* The use of a reverter does not alter the tax treatment of a transaction if it is assigned to an exempt organization. Thus the value of a deduction is not changed because a reverter is used to give a charity enforcement responsibility.

ii. *Impact on the charity.* Reverters assigned to charities can assist in enforcing conservation restrictions. They can also limit the use of land that has been donated to another charity.

d. *Gifts of undivided interests (installment gifts)*

One of the partial interests in property that is deductible for federal tax purposes when given to a charitable organization is an undivided portion of the donor's property.[31] Installment gifts of undivided interests may be used to convey a piece of land over several years. For example, a donor could contribute one-third of his ownership interest every other year for six years.

Joint ownership of undivided interests may include timesharing, with the charity given the right to possession and control of the property for a portion of the year appropriate to its interest and with the donor retaining possession for the balance of the year.[32] Or it may mean that both parties exercise supervisory control over the property as co-owners.

A donor may also transfer subdivided portions of a property, in which case he is transferring the entire interest in a smaller piece of land.

i. *Impact on donor.* A donor may realize several advantages from gifts of undivided interests. The partial transfer of control may protect the land while the owner continues to use it and realizes tax benefits. The donor can spread the deductions over more than the six years permitted for outright gifts to qualified organizations. Finally, if the charity is not qualified as a public charity or a private operating foundation, the donor will still be able to spread the deductions over several years by using the installment mechanism.[33]

ii. *Impact on the charity.* Sharing control of property creates potential problems for a charity, so the charity should try to limit the period during which control is shared. Although joint management decisions with the conservation-minded donor who established the arrangement may not be difficult, dealing with the donor's heirs may not be so easy. The charity should urge the donor to accompany the gift with a gift of the remainder interests or to donate the balance of the property in his will.

There should be a written understanding concerning the management and use of the land during the period of joint ownership. Issues such as access, times of possession, and liability for insurance and taxes should be resolved in advance. These issues may be simplified if the donor leases the property to the charity until the gift is fully completed.

e. *Charitable trusts*

A charitable trust is an entity that owns and administers for charitable purposes; those purposes are spelled out in the trust document.[34] A trust can take effect during the donor's lifetime or through provisions in his will. Because of the flexibility of trusts, a donor can often exert more control over property than if it were transferred directly. When this device is used to donate property to a charity, the charity becomes the trustee responsible for effectuating the donor's wishes.

Charitable trusts are dedicated forever to the uses and purposes for which they were established.[35] This means the charity may not sell the land and buy another parcel. If the land is taken by eminent domain, the compensation paid to the charity is to be applied for the purposes of the trust.

If a charity violates the terms of the charitable trust, it can be sued for breach of fiduciary duty. However, in most instances, the only person legally authorized to sue is the state attorney general. If the trust includes a reverter, the holder of the reverter can also sue.

If circumstances change so that the donor's specific wishes can no longer be carried out, the courts will try to find an alternative means to fulfill his general intent.[36] For instance, if the donor wished to preserve a stand of virgin timber and the trees burned down, the courts could order the land sold and the money used either to buy other timber-bearing land or to buy and plant seedlings.

On the whole, charitable trusts have become less attractive. First, a conservation restriction combined with a reverter to another charitable organization allows the donor to achieve the same goal in a simpler fashion. Second, charities fulfill similar goals because of their charitable purposes. The existing tax laws discourage use of charitable trusts. Properly drafted trusts contain provisions called remainders, which dispose of any property remaining when and if the trust expires, and often these remainders are assigned to charities. Because of the extremely strict rules pertaining to charitable remainder trusts, such a remainder is not likely to qualify if it is in the form of land.[37]

f. *Mortgaged land*

A charity may receive land that is encumbered by a mortgage in either of two situations. The donor may be unwilling to pay off the mortgage, and in this case the charity has to decide if it wishes to and can assume the burden of the mortgage.

The other situation arises when the donor is willing to give the land, in effect, unburdened. If the mortgaged land plus sufficient cash or appreciated property to pay off the mortgage is given to a charity, the donor may benefit. Donating cash will increase the annual deduction limit for the cash contribution to 50 percent of the adjusted gross income, instead of the 30 percent allowed for gifts of appreciated property.[38] Giving appreciated property such as stocks enables the donor to avoid the capital gains tax on stocks he would incur by selling the property and using the proceeds to pay off the mortgage. On the other hand, the assumption of mortgaged land by a charity constitutes a sale of the property to the extent of the unpaid mortgage

note balance. Thus, such a transaction will usually be treated as a bargain sale.

g. *Leases*

A charity may be either a landlord or a tenant of property.

i. *Land leased from a charity.* This kind of lease was mentioned above in the discussion on leasebacks, where the charity first places conservation restrictions on the property, then leases it either to the original owner or to a third party. The charity may also wish to lease asset land or land acquired in some other manner.

Must the charity pay property taxes on leased land?[39] If the land carries a strong conservation easement and the rent is nominal, it might be said to be "used exclusively" for charitable purposes and thus should be exempt from property taxes.[40]

However, the exemption has been narrowly interpreted so that land used for activities closely related to the charitable purpose has been held nonexempt.[41] Property leased to another charitable organization should remain exempt as devoted to that organization's purposes.[42] Rents derived from real property are usually not subject to the federal tax on "unrelated business income" of charitable corporations unless the property is subject to a mortgage.[43]

Charities qualifying as private operating foundations may not be able to classify leased property as part of the 65 percent of assets that must be devoted directly to the charitable purposes.

ii. *Land leased by a charity.* Although a trust may legally lease land from an owner at either nominal or market rent, this is generally done only as an adjunct to another transaction. For owners, the fact that no income tax deduction is available for donation of a leasehold interest makes other techniques more attractive. For trusts, the temporary nature of leases is a major drawback, although leases for long terms are possible.

Leases can be useful to secure charitable management and control over property to be donated in the future. The charity could lease the remaining undivided interests in property being donated over time or the life estate in property that will pass to the trust at the owner's death. An owner who leases property to a charitable organization may be relieved of property taxes if a locality has an appropriate ordinance.[44]

Notes

1. One example is a small parcel that later becomes surrounded by development, creating severe management problems.

2. "Fee simple" means a total transfer of the land and all rights attached to it, so that no elements of ownership remain with any other party.

3. To the extent property has been subject to accelerated depreciation or has been held less than one year, or if the donor is a "dealer" in property, a sale of the property would be taxed as ordinary income and no capital gains tax would be avoided by a gift. I.R.C. §§1221, 1222, 1250. Charitable deductions are

decreased by any amount that would have been treated as ordinary income. I.R.C. §170(e).

4. *See, e.g.,* Conn. Gen. Stat. §12-498(3).

5. I.R.C. §2522 (gift tax); *see, e.g.,* Conn. Gen. Stat. §12-347 (transfer tax).

6. In all discussions of the tax ramifications of various forms of land transfers, it is assumed that the charity meets the Internal Revenue Code's requirements for a public charity or a private operating foundation and that the donor is an individual, not a corporation.

7. I.R.C. §170(b)(1)(C)(ii) (carryover for gifts of appreciated capital gain property); §170(d)(1)(A) (regular carryover).

8. I.R.C. §170(e).

9. Note that the latter method is advantageous for donors with relatively high incomes and relatively low appreciation on their property. Also, if the donor makes other charitable contributions of land, the ability to deduct up to 50 percent of gross income is more likely to compensate for the reduced total.

10. The tax on long-term capital gains is computed by adding 40 percent of the capital gain to taxable income. Here the 40 percent is taxed at 50 percent, for an effective rate of 20 percent of the total capital gain. I.R.C. §1202.

11. Gifts accomplished through a will are termed "devises" when they involve real property and "bequests" when they involve personal property such as cash or securities.

12. I.R.C. §2055; *see, e.g.,* Conn. Gen. Stat. §12-347.

13. Generally, the adjusted basis used to determine capital gains or losses is the cost to the owner including improvements and less depreciation taken.

14. I.R.C. §453.

15. Similar results can be obtained with an inter vivos trust, described later in this article.

16. *See* Rev. Rul. 77-305, 1971-2 C.B. 72, which held that when the deed of gift contained a condition that if the donors decided to sell the property, the donee would have to sell its remainder and would get cash instead, no deduction was allowable.

17. I.R.C. §170(f).

18. A time-sharing arrangement that is particularly useful for vacation homes involves the donor's making an outright gift to the charity of a portion of the undivided interest in the land, allowing the charity use and occupancy during much of the year. The donor gets a tax deduction for the full value of the portion deeded to the charity, plus the value of the remainder interest. *See* Rev. Rul, 75-240, 1975-2 C.B. 78, for one example of such an arrangement. Careful drafting is necessary to make sure that what is deeded is a portion of the undivided interest, rather than a partial interest, which is nondeductible.

19. I.R.C. §170(f)(4); 26 C.F.R. §1.170A-12.

20. *See, e.g.,* Conn. Gen. Stat. §52-563. This means that if the donor commits greater waste than is allowable, he can be sued by the charity for depreciating the land's value.

21. *See, e.g.,* Conn. Gen. Stat. §12-48.

22. *See, e.g.,* Conn. Gen. Stat. §§47-42a to 42c. These statutes greatly simplify legal drafting by abolishing most technical problems caused by archaic legalisms such as privity, alienation, and appurtenant/in gross.

23. The test is applied to the value of the entire tract even though the restriction applies to only part of the tract. Rev. Rul. 76-376, 1976-2 C.B. 53.

24. I.R.C. §§170(f)(3)(B)(iii) and 170(h).

25. S. Rep. No. 96-1007, 96th Cong., 2d Sess. 9-14 (1980).

26. *See, e.g.,* Conn. Gen. Stat. §47-2.

27. A federal gift tax return must be filed without regard to the value of a gift, even though the donation is to a charity and may qualify as a deduction for income tax purposes. If it qualifies for an income tax deduction, it will also be deductible for gift tax purposes. If a gift fails to qualify for the gift tax charitable deduction, it is taxable unless it is given to a natural person, is worth less than $10,000, and is the only gift to such person. No gift tax will be payable, however, to the extent the "unified credit," set forth in I.R.C. §2505(a), is available. However, a nonqualifying donation will diminish the amount of the unified credit for gift tax purposes available for subsequent lifetime gifts. Furthermore, the value of a nondeductible donation made after January 1, 1977, will be included for purposes of computing a decedent's estate tax under I.R.C. §§2001(b) and (c), although a credit is allowed for any gift tax paid with respect to such gift. The value of a nondeductible testamentary donation must be included in the taxpayer's estate for federal estate tax purposes. I.R.C. §§2522(c)(2), 2055(c)(2).

28. *But see* Conn. Gen. Stat. §7-131b(b), which gives statutory authorization for an immediate revaluation of any land on which an easement has been granted to a town.

29. I.R.C. §170(f)(3). This is because such a gift would be of a partial interest in property that does not fall within any of the permissible classifications.

30. Conn. Gen. Stat. §45-97.

31. *See, e.g.,* I.R.C. §170(f)(3)(B)(iii).

32. I.R.C. §1.170A-7(b)(1).

33. Contributions to charitable organizations that are not qualified as public charities or private operating foundations are deductible only up to 20 percent of the donor's income, and the undeducted balance may not be carried forward. I.R.C. §170. However, a series of annual gifts of undivided interest can achieve the same effect as carrying deductions forward.

34. Whether a document creates a trust is a question of state law.

35. *See, e.g.,* Conn. Gen. Stat. §45-79.

36. This is referred to as the "cy pres doctrine."

37. *See* I.R.C. §§664(d)(1) and (d)(2). The regulations require yearly cash outlays of more than 5 percent of the value of the trust. If the principal is in land, this level of outlay is unlikely since no interest will be earned.

38. I.R.C. §170.

39. In Connecticut a lessee does not pay taxes unless the lease is for more than one hundred years. Conn. Gen. Stat. §12-81(7).

40. *See, e.g.,* Conn. Gen. Stat. §§12-81(7), 12-88. However, below-market rents in a leaseback to an original owner can eliminate his federal tax deduction.

41. *See, e.g., Property Tax Exemption for Charitable, Educational, Religious and Governmental Institutions in Connecticut,* 4 Conn. L. Rev. 242-44 (1971).

42. *See, e.g.,* Conn. Gen. Stat. §12-81(7).

43. I.R.C. §512(b)(4). Although income of a qualified charitable organization resulting from its charitable activities is not taxed, certain types of income resulting from the organization's operation of a business unrelated to these purposes are taxed.

44. *See, e.g.,* Conn. Gen. Stat. §12-81(58).

PART IV
FEDERAL TAXATION

Federal tax law permeates the land conservation field. Part IV presents a number of different perspectives on various facets of the tax code and their influence on land-saving programs. However, nothing in this section can substitute for professional consultation, whether with attorneys, accountants, or appraisers, when a particular transaction must be evaluated. The collective contribution of these articles is to provide a sensitivity to the tax elements present in any given conservation effort, a framework for analyzing tax issues as they emerge, and an appreciation of the technical skills needed for proper tax management. With this preparation, individuals at every level of sophistication in the land-saving community can amplify their contribution by harnessing powerful tax incentives to their goals.

The opening article, "Taxes as a Form of Public Financing," sets the conceptual stage by describing the tax law as an integral part of the land conservation movement in this country, indeed, as its financial basis and not as a separate statutory scheme. Such a comprehensive formulation is required to understand the practical significance of particular tax requirements, the land-saving community's role in influencing tax policy, and its responsibility for safeguarding this federal assistance program.

The following article, "Working with the 1980 Amendments to the Internal Revenue Code," delves more deeply into the mechanics of the Code, especially those sections pertaining to the donation of conservation easements. The emphasis is on making a given statutory scheme work as productively as possible for the landowner wanting to donate easements and for the organization wanting to receive them. A collaborative approach with the Internal Revenue Service is espoused as the most effective and least costly path to certainty in the regulatory process. This article offers guidance not only to the comparatively few who will engage in some sort of proceedings with the Internal Revenue Service but also for the movement as a whole in its philosophical orientation to the Treasury Department.

The third article, "Gifts of Partial Interests in Real Property," examines in detail the tax law pertaining to this type of charitable contribution. A more general discussion of less than fee approaches and the development of federal tax law precedes the treatment of the rules governing these contributions. This article provides a comprehensive analysis of the tax law considerations, both technical and conceptual, inherent in the case of less than fee approaches to land conservation. It identifies the areas of certainty and areas of doubt that must be grappled with by those contemplating the tax consequences of a contribution of partial interests as well as by those wishing to reform the process. The following article is a lengthy note by Russell L. Brenneman on the proposed regulations to Section 170(h) of the Internal Revenue Code, the section concerning the donation of easements.

The fifth article, "Easements and Artifacts," looks at the particular impact of the tax law on easements pertaining to archaeological sites. The immediate purpose of this article is to educate archaeologists in the use of easements and the associated charitable contribution advantages as an alternative to the sale and dispersal of archaeological resources. The description of tax concepts is useful to anyone for whom this is especially new terrain and alerts every reader to the possibility of novel applications of easements.

Three articles follow, each of which discusses the appraisal of partial interests. All of the charitable contributions associated with partial interests must rest upon an appraisal of the monetary value of those interests when a deduction is actually claimed. The appraisal of partial interests and the assignment of a market value to the nonmonetary values they possess are difficult tasks. Although valuation must be performed largely on a case-by-case basis, it must be performed credibly if favorable tax treatment is to continue for the donation of partial interests. The first article on appraisals discusses restrictions on the basis of their severity and interjects the notion that market data may lead to the conclusion that restrictions have a greater effect on value than ordinarily supposed. The second and third articles in this group discuss theories of valuation and provide a series of examples illustrating various approaches to the appraisal issue.

"Increased Tax Penalties for Valuation Overstatements," the concluding article in Part IV, addresses the punitive effect the tax code can have on transactions that are improperly effected or that rest upon improper valuations. As these penalties have increased and as the valuation questions remain shadowy, it is critical that both landowners who wish to avail themselves of tax deductions and organizations that use tax incentives as a means of encouraging private stewardship have a clear sense of possible abuses and their negative tax consequences. This is imperative not only if individual donors are to be protected but also if the legitimacy of the tax deduction as a preservation device is to be maintained.

Taxes as a Form of Public Financing: Treasury's Open Space Protection Program

Kingsbury Browne, Jr.

There are well-known programs in the Departments of the Interior and Agriculture for acquisition and protection of critical open space. There is a lesser-known one at Treasury, the parameters of which are difficult to perceive because they are hidden in the complexities of the Internal Revenue Code. Treasury offers tax reductions—through the charitable deduction, for example—to encourage the acquisition and protection of critical open space. It could accomplish the same result by eliminating the charitable deduction and offering cash in its place. Treasury's program is the same as those of the other agencies in the sense that all employ tax revenues, but a unique feature of Treasury's is that its land acquisition costs are structured at less than 70 percent of the fair market value of the lands acquired. The other 30 percent or more is contributed by landowners.[1] Of all the federally supported land protection programs, Treasury's is thus the most economical. The Treasury program also differs from those of the other agencies because the stewardship of the acquired lands is largely entrusted to private, tax-exempt, charitable organizations that specialize in land conservation. These private organizations relieve the federal government of stewardship responsibilities and their attendant costs. In effect, Treasury through tax incentives provides these organizations with the means of acquiring land at below-market costs.

Treasury, land conservation organizations (so-called land trusts), and conservation-minded landowners jointly engage in the protection of critical open space. The number of such land trusts so engaged prior to 1950 reached 36 operating in twenty states, but today there are more than 400 organizations identified in some forty-three states. There are undoubtedly more.[2]

Until quite recently Treasury's role remained purely financial; it supplied the land acquisition funds. The land trust's role was to select the land or interests in land, to take title, and to accept responsibility for on-going management and stewardship in the public interest. The landowner was the third participant, for even though payment was accepted in Treasury dollars for part of the land, the balance had to be a charitable contribution motivated by conservation concerns. The contribution or bargain purchase feature of Treasury's land protection program necessarily limited its scope to landowners financially able to contribute at least 30 percent of their property. That feature also reduced the risk that vast areas of open space would be gobbled up by land trusts and lead to unfair competition with developers and other commercial interests.

Recently, however, Treasury's role has changed in ways that have adversely affected the open space protection work of land trusts. Congress in 1980 expanded on Treasury's passive financial role by shifting to Treasury some of the land selection and management decisions previously made by land trusts.[3] Thus, many final decisions with respect to scenic, recreational, habitat, and other qualities are now made for tax purposes not by land trusts but by administrative personnel in Treasury who write regulations, issue rulings, and conduct tax audits. Congress made this change in 1980 notwithstanding a paucity of hard evidence of any need to relieve the land trusts of their traditional selection responsibilities. At the same time the unorganized land trust community failed to defend and explain the dimensions and quality of its work.

The Department of the Interior became concerned with Treasury's assumption of selection and certification responsibilities and in June of 1982 suggested that the joint land protection effort of Treasury, land trusts, and landowners be expanded to include Agriculture and Interior, each of which would then be given the role of certifying as to the desirable qualities of land interests proposed for acquisition.[4] That suggestion focused on the acknowledged deficiencies in expertise at Treasury but proposed to fill the gap with another level of federal bureaucracy. An obvious alternative would be to return the certification process to the land trusts themselves, subject to the possible addition of statutory safeguards to assure sufficient expertise and financial responsibility on the part of participating land trusts. For now, however, a promising land protection program conducted by Treasury, land trusts, and conservation-minded landowners has lost headway as a result of the 1980 tax law changes. In the Commonwealth of Virginia, for example, use of conservation easements by the Virginia Outdoors Foundation, a state agency, has been temporarily suspended pending issuance of explanatory regulations.[5] While tax incentives gain popularity as a means of stimulating construction, rehabilitation of older buildings, energy conservation, education, and other economic and social goals, their use as a mainstay in land protection has declined.

This breakdown of a promising relationship between the federal government and state and private initiatives may be unintended. Some, however, deny that Treasury ever had an open space conservation program, concealed as it is in the complexities of the Internal Revenue Code. Others question whether land trusts effectively assure the public of benefit commensurate with the public revenues invested. The land trusts themselves are partly responsible for the present problem since many reject accepting any responsibility for policing the use of the federal land acquisition funds provided by Treasury. In any event a number of aspects deserve closer examination, including the mechanics by which the land conservation role of Treasury is conducted through the federal tax system; the vigorous response of the land trust movement to Treasury support; and the growth in the use of conservation easements until changes in tax policy in 1980 adversely affected their use. Finally, some suggestions for reviving cooperation between the Treasury and the private sector in the very small but important area of protecting critical open space deserve attention.

Congress Designs and Treasury Administers a Federal Tax System for the Acquisition of Open Space

In the formative years of Oz, the Wizard of Oz (the WOZ) decided to encourage the conservation of critical open space (WOZACRES) by Oz Private Land Trusts (OPLTs). So he gave each OPLT the right to draw funds from the Treasury of Oz (the TOZ) to be used to purchase open space. Since the WOZ thought the private sector should bear directly some part of the cost of open space conser-

vation, he ordered his legislative draftsmen to provide that no OPLT would be permitted to draw on the TOZ and pay a selling landowner an amount greater than 70 percent of the fair market value of the WOZACRE involved. The landowner would be required to contribute the other 30 percent of value to the OPLT. When the legislative draftsmen prepared the statute, they incorporated that scheme, but (for reasons never disclosed) they added a limitation that the draw and payment by the OPLT should not exceed a graduated percentage of the landowner's income in Oz (OINC). Thus, in the case of a landowner proposing to transfer WOZACRE worth $10,000, the OPLT could, if the landowner had $100,000 of OINC, draw down $7,000 from the TOZ and acquire the land. But if the owner of WOZACRE had only $50,000 of OINC, then the second limitation permitted a draw and payment of only $4,000. This limitation had the curious result of enabling an OPLT to draw down from the TOZ and pay 70 percent of fair market value for WOZACRE if the landowner had lots of OINC but less than 70 percent if OINC was less. It was strange that in the case of two landowners owning WOZACRES of identical value, a larger payment would be made to the one with the greater OINC. Despite these problems, OPLTs multiplied, drew substantial sums from the TOZ, and made bargain purchases of many fine WOZACRES.

In 1912 the United States enacted an income tax and later adopted WOZ's method of subsidizing the preservation of open space by land trusts. Congress, however, "simplified" the WOZ's scheme: it said that since most landowners would be filing tax returns with Treasury and paying taxes on net income, the two-step process in OZ of first authorizing a land trust to draw funds from Treasury and then to pay the funds over to the landowner should be consolidated by simply effecting a commensurate reduction in the landowner's tax liability. The reduction would be achieved mechanically by allowing a charitable deduction for the value of the land in computing the landowner's taxable income. Part of the reduction in tax liability would also be achieved by foregoing capital gains tax with respect to any unrealized appreciation. Thus, in the case of a landowner proposing to transfer land having a cost basis of zero but worth $10,000, Treasury would allow a charitable deduction of $10,000; and if the landowner had sufficient taxable income so as to be subject to the 50 percent maximum tax rate, the resulting $10,000 reduction in taxable income would reduce taxes by 50 percent of $10,000, or $5,000. The landowner would receive $5,000 indirectly through tax return adjustments and would contribute the balance of the land. In fact, the benefit becomes $7,000 (as would have been the result in Oz) because Treasury does not seek to impose a 20 percent tax on the unrealized appreciation.[6]

The fact that the payment, incentive, or subsidy—whatever it is termed—is achieved by the allowance of a charitable deduction that reduces taxes should not conceal the bargain purchase nature of the acquisition. The effect on a landowner of a dollar reduction in taxes otherwise payable is exactly the same as a direct dollar payment without a tax reduction. Nor should the fact that the land trust never actually receives the payment obscure the fact that Treasury is financing land acquisitions by land trusts. Every Treasury payment is controlled by and is therefore constructively made to the land trust because it is the decision of the land trust to accept the responsibilities of owning and managing the critical open space that triggers the tax benefit to the landowner. In this sense charitable gifts of land and cash are quite different. The acceptance of a cash gift by any charity is a foregone conclusion. That is less true, however, with land because a proposed gift of land presents burdens of stewardship that the land trust may or may not wish to assume. Thus, the land trust controls and therefore makes the acquisition payment using funds provided by Treasury through the tax system.

It is this reasoning that provides the basis for asserting that Treasury is engaged in financing a land acquisition and conservation program within the framework of the Internal Revenue Code. It is no less a Treasury land conservation program because title to the land lodges in private land trusts. Most, if not all, enjoy favored tax status because of widespread public support; one of the grounds for tax-exempt status is "the lessening of the burdens of Government."[7] The land trust in one sense is an extension of the federal government.

There are problems in Treasury's open space protection program. The first is the skewing of "purchase" prices in favor of high-tax-bracket landowners. The lands of ranchers in Jackson Hole need protection, but the financial assistance otherwise available from Treasury for conservation acquisitions by the Jackson Hole Land Trust cannot reach many ranchers because they have little or no taxable income to shelter with charitable deductions. A second problem is the opportunity for abuse through aggressive valuations. In direct acquisition programs there is hard bargaining and use of independent appraisers by both sides. These elements are lacking in Treasury's program unless and until the landowner's tax return is audited. The result of inflated values that escape audit and correction is the loss of the bargain element in Treasury's program and thus the elimination of an important public benefit. Thus, if land having a fair market value of $1,000 is "aggressively" appraised for charitable deduction purposes at $1,430, Treasury's financial contribution (70 percent) equals the full fair market value.

The 1980 tax law changes introduced a third problem in the Treasury open space protection program by shifting the administration of part of the program from land trust personnel to employees of the Internal Revenue Service. Until 1980 all decisions of scenic, recreational, and habitat qualities rested in the recipient land trusts. Now those decisions in many acquisitions have shifted to Treasury.[8]

Finally, Treasury's open space protection program has been criticized on the ground that it is hidden from public scrutiny, whereas a direct land acquisition program (by the National Park Service, for example) would be visible, understandable, and a part of the budget process.

The first three problems are real, but it is unlikely that the substitution of a direct federal program for the present tax program will occur; and if it did occur, the third problem would still persist. Budget constraints have already curtailed Federal Land and Water Conservation funding of state and local open space protection programs. The fundamental question is whether land conservationists should and can maintain, indeed restore, long-standing, tax-incentive-based programs for which there are no viable direct alternatives in sight.

The response to Treasury's financial program for the support of land conservation, whatever its problems, has been significant. The rapid growth in the number, diversity, and geographical distribution of land trusts suggests that Treasury's program has been well received. The suspension of many conservation easement programs since the 1980 tax law changes supports the perception that tax incentives can be a major factor.

Treasury's Support of Open Space Protection Encouraged the Rapid Growth of Land Trusts—That Growth Was Slowed Down by the Tax Law Changes in 1980

Land trusts now number more than 400 and are located in forty-three states. Ninety-two percent of these local organizations are membership organizations supported by more than a quarter of a million members. With few exceptions they have qualified for federal tax purposes as publicly supported organizations and therefore are favored over private foundations in terms of tax incentives and freedom from many burdensome administrative requirements. What is also noteworthy is their rate of growth. Before 1950 there were 36 organizations in twenty states, some of them, such as the Trustees of Reservations in Massachusetts, dating back to the nineteenth century. By 1965 the number of such organizations had reached 100. Between 1965 and 1975 an additional 174 land trusts were established. In the six-year period from 1976 to 1981, another 100 appeared, bringing the total to 418. Twenty-three percent of the most recent growth was in the Far West, with matching rates of growth in the Great Lakes and Mid-Atlantic regions.[9]

These 418 private charitable organizations, or land trusts, now protect over 680,000 acres of wildlife habitat, scenic and recreational lands, lava rock formations, wetlands, riparian lands, agricultural and forestlands, grasslands, rights-of-way for trails, historic and archaeological sites, caves, sand dunes, water recharge areas, community gardens, and neighborhood open space. Forty-one percent of the land trusts operate within a single town or community, 17 percent at the county level, and the rest over larger areas.

Until fairly recently the tax-exempt status of a land trust was not difficult to establish. But beginning sometime in the 1970s Treasury refused to grant tax-exempt status to land trusts organized simply to acquire and protect open space. Acceptable charitable purposes had to be limited to the protection of "ecologically significant" lands. The reason for this policy change was obscure, but, consistent with it, Treasury in 1978 denied tax-exempt status to organizations concerned solely with the protection of farmlands.[10] However, organizations simply broadened their purposes to include educational and scientific goals, and the difficulty was largely avoided. Nevertheless, this development was a warning that the scope of Treasury's financial support for land acquisition programs was narrowing, not because of congressional or public dissatisfaction, but because of changing views from within the Treasury. There were other warnings as well, especially in connection with conservation easements.

Most of the land trusts surveyed have widespread public support and thus escape the burdens associated after 1969 with private foundation status. The Tax Reform Act of 1969 reflected congressional concern with exempt-organization abuses. It focused on specific transactions such as income accumulations, self-dealing between donors, and foundations and investments in closely held family companies. Strict rules were laid down and a system of penalties was instituted, but they were limited to a class of exempt organizations called private foundations, of which the so-called family foundation is an example. Land trusts, almost without exception, establish broad-based public support and thus escape the transactional restraints imposed on private foundations. The 1980 tax restrictions, however, introduced transactional limitations into the non-private foundation sector.

The Treasury program that uses tax incentives to assist land trusts is not an isolated example of governmental support of the private initiatives of land trusts. There are numerous examples at state levels of cooperative undertakings for the protection of open space. Relationships between state governments and land trusts do vary. Some land trusts are quasi state agencies supported by state funds. The Maryland Environmental Trust and the Virginia Outdoors Foundation are examples.[11] The activities of land trusts in some states are more closely regulated than in others. In Massachusetts, for example, state approval is required for gifts of conservation easements.[12] Most land trusts, however, are independent, self-supporting, and self-directing. Within this category there are many that voluntarily assist federal and state open space protection programs. Acadia National Park is protected by more than fifty conservation easements given to the National Park Service as a result of the work of the Maine Coast Heritage Trust. The Commonwealth of Massachusetts has a funded program for the protection of critical farmlands through the purchase and retirement of farmers' development rights. (The acquisition of development rights and conservation easements accomplishes the same conservation purpose.) The Massachusetts Farm and Conservation Lands Trust, an affiliate of the Trustees of Reservations, has provided expertise and support in many of the Commonwealth's acquisitions to date. (It is interesting to note that the Massachusetts development rights program relies on direct payments rather than indirect ones through tax benefits.) The State Coastal Conservancy, an arm of the State of California, makes direct grants of state funds to California land trusts to support their work. Thus, Treasury is only one of many governmental agencies working with and providing financial support for private land trusts across the country.[13]

In addition to the rapid growth, an examination of the land trust educational literature points up the importance of Treasury support of open space protection. Almost all of this material stresses the tax incentives available to landowners who work with land trusts. Yet another rough measure of the importance of Treasury assistance through tax incentives may be seen in the rapid rise and fall in the use of conservation easements before and after the 1980 tax law changes.

Conservation Easements—Congress in 1980 Curtails a Promising Land Trust Technique, Perhaps Unintentionally

A conservation easement restricts the use of land, generally by prohibiting development. It is usually negative in the sense that it does not give the holder affirmative rights with respect to the land affected, such as a right of access. After the easement extinguishes the landowner's opportunity to develop the land, the land trust holding the easement is obligated to take remedial action if the landowner or a successor tries to undertake development.

The conservation easement has become a widely accepted conservation technique. It can be tailored to many situations, including the protection of animal and plant habitat, scenic vistas, historic properties, farmlands, and fragile properties such as dunes and water recharge areas, to name but a few of the environs where development can be highly destructive of natural qualities. It appeals to landowners who are not prepared to convey outright ownership and relinquish possession. Thus, a farmer owning a field with a rock outcrop that provides important habitat may be willing to give a conservation easement but not otherwise surrender title to and control of the outcrop.

From the point of view of the recipient land trust, escape from the burdens of fee simple ownership may be important. A 1979 study by the General Accounting Office criticized the Department of the Interior for failing to make wider use of conservation easements for park protection, noting that acquisition costs are less and the burden of maintaining the land does not shift from the donor to Interior.[14]

The use of conservation easements grew slowly beginning in the mid-1950s but by 1980 was well known and widely acclaimed among conservationists.

The conservation easement is a partial interest in land. It can be sold as well as given to charity. Several farmland protection programs are funded at state or local levels for the purpose of purchasing conservation easements from farmers.[15] Whether the development rights involved are sold and extinguished to protect a critical piece of farmland or given by the farmer to a land trust in the form of a conservation easement, the result is the same: the future use of the land is restricted.

Favorable capital gains tax treatment in the case of easement sales and the allowance of an income tax deduction for charitable gifts of easements both require a finding that the development rights or conservation easement constitute "property." The Internal Revenue Service so ruled in 1964 and again in 1974.[16]

For perhaps a decade after 1964, Treasury liberally supported the private land protection initiatives of land trusts. Many of these involved partial or less than fee interests of which the conservation easement was only one example. As time passed, Congress and Treasury were presented with a bewildering variety of such partial interests: life estates, remainders, leaseholds, covenants, undivided interests, mineral interests, and, finally, development rights or scenic easements. Each of these offered a means of identifying and reconciling private ownership objectives with public conservation concerns. Perhaps not since feudal times in England has there been such a resurgence in the use of partial interests to control land use.

In 1969 Congress, sensing abuses on the part of some exempt organizations and donors (largely, however, in areas not involving land conservation), sought to curtail them by a series of penalties in the form of excise taxes. But, as earlier noted, organizations enjoying widespread public support were excluded from the targeted class of so-called private foundations. The risk of tax abuses in the case of publicly supported organizations such as land trusts was considered minimal. The quality of the exempt organization itself rather than the transactions in which it engaged was the determinant of favored tax treatment. Land trusts almost without exception have broad-based public support and escape the restraints imposed on private foundations.

In one important respect, however, even the organizations enjoying widespread public support were faced after 1969 with tax problems relating to certain transactions. These involved the bewildering variety of charitable gifts of partial interests. With no thought of conservation easements in mind, the 1969 House and Senate decided to disallow tax deductions for charitable gifts of partial interests in land, with the exception of certain remainder interests and undivided interests. Not until the tax bill reached the conference committee charged with resolving the differences between the House and Senate versions was it realized that charitable gifts of conservation easements would no longer qualify for tax deductions because the easements did not constitute undivided interests in land under general principles of property law. The committee salvaged the situation by inserting in its report its view (one that is at complete variance with the common law of property) that "easements in gross, in perpetuity" constituted undivided interests. Thus, the deductibility of conservation easements survived the 1969 tax reforms.[17] The eleventh-hour rescue pointed up the immaturity of the growing land trust movement and its lack of voice in the legislative process. That problem would persist into the 1980s.

In 1972 Treasury responded to the 1969 tax law changes with broad and favorable regulations. As a result, any partial property interest cast in the form of an easement to protect open space—any open space—was eligible for the charitable contribution deduction if it was perpetual. Thus, gifts of air rights, in order to limit the height of a building, qualified. The 1972 regulations did not talk about "scenic" land, "ecosystems," "unique habitat," "significant public benefit," or "clearly delineated governmental conservation policy." Those concepts would not surface for another decade.[18]

The partial interest rulings that followed the extraordinary notion that easements constituted undivided interests were just as liberal as the notion itself. The question was frequently asked of the Internal Revenue Service whether the reservation of a personal right to continue to use land donated in fee had the effect of converting the gift into a nondeductible gift of a partial interest. It was usually resolved in the taxpayer's favor. One landowner had conveyed his land to the Department of the Interior, reserving, however, the right to train his hunting dog on the property. Although the reservation literally converted the fee gift into one of a partial interest that would be nondeductible, the Internal Revenue Service ruled in favor of a deductible gift by disregarding the reservation on *de minimis* grounds.[19] Favorable private letter rulings followed, involving such retained partial interests as access to beaches.[20] In another situation, Treasury applied the undivided interest rule to facilitate a charitable gift of land to an educational organization under the terms of which the owner reserved the right to inhabit the property six weeks of each year.[21] It is hard to imagine a more liberal ruling. Rulings of this kind were widely viewed as evidence of a sympathetic attitude at Treasury for the use of tax incentives to encourage open space protection.

There were occasional warnings in the 1970s that internal attitudes at Treasury might be changing. As noted, exempt status rulings for organizations engaged in farmland protection were denied unless the land to be acquired was "ecologically significant." A 1975 ruling allowed a conservation easement deduction but required a representation that the landowner would not disturb conservation qualities by oil drilling on the restricted land.[22] This limitation had no basis in the regulations. Again, it should have been another warning to the land trust movement of changing attitudes at Treasury.

Congress, however, remained supportive of private initiatives for open space protection. Thus, in 1976 it added a specific easement provision to allow deductions in the case of charitable gifts of term easements. Such easements had to be of at least thirty-years' duration but not perpetual. Unlike perpetual easements, deductible term easements had to be supportive of recreational, scenic, historic, or natural environmental qualities. The land conservation community correctly took the position that these new criteria applied only to term easements. The notion that the 1976 legislation somehow narrowed or supplanted the 1969 undivided interest limitation and the broad views expressed in the 1972 regulations simply did not square with the obvious intent of Congress to liberalize the conservation easement tax rules.[23]

In 1977 there occurred an event that confused matters. Through oversight the 1976 tax law establishing term easements was due to expire in June of 1977 instead of 1981 as originally intended. The one-year period was much too short for any fair test of the 1976 liberalization. The 1977 Congress corrected the oversight but restored the 1969 perpetual requirement—the "price" of the amendment. All this happened in a period of three days, without hearings or floor debate. Again, the land trust community was largely unaware of events. At least one of the national conservation organizations believed that term easements were counterproductive and therefore supported the change. (The concerns of organizations conducting conservation on a national scale may differ from those of local land trusts, but those differences often go unnoted at the federal level when only the former have a Washington presence.) There was no suggestion that the 1977 amendment was intended to supplant the 1969 undivided interest rule, and a private letter ruling by the Service followed to that effect.[24] The Service's position changed, however, after a statement appeared in the committee report accompanying the 1980 tax law changes to the effect that "doubt" existed whether the 1976/1977 legislation supplanted the 1969 version.[25]

The 1976/1977 statutory fumbling should have been another warning to the land trust community that tax benefit support among Treasury staff and perhaps the staff of the Joint Committee on Taxation was shaky. The eroding support at those staff levels probably was influenced by the then well-established methodology of tax expenditure analysis. In the first meeting of its kind between Treasury staff and land trusts, sponsored by the Brandywine Conservancy at Chadds Ford, Pennsylvania, in 1979, tax expenditure analysis was explained to the land trust community for the first time.[26] Most of those present were startled to learn that tax scholars question on policy grounds the use of tax incentives for nontax policy purposes, conservation purposes included; conservation concerns should have no place in a tax system intended to raise revenue.

Tax expenditure analysis asks hard questions and calls for careful preparation and skills on the part of any who argue for retention of tax incentives. Is federal financial support desirable and, if so, in what amount? Can it just as well (or perhaps better) be delivered by a direct expenditure program rather than indirectly through tax benefits? The 1980 tax legislation would prove to be a victory for tax expenditurists largely because of the failure of the land trust community to prepare cogent answers to these questions.

As the decade of the 1970s concluded, tax rulings in the land conservation sector generally continued to be favorable to contributors. Even in the area of reserved mineral rights, the Service was sympathetic and sought to be liberal. Thus, the charitable gift of a fee interest was deductible notwithstanding the retention of mineral rights by the donor. Those rights could be exercised only with the consent of the Department of the Interior and the likelihood that Interior, holder of the easement, would assent to the exercise of the mineral rights if wildlife habitat were to be degraded was deemed too remote to be worthy of consideration. As a consequence, the gift was a deductible gift of a fee interest instead of a nondeductible partial interest.[27] The ruling presaged a growing problem. In parts of the United States landowners were prepared to make charitable gifts of large, important tracts of land but only if the mineral rights could be retained without loss of charitable deductions. Donors were not prepared, however, to condition exercise of the retained mineral rights on the consent of the charitable owner of the fee. Late in the 1970s efforts began at the national level to obtain a legislative solution to the problem. The land trust community was not initially involved. The strategy evolved of incorporating the liberalizing measure (which it certainly was) in a bill that would make permanent the conservation easement provisions of the 1977 tax act that would otherwise expire in June of 1981. The piggyback provision to permit retention of mineral rights on a bill to make permanent an otherwise expiring tax measure was superficially appealing until the redundancy view of the expiring law was recalled; if the 1976/1977 conservation easement legislation had expired, it would have left in place the broad easement provisions of the 1969 act and the equally broad treatment in the 1972 regulations.

Nevertheless, the measure was enacted on December 17, 1980, and indeed did contain the much sought-after liberalizing mineral rights provision. It also, however, contained formidable new restrictions with respect to the deductibility of charitable gifts of conservation easements. The mineral rights exception was the only liberalizing aspect of the new law; in other material respects the measure cut back on the availability of tax incentives to support land conservation. The broad provisions of the 1969 act and the liberal regulations interpreting them were explicitly supplanted and new limitations were added. Deductibility after 1980 turned on concepts of "scenic enjoyment";

"unique habitat"; "clearly delineated Federal, State, and local governmental conservation policy"; and "significant public benefit."[28] Explanatory regulations comprising more than eighty pages were reported to be in draft form but as of November 1, 1982, had not been issued, notwithstanding a concerned Congress's demand that they be given highest priority.

The new limitations appeared to reflect the concern of staff at Treasury and at the Joint Committee on Taxation with "aggressive valuations" and suspected abuse of easements by landowners more interested in private protection than public benefit.[29] In the meantime important land protection programs involving easements in Virginia and Maryland, among others, were suspended. Under the 1980 statute, easements that respond to human desires for play and recreation and that preserve endangered animal species seem more likely to receive favorable tax treatment than easements that prohibit the destruction of the farmlands and water resources on which human beings increasingly depend.

The widespread concern with the 1980 tax changes rests with their vagueness: the use of terms and concepts not found elsewhere in the Internal Revenue Code. Lawyers may not be qualified to opine on what is "scenic"; opinions of landscape architects may be necessary. "Clearly delineated" governmental policy of any kind is hard to identify at any level of government. Potential donors will not be persuaded by lawyers' opinions couched in "more probable than not" language; they want assurances of no loss of tax benefits and no risk of gift tax.[30]

The passage of time may help to ameliorate the problem as case law develops and rulings are issued, but in the meantime, many land protection programs, or potential programs, will not be undertaken. Uncertainties, the delays and legal costs attendant upon obtaining rulings, and a growing irritation with added complexities do not bode well for the conservation easement programs of many land trusts. The cutback in Treasury's land protection program is particularly disappointing because the result may not have been intended. On May 26, 1982, Mr. Rostenkowski, Chairman of the House Ways and Means Committee, wrote to the Secretary of the Treasury apropos of the 1980 legislation and said, "It would be regrettable if a provision . . . which was intended to encourage charitable gifts of easements actually caused them to decline."[31] It is conceivable that the eventual regulations will restore vitality to easement programs, but it seems unlikely given the inherent ambiguities of the statute and the lack of safe harbors. Tax rulings will help guide landowners, but they are costly and time consuming, and those in private letter form (the general rule) have no value as reliable precedent.[32]

As of November 1, 1982, several bills had been filed to correct bits and pieces of the problem. If the land trust movement in which Treasury once was a strong participant has in fact the vitality its numbers and rate of growth suggest, then the whole matter of tax incentives and Treasury's role is worth congressional reexamination. If that begins with the view that Treasury is supporting a land acquisition program at bargain prices with the aid of land trusts and conservation-minded donors, then it may be possible to deal with the understandable concerns within Treasury and at the same time encourage private initiatives at local and regional levels without the unmanageable impediments of the 1980 act.

New Approaches Can Be Taken to Tax Incentives for Open Space Protection

The use of tax incentives to encourage open space protection really means that Treasury is engaged in financing the acquisition of land at bargain prices by land trusts. Tax incentives reduce the taxes otherwise payable by a landowner and constitute an indirect payment for the land or interest in land. Because of tax rate ceilings and a forbearance to tax gains, the program, properly conducted, reimburses a landowner for up to 70 percent of the value of the land but no more. The rest must be contributed. An important aspect of the program is Treasury's policy of allowing the land to be assigned to private charitable conservation organizations having broad-based public support. The federal government is relieved of stewardship responsibilities and the attendant costs. The public benefit derives from the charitable purposes and operations of the recipient land trusts.

When this approach is taken to existing tax incentives and those that may emerge, a number of propositions can be postulated.

1. The bargain element—the 30 percent private contribution—is what gives Treasury's program its principal appeal over other federal programs that pay full fair market value. The public dollar goes farther; private initiative and involvement is encouraged; and the requirement that the landowner make a partial contribution restrains an acquisition program that is not otherwise subject to normal budget restraints.

2. The bargain element is eroded or eliminated by "aggressive" valuations, and the likelihood this will occur is aggravated by the inability of Treasury to audit all returns. Since the Treasury program partially finances land trust acquisitions and enables the land to remain in private charitable hands, some responsibility may reasonably be assigned to land trusts to police the aggressive valuations that undermine the bargain feature of Treasury's program. One means of accomplishing this objective would be to require each recipient land trust to acquire its own appraisal. Landowners might then by regulation be required to attach copies of the land trust's appraisal to their tax returns. Regulations pertaining to the exempt status of a land trust might warn that a pattern of unreasonably high appraisals obtained by the land trust would be viewed as evidence of operation of the land trust for private inurement and thus grounds for loss of exempt status.

3. Any subsidized land purchase program—Treasury's included—should pay the same amount for all properties of the same value. The present method that provides payment through tax deductions does not meet that test because the tax brackets of landowners vary. Treasury should not pay more for a piece of land in the hands of an affluent landowner than it would for the same piece of land in the hands of a lower-tax-bracket landowner. Correction can be made by substituting a charitable tax credit for the present tax deduction. If it is set at a percentage of the fair market value of the land (perhaps at a point not expected to affect present revenues), the bargain and contribution features of Treasury's land acquisition program would be retained. Discrimination among taxpayers would be eliminated if the credit were refundable in the case of landowners without tax liability sufficient to absorb the credit.

4. It seems necessary as a practical matter to leave entirely to acquiring land trusts determinations of recreational, habitat, scenic, historic, and other such qualities in the case of a gift of a partial interest. That decisionmaking is already lodged entirely in land trusts receiving gifts of fee interests. Treasury, however, as the funding source, is entitled to reassurance that the land trust recipient is experienced, responsive to local public concerns, and financially capable of carrying out responsible stewardship. Furthermore, should the land trust fail financially, means must exist for the transfer of responsibilities. Land trusts can acquire experience without actually accepting stewardship. The Maine Coast Heritage Trust, for example, arranges for conservation easements that are actually deeded to the National Park Service. The Society for the Protection of New Hampshire Forests, organized in 1911, accepts easements but will transfer them to local organizations when they are ready to accept management responsibility. Thus a new approach to the easement tax problem might limit acceptance of easements to experienced organizations. There would be no discrimination against fledgling land trusts if the seasoned ones were prepared to accept responsibility initially for a period of years sufficient to give the new organization an opportunity to prove itself. Financial capability standards can be worked out but should not be onerous. Thus a demonstrated level of annual support—a percentage of assets—might suffice. In the event a land trust fails, a deed provision to a surviving land trust (if agreeable) or to a governmental body should help to meet the genuine concerns of Treasury.

There are difficult problems in meeting the test of public benefit without at the same time stultifying conservation easement programs. But arguably the problem of assuring public benefit can better be dealt with in the context of the institutional qualities of the exempt organizations than as part of land acquisition transactions, the variety of which among fifty states must be mind-boggling. The problem should be reexamined, especially in the context of the promising initiatives of the expanding land trust movement.

Notes

1. To illustrate the cost to Treasury of acquiring a parcel of land via the charitable deduction route, assume the parcel has a fair market value of $1,000 and a zero cost basis to the owner who has a contribution base in excess of $3,333 and has a marginal tax bracket of 50 percent. In the event of a charitable contribution of the parcel, the fair market value of $1,000 is fully deductible and the resulting tax benefit or tax reduction is $500. That is also an acquisition cost to Treasury. It is not, however, the full cost because the unrealized appreciation of $1,000 escapes a capital gains tax of $200. When that is considered, the total cost to Treasury is $700, or 70 percent of the fair market value of the property. The landowner's contribution is 30 percent. The landowner in a 50 percent tax bracket tends to think of the tax benefit or "purchase price" as measured only by 50 percent of the value of the donated property; the foregone capital gains tax of as much as 20 percent is overlooked.

2. 1981 National Directory of Local Land Organizations published in 1981 by the Land Trust Exchange, Mount Desert, Maine 04660. See also Bremer, A Review of the 1981 National Survey of Local Land Conservation Organizations, Private Options: Tools and Concepts for Land Conservation 177 (Island Press, Covelo, Cal. 1982).

3. Tax Treatment Extension Act of 1980, Pub. L. No. 96-541, 94 Stat. 3204 (1980) (Temporary Tax Provisions).

4. See Subcomm. on Public Lands and Reserved Water of the Senate Comm. on Energy and Natural Resources, 97th Cong., 2d Sess., Workshop on Land Protection and Management (Comm. Print June 15, 1982) (statement of Kingsbury Browne).

5. Statement by Tyson Van Auken, Director, Virginia Outdoors Foundation, to Kingsbury Browne (Nov. 10, 1982).

6. See supra note 1.

7. Treas. Reg. §1.501(c)(3)-1(d)(2).

8. Prior to December 17, 1980, charitable gifts of conservation easements were thought to be deductible as long as the easements were in gross and in perpetuity. But after that date deductible easements required compliance with exceptions involving consideration of a variety of actual or desired uses ranging from the protection of habitat to the maintenance of scenic qualities. The audit task now confronting examiners is far more difficult—and the outcome far less predictable—than it was prior to December 17, 1980. For a discussion of the pre-1980 tax laws affecting conservation easements, see Browne and Van Dorn, Charitable Gifts of Partial Interests in Real Property for Conservation Purposes, 29 Tax Law. 69 (1975).

9: See supra note 2.

10. In Rev. Rul. 76-204, 1976-1 C.B. 152, the Internal Revenue Service granted exempt status to an organization formed for the purpose of preserving the natural environment by acquiring "ecologically significant" undeveloped land. Farming was not involved.

In Rev. Rul. 78-384, 1978-2 C.B. 174, exempt status was denied an organization that restricted its land use to farming or other uses the organization deemed compatible with the ecology of the area. Such restricted use was considered too indirect a public benefit. The land must be ecologically significant.

On January 9, 1980, the United States Tax Court in Dumaine v. Comm'r, 73 T.C. 650 (1980), overruled the Internal Revenue Service and upheld exempt status under Section 501(c)(3) in the case of an organization conducting research projects designed to demonstrate that (1) marginally productive land should be held as conservation land so as to improve the watershed, provide ground cover and food for wildlife, and to produce timber; and (2) modern, ecologically sound farming techniques can restore to productive use land exhausted by repetitive cash-crop farming. The Service is apparently not persuaded that preservation of farmland is in and of itself a proper basis for granting exempt status. For a discussion of protecting farmlands through tax incentives, *see* Thompson, *Protecting Farmland and Farming Enterprise: Federal Tax Incentives*, Private Options: Tools and Concepts for Land Conservation 93 (Island Press, Covelo, Cal. 1982).

11. For a description of the Maryland Environmental Trust, *see* Miller, *Public/Private Relationships: Land Saving by a Quasi-Public Agency*, Private Options: Tools and Concepts for Land Conservation 222 (Island Press, Covelo, Cal. 1982).

12. Mass. Gen. Laws Ann. ch. 184, §§31-33 (West).

13. Rubenstein, *Areas of Cooperation Between Government Agencies and Nonprofit Organizations*, Private Options: Tools and Concepts for Land Conservation 84 (Island Press, Covelo, Cal. 1982).

14. *The Federal Drive to Acquire Private Lands Should Be Reassessed.* Report by the Comptroller General of the United States, CED 80-14, December 14, 1979.

15. Massachusetts; Suffolk County, N.Y.; and King County, Washington have funded programs for the purchase of development rights from farmers.

16. Rev. Rul. 64-205, 1964-2 C.B. 62; Rev. Rul. 74-583, 1974-2 C.B. 80.

17. Browne and Van Dorn, *Charitable Gifts of Partial Interests in Real Property for Conservation Purposes*, 29 Tax Law. 69, 72 (1975).

18. *Id.* at 75; Regulations, Treas. Reg. §1.170A-7(b)(1)(ii).

19. Rev. Rul. 75-66, 1975-1 C.B. 85.

20. *See* Private Letter Ruling (Apr. 20, 1976) (T:I:I:1:1).

21. Rev. Rul. 75-420, 1975-2 C.B. 78; Private Letter Ruling 8204220 (Oct. 30, 1981).

22. Rev. Rul. 75-373, 1975-2 C.B. 77.

23. The extension of deductibility to thirty-year or longer easements was not explained in the Committee Reports. It appears to have been a last-minute addition to the Tax Reform Act of 1976. *See* House Conf. Report No. 94-1515 at 505 (Sept. 13, 1976), *reprinted in* 1976 U.S. Code Cong. & Ad. News 4207-08.

24. Private Letter Ruling 8012026.

25. In a Technical Advice Memorandum dated October 22, 1981, Private Letter Ruling 8204020, the Internal Revenue Service determined the deductibility of an easement granted in 1978 under the 1976/1977 statute, thus denying vitality to the 1969 provision.

26. *See Federal Tax Benefits and Land Conservation, A Transcript of a Colloquy Between Tax Lawyers from the United States Treasury Department and Internal Revenue Service and Leaders of Some Twenty or More Land Conservation Organizations* (K. Browne, ed., Dec. 15, 1979) (sponsored by the Brandywine Conservancy; published by the Maryland Environmental Trust, Baltimore, Md.).

27. The private letter ruling was issued in the mid-1970s and involved the Great Dismal Swamp. It has not yet been published by the Internal Revenue Service.

28. Pub. L. No. 96-541, §6(b), 94 Stat. 3204 (1980), introduced new criteria cast in terms of "qualified real property interest" and "qualified organization" "exclusively for conservation purposes." The last is defined as follows:

(4) *Conservation purpose defined.*

(A) *In general.* —For purposes of this subsection, the term "conservation purpose" means—

(i) the preservation of land areas for outdoor recreation by, or the education of, the general public,

(ii) the protection of a relatively natural habitat of fish, wildlife, or plants, or similar ecosystem,

(iii) the preservation of open space (including farmland and forest land) where such preservation is—

(I) for the scenic enjoyment of the general public, or

(II) pursuant to a clearly delineated Federal, State, or local governmental conservation policy, and will yield a significant public benefit, or

(iv) the preservation of an historically important land area or a certified historic structure.

29. *Hearings on H.R. 7318 Before the Subcomm. on Select Revenue Measures of the House Comm. on Ways and Means*, 96th Cong., 2d Sess. 165, 167 (June 26, 1980) (testimony of Daniel I. Halperin, Deputy Assistant Secretary of the Treasury for Tax Policy).

30. The charitable gift of a conservation easement that fails to qualify for an income tax deduction is subject to gift taxes. I.R.C. §2522(c)(2).

31. Letter from Treasury Secretary Regan to Chairman Dan Rostenkowski, H.R. Comm. on Ways and Means (May 26, 1982) (H.R. Doc. No. 82-6580).

32. Four private letter rulings had issued as of November 1, 1982. Three addressed the meaning of "clearly delineated . . . governmental conservation policy" and a fourth the meaning of "habitat." All involved spectacular facts; the middle of the road remains to be defined. For a more optimistic view of the rulings process, *see* Small, *Working with the 1980 Amendments to the Internal Revenue Code*, Land-Saving Action (Island Press, Covelo, Cal. 1984).

Working with the 1980 Amendments to the Internal Revenue Code*

Stephen J. Small

The Internal Revenue Service is not well liked. In fact, it has been suggested that the Service does nothing to change this reputation since the perception of the Service as ogre may even encourage voluntary compliance with our tax collection system. I worked at the Service for four years, and I still get nervous every time I see a letter from the IRS in my mail at home.

What may be a useful image for tax collection purposes, however, has had a detrimental side effect. There seems to be a widespread assumption in the conservation movement that if the IRS has anything to say about a conservation easement donation, the deduction will be either reduced or denied entirely, with the additional stiff penalty in this latter case of a gift tax to pay.[1] I must tell you that my own experience at the Service leads me to say that assumption is not true. Congress passed the statute allowing these deductions; it was Congress's intention that the statute encourage the protection of conservation interests;[2] and it is the job of the IRS to administer the statute in a manner consistent with congressional intent.

Of course, donors and donees are right to be wary of terms and concepts that are breaking new ground in the Internal Revenue Code.[3] Conceded, it is difficult to work with a statute that calls for subjective judgments on criteria ranging from "scenic enjoyment" to "significant public benefit." But the fact is that we do have a new statute, and whenever Congress passes a new tax law, there is uncertainty about its application and effects and there is hesitation among taxpayers. Let me give one relevant illustration.

In the Tax Reform Act of 1969, while amending the law in a rather obscure area of the tax code, Congress inadvertently nipped in the bud the growing use of easements for land conservation. The effect of this change in the law through subsequent years is well documented and

need not be repeated here.[4] The fact is that in 1970 and for some years thereafter it was perceived to be a damaging and narrow piece of legislation in the conservation field.[5] In response to this perception, in 1970 the Treasury Department and the Council on Environmental Quality began to work together to develop a new and what was intended to be a broader deduction in the tax code for easement donations. The legislation that came out of that dialogue was first introduced in 1972 and was reintroduced every year thereafter until it became law as part of the Tax Reform Act of 1976. That statute gave us the "conservation purposes" test[6] and was the predecessor of the current statute.

Were the "ill effects" of the 1969 legislation remedied by the new law in 1976? Hardly. Between 1969 and 1976 the Internal Revenue Service issued a series of revenue rulings[7] interpreting the 1969 statute (and the regulations implementing the statute) that were not restrictive at all but in fact had a positive effect on the conservation movement.[8] With a great deal of hindsight it now seems that while proposed legislation was being reintroduced annually to remedy an earlier error, the Internal Revenue Service, in its administrative positions, was making the "remedy" unnecessary. After the new legislation was finally enacted in 1976, conservationists who were doing easement work realized that suddenly they had a vaguely defined "conservation purposes" test to meet, while prior to 1976 the deductibility of an easement donation had been considerably easier to establish.[9]

This leads to my main point: Rather than lamenting the vagueness and unworkability of the new statute and rather than spinning wheels thinking of ways to amend the statute (which involves going through a legislative process notorious for shifting congressional coalitions and fickle executive branch support), the conservation movement ought to devote careful attention over the next few years to making the statute work. Let me offer a few thoughts on how to do this, based on my perceptions of the conservation movement and my understanding of the regulatory process at IRS. I ought to say that while the approach I propose is directed at the current conservation easement statute, it is also generally applicable to other areas of the tax code.

In an ideal world we would be aiming for certainty, certainty that a particular easement donation meets (or does not meet) the requirements of the statute for a deduction. In the world under this statute, we are not going to get certainty (because conservation is hardly an exact science), but what we can get is reassurance that donations that look good under the statute and the regulations to conservation professionals in the field also look good to the Internal Revenue Service. It seems to me that if the prevailing view becomes "it works" rather than "it doesn't work," conservationists can stop worrying about the statute and devote more time and energy to their own vital programs.

The foundation for making the statute "workable" begins with the letter ruling process. Very briefly, the process works like this. The Internal Revenue Service is given, in writing, the facts of a proposed transaction ("Mr. and Mrs. A. own 200 acres of undeveloped coastland . . .") and what the writer believes to be the controlling law ("Under section 170(h) of the Internal Revenue Code, a deduction is allowed for the donation of . . ."). The Service is then asked to rule, in writing, that the proposed transaction will meet the requirements of the Code and that the tax treatment suggested by the taxpayer will apply.[10] The closer the proposed transaction comes to meeting the terms and intent of the relevant tax statute and the regulations implementing that statute, the more likely it is that the Service will issue a favorable letter ruling. Letter rulings are a standard part of tax practice. Even with prominent disclaimers by the Service on each letter ruling that the ruling may not be cited as precedent for other transactions, letter rulings are in fact very valuable guides for taxpayers. The Service knows this and tax practitioners know this.

The starting point for this approach, for purposes of the conservation movement, ought to be somewhere inside the "network" that is growing among land trusts and the land conservation movement generally. I am convinced that within this network there are at least a handful of organizations that can identify a total of four or five or six donors who have the resources to apply for a letter ruling from the Internal Revenue Service and easement donations to make that clearly qualify for a deduction. I am not thinking of six donations of easements on privately held land within national parks or five donations with very simple, clearly defined issues. I have in mind a series of donations about which the professionals in the conservation movement can say (1) these are good donations under

this statute and (2) favorable letter rulings on these donations will have widespread applicability both to illustrate the kinds of transactions the statute encourages and to reassure the conservation community that the IRS is administering the statute in a constructive way. Naturally, this sorting-out process ought to begin as soon as possible. Uncertainty and delay are costly for the land conservation movement: not only are particular tracts of land threatened, but the very viability of some land conservation groups is threatened if their programs are stalled.

A number of proposed transactions ought to be scrutinized so the ones that best meet these two criteria can be chosen.[11] The attorneys representing these taxpayer-donors ought to be familiar with the needs of the donee organizations and with the letter ruling process. The donors involved ought to be flexible enough to make the modifications in their original plans that are a part of the give-and-take between the Service and the taxpayer that inevitably precedes the issuance of a favorable ruling. Finally, it is not unreasonable to suggest that this kind of coordinated effort be brought to the attention of the Service. It is not unusual for the Service to work with interest groups in an effort to promote efficient and effective administration of the tax system.

In a sense it could be said that we are making new law. However, I would suggest rather that we are merely confirming that the statute works, that the system works.

It is important to mention that a number of perfectly good easement donations have already been completed without advance approval from the IRS, and of course these should continue. However, these individual transactions do not provide the reassurance many conservationists seem to need. Additionally, even with a reliable vehicle for disseminating news among donee organizations about particular private easement donations, the law is still so new that without a clear understanding of the IRS's position (made evident in the regulations and letter rulings) groups might be reluctant to follow one another's lead with respect to innovative techniques.

I anticipate two responses to my proposal (and I'm sure there will be additional unanticipated responses). First, I will be reminded that the letter ruling process is not for everyone because it costs money and that a conservation program cannot succeed if it must rely on letter rulings. Second, it will be suggested that things would be much simpler if we could (1) amend the law to have some kind of certification process so a donor would know for sure that the gift qualifies for the deduction; or (2) amend the law to reflect the simple proposition that something valuable is given up when an easement is donated to a conservation organization, and the only question that ought to be outstanding is the value of the gift; or (3) amend the law so that an easement donation that fails to meet the requirements of the statute is not then subject to a gift tax (in technical terms, to "uncouple" the gift tax liability).[12]

Let me answer these in order. I recognize that the letter

ruling process can be expensive. What I am suggesting is that in the universe of potential donors with good transactions there are at least a handful who are in a position to bear the cost of a letter ruling (which is tax deductible), both for the security of their own transactions and in order to do some additional good for others who will follow. When there is a body of law in this area, I believe that with few exceptions donors and donee organizations will be comfortable about future donations.

As far as additional statutory amendments are concerned, one general observation is in order before dealing with the three specific suggestions above. Every time Congress has touched this area the conservation movement has paid a price. In 1969, although over a period of years things did work out well, the early impression was of a setback. In 1976, as I noted above, what was intended to be a liberalizing statute did not have that effect at all. In 1977, starting with what was supposed to be a simple technical amendment to the 1976 statute, Congress eliminated the deduction for the donation of easements of thirty years or more and required that all easements be perpetual to qualify for a deduction.[13] And in 1980 the thorough revision of the existing law at the very least cost the conservation movement valuable time until uncertainty over the new statutory scheme could be worked out. The fact of the matter is that the land conservation movement hardly enjoys the legislative clout of the defense lobby or the tobacco lobby and for the time being ought to stay away from the federal legislative process.[14]

This does not mean, however, that conservationists ought to stay away from Capitol Hill. One of the reasons the land conservation movement does not have a better track record with respect to federal legislation is that conservation groups generally (there are exceptions) have not taken the time to develop good working relationships with federal legislators. For a group without a lot of political clout, success in the legislative arena often depends on taking the time to educate legislators. Congressmen and senators truly are very busy people and can only infrequently set their own legislative priorities. They often look to the constituents' priorities to determine how to allocate their own time. A land conservation group is in fact uniquely situated to maintain some kind of regular personal contact with its own congressional delegation. A congressman always welcomes an opportunity to make a statement on the House floor about the rolling hills, or the pleasant valleys, or the majestic mountains, or the historic character of his or her own district. One meeting a year in Washington and, for example, a short, informal tour of the local protected holdings with the congressman every six months (accompanied by a few well-connected, satisfied donors and the local press) could turn out to be mutually rewarding. Occasional telephone calls, not letters,[15] to the appropriate staffer in the congressman's office are also an important way to keep in touch. It is difficult for an interest group to approach a congressman who knows little about its needs

and expect cooperation on any legislation, let alone on some esoteric amendment to the tax code.

It would also be useful for the "network" to explore the possibility of more sophisticated lobbying as time goes by. Strong support from a junior congressman has a fraction of the impact of a nod from the committee chairman. A successful interest group does not approach Chairman Smith of Texas with a delegation from Michigan. Successful interest groups identify the key committee chairmen, ranking minority members (senior members of the committee from the minority party), and other powerful members of Congress and find articulate spokespeople in those particular congressional districts or states to carry on the "education" process. The conservation movement must learn over time to do no less. An interest group that has key legislators who are genuinely supportive of the group's efforts and knowledgeable about the group's needs will often fare quite well in the legislative arena.

With regard to the specific suggestions for legislation I referred to earlier, the first proposal is for some kind of certification process. What is envisioned, broadly speaking, is that at some level of government an agency, department, or office would "certify" donations when those donations meet criteria established by the government. It is suggested that such certified donations, as part of important conservation programs, ought to qualify automatically for a deduction. In some situations that may be useful. However, my personal view is that in most cases such a process won't add much to the section of the statute that allows a deduction for the donation of an easement pursuant to a "clearly delineated governmental policy." Further, in local, state, or federal government a certification process needs continuing executive branch support and appropriations from the legislative branch. It would be distressing, for example, to see conservationists place a lot of emphasis on a Department of the Interior certification process that would always be subject to the kind of executive branch politics that caused the National Register of Historic Places to be frozen shut by administrative fiat through most of 1981.

The second suggestion is to amend the law to eliminate the "conservation purposes" test and other requirements of the statute and to recognize an easement as a separate, severable right. Under this approach, it is argued, there need be only two questions: (1) Was something of value given up? and (2) Did it go to a qualified conservation organization? I think that is a valid approach conceptually. However, it does not take into account the history of congressional and Treasury Department concern over charitable contributions of "partial interests." The donation of a partial interest, in the context of the tax code, is the donation of something less than the entire property. Whether a donor gives cash to the alma mater or used clothing to the Salvation Army, the donor has given up all control over that property (or cash) and, accordingly, has given up any enjoyment of the property. It is clear that the public benefit from these gifts outweighs any private one and that most charitable contributions fall into this framework. The theme of "public benefit" is implicit throughout the charitable contributions section of the Internal Revenue Code.

However, when a taxpayer donates a partial interest, less than the entire property, to a charitable organization, the taxpayer may retain considerable control over and enjoyment of the property. The taxpayer gets a double benefit: an income tax deduction *and* continued (albeit perhaps limited) use of the property. It is no longer clear that the public benefit from such a gift outweighs the private benefit, specifically, the benefit to the taxpayer.

Even if an easement is a separate, severable property right, it is also a partial interest; that is, it is something less than the entire property. As far as Congress and Treasury are concerned, a taxpayer who donates an easement continues to use and enjoy the property, and the requirements for taking an income tax deduction simply must be tighter to ensure that there is also a significant long-term public benefit associated with the donation. This is the kind of analysis that conservation easements have been subject to in the legislative process and will continue to be subject to, whether or not easements are regarded as separate property rights. This point of view does not spring from a new congressional bias against conservation organizations. The bias is a continuing one against the property owner who takes an income tax deduction, then sits on the back porch looking over the unspoiled acreage that was the subject of the deduction.

Finally, it is suggested that a lot of the anguish would be eliminated from this area if donors didn't have to worry about a gift tax liability for failure to meet the requirements of the statute.[16] It is quite arguable that when a taxpayer does in fact donate something of value (partial interest or not) to a charitable organization, if the donation doesn't meet the requirements of the Internal Revenue Code, that taxpayer ought to lose the deduction but ought not be penalized with a gift tax. There are two responses. First, much of the congressional and Treasury Department concern in this area has been over unenumerated abuses, not merely aggressive valuation of donations[17] and, more significantly, the undefined fear that people somewhere out there are taking deductions for easement donations that don't serve any genuinely useful conservation purpose. The threat of a gift tax liability, it is argued, is a strong deterrent to abuse, and one that should be retained.

Even assuming that argument can be overcome, there is a further reason why any amendment to "uncouple" the gift tax liability should be viewed with great caution by the conservation movement. For a truly beneficial amendment such as that, there would almost certainly have to be a trade-off, and that trade-off might be in the form of a considerably narrower easement statute. This is not the place to suggest the array of changes that could achieve such narrowing, but this is the place to reiterate what I said earlier: Every time the Congress has touched this area the conservation movement has paid a price. Until the land conservation movement has a wider range of knowledgeable supporters in Congress, I don't think the movement can risk another major legislative change to this statute and the consequent uncertainty and delay. The rule that Barry Commoner is fond of applying to the environment also applies to the legislative process: There's no such thing as a free lunch.[18]

The proposal to follow the administrative route rather than the legislative route, at least for the short term, is based on two assumptions. One is that the IRS will in fact administer the statute in a reasonable fashion.[19] The other is that the lines of communication recently opening up among conservation groups are sufficient to plan this kind of methodical approach. If these assumptions are correct, I am certain that as time goes by, this statute will turn out to be one of a number of useful tools available to the conservation movement in its continuing effort to improve the quality of life.

Notes

*The publication of *Land-Saving Action* before the publication of final Internal Revenue Service regulations on the donation of conservation easements creates a bit of a timing problem. I resolved the problem by writing my article on the assumption that the final regulations would not be dramatically different from the proposed regulations, published in May 1983.

1. Under the Internal Revenue Code, any transfer of property without "full and adequate consideration" (that is, without payment for the property) is a gift. Gifts are subject to the gift tax imposed by the Code unless there is an exclusion in the Code for such gifts (for example, a gift between spouses) or unless the gift is specifically deductible (for example, a charitable contribution). A gift (to a charity) that is not specifically deductible, then, is subject to the gift tax.

2. "The committee believes that the preservation of our country's natural resources and cultural heritage is important, and the committee recognizes that conservation easements play an important role in preservation efforts. . . . In particular, the committee found it appropriate to expand the types of transfers that will qualify as deductible contributions in certain cases where the contributions are likely to further significant conservation goals without presenting significant potential for abuse." S. Rep. No. 96-1007, 96th Cong., 2d Sess. 9 (1980).

3. It is helpful at this point to include the text of the statute we are discussing.

[Sec. 170(h)]

(h) *Qualified Conservation Contribution.* —

(1) *In general.* —For purposes of subsection (f)(3)(B)(iii), the term "qualified conservation contribution" means a contribution—

(A) of a qualified real property interest,

(B) to a qualified organization,

(C) exclusively for conservation purposes.

(2) *Qualified real property interest.* —For purposes of this sub-

section, the term "qualified real property interest" means any of the following interests in real property:

(A) the entire interest of the donor other than a qualified mineral interest,

(B) a remainder interest, and

(C) a restriction (granted in perpetuity) on the use which may be made of the real property.

(3) *Qualified organization.*—For purposes of paragraph (1), the term "qualified organization" means an organization which—

(A) is described in clause (v) or (vi) of subsection (b)(1)(A), or

(B) is described in section 501(c)(3) and—

(i) meets the requirements of section 509(a)(2), or

(ii) meets the requirements of section 509(a)(3) and is controlled by an organization described in subparagraph (A) or in clause (i) of this subparagraph.

(4) *Conservation purpose defined.*

(A) *In general.*—For purposes of this subsection, the term "conservation purpose" means—

(i) the preservation of land areas for outdoor recreation by, or the education of, the general public,

(ii) the protection of a relatively natural habitat of fish, wildlife, or plants, or similar ecosystem,

(iii) the preservation of open space (including farmland and forest land) where such preservation is—

(I) for the scenic enjoyment of the general public, or

(II) pursuant to a clearly delineated Federal, State, or local governmental conservation policy, and will yield a significant public benefit, or

(iv) the preservation of an historically important land area or a certified historic structure.

(B) *Certified historic structure.*—For purposes of subparagraph (A)(iv), the term "certified historic structure" means any building, structure, or land area which—

(i) is listed in the National Register, or

(ii) is located in a registered historic district (as defined in section 48(g)(3)(B)) and is certified by the Secretary of the Interior to the Secretary as being of historic significance to the district.

A building, structure, or land area satisfies the preceding sentence if it satisfies such sentence either at the time of the transfer or on the due date (including extensions) for filing the transferor's return under this chapter for the taxable year in which the transfer is made.

(5) *Exclusively for conservation purposes.*—For purposes of this subsection—

(A) *Conservation purpose must be protected.*—A contribution shall not be treated as exclusively for conservation purposes unless the conservation purpose is protected in perpetuity.

(B) *No surface mining permitted.*—In the case of a contribution of any interest where there is a retention of a qualified mineral interest, subparagraph (A) shall not be treated as met if at any time there may be extraction or removal of minerals by any surface mining method.

(6) *Qualified mineral interest.*—For purposes of this subsection, the term "qualified mineral interest" means—

(A) subsurface oil, gas or other minerals, and

(B) the right to access to such minerals.

4. *See* Browne and Van Dorn, *Charitable Gifts of Partial Interests in Real Property for Conservation Purposes,* 29 Tax Law 69 (1975);

Small, *The Tax Benefits of Donating Easements in Scenic and Historic Property,* 7 Real Est. L.J. 301 (1979).

5. "Returning to the conservation of scenic easements and restrictions whose deductibility had been acknowledged and publicized by the Service in 1964 and 1965, their future, as determined strictly by Code provisions, was, and is, bleak indeed." Browne and Van Dorn, *supra* note 4, at 73. *See also* Wiggins, Jr. & Hunt, *Tax Policy Relating to Environmental Activities and Public Interest Litigation* (1975), in Department of the Treasury, 4 Research Papers Sponsored by the Commission on Private Philanthropy and Public Needs 2045 (1977).

6. That is, the statute says a deduction is allowed for the donation of an easement "for conservation purposes" and then goes on to enumerate the definitions of "conservation purposes."

7. A revenue ruling is a published statement that represents the conclusions of the Internal Revenue Service on what the law is with respect to the set of facts presented in the revenue ruling. A revenue ruling may be cited by any taxpayer as authority for any transaction fitting that particular set of facts, while a "letter ruling" (see text) may not. Although revenue rulings are official statements of the Service, they do not carry the same legal weight as regulations. The difference in legal force and effect of regulations, revenue rulings, and letter rulings exists generally because regulations (for all federal agencies) are issued under a specific delegation of authority from the Congress and must be promulgated in accordance with the Administrative Procedure Act, the federal statute requiring publication of proposed regulations for comment, and, if requested, public hearings. At the Internal Revenue Service a very extensive review and "sign-off" are required before a regulation can be published. A revenue ruling is reviewed at fewer levels, a letter ruling at fewer still. Revenue rulings are published in final, not proposed, form (unlike regulations), and public hearings are not required. It should be noted that some noncontroversial regulations in fact receive very limited review and some letter rulings turn out to be major projects within the Service, depending on the issues involved.

8. *See, e.g.,* Rev. Rul. 75-358, 1975-2 C.B. 76, holding that an easement to preserve the facade of a state landmark was an "open space" easement under Treas. Reg. §1.170A-7(b)(1)(ii), the regulations promulgated under the 1969 amendment. *See also* Brenneman, *Easements and Their Taxation,* Preservation News (May 1976), where Brenneman commented that Rev. Rul. 75-358 "demonstrates that the Internal Revenue Service is willing to go a long way" in its interpretation of the law.

9. I have taken the liberty of compressing history a bit, and a lengthy footnote is in order. Specifically, the regulations implementing the 1969 legislative change allowed a deduction for the donation of an "open space easement in gross" where the easement was in perpetuity. The 1976 legislation allowed a deduction for the donation of an easement "for conservation purposes." A critical question was left unanswered in the 1976 statute and in its legislative history: whether the 1976 legislation was intended to *supplement* the 1969 legislation (that is, give donors an additional way to deduct an easement donation) or *replace* the 1969 legislation (that is, make the "conservation purposes" test the exclusive one for a deduction). It is understood that during consideration of the 1977 amendment to the "conservation purposes" statute, this question was raised at the *staff* level of the congressional tax-writing committees but was, to be blunt, explicitly ducked. Accordingly, the question was delegated to the Internal Revenue Service to resolve in regulations on the 1976 statute. For a variety of reasons not relevant here, regula-

tions on the 1976 statute were never published. In rewriting the "conservation purposes" statute in 1980, Congress specifically directed that the new statute was henceforth to be the exclusive one for the deductibility of easement donations.

It is, of course, unknown how the Internal Revenue Service and the Treasury Department would have answered the question of which statute controlled if regulations had in fact been published under the 1976 statute. Letter rulings were issued between 1976 and 1980 allowing taxpayers to deduct easement donations based on the 1969 law and regulations, but this would not have prevented the Service and Treasury Department from taking a different position for future transactions in subsequent regulations. Suffice it to say that absent a definite answer from the Service on how to proceed, the state of the law was muddled at best.

10. A sample letter ruling issued by the IRS:

Dear Mr. and Mrs. _____

This is in reply to a request for a ruling that a certain contribution will be a qualified conservation contribution under section 170(h) of the Internal Revenue Code.

We understand the facts to be substantially as follows.

H and W own 245 acres of land (hereinafter referred to as the "property") in J, a valley about 60 miles long and up to 12 miles wide, encompassing most of the county in which it is located, T, in the state of X. The property is leased to R, a corporation. H and W are the sole shareholders of R. R owns approximately 40 acres of land adjoining the property.

The topography of the property is mostly level with small amounts of gentle slopes making the property suitable for ranching, other agricultural uses, or for subdivision or development. The property and the land owned by R is being used for purposes related to the operation of a guest ranch, including the grazing of horses, cattle and other livestock. Approximately 200 families visit the guest ranch annually.

The property is bordered by a national park, P, on the north; a river, S, on the east; and large privately-owned ranches on the south and west. In 1979 over 3,500,000 visits were made to P by members of the general public. Various outdoor recreational pursuits are enjoyed at P, such as boating, fishing, camping, swimming, hiking, mountain climbing, horseback riding and motoring along paved as well as unpaved routes. In addition to the various boating, fishing, and floating opportunities available on S, sightseeing and camping-picknicking are also enjoyed. Not only are portions of both P and S visible, as well as accessible, from the property, the property is also part of the scenic panorama that is the setting of P.

Aspen, willows and meadow have been identified as the three major vegetation types located on the property. The aspen provides a habitat for a wide variety of birds and escape and resting cover for large mammals. The willow vegetation is used as browse by moose that also breed on the property. Elk migrate across the property, crossing from P to islands in S in order to breed. The property has been observed as being in an elk migration corridor. It has also been recognized as a substantially unaltered natural setting of the nearby rugged mountains of southern P and the adjacent S flood plain and its riparian community.

The United States Department of Agriculture Forest Service Draft Environmental Statement for the Wild and Scenic River Study for the S of X in describing S in the area adjacent to the property states:

"Pastoral development along the river lends to the river character. Occasionally, the glimpse of a ranch house, barn or fence may register in the viewer's mind. Cattle and horses may also occasionally be seen grazing the river banks.

Identified outstandingly remarkable values include the scenic presence of a variety of wildlife, the ranching atmosphere and scenic, solitary recreation experience that can easily be experienced by float boat. . . .

This stretch is believed to have 'scenic river' classification potential due to its development level, outstanding scenic view, associated wildlife values, and recreation opportunity."

The area in which the property is located is a mecca for outdoor recreation and attracts millions of visitors annually. Winter activity has increased as a result of developing ski facilities. National attention has been focused on J as a desirable place to live by many who wish to escape a polluted environment and the rapid pace of metropolitan areas. Real estate values have increased by about 400 percent during the past 15-year period. However, only a very limited supply of deeded land is available that is adaptable for development and subdivision in the area. About 3–4 percent of the land in T is privately owned, and it is held by relatively few owners; therefore, the available land for homesites and private development is scarce.

For zoning purposes T is divided into residential, commercial, and industrial districts pursuant to its comprehensive plan and implementation program adopted January 1, 1978. The property is within the residential-agricultural district, having a density of one unit per three acres. Authorized uses in any of the land use districts are agricultural, single-family residences, guest house, home occupations, incidental and accessory structures on the same site that are for the exclusive use of residents and their guests or that are necessary for the operation of a permitted use, public facilities, institutional uses and utilities installations. In addition, the residential-agricultural district permits clustered residential developments, planned unit developments, mobile home parks, dude ranches, outfitters, commercial stables, ski tows and other privately owned outdoor recreational facilities. The present use of the property conforms to the uses within T's comprehensive plan. A 1975 National Park Service study reports that the countryside adjacent to P generally complements the natural and scenic attributes of P.

T has adopted a comprehensive plan and implementation program containing a scenic preservation element that specifically calls for the preservation of the county's scenic resources and sets priorities for the acquisition of fee title or lesser interests in privately owned open space lands for the purpose of preserving the county's scenic resources. In order to implement the scenic preservation element the Board of County Commissioners established the Scenic Preserve Trust of T.

In 1980 residents of the area organized, under the laws of X, a private, nonprofit, tax-exempt corporation, the J Land Trust. One of its purposes was the conservation and acquisition of land, and interests in land within and surrounding J, in order to preserve, protect, and enhance wildlife habitat and natural, scenic, recreational and productive values that benefit the citizens of X and of the United States. The J Land Trust has been determined to be exempt from federal income tax under section 501(c)(3) of the Code and has received an advance ruling that it can reasonably be expected to be a publicly supported organization described in section 509(a)(1) and 170(b)(1)(A)(vi).

H and W propose to grant to J Land Trust, by a properly recorded warranty deed, the fee in one acre of property and a conservation easement over and across 39 acres of property to preserve and protect in perpetuity the open space and its scenic and wildlife habitat values. The one acre of property proposed to be granted is subject to an easement for a private roadway. The easement would confine the use of the property solely to agricultural, dude ranching, natural, open space, wildlife habitat and such other uses consistent with the easement. The easement would authorize one 3 acre residential site on the 39 acre tract, the location of which would be subject to the approval of J Land Trust. A 3 acre lot is the minimum lot size permitted in the district in which the property is located. The easement prohibits subdivision of the property, construction or location of any buildings, mobile homes or other structures, except on the permitted 3 acre residential site, and any filling, excavating, dredging, mining, drilling, removal of topsoil, sand, gravel, rock or other materials, or other changes of the topography of the property. The 39 acre tract is visible from P (looking south) and S (looking west), appearing as partially wooded and partially open graze land. The tract is part of the scenic panorama viewed from both P and S.

Contemporaneous with the grant of the open space easement, the lease with R will be amended to make it subject and subordinate to the open space easement.

The terms of the warranty deed give J Land Trust the right to prevent any activity that is incompatible with the purpose or intent, or authorized uses or prohibitions against use of the conservation easement. The easement is being granted as an appurtenant easement in order to create an enforceable property right under the law of X.

Section 170(a) of the Code provides, subject to certain limitations, a deduction for contributions and gifts to or for the use of organizations described in section 170(c), payment of which is made within the taxable year.

Under section 170(f)(3)(A) of the Code, a taxpayer who contributes less than the taxpayer's entire interest in property (that is, a partial interest) is allowed a deduction only to the extent that a deduction for the contributed interest would have been allowable if the taxpayer had contributed the interest in trust. Section 170(f)(2) generally restricts the deduction for contributions in trust to certain kinds of partial interests. Under section 170(f)(3)(B)(iii), however, the general restriction on partial interests does not apply to a qualified conservation contribution.

Under section 170(h)(1) of the Code, the term "qualified conservation contribution," for purposes of section 170(f)(3)(B)(iii), means a contribution of a qualified real property interest, to a qualified organization, exclusively for conservation purposes.

Under section 170(h)(3)(A) of the Code, the term "qualified organization" includes an organization described in section 170(b)(1)(A)(vi). Because J Land Trust is an organization described in section 170(b)(1)(A)(vi), it is a qualified organization under section 170(h)(1).

Under section 170(h)(2)(C) of the Code, the term "qualified real property interest" includes a restriction granted in perpetuity on the use of real property. With respect to the qualified real property interest requirement, the Senate Finance Committee Report (S. Rep. No. 96-1007, 1980-2 C.B. 599) in Pub. L. 96-541 (codified in part as section 170(h) of the Code) states that the contribution must involve legally enforceable restrictions on the interest in the property retained by the donor. The Report also indicates that the Committee contemplated that the restrictions would be recorded.

In the instant case the easement is being granted as an appurtenant easement. Section 414(5), 3 *Powell on Real Property* (1979), states that the burden of an appurtenant scenic easement will run with the servient land if the instrument creating the scenic easement is properly recorded and that if the requirements of the local recording statute are satisfied, a legal negative easement will be protected against interference by both legal and equitable remedies. The easement here being granted is to be over and across the property and in perpetuity. The easement does not permit mining or drilling, removal of topsoil, sand, gravel, rock, minerals or other materials or other change of the topography of the property. Therefore, we conclude that the easement will be qualified real property interest within the meaning of section 170(h)(2)(C) of the Code.

Under section 170(h)(4)(A)(iii)(II) of the Code, the term "conservation purpose" includes the preservation of open space, including farmland and forest land, if the preservation is pursuant to a clearly delineated federal, state, or local governmental conservation policy and will yield a significant public benefit. With respect to this purpose, the Report states that such purpose is intended to protect property that representatives of the general public identify as worthy of protection. A broad declaration by a legislative body, such as a state legislature, that land should be conserved is not sufficient, but the governmental conservation policy need not be a certification program that identifies particular lots or small parcels of individually owned property. The Report states that public benefit will be evaluated by considering all information germane to the contribution. Factors germane to one contribution may be irrelevant to another contribution. The Report mentions the following specific factors, without limitation, that may be considered:

(1) the uniqueness of the property;

(2) the intensity of land development in the vicinity of the property;

(3) the consistency of the proposed open space use with public programs for conservation in the region, including programs for water supply protection, water quality maintenance or enhancement, and shoreline protection;

(4) the opportunity for the general public to enjoy the use of the property or to appreciate its scenic values.

Based on the facts in the instant case, the public goals of protecting T's environmental quality and scenic beauty are expressed through a governmental policy favoring the preservation of the county's scenic resources pursuant to its comprehensive plan and implementation program that contains a scenic preservation element. Consequently, we conclude that the contribution to J Land Trust will be made for a conservation purpose within the meaning of section 170(h)(4)(A)(iii)(II) of the Code.

The Report states that a conservation purpose is not protected in perpetuity if the contribution would accomplish one of the enumerated conservation purposes, but would allow uses of the property that would be destructive of other significant conservation interests. This requirement, however, is not intended to prohibit uses of the property retained by the donor if under the circumstances the uses are not destructive of significant conservation interests.

Because the easement is perpetual and permits no use of the

donor's retained interest that will be destructive of any significant conservation interest, we conclude that the conservation purposes of the proposed easement will be protected in perpetuity.

Accordingly, based solely upon the facts submitted and representations made in your ruling request, we conclude that the contribution of the easement will be a qualified conservation contribution under section 170(h) of the Code. Therefore, under section 170(f)(3)(B)(iii), section 170(f)(3)(A) does not apply to the contribution, and a deduction is allowed under section 170(a) and section 1.170A-1(c)(1) of the Income Tax Regulations for the fair market value of the easement.

With regard to the fair market value of the easement contributed, see Rev. Rul. 76-376, 1976-2 C.B. 53, which provides that if a taxpayer grants an easement in land and owns adjoining land in which an easement was not granted, the fair market value of the easement granted is the difference between the fair market value of the entire tract of land before and after the granting of the easement.

Rev. Rul. 75-66, 1975-1 C.B. 85, concludes that the contribution of a tract of land to the United States by an individual who retained the right during his lifetime to train his personal hunting dog on the trails extending over the entire tract, and to maintain paths and lanes relating to the reserved use, is deductible in the manner and to the extent provided by section 170 of the Code. The rights retained by the donor were not substantial enough to affect the deductibility of the property contributed.

Similarly, we conclude that the contribution of the fee in one acre, subject to an easement for a roadway, is deductible in the manner and to the extent provided by section 170 of the Code.

This ruling is addressed only to the taxpayer who requested it. Section 6110(j)(3) of the Code provides that it may not be used or cited as precedent. Temporary or final regulations pertaining to one or more of the issues addressed in this ruling have not yet been adopted. Therefore, this ruling will be modified or revoked by adoption of temporary or final regulations, to the extent the regulations are inconsistent with any conclusions in this ruling. See section 17.04 of Rev. Proc. 80-20, 1980-1 C.B. 633, 644. However, when the criteria in section 17.05 of Rev. Proc. 80-20 are satisfied, a ruling is not revoked or modified retroactively, except in rare or unusual circumstances.

Except as specifically ruled upon above, no opinion is expressed as to the federal income tax consequences of the transaction described above under any other provision of the Internal Revenue Code.

You should attach a copy of this ruling to your tax return for the taxable year in which the transaction covered by this ruling is consummated. We are enclosing a copy for that purpose.

In accordance with the power of attorney submitted, we are sending a copy of this ruling to your authorized representative.

Sincerely yours,

Director, Individual Tax
Division

Enclosures 2
  Copy of this letter
  Copy for 6110 purposes

11. The Service does not look only at the obvious issues in a letter ruling request; complex transactions are studied for hidden issues as well. In the case of a conservation easement, for example, while a donor might be primarily interested in a ruling on the question of whether the donation meets the "significant public benefit" test of the statute, the Service might be concerned about spelling out the legal rights of the donee organization to monitor and enforce the easement. Or, as another example, assume the donor owns mostly undeveloped land that helps to support elk and bighorn sheep and serves as an occasional habitat for bald eagles. The donor might be requesting a ruling that a conservation easement on the property meets the statutory requirement of "protection of a relatively natural habitat of fish, wildlife, or plants," while the Service might be concerned that some rights reserved by the donor would interfere with the very habitat the gift is intended to protect.

12. A variety of amendments have also been suggested around the general theme of increasing the dollar value of the deduction to the donor. Generally speaking, there are limits in the tax code to the amount of taxable income that may be offset by a charitable contribution, so a donor cannot eliminate his or her tax bill by making an enormous charitable donation. The limits take the form of restricting the size of the charitable contribution deduction to a percentage of the taxpayer's income, generally either 30 percent or 50 percent. Proposals to raise some of these percentage limits in the case of easement donations, while important, are separate and aside from the problems I am considering here.

13. In an article I published in 1979 (see supra note 4) on this legislative change, I suggested that the change was more to the detriment of historic preservationists than to the land conservation movement, but I also noted that the two areas are not mutually exclusive and that Internal Revenue Code provisions for both can easily exist side by side.

14. I hear distressing stories about syndicated historic rehabilitation projects combining the investment tax credit and significant depreciation benefits with the "proper timing" of an easement donation for maximum tax advantage. Certainly until the air clears in this questionable area, the subject of conservation easements ought not be raised before congressional committees.

15. When I first began work on Capitol Hill in 1969, the congressman I worked for received about 30 letters a day. The congressman saw all his mail and the good letters made an impression. When I left Capitol Hill in 1978, the senator I worked for received 2,000 to 3,000 letters a week. The staff was so swamped by the sheer volume of mail that the good letters evoked about a four-second positive response. Unless an interest group can generate literally hundreds or thousands of letters—and that *will* make a point—a telephone conversation with a congressional staffperson followed by a letter marked to the attention of that staffer is about the only way to make a point long distance.

16. In fact, because of other Code provisions (in technical terms, the "exemption equivalent") allowing a certain dollar amount of property to be given away tax free during life or at death, there may be no *current* tax due if an easement donation fails to qualify for a deduction. In traditional tax planning, however, the use of this exemption equivalent generally is saved for when a taxpayer dies, so that as much of the estate as possible can be passed on tax free. While a "bad" easement donation may not actually trigger the current payment of a gift tax, it will use up some or all of the exemption equivalent and will have an undesirable effect on future tax planning for the donor.

17. "Aggressive valuation" is a euphemism for attempting to

have easements appraised for more than their actual fair market value. The fair market value of an easement is generally equal to the difference between the value of the property before and after the property is encumbered by the easement. In other words, the value of the easement is the value the donor has given up. Obviously, the higher the value of the easement, the larger the tax deduction.

18. I would suggest, however, that with the passage of time and with the collection of some meaningful data on the donations that are actually being made and the important conservation goals that easements are serving (data which the Treasury Department has the capability to collect), concern over vague abuses will become less pronounced. If the land conservation movement uses this time and its own hard data to broaden its base of support in Washington, an amendment to uncouple the gift tax liability from conservation easement donations may be better received in Congress. Only by emphasizing the truly constructive nature of these programs can the "abuses" be put in proper perspective.

19. Merely because a taxpayer who donates a conservation easement is audited does not mean that the Service is being unreasonable. An audit is not always an "us against them" proceeding. Often the auditor is simply looking for more information. In this regard remember that an easement donation represents a very specialized area of the tax code. Administrators of the conservation organization that accepted the gift can play a valuable role in turning an audit into a constructive and educational process for the auditor.

Gifts of Partial Interests in Real Property

Russell L. Brenneman

§6.01 Introduction

[1] Applying Less than Fee Approaches

Charities involved in conserving land or protecting historical properties have learned that it is not necessary in all cases to own land or buildings in order to protect them. Ownership may be required for charitable purposes that contemplate the active use of property, for example, use as a museum or a public park. However, a close look at a particular resource may convincingly establish that the central concern (whether on the part of a governmental agency or a charitable organization) is not its present use and ownership but rather what might happen to it in the future. There are many examples. Natural areas providing habitat for plants or animals that are in the hands of private owners who are committed to their protection and willing and able to hold the land in its present use do not require additional shelter in the form of ownership by a governmental body or land-conserving charity. A historic building in the hands of an owner aware of its historic value and committed to its preservation (the owner, perhaps, also being the person who has invested in the restoration of the building) does not, for the time being, need the additional reassurance of ownership by a preservation charity. Indeed, the case can be made that much of what is left of many of America's natural and cultural treasures is precisely the result of the caring attention of private owners; and a persuasive argument can also be made that many properties are best looked after by their present owners and users, whether they be residential occupants concerned about historic preservation, farmers, owners of wood lots, or what have you. The conservation/preservation issue may boil down to: What will happen in the future? What will happen in the event that circumstances or the intentions of the present owners change? What will happen in the case of death or bankruptcy? What will happen if the market value of potential uses for the property so counterbalances its value for a present use that the pressure for change becomes irresistible? In each of these situations the owner may wish to and be able to change the status of the property, thus defeating a conservation or preservation objective.

The purposes of the conservation or preservation charity (or a governmental agency having the same aims) can be served if it becomes the owner of an "interest" in property that vests upon the death of the owner or upon the happening of a condition that would frustrate the protection of the land or building (for example, bankruptcy) or that requires the consent of the charity to a change in status of the property, as in the case of shared ownership, or that sequesters in the hands of the charity the right that the owner would otherwise have to deal with his property in a way that would frustrate conservation or preservation of the property or the attribute of it that is deemed by the charity to be of importance. The control of property through joint ownership and through the creation of remainder interests presents familiar legal ground. Less familiar, perhaps, is the notion that by means of an enforceable promise running with the land (in whatever form) an owner can surrender, on behalf of himself and all future owners, the right to use property as he or they might choose. Such is the jurisprudential soil in which the conservation or preservation "easement" is planted.[1] The charity (or government agency) holding such a right may achieve its goal of controlling the future use of property without owning it.

"Less than fee" controls on the future of property in the hands of the charity may also be attractive to the present owner of the property in that the owner's present personal use and objectives may be little affected. Like the charity, an owner may be concerned principally about the future, and he may achieve his goal of protecting his property by transferring a remainder interest after one or more life estates or after a term of years. The owner may be comfortable with a joint tenancy that does not disturb existing uses and even more so with the less intrusive approach of a conservation easement, which at bottom simply transfers to the charity the right to enforce a "running" promise in respect to land, a promise that (presumptively) the owner himself has no intention of breaking, that is consistent with his own view of the use of his property, and that, to him, represents the lightest of personal burdens. Yet, beyond question, that burden has an economic cost; value, though it may be latent, is stripped from property in a proportion great or small depending upon the nature and gravity of the restriction.

If the gift is to a charity, something of value passes from the owner to the charity, whether we speak of the creation of a joint ownership, a remainder interest, or an "ease-ment." (Yet a present-use value, conforming to the owner's present needs and wishes, remains.) What "something" has been contributed? Again, in the case of joint tenancies and remainders we find familiar ground. But what of something so ephemeral as the right of a promisee to enforce a promise that property is to be used or is not to be used in a particular way? And if that really is a "something" that can be contributed, what is its economic value? From the standpoint of tax policy, should the transfer of such an interest as a contribution be deductible merely because it passes to a charity and despite the reservation of a private use or benefit? This is the philosophical environment within which the income, estate, and gift tax consequences of such transactions must be considered.

[2] Development of Federal Tax Law

[a] *Before 1969.* In 1964 a taxpayer sought advice from the Internal Revenue Service that resulted in the first ruling on contributions of restrictions on real property.[2] The taxpayer's land was adjacent to a federal highway and presented an attractive wooded and scenic appearance. The interest of the United States was to maintain the scenic view from the highway. The taxpayer and a number of neighboring landowners gave to the United States "perpetual restrictive easements" that restricted the development of their properties in respect to the type and height of buildings that could be constructed and the use of the property, including controls on the removal of trees, placement of utility lines, dumping of trash, and the like. Under the applicable law the "restrictive easement" constituted a valuable property right or interest in favor of the party for whose benefit the easement was created and was enforceable by that party. A valuable property right having passed to the United States, it was ruled that the taxpayer was entitled to a deduction under Section 170 for a charitable contribution. While the circumstances of the transaction were discussed, while the purpose of the restriction was to protect "scenic" amenities, and while the restriction benefited the use of a federal highway, these aspects were seemingly not particularly integral to the central premise of the ruling, which primarily asked and answered the question of whether a valuable property right had been given.

Assuming that, under local law, the rights transferred were a valuable "something," the 1964 ruling rested comfortably on familiar foundations. In the case of a charitable contribution, the questions to be asked, under general principles, are: (1) Is there a transfer of something of value?[3] (2) Is the transfer a gift with the requisite donative intent?[4] (3) Is the transfer to or for the use of an organization, contributions to which qualify for the deduction? So secure was the Service in its interpretation of the Code as it stood in 1964 that it formally announced the availability of income tax deductions for "scenic easements."[5]

[b] *After 1969.* The Tax Reform Act of 1969[6] brought dramatic changes.[7] No longer was the test to be simply

whether or not a valuable property right was donated to an appropriate organization. Instead, to qualify for the charitable contributions deduction, the contribution could not be of a partial interest constituting less than the contributor's entire ownership of the property. The "partial interest" rule was born. While the stated purpose of the law change was to preclude a taxpayer from taking a deduction for a contribution of the use of property for a period of time, with the taxpayer retaining all other present and future ownership rights (as in the case of a leasehold),[8] the effect upon contributions of property interests other than leaseholds was substantial. There were two stated exceptions to the partial interest rule: (1) a gift of a remainder interest in a personal residence or farm qualified for the deduction, and (2) a gift of an undivided portion of the taxpayer's entire interest in the property. A further exception, that for an "open space easement in gross in perpetuity," emerged from a very generous but authoritative gloss upon the statutory language.

By safeguarding the deduction for a contribution of an undivided portion of the taxpayer's entire interest in the property, the Tax Reform Act conformed to prior law,[9] while it additionally specified that the mere right to the use of property is not to be considered such an undivided portion.[10] At the same time, it was clear that where the only interest owned by the taxpayer was itself a "partial" interest, a gift of the taxpayer's entire ownership in that interest would be a gift of his "entire interest."[11] By stipulating that the only type of remainder interest that qualified for the charitable contribution deduction would be a remainder interest in a personal residence or farm, the Tax Reform Act limited prior law, which had allowed a deduction for the contribution of any type of remainder. The act did not define what was meant by "residence" or "farm" or limit the term "residence" by any qualifier such as the word "principal."[12]

More conjectural, and of interest principally because it set the stage for what followed, was the deduction allowed after the enactment of the Tax Reform Act for "open space easements in gross in perpetuity." To the puzzlement of property lawyers and possibly to the surprise of some congressmen, the initial conference report on the act contained the observation that an "open space easement in gross" that is also "in perpetuity" was, for the purposes of the act, to be considered an undivided portion of the taxpayer's entire interest.[13] While the conferees did not define any of those terms, regulations subsequently adopted added: "An easement in gross is a mere personal interest in, or right to use, the land of another; it is not supported by a dominant estate but is attached to, and vested in, the person to whom it is granted."[14] While evidently intending to preserve the deduction for situations such as that presented in Revenue Ruling 64-205, the conference report and the regulations raised, at the very least, the following problems: (1) What was meant by "open space"? Specifically, did it include the protection of structures? (2) What

was meant by an "easement"? Specifically, did it include all types of "running" promises? Was it sensible to establish an exception to the partial interest rule for easements "in gross" (which are not "recognized" by the law of some jurisdictions), while omitting from the exception the legally well-established category of easements appurtenant? Did the language apply only to negative restrictions, or would an affirmative right, in the form of an easement, also support a deduction? (3) Finally, but by no means exhaustively, what was meant by the term "in perpetuity"? Specifically, where an easement might be terminated by operation of law (for example, the effect of a marketable title act), by events beyond the contributor's control (for example, changed circumstances), or upon a condition whose probability might be remote (destruction of a building), would the "perpetuity" test be met? While subsequent legislation has aimed at resolving some of these difficulties, others remain, as will be seen.[15]

The Tax Reform Act of 1976[16] amended the Code to provide a statutory basis for an easement for conservation purposes. Section 2124 of the act added as an additional exception to the partial interest rule the allowance of a deduction for the contribution of a lease, an option to purchase, or an "easement with respect to real property of not less than 30 years' duration" if granted "exclusively for conservation purposes." Also allowed was a deduction for a remainder interest if granted "exclusively for conservation purposes." The act defined "conservation purposes" as meaning "the preservation of land areas for public outdoor recreation or education, or scenic enjoyment; the preservation of historically important land areas or structures or the protection of natural environmental systems." The 1976 act is noteworthy as imposing an additional requirement for the deductibility of gifts of the interests described, the requirement that the interest must be created for "conservation purposes." The exceptions to the partial interest rule established by the 1969 act related to the "type" of interest created. In 1976 the Congress added to that an additional requirement, that of a purpose test.[17]

The present characteristics of the Code were established by yet another comprehensive revision contained in the Tax Treatment Extension Act of 1980.[18] The deductions for an undivided portion of the taxpayer's entire interest and for a remainder interest in a personal residence or farm were retained as they had been since 1969. However, the language in Sections 170(f)(3)(B) and (C) referring to "conservation purposes" that had been added by the 1976 act was repealed and a new subsection (B)(iii) was substituted in its place; a deduction is now allowed for a "qualified conservation contribution," the prerequisites of which are set forth in a new Section 170(h). As will be noted in greater detail, the new type of contribution deduction is available for transfers for both historic preservation and land conservation purposes, subject to limitations that will be discussed, provided that the restriction is "granted" in perpetuity. A qualified conservation contribution may also be a "remainder interest." That is, under present law this new type of remainder interest qualifies, in addition to the remainder interest in a personal residence or farm. Finally, carrying forward the thoughts first expressed in the 1969 conference report, which were articulated in the regulations subsequently adopted under the 1969 law and reformulated in statutory form in 1976, the "purpose" test was amplified and elaborated upon in 1980. The "qualified conservation contribution" thus is unique among the exceptions to the partial interest rule in requiring that a transaction not merely be of a particular quantum of the taxpayer's property but also that the transfer must be for a particular purpose.[19]

§6.02 The General Rule and Exceptions to It; General Principles; Valuation

[1] Partial Interest Rule

The general rule disallowing a deduction for a contribution of a "partial interest," unless one of the stated exceptions is applicable, remains as it has been since 1969. If the contribution is not made in trust, the deduction is disallowed if the interest is less than the taxpayer's entire interest.[20] On the other hand, if the taxpayer transfers his entire interest in the property (even though the interest itself is less than the fee) the deduction will be allowed.[21] The deduction will also be allowed if it would have been allowable had the contribution been made in trust.

[2] Exceptions to the General Rule

There are three exceptions to the general rule. They are for contributions of: (1) an undivided portion of the taxpayer's entire interest in the contributed property; (2) a remainder interest if the remainder interest is in a personal residence or farm or is a qualified conservation contribution; and (3) a restriction on the use of real property that is granted in perpetuity if the other requirements of a qualified conservation contribution are met.

[3] General Principles

General rules relating to donative intent,[22] completed transfers, and unconditional contributions[23] apply, of course, to partial interest gifts. The donor may not retain "substantial rights,"[24] other than those appropriate to his shared ownership if he has made a gift of an undivided portion of his entire interest, to his life estate if he has donated a remainder interest, or to his rights as a fee owner if he has contributed a "restriction" that is a qualified conservation contribution. Nor may a donor of a qualified conservation contribution retain a mineral interest, as it is defined in Section 170(h), if he also retains the right to extract or remove the minerals through surface mining.[25]

[4] Valuation

The valuation of less than fee interests for which there is no conventional market or transactional history is partic-

ularly difficult.[26] As is the case with other contributions, a partial interest is to be valued at its fair market value at the time of the contribution.[27] In the case of a gift of a remainder interest in real property, depreciation and depletion must be taken into account.[28] Penalties for overstating valuation are applicable.[29]

In valuing contributions of restrictions satisfying the Code definition of qualified conservation contributions, rulings applicable to "easements" will clearly apply. The amount of the deduction is the difference between the value of the taxpayer's property before the restriction is imposed and its value afterward.[30] The "before" value must take into account zoning, land use, and deed restrictions that may limit the use or value of the property even in the absence of the contributed restriction.[31] Similarly, the "after" value must take into account the value of rights that the taxpayer has retained. It is not simply the property that is subject to the restriction or easement that must be appraised. The *total* property of the taxpayer affected by the easement (not just the parcel to which the easement applies) must be appraised on a "before and after" basis to determine the economic value of the donation.[32] It is noteworthy that the hearings on the 1980 legislation contained testimony expressing the concern of the Treasury Department about "aggressive" valuations in the case of open space easement gifts.[33] The Senate Finance Committee Report[34] on the 1980 law also expressed concern in the case of contributions of conservation easements and restrictions about the absence of a market for these interests. While not disapproving of the "before and after" rule, the committee expressed its opinion that the rule should "not be applied mechanically."[35] The Senate committee cautioned that a valuation of the contribution should take into account an objective assessment of how immediate or remote the likelihood might be that the property would be developed in the absence of the restriction. The committee observed that no deduction would be allowable in instances where a grant of an easement might actually enhance the value of the taxpayer's property, citing as possible examples restrictions on historic property and restrictions protecting the seaward vista of ocean-front properties.

[5] Estate and Gift Taxes

By conforming amendments the same requirements for deductibility that apply to the income taxation of contributions of less than fee interests apply to estate and gift taxes.[36] That is to say, a contribution that does not meet the test of income tax deductibility will be a taxable transfer under the gift tax law and will be included in the transferor's taxable estate for estate tax purposes; thus, the failure to clear the income tax hurdle will not only result in a lost deduction but also, to the taxpayer's undoubted surprise, a potential gift tax liability as well.[37] This is particularly important to bear in mind in connection with gifts of easements and restrictions under the 1980 law because, as will be noted, many gray areas remain, and regulations have not yet been proposed.

In the case of a gift or a devise of a remainder interest in a personal residence or a farm or a remainder interest constituting a qualified conservation contribution preceded by a life estate in the spouse of the donor or testator, the donor or his executor may elect that the property be considered "qualified terminable interest property" (Q-TIP), assuming that the life estate meets the requirements of the Code.[38] The entire value of the property (not just the value of the spouse's life interest) will be deductible for estate and gift tax purposes.[39] When the surviving spouse dies, the value of the Q-TIP must be included in his or her gross estate.[40] While the present law is not entirely clear, the best interpretation appears to be that a charitable-contribution estate-tax deduction will be available to the surviving spouse.[41]

§6.03 Undivided Portions of the Taxpayer's Entire Interest

In the words of the Code as they have existed since 1969, a deduction will be allowed for a contribution of a partial interest that constitutes "an undivided portion of the taxpayer's entire interest in property. . . ."[42] Because the predicate of the Tax Reform Act of 1969 was the restriction of the contribution deduction for gifts of the *use* of the property, language was incorporated in the act to make sure that transfers of fractional interests would be exempt from the partial interest rule.[43] Such an undivided portion must consist of a fraction or percentage of every substantial interest or right owned by the taxpayer in the property, and the interest constituting the portion must extend over the entire term of the taxpayer's interest in the property.[44] On the other hand, if the taxpayer transfers some specific rights (other than such an undivided portion) and retains other substantial rights, the deduction will not be allowed.[45]

While a contribution of a right to use property, by the terms of the Code, is to be considered a contribution of less than the taxpayer's entire interest,[46] if the recipient organization "is given the right, as a tenant in common with the donor, to possession, dominion, and control of the property for a portion of each year appropriate to its interest in such property," the deduction will be allowed.[47] Revenue Ruling 75-420[48] demonstrates the distinctions and provides an example of a transaction combining a contribution of a remainder interest with a contribution of an undivided portion of the taxpayer's entire interest. The property at issue consisted of twenty acres of land, a large dwelling house, appropriate outbuildings, and amenities such as a swimming pool, gymnasium, and tennis court. The property had been used by the taxpayer as a vacation home. The recipient of the inter vivos gift was a college. The taxpayer granted to the college his entire interest in the property but reserved the right to use it exclusively each year during his lifetime from August 1

through September 15 and the right to store personal property in the home at all times of the year. The deed of gift also provided that the college was not to convey the property until ten years had elapsed from the time of the gift or the taxpayer's death, whichever occurred later. The college was restricted from making structural or decorative changes during the taxpayer's life without his consent. It was ruled that the taxpayer had contributed both a remainder interest in a personal residence to the college and an undivided interest as a tenant in common in his retained life estate. The combination of the gift of the remainder interest with the gift of the fractional share of the life estate was deemed critical; the ruling pointed out that had "the taxpayer . . . given the remainder interest to a relative and limited the life estate in the property by sharing such estate with the college as tenants in common for life or simply made a gift of the life estate to the college, no deduction would be allowable if the partial interest, that is, the remaining life estate, was created in order to avoid the provisions of Section 170(f)(3)(A) of the Code." The ruling points out that where a partial interest is created in order to avoid Section 170(f)(3)(A), the deduction will not be allowed.[49]

§6.04 Remainder Interest in Personal Residence or Farm

[1] General Rule
The contribution of a remainder interest in a personal residence or farm has been deductible as an exception to the partial interest rule since 1969.[50] The deduction is available for contributions made to any organization described in Section 170(c), whereas remainder interests sought to be deducted as qualified conservation contributions may be made only to those organizations described in Section 170(h)(3), as discussed below. Remainder interests are to be valued as prescribed in Section 170(f)(4). The remainder interest may follow a life estate or an estate for a term of years.[51]

[2] Residence
Personal residence does not mean "principal" residence. Thus, a vacation home or other property used by the taxpayer personally as a residence would qualify.[52] By regulation, the term "personal residence" includes stock owned by a taxpayer as a tenant-stockholder in a cooperative housing corporation if the dwelling that the taxpayer is entitled to occupy as such a stockholder is in fact used by him as a personal residence.[53] "Personal residence" connotes a residence used as such by the taxpayer and one which meets that criterion at the time of the contribution.

Of what is a "residence" comprised? Clearly more than a building occupied as a residence and its immediate curtilage. The scope is unclear; perhaps it is what the taxpayer himself regards and uses as a residence. As has been noted, in Revenue Ruling 75-420[54] a deduction was allowed for a residence that consisted of 20 acres of land on which were located a twenty-five-room principal dwelling house, a caretaker's cottage, a barn, a swimming pool, a gymnasium, and a tennis court. A private ruling[55] allowed a deduction for a contribution of a remainder interest (following successive life estates in the taxpayer and his wife) where the property consisted of 77.33 acres. The property included a principal dwelling where the taxpayer lived, a pool and pool-house complex, a barn used as a workshop, a gymnasium and kennel, two separate garages, and a caretaker's cottage. The acreage consisted of 12 acres of lawn, including formal landscaping, and 65 acres divided between open pastures and woodland. The property also comprised a portion of land used as a farm, on other acreage of which the taxpayer had previously granted a "conservation easement" to the same charity that received the gift of the remainder interest. The deduction was allowed with citations to both the "residence" and "farm" language in the Code and regulations.

[3] Farm

A "farm" means land or improvements used for the production of crops, fruits, or other agricultural products or to sustain livestock.[56] The requirement that a farm must be "used by the taxpayer or his tenant" that is contained in the regulations is not to be found in the language of the Code. The only apparent justification for that interpretation would be the argument that "personal" modifies both "residence" and "farm." In a private ruling a deduction was allowed in the case of a 400-acre ranch where the taxpayer did not include in the gift his residence, which was located on the property and constituted the "farmhouse."[57] Inferentially, while "farm" may include improvements, it need not necessarily include all of them. Since property used for the "sustenance of livestock" qualifies, the regulation contains a definition of what is meant by "livestock."

[4] Qualified Terminable Interest Property

As noted above, if a life estate in a personal residence or farm is given or devised to a spouse, with the remainder passing to a qualified organization, the donor or his executor may elect that the property be considered "qualified terminable interest property," in which case the value of the entire property will be deductible by the donor for estate and gift tax purposes.[58]

§6.05 Qualified Conservation Contribution

[1] Qualified Conservation Contribution

In addition to the deductions allowed for a contribution of a partial interest consisting of a remainder interest in a personal residence or farm and an undivided portion of the taxpayer's entire interest, since 1980 there has been allowed a charitable deduction for what is called a qualified conservation contribution.[59] While a major purpose of the new law was to clarify and make explicit how contributions of conservation "easements" are to be treated, the 1980 act also included within the new category other types of partial interests. The Senate Report[60] states that it was considered "appropriate to expand the types of transfers which will qualify as deductible contributions in certain cases where the contributions are likely to further significant conservation goals without presenting significant potential for abuse."[61] A further stated reason for the change was confusion over whether or not the Congress in the 1976 and 1977 laws intended to supersede the "statements" made in the 1969 conference report that (somewhat modified, as has been noted) found their way into the regulations. By way of explaining the limitations that the new law creates, and most particularly in defense of the highly articulated "purpose" test, the Senate committee endorsed the preservation of natural and cultural resources and acknowledged the important role that "easements" may play in their protection, but it also pointed out that it "also recognizes that it is not in the country's best interests to restrict or prohibit development of *all* land areas and existing structures."[62] (Emphasis added.)

The new legislation accomplishes its purpose by defining in considerable detail what is meant by a "qualified conservation contribution."[63] It must meet three tests: (1) the contribution must be of a "qualified" interest in real property, (2) the contribution must be made to a "qualified" organization, and (3) the contribution must be exclusively for conservation purposes.[64]

[2] Qualified Property Interest

A qualified property interest must be an interest in "real" property.[65] Only three such interests are qualified.

[a] Entire Interest of the Donor. The first category of qualified real property interest consists of the "entire interest of the donor other than a qualified mineral interest. . . ."[66] A qualified mineral interest is defined as subsurface oil, gas, or other minerals and the right of access to them.[67] While the meaning of this is not transcendently clear, the Report provides enlightenment: what is meant is that if a taxpayer donates his entire interest in a parcel of real property but retains a "qualified mineral interest" the taxpayer will still be entitled to the contribution deduction. That is, the language is not to be construed as stating that a taxpayer will be denied a deduction if his entire interest consists of a qualified mineral interest that he donates.[68] However, if the donor retains a mineral interest, his contribution will not qualify for the deduction (on the ground that it will not meet the "exclusively for conservation purposes" test) if at any time the minerals may be extracted or removed through surface mining.[69]

[b] Remainder Interest. A remainder interest may qualify if it meets the tests for a qualified conservation contribution. This provides an additional category of remainder interests that are deductible as exceptions to the partial interest rule. The deduction for a contribution

of a personal residence or farm (which need not meet the "qualified conservation contribution" test) remains.

[c] Restriction. A restriction constituting a qualified property interest must be granted in perpetuity. It must restrict the use that may be made of the real property to which it applies. While the Code does not define what is meant by "restriction," quite evidently it is meant to include, at least, restrictions in the form of conservation and historic preservation "easements," as they had been known under prior law.[70] Noting that the 1976 legislation covered leases and options to purchase as well as easements, the Senate committee declared that the language in the 1980 act "would cover easements and other interests in real property that under State property laws have similar attributes (e.g., a restrictive covenant)."[71] An eligible restriction must be *granted* in perpetuity. While this test will be presumably satisfied by the language of the granting instrument, it should be noted that in order to meet the "exclusively for conservation purposes" test the conservation purpose of the contribution must be *protected* in perpetuity.[72]

[3] Qualified Organization

Whereas it is generally the case that a taxpayer will be entitled to a contribution deduction for a gift to any organization described in Section 170(c), with the nature of the organization affecting in some cases the amount that can be deducted but not the deduction itself,[73] a qualified conservation contribution must be made to a "qualified organization."[74] This means a governmental unit, an exempt organization that meets the test of Section 170(b)(1)(vi), an organization described in Section 501(c)(3) and Section 509(a)(2), or an organization described in Section 501(c)(3) and Section 509(a)(3) that is controlled by any of the foregoing. In general, as the Senate committee indicated, the 1980 legislation was intended to restrict the deduction to contributions to governmental bodies and publicly supported charities.[75] It should be noted that no limitation in regard to the recipient organization applies to a gift of a fractional share or a remainder interest in a personal residence or farm.

[4] "Exclusively" and "In Perpetuity"

A restriction, as has been noted, must be granted in perpetuity, and it and all other forms of qualified conservation contributions must be "protected in perpetuity."[76] A number of significant questions are raised. According to the Senate committee, the requirement that the contribution be "exclusively for" conservation purposes would not be met if, for example, in the case of a remainder interest the tenants for life or for a term of years could use the property for the duration of the estate preceding the remainder in a manner that might diminish the conservation values intended to be protected.[77] So, also, if a contribution would meet "one of the enumerated conservation purposes, but would allow uses of the property that would be destructive of other significant conservation interests,"[78] the require-

ment would not be met. An example given involves the preservation of farmland. The Report indicates that the requirement would not be met if the use of pesticides in the operation of the farm could significantly injure or destroy a "natural ecosystem."

The coupling of the word "exclusively" with the purpose test raises questions about the materiality of collateral effects or benefits. For example, if an effect of the contribution is to enhance the value of other remaining lands of the donor, is it "exclusively for" conservation purposes (whatever the effect this circumstance might have on the amount of the deduction)? Under the same circumstance, if the contribution enhances the value of other lands of the donor's family or his or her neighbors, is it "exclusively for" conservation purposes?

The requirement that the conservation purpose be "protected in perpetuity" raises additional issues. The Senate committee indicates that there must be "legally enforceable" restrictions that would prevent uses of the property that are inconsistent with the conservation purposes for which the contribution is made. Legal enforceability will, of course, be determined by applicable local law, and note should be taken of the problems in some jurisdictions with the enforceability and transferability of easements "in gross." Even where questions of enforceability can be answered, questions of durability will remain. For example, if by its terms a restriction is terminable upon a condition (for example, the destruction of a historic building), is it to be considered "in perpetuity"? If a restriction may be terminated upon the exercise of eminent domain by government authority, is it "in perpetuity" (presuming the proceeds of the condemnation pass to a qualified charitable recipient)? Must the recipient affirmatively accept the obligation to provide "perpetual" protection?[79] If the recipient organization is willing to undertake protection of the resource but as a practical matter can be demonstrated to be unable to provide protection in fact, will the conservation purpose be found to be protected "in perpetuity"?[80]

As has been noted above, the "exclusively" test will not be found to have been met where the taxpayer retains a qualified mineral interest if at any time the taxpayer or his successors may extract or remove minerals through surface mining.[81]

[5] Conservation Purpose: Historic Preservation

Historic preservation is included within the term "conservation purpose," provided that rather specific requirements of the Code are met. Specifically, a conservation purpose includes the preservation of "an historically important land area" *or* "a certified historic structure."[82] "Certified historic structure" means "any building, structure, or land area"[83] that either (1) is listed in the National Register; or (2) is located in a registered historic district, as defined in Code Section 191(d)(2), *and* is certified by the Secretary of the Interior to the Secretary of the Treasury as "being of historic significance to the district." The test is met if the property satisfies one of the requirements, either when the interest is transferred or on the due date of the contributor's return for the taxable year in which the transfer is made (including any extension of the due date).

While the Code is not entirely clear, it appears that a contribution would be allowed for a transfer of an interest in a "historically important land area" that does not meet the "certified historic structure" definition because the terms are used disjunctively in Section 170(h)(4)(A)(iv). According to the Senate committee, the term is intended to include land areas that are independently significant apart from historic structures, suggesting, however, that there must be some relationship between the land area and certified historic resources.[84]

It should be noted that if a contribution meets the Section 170(h)(4)(A)(iv) test, it need not meet the tests relative to land protection discussed below, including the "public benefit" requirement.[85]

[6] Conservation Purpose: Land Protection

The other three categories within the term "conservation purpose" all relate to the protection, conservation, and preservation of land. They are (1) the preservation of land areas for outdoor recreation by, or the education of, the general public; (2) the protection of relatively natural habitats and ecosystems; and (3) the preservation of open space, including farmland and forestland. While many contributions will serve more than one of these purposes, an eligible contribution need serve only one of them.

[a] Outdoor Recreation and Education. Section 170(h)(4)(A)(i) provides that a conservation purpose includes "the preservation of land areas for outdoor recreation by, or the education of, the general public. . . ." The example given by the Senate committee is the preservation of a water area for public boating and fishing or a hiking trail for public use.[86] Because only a "restriction" qualifies as a deductible interest, the anomaly presents itself that under the partial interest rule an affirmative easement for hiking or recreation would not be deductible, whereas a negative restriction in order to protect that use would be. A sensible construction would be that such an affirmative interest would be considered a "restriction" in that by granting it the property owner would restrict himself from interfering with the exercise of the easement. Because public use sometimes must be limited in order to protect a resource, would any limitation be an unacceptable exclusion of the "general public"?

[b] Habitats and Ecosystems. Section 170(h)(4)(A)(ii) includes within the term "conservation purpose" "the protection of a relatively natural habitat of fish, wildlife, or plants, or similar ecosystems. . . ." "Relatively natural" does not mean pristine, but it is not clear the extent to which some disturbance might be disqualifying. The Senate Report states that the habitat or environment may be

"to some extent" altered by human activity, giving as an example a lake that has been formed by a man-made dike if a fish, wildlife, or plant community exists there in "relatively natural condition." The committee's intention is that contributions protect and preserve "significant" natural habitats and ecosystems, such as those of rare, endangered, or threatened species; "high-quality" natural areas; and land areas that are within or contribute to the "ecological viability" of a park, nature reserve, wildlife refuge, wilderness area, or similar conservation area.[87]

[c] Open Space. The third category of land conservation purpose is the preservation of open space, including farmland and forestland.[88] A contribution for the preservation of open space must be "for the scenic enjoyment of the general public" *or* it must be created pursuant to a clearly delineated government conservation policy. Whether created for scenic enjoyment or pursuant to a government conservation policy, there must be a "significant public benefit." These strictures express as much as any other provision of the 1980 legislation the view of the Congress, as stated in the Senate Report, "that it is not in the country's best interest to restrict or prohibit the development of all land areas and existing structures."[89]

[i] Scenic Enjoyment. Scenic enjoyment does not require physical access. However, the enjoyment contemplated is by the "general public." Visual access is the requirement, such as might be enjoyed from a road, a river, a trail, or a park if the places from which the vista may be enjoyed are open to the public.[90] Authentication of the "scenic" nature of a resource raises questions of aesthetics best discussed elsewhere.[91]

[ii] Government Policy. If an open space contribution does not meet the scenic enjoyment test, for the contributor to be eligible for the deduction the interest must be granted "pursuant to a clearly delineated Federal, State, or local governmental conservation policy."[92] The intention, according to the Senate committee, is to use as a reference identification of resources by "representatives of the general public" through administrative or legislative action.[93] A significant commitment to the conservation project by the government must be present, although this need not necessarily include funding. Broad declarations of general policy will be insufficient. Yet it is, according to the committee, unnecessary that the government policy include a certification program identifying particular lots or small parcels of property.

Because there are many types of public programs showing various levels of commitment to a conservation objective, many questions remain. For example, in a state that has a plan of conservation and development that broadly identifies objectives to be followed in making public capital investments, would the requirement be met if the plan delineated general categories of resources the protection of which is in the public interest (for example, forestland)? If a state has a preferential tax treatment program for agricultural, forest, or open space land that is certified by the state forester or local assessors, would the test be met? Would the test be met if a municipality classified land as "open space" under a zoning bylaw?[94]

[iii] Public Benefit. "Open space" contributions for either purpose must meet the requirement that they "yield a significant public benefit. . . ." Thus, it is not sufficient that a contribution be for "scenic enjoyment" in and of itself, or even that it be pursuant to a clearly delineated policy adopted by government. An additional layer of "public benefit" is required. The Code does not disclose the nature of this test, and the Senate Report simply, and unsatisfactorily, observes that such a benefit will be evaluated by the consideration of all germane factors in a given case, including the uniqueness of the particular property, the intensity of land development (including foreseeable trends), consistency with public programs, and opportunities for public use and enjoyment. The illustrations discussed below suggest that the "public benefit" will be established by cumulative reference to many factors.

§6.06 Illustrations

Private rulings promulgated in the summer of 1982 provide examples of the view of the Internal Revenue Service toward the 1980 legislation.[95]

The first ruling[96] held deductible a gift of a conservation easement on a thirty-acre farm used for agriculture and dairy farming. The shareholders of the corporation that owned the farm proposed to donate a perpetual open space easement, reserving, however, two waterfront residential sites comprising a portion of the farm. The recipient organization was created by a state statute declaring it to be in the public interest to protect open space and empowering the organization to accept contributions for that purpose. In furtherance of this program, the recipient organization had already accepted a number of easements, had developed an easement form that could be used by donating landowners, and had developed a policy relating to acceptance of open space easements, stressing easements on waterfront land where development pressure was intense and agricultural land where the landowner was particularly interested in preserving it, as well as the protection of historic districts.

The farm included frontage on tidal waters, was visible from a much frequented nearby bridge, and was proximate to two public parks. Development pressure in the vicinity was intense. Several years earlier the planning commission of the state adopted a regional open space plan, noting the need to preserve important environmental resources such as wetland, farmland, and open space buffers. This plan, however, did not identify specific sites. The state planning commission had also endorsed a housing and land-use plan and an environmental impact assessment in satisfaction of

requirements of the U.S. Department of Housing and Urban Development that implied that appropriate open space preservation was a significant factor in accommodating expected growth. A water quality plan adopted by the state planning commission identified the water areas in the vicinity of the farm as of critical importance and made general recommendations in support of open space preservation, including the use of open space buffer zones adjacent to water bodies. The municipality had adopted a comprehensive development plan, as required by state laws, whose general purposes included protection of open space, water quality, and the preservation of environmentally sensitive areas, such as wetlands.

The easement, as an easement in gross, was enforceable under applicable local law. Under the circumstances it was found that the recipient organization was an integral part of the state government and that the easement granted to it was deductible as a qualified conservation contribution. In the ruling it was noted that the easement on the farm did not permit the contributor to develop or extract oil, gas, or other minerals. The ruling quoted extensively from the Report and concluded that the "conservation purpose" and "perpetuity" tests were met.

A second private letter ruling[97] involved a contribution of an easement on an 860-acre ranch, much of which is accessible from an adjacent public highway and from a river that traverses the ranch. Small and big game and nongame animals are present, including endangered species such as the bald eagle. An adjacent river, heavily used by the public for fishing, is a "renowned trout fishing stream"; and a tributary located entirely on the ranch is both an outstanding trout fishing stream and a significant spawning place for trout, as has been noted by the state department of fish and game. The county commissioners have authorized the county planning board to pursue a scenic easement program along the river, including those parts of the river along the ranch. Both the commissioners and the board have expressed the opinion that the donation of a conservation easement would be of great significance to the easement program, in which it was the intention of the county planning board to interest approximately 100 landowners. This program, for which funds have been budgeted for necessary personnel and activities and professional assistance, was supported by a grant from the state department of natural resources and conservation. Development pressure for residential housing in the vicinity of the ranch is significant, with approximately 50,000 acres in the area recently having been subdivided into parcels of 20 acres or less. The terms of the easement provided for certain reserved interests, including the reservation of mineral rights. However, the surface covered by the easement could not be used for exploration or extraction. The restrictions were granted in perpetuity. Such easements are recognized as enforceable under the state law. The recipient charity had been classified as a "public charity" under Sections 509(a)(1) and 170(d)(1)(A)(vi) of the Code. (A portion of the ruling not here material finds that the contribution to the organization was an "unusual grant.")

The interest was held to be a qualified real property interest notwithstanding the retention of the qualified mineral interest, and it was further held that the "conservation purpose" test was met. Again, liberal reference to the Senate Report was made and much stress laid on the fact that the "clearly delineated" government program was funded.

A third private ruling[98] involved property comprising 245 acres that were used for a guest ranch, as well as the grazing of horses, cattle, and other livestock. The property was bordered by a national park with extensive public visitation and recreational use. A river forming another border of the ranch was used for boating, fishing, and floating by the general public and is the subject of a Wild and Scenic River study. The property formed a part of the scenic panorama of the park and the river. Millions of visitors were attracted to the area for both summer and winter activities; one result of this had been an escalation in land values of 400 percent over a few years.

A comprehensive plan has been adopted by the county where the property is located, calling for the preservation of the county's scenic resources, and the county has established a Scenic Preserve Trust to carry out the plan. In addition, in 1980 residents organized a land trust that qualified as a publicly supported exempt organization under the Code. The easement was donated to the land trust. Pursuant to its terms, 39 acres were designated for protection of scenic and wildlife values. Retained uses include only agriculture, dude ranching, and natural, open space, and wildlife habitat.

The ruling holds the easement gift deductible. It particularly discusses the public benefit test and relies extensively on the Report. Again stressed is the case-by-case nature of judgments on these transactions. ("Factors germane to one contribution may be irrelevant to another contribution.") The retention of some significant uses was not disabling because the retained uses "are not destructive of significant conservation interests" and the retained rights are not "substantial enough to affect deductibility. . . ."

The rulings are notable for the detail with which the factual situation is considered, the precision of legal analysis, and their length; and they seem to underscore by these qualities the assertion of the Senate committee that the measurement of the "public benefit" must be accomplished on a case-by-case basis.

§6.07 Conclusion

While the law applicable to the contribution of a partial interest constituting an undivided portion of the taxpayer's entire interest in property and a remainder interest in a personal residence or farm has remained consistent since the Tax Reform Act of 1969, the status of easements or restrictions on real property for conservation or historic

preservation purposes has undergone significant change in the same period, culminating in the 1980 law. Although the intention of Congress to assure a future in the tax law for such interests and to clear up past confusion is praiseworthy, the result leaves many questions unanswered. The notion that transactions will pass muster if they are for a particular purpose, hinted at in the 1969 conference report and brought into statutory language in 1976, has burgeoned into elaborate requirements that fall far short of general rules providing for predictable outcomes.

Ill met, it would seem, were the congressional intention to establish easements and restrictions more firmly as deductible interests and to clarify past confusion, the concern by the Treasury about private windfalls that particularly centered upon assertedly "aggressive" evaluations,[99] the participation of conservation and preservation organizations ill-equipped and unaccustomed to dealing with Washington tax issues, and authentic difficulties in understanding an unfamiliar property law concept. The encounter with the issue in 1980 was made more difficult by the absence of good information on how extensively easements and restrictions have in fact been used by taxpayers, what in fact the valuation experience has been, whether or not hypothetically imaginable instances of potential abuse have occurred or are occurring, and much other information needed by a thoughtful legislature. Indeed, the Senate committee noted that it was "hindered . . . by the absence of a comprehensive data base concerning the nature and scope of conservation easements and remainder interests."[100]

The uncertainty places potential contributors at risk because a failure to qualify for the contribution deduction does not mean merely the loss of an income tax deduction; but it also means the exposure to gift tax liability. The situation is made much more difficult by the absence of regulations. The Senate Report recognizes "the need of potential donors to be secure in their knowledge that a contemplated contribution will qualify for a deduction."[101] In the meantime, the committee notes its expectation that taxpayers will avail themselves of a "prior administrative determination" as to deductibility and its further expectation that regulations "will be classified among those regulation projects having the highest priority. . . ."[102] The Report is dated June 12, 1980, and the 1980 law became effective with President Carter's signature December 17, 1980.

Notes

1. There is substantial literature on the use of restrictions, easements, and other less than fee techniques for conservation and historic preservation purposes. *See generally* Brenneman, "Private Approaches to the Preservation of Open Land" (Conservation and Research Foundation, 1967); Netherton, "Environmental Conservation and Historic Preservation Through Recorded Land-Use Agreements," 14 Real Prop. Prob. & Tr. J.

540 (1979); *Note,* "Techniques for Preserving Open Spaces," 75 Harv. L. Rev. 1622 (1962); Whyte, "Securing Open Space for Urban America: Conservation Easements," Urb. Land Inst. Bull. No. 36 (1959); Brenneman, "Techniques for Controlling the Surroundings of Historic Sites," 36 Law & Contemp. Prob. 416 (1971). By statute in many states such restrictions are declared to be interests in real property. *See, e.g.,* Conn. Gen. Stat. §§47-42a through 47-42c (1981); Uniform Conservation Easement Act, §1(1), 12 U.L.A. 44 (Supp. 1981). The Uniform Act has been adopted by the State of Wisconsin. 1981 Wis. L., ch. 261 (1981).

2. Rev. Rul. 64-205, 1964-2 C.B. 62.

3. Woodside Mills v. United States, 160 F. Supp. 356 (W.D.S.C. 1958), *aff'd per curiam,* 260 F.2d 935 (4th Cir. 1958); Mattie Fair v. Comm'r, 27 T.C. 866 (1957), *acq.* 1957-2 C.B. 4.

4. Ottawa Silica Co. v. United States, No. 272-78, 49 AFTR 2d 1162 (Ct. Cl. 1982); Perlmutter v. Comm'r, 45 T.C. 311 (1965); Transamerica Corp. v. United States, 254 F. Supp. 504 (N.D. Cal. 1966), *aff'd* 392 F.2d 522 (9th Cir. 1968). *Cf.* Citizens & S. Nat'l Bank of S.C. v. United States, 243 F. Supp. 900 (W.D.S.C. 1965).

5. IRS News Release No. 784, Nov. 15, 1965, 657 CCH 6787.

6. Pub. L. No. 91-172, 83 Stat. 487, hereinafter "Tax Reform Act."

7. *See generally* Browne & Van Dorn, "Charitable Gifts of Partial Interests in Real Property for Conservation Purposes," 29 Tax Law. 69, 72-85 (1975).

8. *See* H.R. Rep. No. 413 (Part 1), 91st Cong., 1st Sess. 58 (1969) *reprinted in* 1969 U.S. Code Cong. & Ad. News 1645; S. Rep. No. 552, 91st Cong., 1st Sess. 83 (1969).

9. Mattie Fair v. Comm'r, 27 T.C. 866 (1957), *acq.* 1957-2 C.B. 4.

10. I.R.C. §170(f)(3)(A).

11. Rev. Rul. 72-419, 1972-2 C.B. 104.

12. Problems presented by the language of the Tax Reform Act of 1969 are discussed in Browne & Van Dorn, *supra* N. 7 at 81-85.

13. Conf. Rep., H.R. Rep. No. 782, 91st Cong., 1st Sess. 294 (1969), *reprinted in* 1969 U.S. Code Cong. & Ad. News 2392.

14. Treas. Reg. §1.170A-7(b)(1)(ii).

15. Rev. Rul. 75-358, 1975-2 C.B. 76, held that an owner of a landmark building was entitled to deduct the value of a grant to a state of the right to prevent the alteration of the building's "historically significant appearance." *Id.* The easement was found to be an "open space easement." *Id* at 77.

In the case of a contribution of a conservation or historic preservation easement or restriction, the Service ruled that the taxpayer's basis must be reduced by the portion of the total basis that is "properly allocable" to the easement granted. Rev. Rul. 64-205, 1964-2 C.B. 62. *See also* Rev. Rul. 73-339, 1973-2 C.B. 68. The applicable principles where the taxpayer receives consideration are authoritatively discussed in Browne & Van Dorn, *supra* N.7 at 89-93.

16. Pub. L. No. 94-455, 90 Stat. 1520.

17. The 1976 act allowed a deduction for a thirty-year term easement. The provision was short-lived. The Tax Reduction and Simplification Act of 1977, Pub. L. No. 95-30, 91 Stat. 126, further amended the Code to require that a deductible easement must be "granted in perpetuity." For a discussion of the legislative history of the 1976 and 1977 acts, *see* Small, "The Tax Benefits of Donating Easements in Scenic and Historic Property," 7 Real Est. L.J. 304, 310-18(1979).

18. Pub. L. No. 96-541, 94 Stat. 3204. Action by the Congress in 1980 was necessary to avoid the June 14, 1981, "sunset" provision relating to conservation easements in the 1976 law. However, even if the "sun" had set on the 1976 provisions, the 1969 act and 1972 regulations would have remained in effect.

19. For a discussion of the legislative history of the 1980 act, *see* Coughlin, "Preservation Easements: Statutory and Planning Issues," 1 Preservation L. Rep. 2011(1982).

20. I.R.C. §170(f)(3).

21. Treas. Reg. §1.170A-7(b)(1)(i).

22. Ottawa Silica Co., Ct. Cl. No. 272-78, 49 AFTR 2d 1160 (Ct. Cl. 1982).

23. Treas. Reg. §1.170A-1(e).

24. Treas. Reg. §1.170A-7(b)(1).

25. I.R.C. §170(h)(5)(B).

26. Appraisals of restrictions and other less than fee interests are notoriously difficult. For an appraiser's view that includes an excellent bibliography, *see* Smith, "Some Enchanting Easements," Appraisal J. (October 1980). *See also* Reynolds, "Preservation Easements," Appraisal J. 356 (July 1976). On valuation of historic preservation restrictions, *see* Roddewig & Shales, "Appraising the Best Tax Shelter in History," Appraisal J. 50 (1982).

27. Treas. Reg. §1.170A-7(c).

28. I.R.C. §170(f)(4); Treas. Reg. §1.170A-12.

29. I.R.C. §§6659, 6653(a), and 6653(b); *see* United States v. Wolfson, 573 F.2d 216 (5th Cir. 1978).

30. Rev. Rul. 73-339, 1973-2 C.B. 68; Robert H. Thayer, 36 T.C.M. 1504 (1977).

31. *See* George Deukmejian, 41 T.C.M. 738 (1981).

32. Rev. Rul. 76-376, 1976-2 C.B. 53; *cf.* Baetjer v. United States, 143 F.2d 391 (1st Cir. 1944), *cert. denied* 323 U.S. 772 (valuation for condemnation purposes).

33. Daniel I. Halperin, Deputy Assistant Secretary (Tax Legislation) of the Department of the Treasury called attention to the "incentive" for aggressive valuation of conservation easements because of the difficulty in assigning reliable economic values to the private and public benefits said to be involved. *Hearings on H.R. 7318 Before the Subcomm. on Select Revenue Measures of the House Comm. on Ways and Means,* 96th Cong., 2d Sess. 156, 167 (June 26, 1980).

34. S. Rep. No. 1007, 96th Cong., 2d Sess., *reprinted in* 1980 U.S. Code Cong. & Ad. News 6736, hereinafter "Report."

35. *Id.* at 15, 1980 U.S. Code Cong. & Ad. News at 6750.

36. I.R.C. §§2522(c)(2) and 2055(e)(2).

37. *See* Ltr. Rul. 8205019.

38. I.R.C. §§2056(b)(7) and 2523(f).

39. H.R. Rep. No. 201, 97th Cong., 1st Sess. 161 (1981).

40. I.R.C. §2044(b)(1).

41. While the law was unclear about whether or not the estate tax charitable deduction is available to the surviving spouse, it now is available. I.R.C. §2055(a) refers to "bequests, legacies, devises, or transfers." Is there a "transfer" upon the death of the surviving spouse? (Not by the surviving spouse, within the ordinary meaning of the language.) The General Explanation of the Economic Recovery Tax Act of 1981 says that Congress intended that Q-TIP included in the estate of the surviving spouse shall be treated as "passing from" the surviving spouse for the purpose of the estate tax charitable deduction. Joint Comm. Rep. No.

236-37, 97th Cong., 1st Sess., N.4 (1981). Sec. 104 of the House Technical Corrections Bill of 1982 (H.R. 6056, 97th Cong.), which was signed into law by the President, January 12, 1983, amends Section 2044 to make clear that Q-TIP would qualify for the estate tax charitable deduction as a "transfer" from the surviving spouse.

42. I.R.C. §170(f)(3)(B)(ii). While this text primarily addresses gifts of interests in real property, it should be noted that the gift of an undivided portion of the taxpayer's interest in personal property is also deductible. The transfer of a fractional interest in a painting, for example, coupled with the right of the donee to exclusive possession for a period of each year appropriate to its fractional interest, is a deductible gift. Treas. Reg. §1.170A-5(a)(2). *See* Ltr. Rul. 8145085. In this situation there is also no "future interest" within the rule that in the case of a gift of a future interest in tangible personal property the charitable deduction must be postponed until all intervening interests, or rights to possession or enjoyment of the property, have expired or are held by persons other than those in the categories described in I.R.C. §267(b). I.R.C. §170(A)(3); Treas. Reg. §170A-5(a)(1)(ii). The postponement rule does not apply to gifts of real property.

43. S. Rep. No. 552, 91st Cong., 1st Sess. 84 (1969), *reprinted in* 1969 U.S. Code Cong. & Ad. News 2027; Conf. Rep., H.R. Rep. No. 782, 91st Cong., 1st Sess. (1969), *reprinted in* 1969 U.S. Code Cong. & Ad. News 2392.

44. Treas. Reg. §1.170A-7(b)(1)(i).

45. *Id.* Where property was donated in fee, the retention of certain rights of ingress and egress to and from adjacent land of the contributor was not the reservation of a "substantial" interest in which regulations of the U.S. Department of Agriculture, the donee, controlled use of the access. Ltr. Rul. 8216025.

46. I.R.C. §170(f)(3)(A).

47. Treas. Reg. §1.170A-7(b)(1)(i).

48. 1975-2 C.B. 78.

49. Treas. Reg. §1.170A-7(a)(2)(i). Depending upon the age of the contributor and the size of the donated fractional share, the value of the deduction could amount to a significant portion of the fair market value of the property at the time of the gift. For other examples of fractional share gifts, *see* Rev. Rul. 58-261, 1958-1 C.B. 143, and Ltr. Rul. 8204220.

50. I.R.C. §170(f)(3)(B)(i).

51. Treas. Reg. §1.170A-7(b)(3).

52. *Id.*; Rev. Rul. 75-420, 1975-2 C.B. 78.

53. Treas. Reg. §1.170A-7(b)(3).

54. 1975-2 C.B. 78.

55. Ltr. Rul. 8202137.

56. Treas. Reg. §1.170A-7(b)(4).

57. Ltr. Rul. 8217073.

58. I.R.C. §§2056(b)(7), 2523(f); H.R. Rep. No. 201, 97th Cong., 1st Sess. 161 (1981).

59. I.R.C. §170(f)(3)(B)(iii).

60. Report, *supra* N.34.

61. *Id.* at 9, 1980 U.S. Code Cong. & Ad. News at 6745.

62. *Id.* at 9, 1980 U.S. Code Cong. & Ad. News at 6744-45.

63. I.R.C. §170(h).

64. I.R.C. §§170(h)(1)(A), (B), and (C).

65. I.R.C. §170(h)(1)(A).

66. I.R.C. §170(h)(2)(A).

67. I.R.C. §§170(h)(6)(A) and (B).

68. "The Committee intends that a contribution will not qualify under this new provision if the donor has reduced his 'entire interest in real property' before the contribution is made by, for example, transferring part of his interest in the real property to a related person in order to retain control of more than a qualified mineral interest in the real property or reduce the real property interest donated." Report, *supra* N.34 at 10 (citing Treas. Reg. §1.170A-7(a)(2)(i)), 1980 U.S. Code Cong. & Ad. News at 6745.

69. I.R.C. §170(h)(5)(B). Under pre-1980 law a taxpayer who granted an open space easement on the land surface but retained mineral rights in the subsurface (subject to the proviso that any drilling or mining would be done "by slant" from adjacent property so as not to disturb the surface controlled by the easement) was held entitled to a deduction for the contribution of an "open space easement in gross." Rev. Rul. 75-373, 1975-2 C.B. 77. In Rev. Rul. 76-331, 1976-2 C.B. 52, the contributor retained all mineral rights while making a gift of all remaining rights of fee ownership; the contributor was held not entitled to a deduction because of the retention of a "substantial" right, this ruling distinguishing Rev. Rul. 75-373. Treasury noted its concern about the retained mineral rights issue in 1979. *Hearings on H.R. 4611 Before the Subcomm. on Select Revenue Measures of the House Comm. on Ways and Means*, 96th Cong., 1st Sess. 6-7 (Nov. 9, 1979). Report, *supra* N.34. *Id.* at 10-11, 1980 U.S. Code Cong. & Ad. News at 6745-46, suggests that the act codifies the distinction. In Ltr. Rul. 8247024, discussed *infra* at 6-34, the taxpayer donating a conservation restriction reserved subsurface mineral rights, but no surface mining was permitted; the deduction was allowed in a ruling that compatibly includes discussion of the Report, Rev. Rul. 75-373, and Rev. Rul. 76-331. In summary, the contribution of a restriction will support the deduction even if mineral rights are reserved when there is a restriction against surface mining and extraction.

70. Selecting a uniformly acceptable name for a "property interest" that may consist of little more than the right to prevent a particular use of property by its owner has proved challenging. *See* Commissioners' Prefatory Note, Uniform Conservation Easement Act, 12 U.L.A. 44 (Supp. 1981). The Uniform Act elects to use "easement." Some state laws use the term "restriction." E.g., Conn. Gen. Stat. §§47-42a to 47-42c. *See generally* Netherton, *supra* N.1.

71. Report, *supra* N.34 at 10, 1980 U.S. Code Cong. & Ad. News at 6745.

72. I.R.C. §170(h)(5)(A).

73. I.R.C. §170(b)(1)(B).

74. I.R.C. §170(h)(3).

75. Report, *supra* N.34 at 14, 1980 U.S. Code Cong. & Ad. News at 6749.

76. "A contribution shall not be treated as exclusively for conservation purposes unless the conservation purpose is protected in perpetuity." I.R.C. §170(h)(5)(A).

77. Report, *supra* N.34 at 13, 1980 U.S. Code Cong. & Ad. News at 6748.

78. *Id.*, at 13, 1980 U.S. Code Cong. & Ad. News at 6749.

79. Section 2(b) of the Uniform Conservation Easement Act, 12 U.L.A. 44, 47 (Supp. 1981) requires acceptance by the holder.

80. The 1977 Conf. Rep., H.R. Rep. No. 263, 95th Cong., 1st Sess. 30 (1977), in discussing the "exclusively" test stated that the deduction would be limited to situations where the donee organization was required to hold the easement (for exam-

ple, the easement could not be transferable). *See* Small, *supra*
N.17 at 318, N.38.

81. I.R.C. §170(h)(5)(B).

82. I.R.C. §170(h)(4)(A)(iv).

83. I.R.C. §170(h)(4)(B).

84. "The term 'historically important land area' is intended
to include independently significant land areas (for example, a
civil war battlefield) and historic sites and related land areas, the
physical or environmental features of which contribute to the
historical or cultural importance and continuing integrity of certified historic structures such as Mount Vernon, or historic districts, such as Waterford, Virginia, or Harper's Ferry, West Virginia." Report, *supra* N.34 at 12, 1980 U.S. Code Cong. & Ad.
News at 6749.

85. I.R.C. §170(h)(4)(A)(iii).

86. Report, *supra* N.34 at 10, 1980 U.S. Code Cong. & Ad.
News at 6745.

87. *Id.* at 11, 1980 U.S. Code Cong. & Ad. News at 6746.

88. I.R.C. §170(h)(4)(A)(iii).

89. Report, *supra* N.34 at 9, 1980 U.S. Code Cong. & Ad.
News at 6744-45.

90. *Id.* at 11, 1980 U.S. Code Cong. & Ad. News at 6746.

91. *See generally* Costonis, "Law and Aesthetics: A Critique
and a Reformulation of the Dilemmas," 80 Mich. L. Rev. 355
(1982).

92. I.R.C. §170(4)(A)(iii)(II).

93. Report, *supra* N.34 at 11, 1980 U.S. Code Cong. & Ad.
News at 6747.

94. The effect of land-use classifications that preclude owners
from maximizing value through land development or that allow
owners a preferential assessment for the ad valorem property tax
as a public "investment" in the form of foregone tax revenues
should not be overlooked.

95. Each ruling is addressed solely to the taxpayer requesting
it. I.R.C. §6110(j)(3) provides that such a ruling may not be
used or cited as precedent.

96. Ltr. Rul. 8233025.

97. Ltr. Rul. 8247024.

98. Ltr. Rul. 8243125.

99. *See Hearings on H.R. 4611 Before the Subcomm. on Select
Revenue Measures of the House Comm. on Ways and Means*, 96th
Cong., 1st Sess. 5-6 (Nov. 9, 1979); *Hearings on H.R. 7318
Before the Subcomm. on Select Revenue Measures of the House
Comm. on Ways and Means*, 96th Cong., 2d Sess. (June 26,
1980).

100. Report, *supra* N.34 at 15, 1980 U.S. Code Cong. &
Ad. News at 6751.

101. *Id.* at 13, 1980 U.S. Code Cong. & Ad. News at 6748.
The elaboration of the "purpose" test leads to substantive judgments on natural resource issues being rendered by officials in
the Department of the Treasury.

102. *Id.*

Note on Regulation Under I.R.C. Section 170(h)

Russell L. Brenneman

As the previous article discusses, Section 6 of the Tax Treatment Extension Act of 1980, which became effective December 18, 1980, substantially changed the rules hitherto applicable to charitable contributions of less than the donor's entire interest in property in the case of gifts for land conservation and historic preservation purposes. The text of Section 170(h) as it stands following the passage of that law is as follows:

§170(h) Qualified Conservation Contribution.—
(1) *In general.*—For purposes of subsection (f)(3)(B)(iii), the term "qualified conservation contribution" means a contribution—
(A) of a qualified real property interest,
(B) to a qualified organization,
(C) exclusively for conservation purposes.
(2) *Qualified real property interest.*—For purposes of this subsection, the term "qualified real property interest" means any of the following interests in real property:
(A) the entire interest of the donor other than a qualified mineral interest,
(B) a remainder interest, and
(C) a restriction (granted in perpetuity) on the use which may be made of the real property.
(3) *Qualified organization.*—For purposes of paragraph (1), the term "qualified organization" means an organization which—
(A) is described in clause (v) or (vi) of subsection (b)(1)(A), or
(B) is described in section 501(c)(3) and—
(i) meets the requirements of section 509(a)(2), or
(ii) meets the requirements of section 509(a)(3) and is controlled by an organization described in subparagraph (A) or in clause (i) of this subparagraph.

(4) *Conservation purpose denied.*—
(A) *In general.*—For purposes of this subsection, the term "conservation purpose" means—
(i) the preservation of land areas for outdoor recreation by, or the education of, the general public,
(ii) the protection of a relatively natural habitat of fish, wildlife, or plants, or similar ecosystem,
(iii) the preservation of open space (including farmland and forest land) where such preservation is—
(I) for the scenic enjoyment of the general public, or
(II) pursuant to a clearly delineated Federal, State, or local governmental conservation policy, and will yield a significant public benefit, or
(iv) the preservation of an historically important land area or a certified historic structure.
(B) *Certified historic structure.*—For purposes of subparagraph (A)(iv), the term "certified historic structure" means any building, structure, or land area which—
(i) is listed in the National Register, or
(ii) is located in a registered historic district (as defined in section 191(d)(2)) and is certified by the Secretary of the Interior to the Secretary as being of historic significance to the district.

A building, structure, or land area satisfies the preceding sentence if it satisfies such sentence either at the time of the transfer or on the due date (including extensions) for filing the transferor's return under this chapter for the taxable year in which the transfer is made.

(5) *Exclusively for conservation purposes.*—For purposes of this subsection—
(A) *Conservation purpose must be protected.*—A con-

tribution shall not be treated as exclusively for conservation purposes unless the conservation purpose is protected in perpetuity.

(B) *No surface mining permitted.*—In the case of a contribution of any interest where there is a retention of a qualified mineral interest, subparagraph (A) shall not be treated as met if at any time there may be extraction or removal of minerals by any surface mining method.

(6) **Qualified mineral interest.**—For purposes of this subsection, the term "qualified mineral interest" means—

(A) subsurface oil, gas or other minerals, and

(B) the right to access to such minerals.

Proposed Regulations for Section 170(h) were published in the Federal Register May 23, 1983. These regulations add, following Treas. Reg. Sec. 1.170A-12, an additional provision, the text of which is as follows:

§1.170A-13 Qualified conservation contributions.

(a) **Qualified conservation contributions.** A deduction under section 170 is generally not allowed for a charitable contribution of any interest in property that consists of less than the donor's entire interest in the property other than certain transfers in trust (see §1.170A-6 relating to charitable contributions in trust and §1.170A-7 relating to contributions not in trust of partial interests in property). However, a deduction may be allowed under section 170(f)(3)(B)(iii) for the value of a qualified conservation contribution if the requirements of this section are met. A qualified conservation contribution is the contribution of a qualified real property interest to a qualified organization exclusively for conservation purposes. To be eligible for a deduction under this section, the conservation purpose must be protected in perpetuity.

(b) **Qualified real property interest**—

(1) Entire interest of donor other than qualified mineral interest.

The entire interest of the donor other than a qualified mineral interest is a qualified real property interest. A qualified mineral interest is the taxpayer's interest in subsurface oil, gas, or other minerals and the right of access to such minerals. A property interest shall not be treated as a qualified real property interest by reason of section 170(h)(2)(A) or this paragraph (b)(1), if at any time over the entire term of the taxpayer's interest in such property the taxpayer transferred any portion of that interest (except in the case of a donation of a perpetual conservation restriction under paragraph (b)(3) of this section) to any other person (except for minor interests, such as rights-of-way, that will not interfere with the conservation purposes of the donation).

(2) Remainder interest in real property.

A remainder interest in real property is a qualified real property interest. A property interest shall not be treated as a qualified real property interest by reason of section 170(h)(2)(B) or this paragraph (b)(2), if at any

time over the entire term of the taxpayer's interest in such property the taxpayer transferred any portion of that interest (except in the case of a donation under paragraph (b)(3) of this section) to any other person (except for minor interests, such as rights-of-way, that will not interfere with the conservation purposes of the donation).

(3) Perpetual conservation restriction.

A perpetual conservation restriction is a qualified real property interest. A "perpetual conservation restriction" is a restriction granted in perpetuity on the use which may be made of real property—including an easement or other interest in real property that under state law has attributes similar to an easement (e.g., a restrictive covenant or equitable servitude). For purposes of this section, the terms "easement," "conservation restriction," and "perpetual conservation restriction" have the same meaning. The definition of "perpetual conservation restriction" under this paragraph (b)(3) is not intended to preclude the deductibility of a donation of affirmative rights to use a land or water area under §1.170A-13(d)(2). Any rights reserved by the donor in the donation of a perpetual conservation restriction must conform to the requirements of this section. See, e.g., paragraphs (d)(4)(ii), (d)(5)(i), (e)(3), and (g)(4) of this section.

(c) **Qualified organization**—

(1) Eligible donee.

To be considered an eligible donee under this section, an organization must have the resources to enforce the restrictions and must be able to demonstrate a commitment to protect the conservation purposes of the donation. An established group organized exclusively for conservation purposes, for example, would meet this test. A qualified organization need not set aside funds, however, to enforce the restrictions that are the subject of the contribution. For purposes of this section, the term "qualified organization" means:

(i) A governmental unit described in section 170(b)(1)(A)(v);

(ii) An organization described in section 170(b)(1)(A)(vi);

(iii) A charitable organization described in section 501(c)(3) that meets the public support test of section 509(a)(2);

(iv) A charitable organization described in section 501(c)(3) that meets the requirements of section 509(a)(3) and is controlled by an organization described in paragraphs (c)(1)(i), (ii), or (iii) of this section.

(2) Transfers by donee.

A deduction shall be allowed for a contribution under this section only if in the instrument of conveyance the donor prohibits the donee from subsequently transferring the easement (or, in the case of a remainder interest or the reservation of a qualified mineral interest, the property), whether or not for consideration, unless the donee organization, as a condition of the subsequent transfer, requires that the conservation purposes which the contribution was originally intended to advance continue to be carried out. Moreover, subsequent transfers must be restricted to organizations qualifying, at the time of the subsequent transfer, as an eligible donee under paragraph (c)(1) of this section. When a later unexpected change in the conditions surrounding the property that is the subject of a donation under paragraphs (b)(1), (2), or (3) of this section makes impossible or impractical the continued use of the property for conservation purposes, the requirement of this paragraph will be met if the property is sold or exchanged and any proceeds are used by the donee organization in a manner consistent with the conservation purposes of the original contribution. In the case of a donation under paragraph (b)(3) of this section to which the preceding sentence applies, see also paragraph (g)(5)(ii) of this section.

(d) *Conservation purposes*—

(1) In general.

For purposes of section 170(h) and this section, the term "conservation purposes" means—

(i) The preservation of land areas for outdoor recreation by, or the education of, the general public, within the meaning of paragraph (d)(2) of this section,

(ii) The protection of a relatively natural habitat of fish, wildlife, or plants, or similar ecosystem, within the meaning of paragraph (d)(3) of this section,

(iii) The preservation of certain open space (including farmland and forest land) as described in paragraph (d)(4) of this section, or

(iv) The preservation of an historically important land area or a certified historic structure, within the meaning of paragraph (d)(5) of this section.

(2) Recreation or education—

(i) In general. The donation of a qualified real property interest to preserve land areas for the outdoor recreation of the general public or for the education of the general public will meet the conservation purposes test of this section. Thus, conservation purposes would include, for example, the preservation of a water area for the use of the public for boating or fishing, or a nature or hiking trail for the use of the public.

(ii) Public use. The preservation of land areas for recreation or education will not meet the test of this section unless the recreation or education is for the substantial and regular use of the general public or the community.

(3) Protection of environmental system—

(i) In general. The donation of a qualified real property interest to protect a significant relatively natural habitat in which a fish, wildlife, or plant community, or similar ecosystem, normally lives will meet the conservation purposes test of this section. The

fact that the habitat or environment has been altered to some extent by human activity will not result in a deduction being denied under this section if the fish, wildlife, or plants continue to exist there in a relatively natural state. For example, the preservation of a lake formed by a man-made dam or a salt pond formed by a man-made dike would meet the conservation purposes test if the lake or pond were a natural feeding area for a wildlife community that included rare, endangered, or threatened native species.

(ii) Significant habitat or ecosystem. Significant habitats and ecosystems include, but are not limited to, habitats for rare, endangered, or threatened species of animals, fish, or plants; natural areas that represent high quality examples of a terrestrial community or aquatic community, such as islands that are undeveloped or not intensely developed where the coastal ecosystem is relatively intact; and natural areas which are included in, or which contribute to, the ecological viability of a local, state, or national park, nature preserve, wildlife refuge, wilderness area, or other similar conservation area.

(4) Preservation of open space—

(i) In general. The donation of a qualified real property interest to preserve open space (including farmland and forest land) will meet the conservation purposes test of this section if such preservation is—

(A) Pursuant to a clearly delineated Federal, state, or local governmental policy and will yield a significant public benefit, or

(B) For the scenic enjoyment of the general public and will yield a significant public benefit. An open space easement donated on or after December 18, 1980, must meet the requirements of this section in order to be deductible under section 170. See §1.170A-7(b)(1)(ii).

(ii) Scenic enjoyment.—

(A) Factors. A contribution made for the preservation of open space may be for the scenic enjoyment of the general public. "Scenic enjoyment" will be evaluated by considering all pertinent facts and circumstances germane to the contribution. Regional variations in topography, geology, biology, and cultural and economic conditions require flexibility in the application of this test, but do not lessen the burden on the taxpayer to demonstrate the scenic characteristics of a donation under this paragraph. The application of a particular objective factor to help define a view as "scenic" in one setting may in fact be entirely inappropriate in another setting. Among the factors to be considered are:

(1) The compatibility of the land use with other land in the vicinity;

(2) The degree of contrast and variety provided by the visual scene;

(3) The openness of the land (which would be a more significant factor in an urban or densely populated setting or in a heavily wooded area);

(4) Relief from urban closeness;

(5) The harmonious variety of shapes and textures;

(6) The degree to which the land use maintains the scale and character of the urban landscape to preserve open space, visual enjoyment, and sunlight for the surrounding area;

(7) The consistency of the proposed scenic view with a methodical state scenic identification program, such as a state landscape inventory; and

(8) The consistency of the proposed scenic view with a regional or local landscape inventory made pursuant to a sufficiently rigorous review process, especially if the donation is endorsed by an appropriate state agency.

(B) Preservation of a view. To satisfy the requirement of scenic enjoyment by the general public, visual (rather than physical) access to or across the property by the general public is sufficient. Thus, preservation of land may be for the scenic enjoyment of the general public if development of the property would impair the scenic character of the local rural or urban landscape or would interfere with a scenic panorama that can be enjoyed from a park, nature preserve, road, waterbody, trail, or historic structure or land area, and such area or transportation way is open to, or utilized by, the public.

(C) Visible to public. Under the terms of an open space easement on scenic property, the entire property need not be visible to the public for a donation to qualify under this section, although the public benefit from the donation may be insufficient if only a small portion of the property is visible to the public.

(iii) Governmental conservation policy—

(A) In general. The requirement that the preservation of open space be pursuant to a clearly delineated Federal, state, or local governmental policy is intended to protect the types of property identified by representatives of the general public as worthy of preservation or conservation. A general declaration of conservation goals by a single official or legislative body is not sufficient. This requirement will be met by donations that further a specific, identified conservation project, such as the preservation of land within a state or local landmark district that is locally recognized as being significant to that district; the preservation of a wild or scenic river; the preservation of farmland pursuant to a state program for flood prevention and control; or the protection of the scenic, eco-

logical, or historic character of land that is contiguous to, or an integral part of, the surroundings of existing recreation or conservation sites. For example, the donation of a perpetual conservation restriction to a qualified organization pursuant to a formal declaration (in the form of, for example, a resolution or certification) by a local governmental agency established under state law specifically identifying the subject property as worthy of protection for conservation purposes will meet the requirement of this paragraph. A program need not be funded to satisfy this requirement, but the program must involve a significant commitment by the government with respect to the conservation project.

(B) Effect of acceptance by governmental agency. Acceptance of an easement by an agency of the Federal Government or by an agency of a state or local government (or by a commission, authority, or similar body duly constituted by the state or local government and acting on behalf of the state or local government) tends to establish the requisite clearly delineated governmental policy, although such acceptance, without more, is not sufficient. The more rigorous the review process by the governmental agency, the more the acceptance of the easement tends to establish the requisite clearly delineated governmental policy.

(iv) Significant public benefit—

(A) Factors. All contributions made for the preservation of open space must yield a significant public benefit. Public benefit will be evaluated by considering all pertinent facts and circumstances germane to the contribution. Factors germane to the evaluation of public benefit from one contribution may be irrelevant in determining public benefit from another contribution. No single factor will necessarily be determinative. Among the factors to be considered are:

(1) The uniqueness of the property to the area;

(2) The intensity of land development in the vicinity of the property (both existing development and foreseeable trends of development);

(3) The consistency of the proposed open space use with public programs (whether Federal, state or local) for conservation in the region, including programs for outdoor recreation, irrigation or water supply protection, water quality maintenance or enhancement, flood prevention and control, erosion control, shoreline protection, and protection of land areas included in, or related to, a government approved master plan or land management area;

(4) The consistency of the proposed open space use with existing private conservation programs in the area, as evidenced by other land, pro-

tected by easement or fee ownership by organizations referred to in §1.170A-13(c)(1), in close proximity to the property;

(5) The likelihood that development of the property would lead to or contribute to degradation of the scenic, natural, or historic character of the area;

(6) The opportunity for the general public to use the property or to appreciate its scenic values;

(7) The importance of the property in preserving a local or regional landscape or resource that attracts tourism or commerce to the area;

(8) The likelihood that the donee will acquire equally desirable and valuable substitute property or property rights;

(9) The cost to the donee of enforcing the terms of the conservation restriction;

(10) The population density in the area of the property; and

(11) The consistency of the proposed open space use with a legislatively mandated program identifying particular parcels of land for future protection.

(B) Illustrations. The preservation of an ordinary tract of land would not in and of itself yield a significant public benefit, but the preservation of ordinary land areas in conjunction with other factors that demonstrate significant public benefit or the preservation of a unique land area for public enjoyment would yield a significant public benefit. For example, the preservation of a vacant downtown lot would not by itself yield a significant public benefit, but the preservation of the downtown lot as a public garden would, absent countervailing factors, yield a significant public benefit. The following are other examples of contributions which would, absent countervailing factors, yield a significant public benefit: the preservation of farmland pursuant to a state program for flood prevention and control; the preservation of a unique natural land formation for the enjoyment of the general public; the preservation of woodland along a Federal highway pursuant to a government program to preserve the appearance of the area so as to maintain the scenic ocean view from the highway; and the preservation of a stretch of undeveloped property located between a public highway and the ocean in order to maintain the scenic view from the highway.

(v) Limitation. A deduction will not be allowed for the preservation of open space under section 170(h)(4)(A)(iii), if the terms of the easement permit a degree of intrusion or future development that would interfere with the essential scenic quality of the land or with the governmental conservation policy that is being furthered by the donation.

(vi) Relationship of requirements—

(A) Clearly delineated governmental policy and significant public benefit. Although the requirements of "clearly delineated governmental policy" and "significant public benefit" must be met independently, for purposes of this section the two requirements may also be related. The more specific the governmental policy with respect to the particular site to be protected, the more likely the governmental decision, by itself, will tend to establish the significant public benefit associated with the donation. For example, while a statute in State X permitting preferential assessment for farmland is, by definition, governmental policy, it is distinguishable from a state statute, accompanied by appropriations, naming the X River as a valuable resource and articulating the legislative policy that the X River and the relatively natural quality of its surroundings be protected. On these facts, an open space easement on farmland in State X would have to demonstrate additional factors to establish "significant public benefit." The specifically [sic] of the legislative mandate to protect the X River, however, would by itself tend to establish the significant public benefit associated with an open space easement on land fronting the X River.

(B) Scenic enjoyment and significant public benefit. With respect to the relationship between the requirements of "scenic enjoyment" and "significant public benefit," since the degrees of scenic enjoyment offered by a variety of open space easements are subjective and not as easily delineated as are increasingly specific levels of governmental policy, the significant public benefit of preserving a scenic view must be independently established in all cases.

(C) Donations may satisfy more than one test. In some cases, open space easements may be both for scenic enjoyment and pursuant to a clearly delineated governmental policy. For example, the preservation of a particular scenic view identified as part of a scenic landscape inventory by a rigorous governmental review process will meet the tests of both paragraphs (d)(4)(i)(A) and (d)(4)(i)(B) of this section.

(5) Historic preservation—

(i) In general. The donation of a qualified real property interest to preserve an historically important land area or a certified historic structure will meet the conservation purposes test of this section. When restrictions to preserve a building or land area within a registered historic district permit future development on the site, a deduction will be allowed under this section only if the terms of the restrictions require that such development conform with appropriate local, state, or Federal standards for construction or rehabilitation within the district. See also, §1.170A-13(h)(3)(ii).

(ii) Historically important land area. The term "historically important land area" includes:

(A) An independently significant land area (for example, an archaeological site or a Civil War battlefield) that substantially meets the National Register Criteria for Evaluation in 36 CFR 60.4 (Pub. L. 89-665, 80 Stat. 915);

(B) Any building or land area within a registered historic district (except buildings that cannot reasonably be considered as contributing to the significance of the district); and

(C) Any land area adjacent to a property listed individually in the National Register of Historic Places (but not within a registered historic district) in a case where the physical or environmental features of the land area contribute to the historic or cultural integrity of the structure.

(iii) Certified historic structure.—

(A) Definition. The term "certified historic structure," for purposes of this section, generally has the same meaning as in section 191(d)(1) (as it existed prior to the Economic Recovery Tax Act of 1981, relating to 5-year amortization of expenditures incurred in the rehabilitation of certified historic structures). However, a "structure" for purposes of this section means any structure, whether or not it is depreciable. Accordingly, easements on private residences may qualify under this section. In addition, a structure would be considered to be a certified historic structure if it were certified either at the time the transfer was made or at the due date (including extensions) for filing the donor's return for the taxable year in which the contribution was made.

(B) Interior and exterior easements. A deduction under this section will not be allowed for the donation of an interior or exterior easement prohibiting destruction or alteration of architectural characteristics inside or on the outside of a certified historic structure unless there is substantial and regular opportunity for the general public to view the architectural characteristics that are the subject of the easement.

(e) *Exclusively for conservation purposes*.

(1) In general. To meet the requirements of this section, a donation must be exclusively for conservation purposes. See paragraphs (c)(1) and (g)(1) through (g)(5)(ii) of this section. A deduction will not be denied under this section when incidental benefit inures to the donor merely as a result of conservation restrictions limiting the uses to which the donor's property may be put.

(2) Access. Any limitation on public access to property that is the subject of a donation under this section shall not render the donation nondeductible if such limitation is necessary for protection of the conservation interests that are the basis of the deduction. For example, a restriction on all public access to the habitat of a threatened native animal species protected by a donation under paragraph (d)(3) of this section would be appropriate if such restriction were necessary for the survival of the species.

(3) Inconsistent use. Except as provided in paragraph (e)(4) of this section, a deduction will not be allowed if the contribution would accomplish one of the enumerated conservation purposes but would permit destruction of other significant conservation interests. For example, the preservation of farmland pursuant to a state program for flood prevention and control would not qualify under paragraph (d)(4) of this section if under the terms of the contribution a significant naturally occurring ecosystem could be injured or destroyed by the use of pesticides in the operation of the farm. A donor is not required to demonstrate that all possible conservation interests associated with the property will be protected; rather, the terms of the donation must not permit destruction of significant conservation interests.

(4) Inconsistent use permitted. A use that is destructive of conservation interests will be permitted only if such use is necessary for the protection of the conservation interests that are the subject of the contribution. For example, a deduction for the donation of an easement to preserve an archaeological site that is listed on the National Register of Historic Places will not be disallowed if site excavation consistent with sound archaeological practices may impair a scenic view of which the land is a part. A donor may continue a preexisting use of the property that does not conflict with the conservation purposes of the gift.

(f) *Examples.* The provisions of this section relating to conservation purposes may be illustrated by the following examples.

Example (1). State S contains many large track forests that are desirable recreation and scenic areas for the general public. The forests' scenic values attract millions of people to the State. However, due to the increasing intensity of land development in State S, the continued existence of forest land parcels greater than 45 acres is threatened. J grants a perpetual easement on a 100-acre parcel of forest land that is part of one of the State's scenic areas to a qualifying organization. The easement imposes restrictions on the use of the parcel for the purpose of maintaining its scenic values. The restrictions include a requirement that the parcel be maintained forever as open space devoted exclusively to conservation purposes and wildlife protection, and that there be no commercial, industrial, residential, or other development use of such parcel. The law of State S recognizes a limited public right to enter private land, particularly for recreational pursuits, unless such land is posted or the landowner objects. The easement specifically restricts the landowner from posting the parcel, thereby maintaining public access to the parcel according to the custom of the State. J's parcel is regarded by the local community as providing the opportunity for the public to enjoy the use of the property and appreciate its scenic values. Accordingly, J's donation qualifies for a deduction under this section.

Example (2). A qualified conservation organization owns Greenacre in fee as a nature preserve. Greenacre contains a high quality example of a tall grass prairie ecosystem. Farmacre, an operating farm, adjoins Greenacre and is a compatible buffer to the nature preserve. Conversion of Farmacre to a more intense use, such as a housing development, would adversely affect the continued use of Greenacre as a nature preserve because of human traffic generated by the development. The owner of Farmacre donates an easement preventing any future development on Farmacre to the qualified conservation organization for conservation purposes. Normal agricultural uses will be allowed on Farmacre. Accordingly, the donation qualifies for a deduction under this section.

Example (3). H owns Greenacre, a 900-acre parcel of woodland, rolling pasture, and orchards on the crest of a mountain. All of Greenacre is clearly visible from a nearby national park. Because of the strict enforcement of an applicable zoning plan, the highest and best use of Greenacre is as a subdivision of 40-acre tracts. H wishes to donate a scenic easement on Greenacre to a qualifying conservation organization, but H would like to reserve the right to subdivide Greenacre into 90-acre parcels with no more than one single-family home allowable on each parcel. Random building on the property, even as little as one home for each 90 acres, would destroy the scenic character of the view. Accordingly, no deduction would be allowable under this section.

Example (4). Assume the same facts as in Example (3), except that not all of Greenacre is visible from the park and the deed of easement allows for limited cluster development of no more than five nine-acre clusters (with four houses on each cluster) located in areas generally not visible from the national park and subject to site and building plan approval by the donee organization in order to preserve the scenic view from the park. The donor and the donee have already identified sites where limited cluster development would not be visible from the park or would not measurably impair the view. Owners of homes in the clusters will not have any rights with respect to the surrounding Greenacre property that are not also available to the general public. Accordingly, the donation qualifies for a deduction under this section.

Example (5). State S has experienced a marked decline in open acreage well suited for agricultural use. In the parts of the State where land is highly productive in agricultural use, substantially all active farms are small, family-owned enterprises under increasing development pressures. In response to those pressures, the legislature of State S passed a statute authorizing the purchase of "agricultural land development rights" from farm owners and the placement of "agricultural preservation restrictions" on their land, in order to preserve the State's open space and farm resources. Agricultural preservation restrictions prohibit or limit construction or placement of buildings except those used for agricultural purposes or dwellings used for family living by the farmer and his family and employees; removal of mineral substances in any manner that adversely affects the land's agricultural potential; or other uses detrimental to retention of the land for agricultural use. Money has been appropriated for this program and some landowners have in fact sold their "agricultural land development rights" to State S. K owns and operates a small dairy farm in State S. K desires to preserve his farm for agricultural purposes in perpetuity. Rather than selling the development rights to State S, K grants to a qualifying conservation organization an agricultural preservation restriction on his property in the form of a conservation easement. K reserves to himself, his heirs and assigns the right to manage the farm consistent with sound agricultural and management practices. K's farm is located in one of the more agriculturally productive areas within State S. Accordingly, a deduction is allowed under this section.

(g) *Enforceable in perpetuity—*

(1) In general. In the case of any donation under this section, the interest in the property retained by the donor (and the donor's successors in interest) must be subject to legally enforceable restrictions that will prevent uses of the retained interest inconsistent with the conservation purposes of the donation. In the case of a contribution of a remainder interest, the contribution will not qualify if the tenants, whether they are tenants for life or a term of years, can use the property in a manner that diminishes the conservation values which are intended to be protected by the contributions.

(2) Remote future event. A deduction shall not be disallowed under section 170(f)(3)(B)(iii) and this section merely because the interest which passes to, or is vested in, the donee organization may be defeated by the performance of some act or the happening of some event, if on the date of the gift it appears that the possibility that such act or event will occur is so remote as to be negligible. See paragraph (e) of §1.170A-1. For example, a state's statutory requirement that use restrictions must be rerecorded every 30 years to remain enforceable shall not, by itself, render an easement nonperpetual.

(3) Retention of qualified mineral interest—

(i) In general. The requirements of this section are not met and no deduction shall be allowed in the case of a contribution of any interest when there is a retention of a qualified mineral interest if at any time there may be extractions or removal of minerals by any surface mining method. Moreover, in the case of a qualified mineral interest gift, the requirement that the conservation purposes be protected in perpetuity is not satisfied if any method of mining that is inconsistent with the particular conservation purposes of a contribution is permitted at any time. See also §1.170A-13(e)(3). However, a deduction under this section will not be denied in the case of certain methods of mining that may have limited, localized impact on the real property but that are not irremediably destructive of significant conservation interests. For example, a deduction will not be denied in a case where production facilities are concealed or compatible with existing topography and landscape and when surface alteration is to be restored to its original state.

(ii) Examples. The provisions of paragraph (g)(3)(i) of this section may be illustrated by the following:

Example (1). K owns 5,000 acres of bottomland hardwood property along a major watershed system in the southern part of the United States. Agencies within the Department of the Interior have determined that southern bottomland hardwoods are a rapidly diminishing resource and a critical ecosystem in the south because of the intense pressure to cut the trees and convert the land to agricultural use. These agencies have further determined (and have indicated in correspondence with K) that bottomland hardwoods provide a superb habitat for numerous species and play an important role in controlling floods and in purifying rivers. K donates to a qualifying conservation organization all his interest in this property other than his interest in the gas and oil deposits that have been identified under K's property. K covenants and can ensure that, although drilling for gas and oil on the property may have some temporary localized impact on the real property, the drilling will not interfere with the overall conservation purpose of the gift, which is to protect the unique bottomland hardwood ecosystem. Accordingly, the donation qualifies for a deduction under this section.

Example (2). Assume the same facts as in example (1), except that K does not own the mineral rights (or the right of access to those minerals) on the 5,000 acres and cannot ensure that the mining and drilling will not interfere with the overall conservation purpose. Accordingly, a deduction for the donation of the easement would not be allowable under this section. The same rule would apply to disallow a deduction by K for the donation of a remainder interest in the land for conservation purposes. A different result would follow if under applicable State law the qualifying organization had sufficient rights to protect the conservation purpose of the gift. Additionally, a donation of K's entire interest in the 5,000 acres to an eligible organization would qualify for a deduction under section 170(f)(3)(A) without regard to this section.

Example (3). Assume the same facts as in example (1), except that K sells the mineral rights to an unrelated party in an arm's-length transaction, subject to a recorded prohibition on the removal of any minerals by any surface mining method and a recorded prohibition against any mining technique that will harm the bottomland hardwood ecosystem. After the sale, K donates an easement for conservation purposes to a qualifying organization to protect the bottomland hardwood ecosystem. Since K can ensure in the easement that the mining of minerals on the property will not interfere with the conservation purposes of the gift, the donation qualifies for a deduction under this section.

(4) Protection of conservation purpose where taxpayer reserves certain rights.

(i) Documentation. In the case of a donation made after [the date final regulations are published in the Federal Register] of any qualified real property interest when the donor reserves rights the exercise of which may have an adverse impact on the conservation interests associated with the property, for a deduction to be allowable under this section the donor must make available to the donee, prior to the time the donation is made, documentation sufficient to establish the condition of the property at the time of the gift. Such documentation may include:

(A) The appropriate survey maps from the United States Geological Survey, showing the property line and other contiguous or nearby protected areas;

(B) A map of the area drawn to scale showing all existing man-made improvements or incursions (such as roads, buildings, fences, or gravel pits), vegetation and identification of flora and fauna (including, for example, rare species locations, animal breeding and roosting areas, and migration routes), land use history (including present uses and recent past disturbances), and distinct natural features (such as large trees and aquatic areas);

(C) An aerial photograph of the property at an appropriate scale taken as close as possible to the date the donation is made; and

(D) On-site photographs taken at appropriate locations on the property. If the terms of the donation contain restrictions with regard to a particular natural resource to be protected, such as water quality or air quality, the condition of the resource at or near the time of the gift must be established. The documentation, including the maps and photographs, must be accompanied by a statement signed by the donor and a representative of the donee clearly referencing the documentation and in substance saying "This natural resources inventory is an accurate representation of [the protected property] at the time of the transfer."

(ii) Donee's right to inspection and legal remedies. In the case of any donation referred to in paragraph (g)(4)(i) of this section, the donor must agree to notify the donee, in writing, before exercising any reserved right, e.g., the right to extract certain minerals which may have an adverse impact on the conservation interests associated with the property. The terms of the donation must provide a right of the donee to enter the property at reasonable times for the purpose of inspecting the property to determine if there is compliance with the terms of the donation. Additionally, the terms of the donation must provide a right of the donee to enforce the conservation restrictions by appropriate legal proceedings, including but not limited to, the right to require the restoration of the property to its condition at the time of the donation.

(5) Extinguishment.

(i) In general. If a subsequent unexpected change in the conditions surrounding the property that is the subject of a donation under this paragraph can make impossible or impractical the continued use of the property for conservation purposes, the conservation purpose can nonetheless be treated as protected in perpetuity if the restrictions are extinguished by judicial proceeding and all of the donee's proceeds (determined under paragraph (g)(5)(ii) of this section) from a subsequent sale or exchange of the property are used by the donee organization in a manner consistent with the conservation purposes of the original contribution.

(ii) Proceeds. In the case of a donation made after [the date final regulations are published in the Federal Register], for a deduction to be allowed under this section, at the time of the gift the donor must agree that the donation of the perpetual conservation restriction gives rise to a property right, immediately vested in the donee organization, with a fair market value that is a minimum ascertainable proportion of the fair market value of the entire property. See §1.170A-13(h)(3)(iii). For purposes of this paragraph (g)(5)(ii), that original minimum proportionate value of the donee's property rights shall remain constant. Accordingly, when a change in conditions gives rise to the extinguishment of a perpetual conservation restriction under paragraph (g)(5)(i) of this section, the donee organization, on a subsequent sale, exchange, or involuntary conversion of the subject property, must be entitled to a portion of the proceeds at least equal to the original proportionate value of the perpetual conservation restriction, unless state law provides that the donor is entitled to the full proceeds from the conversion without regard to the terms of the prior perpetual conservation restriction.

(h) *Valuation*—

(1) Entire interest of donor other than qualified mineral interest. The value of the contribution under section 170 in the case of a contribution of a taxpayer's entire interest in property other than a qualified mineral interest is the fair market value of the surface rights in the property contributed. The value of the contribution shall be computed without regard to the mineral rights. See paragraph (h)(4), example (1), of this section.

(2) Remainder interest in real property. In the case of a contribution of any remainder interest in real property, section 170(f)(4) provides that in determining the value of such interest for purposes of section 170, depreciation and depletion of such property shall be taken into account. See §1.170A-12. In the case of the contribution of a remainder interest for conservation purposes, the current fair market value of the property (against which the limitations of §1.170A-12 are applied) must take into account any preexisting or contemporaneously recorded rights limiting, for conservation purposes, the uses to which the subject property may be put.

(3) Perpetual conservation restriction—

(i) In general. The value of the contribution under section 170 in the case of a charitable contribution of a perpetual conservation restriction is the fair market value of the perpetual conservation restriction at the time of the contribution. See §1.170A-7(c). If no substantial record of marketplace sales is available to use as a meaningful or valid comparison, as a general rule (but not necessarily in all cases) the fair market value of a perpetual conservation restriction is equal to the difference between the fair market value of the land it encumbers before the granting of the restriction and the fair market value of the encumbered land after the granting of the restriction. The amount of the deduction in the case of a charitable contribution of a perpetual conservation restriction covering a portion of the contiguous land owned by a taxpayer and the taxpayer's family (see section 267(c)(4)) is the difference between the fair market value of the entire contiguous tract before and after the granting of the restriction. Accordingly, in the case of the donation of a perpetual conservation restriction in all or a portion of the contiguous land owned by a taxpayer and the taxpayer's family (see section 267(c)(4)), if the donor or the donor's family receives, or can reasonably expect to receive, financial or economic benefits that are greater than those that will inure to the general public from the transfer, no deduction is allowable under this section. However, if the transferor receives, or can reasonably expect to receive, a financial or economic benefit that is substantial, but it is clearly shown that the benefit is less than the amount of the transfer, then a deduction under this section is allowable for the excess of the amount transferred over the amount of the financial or economic benefit received or reasonably expected to be received by the transferor. (See example (11) of paragraph (h)(4) of this section.)

(ii) Fair market value of property before and after restriction. If before and after valuation is used, the fair market value of the property before contribution of the conservation restriction must take into account not only the current use of the property but also an objective assessment of how immediate or remote the likelihood is that the property, absent the restriction, would in fact be developed, as well as any effect from zoning, conservation, or historic preservation laws that already restrict the property's potential highest and best use. Further, there may be instances where the grant of a conservation restriction may have no material effect on the value of the property or may in fact serve to enhance, rather than reduce, the value of property. In such instances, no deduction would be allowable. In the case of a conservation restriction that allows for any development, however limited, on the property to be protected, the fair market value of the property after the contribution of the restriction must take into account the effect of the development. Additionally, if before and after valuation is used, an appraisal of the property after contribution of the restriction must take into account the effect of restrictions that will result in a reduction of the potential fair market value represented by highest and best use but will, nevertheless, permit uses of the property that will increase its fair market value above that represented by the property's current use. The value of a perpetual conservation restriction shall not be reduced by reason of the existence of restrictions on transfer designed solely to ensure that the conservation restriction will be dedicated to conservation purposes. See §1.170A-13(c)(2).

(iii) Allocation of basis. In the case of the donation of a qualified real property interest for conservation purposes, the basis of the property retained by the donor must be adjusted by the elimination of that part of the total basis of the property that is properly allocable to the qualified real property interest granted. The amount of the basis that is allocable to the qualified real property interest shall bear the same ratio to the total basis of the property as the fair market value of the qualified real property interest bears to the fair market value of the property before the granting of the qualified real property interest. When a taxpayer donates to a qualifying conservation organization an easement on a structure with respect to which deductions are taken for depreciation, the reduction required by this paragraph (h)(3)(iii) in the basis of the property retained by the taxpayer must be allocated between the structure and the underlying land.

(4) Examples. The provisions of this section may be illustrated by the following examples. In examples illustrating the value or deductibility of donations, the applicable restrictions and limitations of §1.170A-4, with respect to reduction in amount of charitable contributions of certain appreciated property, and §1.170A-8, with respect to limitations on charitable deductions by individuals, must also be taken into account.

Example (1). A owns Goldacre, a property adjacent to a state park. A wants to donate Goldacre to the state to be used as part of the park, but A wants to reserve a qualified mineral interest in the property, to exploit currently and to devise at death. The fair market value of the surface rights in Goldacre is $200,000 and the fair market value of the mineral rights is $100,000. In order to ensure that the quality of the park will not be degraded, restrictions must be imposed on the right to extract the minerals that reduce the fair market value of the mineral rights to $80,000. Under this section, the value of the contribution is $200,000 (the value of the surface rights).

Example (2). Assume the same facts as in example (1), except that A would like to retain a life estate in Goldacre. A donates a remainder interest in Goldacre to the county government to use Goldacre as a park after A's death, but reserves the mineral rights in Goldacre (with restrictions on extraction similar to those in example (1)). A's gift does not meet the requirements of §1.170A-7, with respect to contributions not in trust of partial interests in property, of §1.170A-13(b)(1), with respect to qualified mineral interests, or of §1.170A-13(b)(2), with respect to remainder interests in real property. Accordingly, no income tax deduction is allowable under this section.

Example (3). In 1982, B, who is 62, donates a remainder interest in Greenacre to a qualifying organization for conservation purposes. Greenacre is a tract of 200 acres of undeveloped woodland that is valued at $200,000 at its highest and best use. Under §1.170A-12(b), the value of a remainder interest in real property following one life is determined under §25.2512-9 of the Gift Tax Regulations. Accordingly, the value of the remainder interest, and thus the amount eligible for an income tax deduction under section 170(f), is $95,358 ($200,000 × .47679).

Example (4). Assume the same facts as in example (3), except that Greenacre is B's 200-acre estate with a home built during the colonial period. Some of the acreage around the home is cleared; the balance of Greenacre, except for access roads, is wooded and undeveloped. See §170(f)(3)(B)(i). However, B would like Greenacre to be maintained in its current state after his death, so he donates a remainder interest in Greenacre to a qualifying organization for conservation purposes pursuant to sections 170(f)(3)(B)(iii) and (h)(2)(B). At the time of the gift the land has a value of $200,000 and the house has a value of $100,000. The value of the remainder interest, and thus the amount eligible for an income tax deduction under section 170(f), is computed pursuant to §1.170A-12. See §1.170A-12(b)(3).

Example (5). Assume the same facts as in example

(3), except that at age 62 instead of donating a remainder interest B donates an easement in Greenacre to a qualifying organization for conservation purposes. The fair market value of Greenacre after the donation is reduced to $110,000. Accordingly, the value of the easement, and thus the amount eligible for a deduction under section 170(f), is $90,000 ($200,000 less $110,000).

Example (6). Assume the same facts as in example (5), and assume that three years later, at age 65, B decides to donate a remainder interest in Greenacre to a qualifying organization for conservation purposes. Increasing real estate values in the area have raised the fair market value of Greenacre (subject to the easement) to $130,000. Accordingly, the value of the remainder interest, and thus the amount eligible for a deduction under section 170(f), is $67,324 ($130,000 × .51788).

Example (7). Assume the same facts as in example (3), except that at the time of the donation of a remainder interest in Greenacre, B also donates an easement to a different qualifying organization for conservation purposes. Based on all the facts and circumstances, the value of the easement is determined to be $100,000. Therefore, the value of the property after the easement is $100,000 and the value of the remainder interest, and thus the amount eligible for deduction under section 170(f), is $47,679 ($100,000 × .47679).

Example (8). C owns Greenacre, a 200-acre estate containing a house built during the colonial period. At its highest and best use, for home development, the fair market value of Greenacre is $300,000. C donates an easement (to maintain the house and Greenacre in their current state) to a qualifying organization for conservation purposes. The fair market value of Greenacre after the donation is reduced to $125,000. Accordingly, the value of the easement and the amount eligible for a deduction under section 170(f) is $175,000 ($300,000 less $125,000).

Example (9). Assume the same facts as in example (8) and assume that three years later, C decides to donate a remainder interest in Greenacre to a qualifying organization for conservation purposes. Increasing real estate values in the area have raised the fair market value of Greenacre to $180,000. Assume that because of the perpetual easement prohibiting any development of the land, the value of the house is $120,000 and the value of the land is $60,000. The value of the remainder interest, and thus the amount eligible for an income tax deduction under section 170(f), is computed pursuant to §1.170A-12. See §1.170A-12(b)(3).

Example (10). D owns property with a basis of $20,000 and a fair market value of $80,000. D donates to a qualifying organization an easement for conservation purposes that is determined under this section to have a fair market value of $60,000. The amount of basis allocable to the easement is $15,000 ($60,000/$80,000 = $15,000/$20,000). Accordingly, the basis of the property is reduced to $5,000 ($20,000 minus $15,000).

Example (11). E owns 10 one-acre lots that are currently woods and parkland. The fair market value of each of E's lots is $15,000 and the basis of each lot is $3,000. E grants to the county a perpetual easement for conservation purposes to use and maintain eight of the acres as a public park and to restrict any future development on those eight acres. As a result of the restrictions, the value of the eight acres is reduced to $1,000 an acre. However, by perpetually restricting development on this portion of the land, E has ensured that the two remaining acres will always be bordered by parkland, thus increasing their fair market value to $22,500 each. If the eight acres represented all of E's land, the fair market value of the easement would be $112,000, an amount equal to the fair market value of the land before the granting of the easement (8 × $15,000 = $120,000) minus the fair market value of the encumbered land after (8 × $1,000 = $8,000). However, because the easement only covered a portion of the taxpayer's contiguous land, the amount of the deduction under section 170 is reduced to $97,000 ($150,000 − $53,000), that is, the difference between the fair market value of the entire tract of land before ($150,000) and after ((8 × $1,000) + (2 × $22,500)) the granting of the easement.

Example (12). Assume the same facts as in example (11). Since the easement covers a portion of E's land, only the basis of that portion is adjusted. Therefore, the amount of basis allocable to the easement is $22,400 ((8 × $3,000) × ($112,000/$120,000)). Accordingly, the basis of the eight acres encumbered by the easement is reduced to $1,600 ($24,000 − $22,400), or $200 for each acre. The basis of the two remaining acres is not affected by the donation.

Example (13). F owns and uses as professional offices a two-story building that lies within a registered historic district. F's building is an outstanding example of period architecture with a fair market value of $125,000. Restricted to its current use, which is the highest and best use of the property without making changes to the facade, the building and lot would have a fair market value of $100,000, of which $80,000 would be allocable to the building and $20,000 would be allocable to the lot. F's basis in the property is $50,000, of which $40,000 is allocable to the building and $10,000 is allocable to the lot. F's neighborhood is a mix of residential and commercial uses, and it is possible that F (or another owner) could enlarge the building for more extensive commercial use, which is its highest and best use. However, this would require changes to the facade. F would like to donate to a qualifying preservation organization an easement restricting any changes to the facade and promising to maintain the facade in perpetuity. The donation would qualify for a deduction under this section. The fair market value of the easement is $25,000 (the fair market value of the property before the easement, $125,000, minus the fair market value of the property after the easement, $100,000). Pursuant to §1.170A-13(h)(3)(iii), the basis allocable to the easement is $10,000 and the basis of the underlying property (building and lot) is reduced to $40,000.

(i) *Substantiation requirement.* If a taxpayer makes a qualified conservation contribution and claims a deduction, the taxpayer must maintain written records of the fair market value of the underlying property before and after the donation and the conservation purpose furthered by the donation and such information shall be stated in the taxpayer's income tax return if required by the return or its instructions.

(j) *Effective date.* This section applies only to contributions made on or after December 18, 1980.

Many organizations provided the Internal Revenue Service with written comments on the proposed regulations, including The Trust for Public Land, the Sonoma (California) Land Trust, the Napa County (California) Land Trust, the Montana Land Reliance, and The Nature Conservancy.

The comments filed by The Trust for Public Land included the following observations:

1. *Preservation of Open Space: A Need for More Safe Harbors.* Despite the lengthy discussion in the regulations of the open space purpose test (§1.170A-13(d)(4)) and despite the numerous factors listed and illustrations provided, the uncertainty you refer to surrounding this part of the statute has not been dispelled. There remains too much room for conflicting interpretations.

The cost of uncertainty for fledgling conservation easement programs is high. Typically, our donors cannot afford the expense of private rulings or appeals. The transaction costs involved in an easement donation—appraisal, resource inventory, monitoring fund—are already substantial. To ask potential donors to undertake the risk that a deduction will be denied, with the resulting exposure to gift tax liability, is in most cases to ask too much.

The source of the problem, we recognize, is the statutory significant public benefit requirement, a concept which does not lend itself to bright-line distinctions. Nevertheless, if because of it the conservation easement approach to open space protection were to founder, most would agree that the public benefit will have been badly served. To prevent such an outcome, we propose that an effort be made to incorporate more safe harbors into the open space provision.

(a) *Governmental Donees.* As a starting point, we think you should reexamine your treatment of donations made directly to, and accepted by, governmental agencies. Unquestionably, the easiest way to administer this section of the statute would be to presume significant public benefit in those cases where the integrity of the

donee itself is sufficient assurance that the gift will yield such benefit. The mandate of governmental agencies is to serve the public good, and they are accountable to it through the political process. The opportunity for abuse in the present context seems limited to us. In our experience, governmental agencies have not been over-eager to take on the burden of maintaining and enforcing a conservation interest. They do it, basically, when the public demands it. The I.R.S. should be able to rely on the determination of public benefit implicit in a governmental agency's acceptance of a gift. As for the clearly delineated governmental policy requirement, no governmental action in this area could be as clearly focused as one that actually involves the government in accepting conservation gifts. The public nature of the donee alone should qualify the gift under the open space purpose provision.

It would be of great benefit to conservation easement programs in California, and other states with similar legislation, if the regulations were to contain unequivocal language indicating that donations made pursuant to statutes like the Open-Space Easement Act [of California], by their nature, satisfy the requirements of the open space provision. In its current form §1.170A-13(d)(4) nearly accomplishes this. To complete the job, we propose amending the language of §1.170A-13(d)(4)(vi)(A) as indicated in paragraph (1) below.

(1) *Section 1.170A-13(d)(4)(vi) Relationship of requirements—(A) Clearly delineated governmental policy and significant public benefit.* Although the requirements of "clearly delineated governmental policy" and "significant public benefit" must be met independently, for purposes of this section the two requirements may also be related. The more specific the governmental policy with respect to the particular site to be protected, the more likely the governmental decision, by itself, will tend to establish the significant public benefit associated with the donation. For example, while a statute in State X permitting preferential assessment for farmland is, by definition, governmental policy, it is distinguishable from a state statute, accompanied by appropriations, naming the X River as a valuable resource and articulating the legislative policy that the X River and the relatively natural quality of its surroundings be protected. * The specificity of the legislative mandate to protect the X River would by itself tend to establish the significant public benefit associated with an open-space easement on land fronting the X River. * *Whereas,* an open-space easement on farmland in State X would have to demonstrate additional factors to establish "significant public benefit." However, if qualifying for the preferential assessment program of State X were contingent on the imposition of conservation restrictions on an individual parcel pursuant to a resolution of a city or county, and maintaining the property as

farmland were consistent with the local governmentally approved general plan, the necessary specificity would exist to establish the significant public benefit associated with a donation made in accordance with such a program. [Transposition indicated "*"; additions indicated by underscoring.]

2. *Access.* The single most troubling aspect of the draft regulations is their treatment of public access. Most people have assumed that, other than for gifts for recreational or educational purposes or where sufficient public benefit is not otherwise apparent, the availability of public access would be irrelevant to the question of deductibility of a conservation contribution. The access rule stated in §1.170A-13(e)(2) has, as far as we can see, no basis in the Code Section, the legislative history, or the Committee Reports. It is, in fact, in direct conflict with the statement that appears in both Committee Reports, which you adopt, that visual, not physical, access by the general public is sufficient to satisfy the scenic enjoyment requirement (H.R. Rep. No. 96-1278 at 17; S. Rep. No. 1007 at 11; §1.170A-13(d)(ii)(B)). Neither of the Committee Reports gives any indication that public access has any bearing whatever on the "exclusively for conservation purposes" requirement. In our opinion, you have imported an access bias into these regulations that is contrary to the intent of the legislation.

Access should be relevant only to recreational and educational gifts. So long as there is a significant public benefit to be derived from a conservation gift that limits or prohibits public access, access should not be an issue. . . . The draft regulations' treatment of access ignores the serious and legitimate concern of private landowners for privacy and the quiet enjoyment of their property. The result could be to discourage gifts of easements over property whose protection would be of over-arching significance to the public, even though allowing access would be of only marginal additional benefit. . . .

We recommend that the access provision of §1.170A-13(e)(2) be deleted. Alternatively, we recommend that it be limited to gifts of entire-interests-less-mineral-rights or matured remainders and relocated in the significant public benefit section (§1.170A-13(d)(4)(iv)) with the addition of the following final sentence:

"The limitation or prohibition of public access to property that is the subject of an easement gift shall not render the donation nondeductible, except that provision for public access may be relevant in certain cases to establishing the significant public benefit to be derived from the donation where other factors are insufficient by themselves to establish the required degree of public benefit."

4. *No Prior Transfer Rule.* The prohibition of prior transfers that §1.170A-13(b)(1) and (2) impose on donations of entire-interests-less-mineral-rights and remainders seems over-broad to us. We note the following statement found in the Senate Finance Committee Report:

"The committee intends that a contribution will not qualify under this new provision if the donor has reduced his . . . interest before the contribution is made by, for example, transferring part of his interest in the real property to a related person in order to retain control of more than a qualified mineral interest in the real property or reduce the real property interest donated." (S. Rep. 1007 at 10.)

If this is the source of the rule, the draft regulations cast their net much wider than is necessary to catch the abuse identified by the Committee Report. A rule similar to Treas. Reg. §1.170A-7(a)(2)(i), which is cited by the Committee Report, should be sufficient.

6. *Deed Restrictions in Gifts of Entire-Interests-Less-Mineral-Rights or Remainders.* The requirement imposed by §1.170A-13(c)(2) that the instrument of conveyance in a gift of a remainder interest or an entire-interest-less-mineral-rights include restrictions on subsequent transfers appears to us to be a futile attempt to control the use qualified donees make of such conservation interests. . . .

The Nature Conservancy also filed written comments on the proposed regulations, as follows:

Section: 1.170A-13(b)(1) and (2). The proposed regulations state that a property interest will not qualify under either subparagraphs 1 or 2 of the above-referenced section "if at any time over the entire term of the taxpayer's interest in such property, the taxpayer transfers any portion of that interest. . . ." It is our opinion that this would create an unworkable, technical standard which would arbitrarily disqualify such interests, regardless of the reason for the transfer of "any portion" of the real property interest. . . .

Section: 1.170A-13(c)(1).

1. The regulations state that an example of a qualified organization would be "an established group organized exclusively for conservation purposes." The regulations should recognize that organizations organized exclusively for conservation purposes are not the only organizations that meet the qualified-organization test. For example, The Nature Conservancy and many other conservation organizations are not organized exclusively for conservation purposes, but conservation purposes entail a substantial portion of the activity. We would suggest that this example language be changed to reflect that to meet the qualified-organization test a substantial portion of the activities of the organization must be dedicated to conservation purposes.

2. We agree that an organization "must be able to demonstrate a commitment to protect the conservation purposes. . . ." However, there is a question as to how this test will be monitored. Will this test require the Internal Revenue Service to regularly monitor the financial resources of the organization? Will the Internal Revenue Service issue a list of the organizations which are deemed to satisfy this test? Will the Internal Revenue Service establish mathematical formulas to demonstrate the required commitment?

Section: 1.170A-13(c)(2).

1. The restriction on transfers by the donee applies to easements, remainder interests, or property subject to the reservation of a qualified mineral interest. Under Section 1.170A-13(h)(3)(ii), there is a statement that "the value of a perpetual conservation restriction shall not be reduced by reason of the existence of restrictions on a transfer designed solely to ensure that the conservation restriction will be dedicated to conservation purposes." Does this provision apply also to the value of a gift of a remainder interest for conservation purposes or a gift of property subject to the reservation of a qualified mineral interest? Application of this valuation provision to remainder interests for conservation purposes and gifts subject to the reservation of a qualified mineral interest, as well as to easements, would seem to be consistent with the intent of this legislation.

2. The sentence addressing "a later unexpected change in the conditions surrounding the property that is the subject of a donation. . ." should be amended to cover situations where the unexpected change is beyond the control of the landowner or the holder of the conservation gift. Otherwise, arguably an action taken by either the holder of the land or the holder of the conservation gift would result in unjust enrichment. A cross reference to Section 1.170A-13(g)(5)(i), which provides for judicial determinations in such cases, would be helpful.

Section: 1.170A-13(d)(4).

1. No weighing mechanism, mathematical formula, or prioritization among the numerous factors differentiates among the criteria indicating scenic enjoyment or significant public benefits (Sections 1.170A-13(d)(4)(ii)(A)(1 through 8) or 1.170A-13(d)(4)(iv)(A)(1 through 11)). For example, if a conservation contribution satisfies the majority of the factors, will it automatically meet the test? Do some of these factors outweigh others? Within the Treasury Department, who will be making the determinations under these tests? . . .

2. Public agencies, federal, state, and local, are required to act in the best interest of the general public. Therefore, it would seem that any conservation contribution made to a public conservation agency would automatically satisfy the significant public-benefit test. We would suggest that the acceptance by a public conservation agency automatically satisfies the significant public-benefit test.

Section: 1.170A-13(e)(2). Public access should not be a necessary factor to meet the test of "exclusively for conservation purposes." The public access is an appropriate factor to consider when working with a contribution "for the scenic enjoyment of the general public." In addition, it may be critical to the deductibility of a contribution for "the preservation of land area for outdoor recreation by, or the education of, the general public." In most other instances, public access should not be a determining factor. For example, the protection of natural habitat, in itself, is the desirable public goal. The same can be said

for the preservation of threatened agricultural land. The agricultural land, in most instances, is being preserved as a valuable natural resource for food supply, not for public access purposes.

The requirement of public access would contradict the historical concept and marketability of conservation easements as an effective resource protection tool. It has been the experience of the nonprofit sector that most donors would not make a gift of a conservation easement if public access was mandatory. We should also note that a requirement of public access would often result in an additional financial and resource drain on the donee organization to cover the additional expenses of day-to-day land management and liability which results from public access.

Section: 1.170A-13(e)(3) and (4). We agree with the concept of looking at inconsistent uses in determining whether or not these uses interfere with the conservation purposes of the donation. However, since this is an area that will require professional natural resource experts, it would make sense to turn this determination process over to the appropriate public agencies. Otherwise, the Internal Revenue Service will have the burden of hiring or contracting for additional staff.

Section: 1.170A-13(g)(3)(ii), Example 2 and Example 3. Both of these examples imply that a contribution under this section will not qualify if the donor and donee cannot control the extraction of the minerals and/or if the limitation has not been imposed that the extraction of the minerals must be accomplished in a manner consistent with conservation purposes. Unfortunately, these examples demonstrate the current land ownership patterns in both the Southeast and the West where the donor often does not have control over the minerals. The application of these examples means that we will not be able to use qualified conservation contributions as a protection tool in areas where they are most needed. We would suggest at a minimum adding a provision to the regulations which would allow the qualified conservation contribution in the event that there are outstanding minerals beyond the control of the donor or donee, provided that there is little likelihood that either a) the minerals will ever be extracted; or b) if the minerals are extracted, it will be done in such a fashion, based on customary practices, that it will not result in significant disturbances to the detriment of the conservation purposes of the gift.

Section: 1.170A-13(g)(5)(ii).

1. The donee organization should not play a role at the time of the gift in determining the proportionate value of the donee's property rights. Otherwise, the donee will indirectly be playing a role in the valuation of the gift, a role that should be avoided at all times by the donee organization. Therefore, the regulations should be clarified to state that the determination of the value and of the proportionate value of the donee's property rights shall be the responsibility of the donor.

2. The proportionate share of the proceeds to which

the donee may be entitled must be "at least equal to the original proportionate value of the perpetual conservation restriction." We think the regulations should be clear that the original proportionate value is the minimum that a donee organization will receive, but that the donee organization will also receive the benefit of any increase in value when the donee interests increase based on changes in the market for such interests.

The historic preservation community was also concerned about certain provisions in the proposed regulations. On behalf of the Philadelphia Historic Preservation Corporation, Robert J. Shusterman, Esquire, addressed a letter to John R. Harman, Esquire, of the Internal Revenue Service, providing the following additional commentary, in pertinent part:

We are pleased to state that most of the proposed regulations are supportive to our program and will assist us in accomplishing our historic preservation goals. The provisions relating to extinguishment of easements, however, are a bit perplexing and appear to be unreasonable as applied to facade easements.

The essence of our concern is two-fold. The first and most important concern is that the straight proportional approach to the distribution of proceeds in the event of an extinguishment is unfair as applied to conservation easements which are comprised substantially of structures. This will be elaborated upon later. Our second concern is that a casualty loss may result in a partial extinguishment of an easement. In the event the historic structure is destroyed, the size, bulk, height, and other limitations governing any replacement structure may remain. This requires an apportionment of the different aspects of the easement to determine the distribution of the proceeds. This adds another level of complication to the process and may overinvolve the donee organization in the appraisal process. Furthermore, it is foreseeable that a facade easement on a building with several valuable facades be extinguished in part by a casualty affecting only one of the subject facades. In this situation a proportional distribution of the proceeds may be appropriate, or could serve to diminish the pool of funds necessary to restore the remaining portions of this historic structure.

I would like to now elaborate on our concern that the straight proportional approach to the distribution of proceeds in the event of an extinguishment is unfair as applied to conservation easements which are comprised substantially of structures. The straight proportional distribution may be fair and equitable as applied to open-space easements, but it is not reasonable when applied to facade easements. It does not take into consideration the increasing maintenance expenditures over time and the effect of a casualty loss on the economics of the donation. The potential adverse effects of an extinguishment due to a casualty loss are so substantial that they may make the

facade easement program unattractive to many possible donors. This can be seen by examining the hypothetical situation below.

A donor may be willing to give away rights resulting in his property being worth 10% less on resale. The impact on the donor is not immediate even though the loss of value is. The donor contemplates realizing this loss when the property is sold and has chosen to take a present tax savings over getting a higher return for the property on resale. Many donors anticipate a general appreciation of property values so that the impact of the contribution on the donor will not result in a cash out of pocket situation. Thus, if the property as subject to the easement appreciated 20% prior to resale, the sale of the property subject to the easement would still result in a positive cash flow. The calculations for a hypothetical situation are set forth below and are simplified by assuming that no depreciation is taken.

	With Easement	Without Easement
Purchase price (1/1/76)	$ 750,000	$ 750,000
Value without easement (1/1/84)		$1,000,000
Value with easement (1/1/84)	$ 900,000	
Basis of property after easement is given	$ 675,000	
Percentage value of easement	10%	
Rate of appreciation of real estate over holding period	20%	20%
Sale (1/1/88)	$1,080,000	$1,200,000
Capital gain (assuming no depreciation)	$ 405,000	$ 450,000
Profit on transaction	$ 330,000	$ 450,000
Capital gains tax at 20%	$ 81,000	$ 90,000
After tax profit	$ 249,000	$ 360,000

In this case, the donor may have made $111,000 less in overall profit, but he has still realized a profit from the property. In this type of situation, a reasonable, prudent businessman might be willing to take a $50,000 tax savings now and give up a potential after tax gain of $111,000 in the future. In making the donation, rights and values are lost, but no out of pocket expenses are incurred. In this instance it may be a reasonable business decision to take the present tax savings instead of waiting to realize a larger profit on the property on resale. On the other hand, the effect of casualty loss as demonstrated below shows that it may not be a reasonable business decision to give a facade easement. Using the same example, should a casualty totally extinguish the easement, the gift of the easement will result in a present out of pocket expense to the donor.

Valuation of building	80% structure	$720,000
with easement	20% land	$180,000
Insurance proceeds based upon full coverage of the structure		$720,000
Insurance proceeds to donor	(90%)	$648,000
Insurance proceeds to donee	(10%)	$ 72,000
Tax savings to donor from easement donation ($100,000 donation at 50% bracket)		$ 50,000
Cash cost to donor		$ 22,000

In this example the donor is out of pocket $22,000. Although there is an increase in the value of the land since the easement has been extinguished, the funds available to the owner are not sufficient to reconstruct the building he has lost. While this example may not appear unconscionable, it is clear that this result would not be deemed a "tax incentive." It is reasonable to assume that a businessman who has considered these factors would decide not to give a facade easement donation.

Accordingly, I urge the Internal Revenue Service to make its proposed regulations more equitable with respect to facade easements. At this time I have no alternate language to offer; however, I suggest that a more flexible standard be adopted.

Easements and Artifacts: An Archaeological Investigation of the Internal Revenue Code

Glenn F. Tiedt

The Internal Revenue Code of 1954 traditionally has been of little interest to archaeologists. Even to historical archaeologists it has been of much too recent vintage to merit investigation. Yet buried in the Code are several important tools that have been used in the past by other disciplines to preserve and protect significant resources. It is the purpose of this report to publicize those tools and demonstrate how they can be used for the good of archaeology.

Full Acquisition: Fee Simple Absolute

The most obvious means of protecting an archaeological site is to obtain full acquisition.[1] Ownership of the entire interest in a property embraces the right to control all uses of the site. In such instances the only activities legally allowed are those expressly authorized by the owner.

The most obvious limitation on acquisition is money—sites cannot be purchased without it. If no money is available, what can then be done? Acquire it by gift. Now, why should anyone give away land? Because a gift to a government agency or a qualified nonprofit organization can generate substantial income tax benefits. Unfortunately, most landowners and nearly all archaeologists are unaware of those benefits.

Tax benefits are a major factor in many gifts. Individual landowners who are entitled to be taxed at capital gains rates on the profit from any sale of their property may also be entitled to deduct the fair market value of the land from income if the same property is donated to a government agency or qualified nonprofit organization.[2] The owner

thus lowers taxes, which would have been raised by the capital gain, by deducting the value of the donation from taxable income. For those in higher brackets, a comparison between what the landowner would pocket after taxes on a sale of the property and the amount he or she would pocket in tax savings on a gift may show an insignificant difference. The greater benefits, of course, will go to those landowners with a highly appreciated site and a high ordinary income, but it is important to note that nearly every landowner can realize some benefit from a gift.

The charitable contribution deduction for capital gain property in any one year is normally limited to 30 percent of the donor's adjusted gross income.[3] If the value of the gift exceeds this limitation, the excess may be carried forward for up to five years.[4] This permits the donor to spread the tax effect of the gift over a six-year period, but the maximum deduction allowable must be taken each year.

Alternatively, a landowner may elect to deduct up to 50 percent of adjusted gross income, but the value of the gift must be reduced by 40 percent of the gain[5] (the amount that would have been subject to tax if the property had been sold). Here there is a loss of the benefit of deducting tax dollars in exchange for taking a larger portion of income as a deduction each year. The giver retains the ability to carry forward any excess for up to five additional years.[6]

Should a landowner decide that he or she cannot afford to donate the property, there remains the possibility of making a partial gift through a bargain sale. A bargain sale is a sale at less than fair market value. The difference between the fair market value and the sale price is treated as a charitable contribution for federal income tax pur-

194

poses.[7] A sale of property with a fair market value of $50,000 at a price of only $30,000, for example, would be a bargain sale in which the seller would be making a $20,000 gift to the buyer. The landowner will realize a taxable gain on the sale, but this will be partially offset by the charitable contribution deduction. There are special rules on allocation of costs and gain between the sale and the gift, which are set forth in the Treasury regulations.[8]

It is important to be aware that these rules apply only to individuals whose profit would be treated as capital gain were their property to be sold. The rules do not normally apply to developers because profit from sales of development property is treated as ordinary income. This does not mean, however, that developers cannot benefit from gifts. Qualified gifts of ordinary income property entitle the donor to a charitable contribution deduction equal to his cost basis in the property.[9] And even developers occasionally own investment property subject to capital gains treatment.

It is also important to recognize that these rules do not apply to corporations. Corporations have different limitations and different tax rates, but corporations can realize one big benefit that is usually of little or no concern to individuals: public relations. If tax savings alone will not do the trick, public relations often will.

Partial Interests: Conservation Easements

Even if money is available to buy a site or the landowner is willing to donate it, acquisition of the "fee simple absolute" interest may not be the most desirable means of protection. Ownership confers not only the right to control uses, but also the burden of responsibility. Having the right to control something does not necessarily confer the ability to do so, and remote sites are not easily protected by absentee landowners.

Such considerations may compel some individuals to investigate the benefits of acquisition of a conservation easement. This involves the ownership of only those rights necessary to protect specific resources. All uses of the site that do not conflict with the easement remain vested in the landowner. Since landowners are usually very vigilant about protecting their property, the owner of the easement has only the landowner to worry about.

If the landowner supports the purpose of the easement—and landowners who donate easements universally support the purpose for which their gifts are made—he or she will protect both his or her own rights and those of the easement owner with equal vigilance. The National Trust for Historic Preservation cites the example of the landowner who protected a highly significant early Indian village site in a farm pasture behind a locked gate for many years: "To keep pothunters off the property, the landowner, who lived nearby, reinforced his determination with a bull and a German shepherd."[10] Few public agencies or nonprofit organizations could explain, much less justify, a bull and a German shepherd on their payroll. Yet these creatures probably protected the site infinitely better than the casual caretaker whose intermittent visits would only confirm that the land was still there.

So what is a conservation easement? The law school explanation compares property rights to a bundle of sticks. Each stick is a right. One stick is the right to develop the property. Another is the right to alter the topography. Still another is the right to remove sand and gravel. The owner of a "fee simple absolute" interest usually owns the entire bundle. The owner can give up some of these sticks and still own fee simple absolute, but he or she cannot exercise the rights represented by the sticks that have been relinquished. The customary way to transfer sticks from the landowner's bundle to someone else is for the landowner to grant a conservation easement. This easement consists only of those sticks expressly given up by the landowner: all the other sticks remain in the landowner's bundle.

The rights represented by the sticks in a conservation easement are of two basic types—negative or affirmative. Negative rights are such rights as the right to prohibit subdivision, the right to prevent development, and the right to prevent the removal of sand and gravel. Affirmative rights are such rights as the right to remove timber, the right to remove sand and gravel, and the right to remove artifacts.

Easements also are classified according to their relationship to other property owned by the holder of the easement. If an easement benefits other property in the same ownership as the easement, it is an easement appurtenant. An example of such an easement would be an easement on property surrounding an archaeological site, prohibiting development and preserving the context within which the site is located. If an easement does not benefit other property in the same ownership, it is an easement in gross. An easement protecting a remote archaeological site, isolated from any other property held by the owner of the easement, is an easement in gross.

Easements in gross that consist solely of negative rights may be extremely vulnerable under the common law. Easements appurtenant and easements consisting solely of affirmative rights are usually secure. A number of state legislatures have enacted statutes to overcome the common law defects of easements in gross, but there is very little consistency among these statutes.[11] The National Conference of Commissioners on Uniform State Laws has just completed work on a Uniform Conservation Easement Act. If enacted by the states, this act will eliminate the major technical problems with conservation easements.

In the absence of state law validating conservation easements in gross, some easements to protect archaeological sites have included affirmative rights to the archaeological materials on the property.[12] In other words, ownership of the unrecovered artifacts has been made an express part of the gift. This has the advantage of creating an affirmative easement, but it deprives the donor of any opportunity to take a charitable contribution deduction for the value of artifacts themselves. Conservation easements are valued by deducting the fair market value of the property as restricted from the fair market value of the property unrestricted:[13] the independent value of specific resources cannot be added to this amount. A technique used by conservation organizations for creating conservation easements appurtenant is to accept a donation of the fee simple interest in one acre of land and then to accept donations of conservation easements on hundreds of acres adjoining it. For archaeological sites this technique would not only overcome the common law problem but it would also allow the donor to make a later gift of the protected resource itself.

Qualified Conservation Contributions

Let us turn now to the federal income tax law. Prior to December 1980, gifts of conservation easements to protect archaeological sites were deductible under some relatively broad provisions of the Internal Revenue Code of 1954 as amended. On December 17, President Carter signed the Tax Treatment Extension Act of 1980,[14] which repealed all prior law on the subject and introduced the new concept of a "qualified conservation contribution."[15]

A qualified conservation contribution is defined as a contribution of a qualified real property interest to a qualified organization exclusively for conservation purposes.[16] This simple definition requires only five more definitions to give it full meaning!

A qualified real property interest is the donor's entire interest other than a qualified mineral interest, a remainder interest, and a restriction granted in perpetuity.[17] A qualified mineral interest is the subsurface oil, gas, or other minerals and the right to access to such minerals.[18] In plain English this means a landowner can donate his entire interest in real property and reserve the mineral interests. But there is a catch. If the minerals may be removed or extricated by any means of surface mining, the deduction will be disallowed.[19]

A qualified organization is a government agency or a "501(c)(3)" (Internal Revenue Code) public charity or an entity controlled by either of these.[20]

This brings us to the definition of conservation purpose. In the words of the statute

. . . the term "conservation purpose" means—

(i) the preservation of land areas for outdoor recreation by, or education of, the general public,

(ii) the protection of a relatively natural habitat of fish, wildlife, or plants, or similar ecosystem,

(iii) the preservation of open space (including farmland and forest land) where such preservation is—

(I) for the scenic enjoyment of the general public, or

(II) pursuant to a clearly delineated Federal, State, or local governmental conservation policy, and will yield a significant public benefit, or

(iv) the preservation of an historically important land area or a certified historic structure.[21]

If by now the reader feels a little confused, he is not alone. Even lawyers find it difficult to unravel the Internal Revenue Code. Rudolf Flesch gives it a score of minus 6 on his readability scale of 0 to 100.[22] But we are not finished yet. Even the definition requires a supplemental definition to complete the meaning:

. . . the term "certified historic structure" means any building, structure, or land area which—

(i) is listed in the National Register, or

(ii) is located in a registered historic district (as defined in section 191(d)(2)) and is certified by the Secretary of the Interior to the Secretary as being of historic significance to the district.[23]

What does all this have to do with archaeology? A charitable contribution of a conservation easement to protect an archaeological site is deductible if the site is either a historically important land area or a certified structure. The Senate Finance Committee report on this legislation said: "The term 'historically important land area' is intended to include independently significant land areas (for example, a civil war battlefield) and historic sites and related land area, the physical or environmental features of which contribute to the historic or cultural importance and continuing integrity of certified historic structures such as Mount Vernon, or historic districts, such as Waterford, Virginia, or Harper's Ferry, West Virginia."[24] We must wait for the Treasury regulations to get the IRS view, but it appears reasonable to consider archaeological sites to be independently significant land areas.

But can an archaeological site also be a certified historic structure? It certainly can. The Code says a land area is a certified historic structure if it is listed in the National Register or is located in a registered historic district and is certified as being of historic significance to the district.[25] If there is any doubt whether a particular site qualifies as an independently significant land area, such doubt can be removed by having it listed in the National Register. The listing requirement is met if the property is listed either at the time the gift is made or on the due date (including extensions) for filing the donor's return.[26]

In reference to the definition of the term "conservation purpose," the Senate committee commented, "Although many contributions may satisfy more than one of these objectives . . . it is only necessary for a contribution to further one of the four."[27] Then it added a little twist: "This requirement is not met if the contribution would accomplish one of the enumerated conservation purposes, but would allow uses of the property that would be destructive of other significant conservation interests."[28] This may mean that a conservation easement protecting an archaeological site on a unique natural area would not be deductible if either the unique natural features or the archaeological resources could be destroyed while the other was fully preserved. Thus the committee has seen fit to require very close coordination among the conservation and preservation disciplines in order to protect the donors as well as the resources.

Artifacts

Most easements on archaeological sites are negative. They prevent the landowner from doing anything that would adversely affect the cultural resources, but they usually do not include any affirmative rights in the resources themselves. There are two good reasons for this. First, the landowner does not want people digging on the property whenever they get the urge, and, second, the artifacts contribute almost nothing to the value of the easement. The method of appraisal prescribed by the IRS simply cannot assign any additional, independent value to the artifacts.

The artifacts and the right to remove them, however, can be the subject of a separate gift, but valuation is still a problem. Archaeologists are reluctant to give artifacts a market value because they fear this will encourage pothunters, and the IRS will not accept an unsupported value in a charitable contribution deduction.

An appropriate solution to the dilemma was used several years ago in Tennessee. As described by Geoffrey Gyrisco: "In the case of Averbuch Site, Tennessee, a large village and cemetery site excavated under contract with Interagency Archeological Services, US Department of the Interior, the developer donated the excavated archeological material to the state. The IRS accepted as the value of the material the total amount expended in the field to recover the data. This is a solution to the problem of determining the value of archeological artifacts."[29] This solution not only avoids the marketplace valuation problem, it also gives the landowner the opportunity to make more than one gift. He or she can donate a conservation easement protecting the site, then later donate the artifacts themselves. But he or she can do this only if the artifacts were not included in the original gift of the easement.

The two-gift approach also can be a means of spreading the charitable contribution deduction over more than six years should the value of the conservation easement and the artifacts together exceed the limitations described earlier.

Note that this approach has not been officially sanctioned by the IRS for general use. Nevertheless, every donee should make sure the donor of a conservation easement is not denied the opportunity to take the deduction for a separate gift of the artifacts by including them in the original easement. The donor should, of course, be given the opportunity to obtain the maximum deduction the law allows.

Conclusion

This short discussion has left out many details. It has identified some new approaches and described their manner of use, but it is not intended to make tax experts of laymen. Just as a skilled archaeologist is needed to extract full meaning from the cultural debris in the archaeosphere, a skilled lawyer or accountant is needed to extract the maximum tax deduction from the legislative debris in the Internal Revenue Code. Archaeologists should not hesitate to ask landowners to seek professional advice. Everyone involved has much to gain and little to lose.

Notes

1. Barnes, Mark R., "Preservation of Archeological Sites Through Acquisition," *American Antiquity* 46 (1981).

2. I.R.C. §170(b)(1)(C)(i).

3. I.R.C. §170(b)(1)(C)(i).

4. I.R.C. §170(b)(1)(C)(ii).

5. I.R.C. §170(b)(1)(C)(iii).

6. I.R.C. §170(d)(1).

7. I.R.C. §170(b)(1)(C).

8. I.R.C. §1011(b).

9. I.R.C. §170(e)(1)(A).

10. *Information Sheet* 28, National Trust for Historic Preservation (1980): 14.

11. Netherton, Ross D., "Environmental Conservation and Historic Preservation Through Recorded Land-Use Agreements," *Real Property, Probate and Trust Journal* 14(3) (1979): 540–580.

12. Gyrisco, Geoffrey M., "Legal Tools to Preserve Archeological Sites," Heritage Conservation and Recreation Service, *11593 Special Issue* (Fall 1980): 4.

13. Rev. Rul. 73-339, 1973-2 C.B. 68 and Rev. Rul. 76-376, 1976-2 C.B. 53.

14. Pub. L. No. 96-541, 94 Stat. 3204 (1980).

15. I.R.C. §170(f)(3)(B)(iii).

16. I.R.C. §170(h)(1).

17. I.R.C. §170(h)(2).

18. I.R.C. §170(h)(6).

19. I.R.C. §170(h)(5)(B).

20. I.R.C. §170(h)(3).

21. I.R.C. §170(h)(4)(A).

22. Flesch, Rudolf, *How to Write Plain English: A Book for Lawyers and Consumers* (Harper & Row: New York, 1979), p. 26.

23. I.R.C. §170(h)(4)(B).

24. S. Rep. No. 96-1007, 96th Cong., 2d Sess. 12 (1980).

25. I.R.C. §170(h)(4)(B).

26. I.R.C. §170(h)(4)(B).

27. S. Rep. No. 96-1007, 96th Cong., 2d Sess. 10 (1980).

28. S. Rep. No. 96-1007, 96th Cong., 2d Sess. 13 (1980).

29. Gyrisco, "Legal Tools," *supra* note 12, at 6.

Appraising Deductible Restrictions

Robert E. Suminsby

The value of a deductible restriction may be defined as the difference between the market value of the property affected, in its entirety, before the imposition of the restriction and the market value of the property immediately after the imposition of the restriction—commonly known as a before and after appraisal. An appraisal of property both before and after imposition of a restriction should employ one or more of the traditional approaches to value—cost, sales comparison, and income. The special problems encountered revolve around the need for a thorough analysis of highest and best use, including subdivision potential, both before and after, and the lack of market data to support the after value.

The value of property is never enhanced by the imposition of a restriction. Any deed restriction removes, or at least shortens, one or more of the straws in the "bundle of rights" that attaches to the ownership of property. In this sense any restriction, no matter how innocuous, will diminish the value of the property affected. The value of a portion of the property affected might be enhanced at the expense of diminishing the value of another portion, but the net effect on the property in its entirety will still be a diminution. Neighboring properties may be enhanced, and a combination of restrictions placed on a number of neighboring properties might have the effect of enhancing the value of them all, but this is a situation not usually encountered in the appraisal of a specific property.

Deed restrictions may be classified in three general categories: (1) highly significant restrictions—those that effect a change in the highest and best use of the property; (2) moderately significant restrictions—those that alter the subdivision potential of the property and prescribe some conditions on use; and (3) relatively insignificant restrictions—those that neither effect a change in use nor alter the subdivision potential, but simply prescribe conditions

for the use of the property in keeping with its current highest and best use.

Highly Significant Restrictions

Restrictions that effect a change in the highest and best use of a property usually cause a dramatic diminution in the property's market value. An example would be a restriction that prohibits any structures on a parcel of land that is suitable for development for residential purposes. An appraisal to determine the value before the restriction is placed can be made by comparing the land with sales of similar property suitable for residential development; whereas an appraisal of the after value might involve a comparison with sales of agricultural land. Such a restriction may make the property virtually unmarketable. An island on the Maine coast with a forever-wild easement held by The Nature Conservancy, which prohibits all structures, is currently being offered for sale at a price that is only about a third of what its value might have been if it were unencumbered by restrictions. The offering has attracted a number of interested buyers, but upon learning of the restrictions, their interest ceases, and to date no offers have been received. The island has aesthetic appeal and may eventually be purchased by somebody simply as a place to tent or picnic, but the eventual sale price will be a small fraction, probably no more than 10 to 20 percent, of the before value.

Moderately Significant Restrictions

Many restrictions do not effect a change in use but will either negate or alter the subdivision potential of the property. An example would be a twenty-acre parcel with a dwelling, with a restriction that does not permit any further dwellings. If the original dwelling is adequately supported by a two-acre parcel and there are several potential building sites, then there is a moderate diminishing of value, usually in the 10-to-30 percent range. The appraisal will involve a careful analysis of the subdivision potential with a valuation accomplished by a valuation of the subdivided parcels through a sales comparison approach to determine a total sale price on subdivision, then deducting for the time required for sale of the property on subdivision, the cost involved, and an allowance for entrepreneurship. Such an analysis will provide a wholesale value of the property in its entirety. A similar procedure may be employed in the after value.

For example, assume a parcel of thirty acres, the highest and best use of which is division into six residential lots of five acres, each potentially selling for a price of $20,000. The gross sale price is $120,000. Assuming subdivision and marketing costs of $20,000, the net income is $100,000, or $50,000 annually if a two-year marketing period is appropriate. Present worth of $50,000 annually for two years, discounted at 20 percent to allow for entrepreneurship profit, is $76,400. If the restriction allowed for subdividing into only two parcels, then it might be determined that both parcels could be sold within one year at $35,000, each with subdivision costs of only $8,000. The present worth of $62,000 discounted at 20 percent for one year is $52,700. The indicated value of the restriction would be the difference between the before and after values ($76,400 less $52,700), or $24,700.

Relatively Insignificant Restrictions

Many deed restrictions do not effect a change in use nor alter subdivision potential but simply prescribe conditions. An example would be a restriction that prohibited any further residences on a two-acre parcel of land with an existing dwelling, located in a neighborhood with two-acre zoning and with physical characteristics such that an additional dwelling would not be desirable in any event. Such restrictions would not appear to cause much diminution in value and frequently defy measurement. Some marketing experience is emerging, however, that suggests that these types of restrictions have a "nuisance effect" that must be considered. Following are three marketing experiences that will illustrate this point.

1. Somesville is a well-preserved New England village on the National Register of Historic Places. Conservation easements to the United States of America have been granted by several of the property owners around the harbor. In 1974 the owner of a property comprising 4¼ acres with a main residence and guest dwelling gave a conservation easement that restricted the property to its current use and prohibited any additional structures, while the owner retained only the right to replace or rebuild or to alter in substantially the same location the existing structures. Subsequently, the guest dwelling with one-half acre

of land was listed for sale. The restriction appeared to be beneficial to the offering because the purchaser would be protected against intense development of the surrounding land, but this did not prove to be the case. After a purchase and sale agreement was signed, the attorney for the buyer raised several questions with regard to the deed restrictions. Clarification of the meaning of those restrictions through the Department of the Interior was necessary, and the closing was delayed several months, resulting in a loss to the owner.

2. A 120-acre parcel of land was offered for sale subject to a deed restriction that would limit development to two residences and appurtenant structures. A buyer was found and a contract was entered into, but the wording of the restriction was left open. The owner wished to convey a conservation easement to the United States of America prior to closing, but the wording of the easement contained "words of art" that were misinterpreted by the buyer; and after protracted negotiations lasting nearly a year, the purchase and sale contract was terminated.

3. In 1974 the owner of a seventy-acre island granted to the United States of America a conservation easement that restricted development to five single-family, residential buildings and appurtenant structures, only two of which could be located within 300 feet of the high-water line. The easement contained additional wording that prescribed use and development of the property. At the time the easement was conveyed, it did not appear that it would significantly alter the market value of the property because five houses are more than are usually constructed on such islands. In 1980 the island was offered for sale and subsequently sold at a price almost 50 percent less than the price obtained for a neighboring island of comparable size and physical characteristics.

Summary

There is no secret formula for the appraisal of a deductible restriction; rather, it simply employs the traditional appraiser's methods with an added emphasis on the concept of highest and best use. If the restriction is one that effects a change in the highest and best use, then the appraiser may be able to find sales of properties with uses comparable to the subject property both before and after the restriction. In the case of the appraisal that negates or alters the subdivision potential, the appraiser may be able to employ the income analysis of subdivision potential both before and after in order to measure the restriction. In many cases, however, the measurement is not clear and the appraiser must rely on his judgment and common sense. With time a sufficient body of market data will emerge to provide more guidelines for the appraisal of the after value. At this time the experience with restrictions along the Maine coast suggests that such restrictions may have a more adverse effect on market value than might normally be assumed. There is a significant difference between voluntarily giving away a portion of one's property rights to a recipient in whom one has faith in order to protect a property for which one has concern, with the additional benefit of a tax deduction, and being a potential purchaser, to whom there is no tax advantage and to whom the holder of the restriction may be unfamiliar. The buyer is investing his money in a property for his, not for the public's, benefit. It is the other side of the coin. Restrictions of any sort do affect market value, and market evidence is just beginning to illustrate that point.

Appraising Deductible Restrictions

M. Eugene Hoffman

There is no well-established method for the appraisal or valuation of tax deductible restrictions as they pertain to land, particularly for conservation or preservation purposes. There is little history as well; it seems to have started during the early-to-mid-1960s. Little instructional literature has been published, and it has been only during the past two or three years that professional appraisal organizations have acknowledged sufficient interest or demand from their members to warrant training seminars for appraisers of such partial interests in real estate. To date, these seminars have been nothing more than brief orientations presented by appraisers who have had local experience. To my knowledge no standard course or instructional material has been formally developed. Each appraiser has apparently adapted an appraisal technique to solve each particular problem. Some have been "far out," to say the least, but have nevertheless been paid a good fee by the trusting and uninformed client.

Appraisals of conservation easements have evolved for the most part from the various federal land management agencies after passage of federal legislation such as the National Wild and Scenic Rivers Act, National Recreation Area Acts, and a multitude of other similar acts. These acts protect certain aesthetic and/or natural values on private lands strategically located within or next to public lands with some consonant value. Hence, most of the initial appraisal standards and techniques were promulgated by federal agencies such as the U.S. Forest Service, National Park Service, and Bureau of Outdoor Recreation. Most of the appraisals were done by staff personnel. As the job loads increased, a few independent fee appraisers were contracted. The contracts usually set forth general instructions, often leaving to the volition of the appraiser

the collection and gathering of evidence of the market value of the sometimes vague interests to be appraised.

The concept of conservation easements is relatively new, and a market for such interests has not been well established. Fee appraisers became more involved as certain property owners became informed of the special moral and financial benefits that could accrue to them from charitable donations made to a qualified public or quasi-public entity that would presumably provide a substantial long-term public benefit. Thus the appraisal methodology for conservation easements developed to its present status, and still it is understood by only a relatively few appraisers.

The following definitions are pertinent to the understanding of the appraisal procedure.

Conservation Easement
Conservation easements are commonly referred to as scenic easements and open space easements. These easements, like any other easement, allow someone else to prohibit or require a limitation upon a portion of the property owner's "bundle of rights." Such an easement is usually negative in character. The holder is allowed to prevent the servient owner from conducting specified acts on his own land to protect the significant natural and/or historical values of the property. These usually include aesthetic, scientific, educational, and ecological values, and the protection of open space and historic buildings.

Conservation easements may be easements appurtenant or easements in gross. An easement appurtenant is an easement created for the benefit of another tract of land, which usually, but not necessarily, adjoins it. The easement appurtenant has the following distinctive characteristics: (1) it always includes dominant and servient tracts or parcels of land, (2) it is irrevocable, (3) the ownership of the easement follows the land to which it belongs (the dominant parcel), and (4) it continues as a servitude to the servient estate when such estate is conveyed.[1]

Easements in gross are usually not appurtenant to any estate in land. They are a personal interest in, or right to use, land of another for a particularly defined purpose. The easement in gross has the following characteristics: (1) it includes only a servient parcel of land; (2) it may be personal or commercial; (3) it is irrevocable; (4) if personal, it is not inheritable, it cannot be mortgaged, it cannot be assigned to a third party, and it terminates upon death of the easement holder; and (5) if commercial, it is inheritable, it may be mortgaged, and it may be conveyed or otherwise transferred to third parties.[2]

The Larger Parcel

In appraising easements or property rights in condemnation,[3] the larger parcel is that portion of a property that has unity of ownership, contiguity, and unity of use. These are three conditions that must be present to establish the larger parcel for purposes of considering the extent of severance damage[4] in most states. However, in federal cases and in some state cases, the matter of contiguity is sometimes subordinated to that of unitary use. Baetjer v. U.S. held: "Integrated use, not physical contiguity, is the test whether land condemned is part of a 'single tract' warranting award of severance damage . . . ." 143 F.2d 391 (1st Cir. 1944), cert. denied, 232 U.F. 772. This is commonly referred to as the unit rule.

Selection of the larger parcel in appraisals of easements follows the same procedure as appraisals of severance damages.

The Remainder

The remainder is a term given to the property rights remaining in possession of the owner after partial rights of the property have been conveyed or divested from the property.

"Before and After" Method

This term applies to the appraisal technique preferred in estimating the value of partial takings in condemnation. It also applies to estimating the value of easements. With this method, which is usually the simplest approach, the market value of the larger parcel is estimated before it is encumbered by an easement; subtracted from that amount is the market value of what remains (the remainder) after the encumbrance by an easement. The difference represents the market value of the easement: diminution or enhancement of the value of the larger parcel caused by the easement.

There are also two basic principles of real property value that are particularly important in the appraisal of conservation easements: the principle of highest and best use and the principle of contribution.

Principle of Highest and Best Use

Of course the principle of highest and best use is basic to appraisals of all real property, but it is of special significance in appraising conservation easements. Briefly, highest and best use is that use that, at the time of the appraisal, is the most profitable likely use. The most profitable likely use cannot always be interpreted strictly in terms of money. Return sometimes takes the form of amenities.[5] Implied within the definition is recognition of the contribution of that specific use to community environment or to the community development goals in addition to wealth maximization of individual property owners. Also implied is that the determination of highest and best use results from the appraiser's judgment and analytical skill, that is, that the use determined from analysis represents an opinion, not a fact to be found.[6]

In order for a conservation easement to have value, a change of highest and best use of the larger parcel by virtue of the imposition of a conservation easement is paramount. Hence the existing use of the property is not its highest and best use. It should be obvious that without a change of highest and best use the value of the larger parcel before the restriction would be the same as its value after the restriction. The change may be in transition. The application of the before and after method of appraising will measure the resulting change of value. For example, the historical and existing use of a property at the date of appraisal is a ranch in the path of growth or development. The highest and best use is trending toward development and partaking development property values. A conservation easement may restrict development and provide that use of the property in the future be limited to its historical and existing use as a ranch, in effect eliminating any accrued development value. It is therefore logical for the appraiser to determine that the highest and best use of the property, or a part thereof, before being restricted by the easement is for development, or imminent potential development, while the highest and best use of the property after the restriction is for continued ranching, or perhaps a single, large homesite if ranching is no longer practical per se. Market data for application of the before and after method should be gathered accordingly.

Principle of Contribution

This is a valuation principle that states that the value of an agent of production, or of a component part of a property, depends upon how much it contributes to the value of the whole (larger parcel), or how much its absence detracts from the value of the whole.[7]

By application of the before and after method, the contribution of those rights of the total "bundle of rights" that are divested (or restricted by the conservation easement) from the larger parcel can be determined. The presence of a conservation easement over part of the larger parcel may indeed contribute value to all or portions of the unencumbered part of the parcel.

When the above definitions as they apply to the appraisal of conservation easements are clearly understood, the appraisal process is thereafter relatively simple. Basically it follows standard, recognized appraisal procedures, where both the before and after appraisals use two of the three standard approaches to value: the cost and market data approaches. The use of the income approach is limited to income-producing properties. This approach may be particularly useful as a check on the after value, or the value of the remainder, and on agriculture and recreational income properties where sufficient income data is available.

The appraisal of conservation easements, like the appraisal of many special-purpose properties, is complicated by the lack of market data involving the buying and selling of similar properties or interests in property. Since the concept of conservation easements is relatively new, sales of similar properties with only a remainder interest are extremely scarce or lacking in most market areas. Market data for properties encumbered by conservation easements or the remainder interests are available in a few isolated areas where a public land management agency has actively purchased conservation easements over an extended period. The Sawtooth National Recreation Area within the Sawtooth National Forest in central Idaho is one such area. Purchases of conservation easements there began about 1972, and since that time a few sales of remainder properties between private parties have occurred. During this same period, a few similar unencumbered properties within the area have also sold; thus a ratio of the value of the larger parcels before the encumbrance and the remainder after the encumbrance can be determined with reasonable accuracy. However, the appraiser must use extreme care and judgment in extending these ratios to other market areas. Similarity of the market areas, the properties, and the remainder interests therein must be carefully considered.

In the absence of market transactions for conservation easements or remainder interests, the appraiser must use logic in his search for other reasonably valid indicators of remainder value. These may include similar properties in the market area on which the particular highest and best use is similarly restricted by either physical or legal limitations. Physical limitations might include those caused by terrain, ground water, and access, while legal limitations may occur from adverse zoning or deed restrictions. A common practice in appraising the remainder in lands being used for agriculture or ranchland, but where the highest and best use has changed or is changing, is to find market data of similar properties in the immediate market area and similar properties beyond the influence of change on which the existing and anticipated highest and best use is agriculture or ranching. The difference between the values of the remainder and the larger parcel then represents the value of the conservation easement. This procedure may apply likewise to property interests other than agriculture.

The appraiser's failure to properly select and identify the larger parcel is a common pitfall observed in the appraisal of conservation easements. An understanding of the unit rule is essential in selecting the larger parcel since it is the ultimate test. An appraisal of less than the larger parcel may significantly distort the market value of a conservation easement. For instance, a property owner may choose to donate, grant, sell, or otherwise dispose of a conservation easement from only a portion of a property, which would not in itself qualify as the larger parcel meeting the critical test of the unit rule. The contribution of the easement to the value of the larger parcel may therefore be either greater or less than its contribution to the part appraised. The existence of a conservation easement on a part of the larger parcel may in fact enhance or diminish the value of the unencumbered part of the larger parcel, thus canceling all or part of the actual loss or gain in market value of the remainder that results from the conservation easement. Losses of value to the unencumbered part of the remainder are seldom encountered, but could conceivably occur by blockage of access or utility easements, or by limiting or restricting future use in some manner. Enhancement of unencumbered remainder value, on the other hand, frequently occurs generally from certain amenities provided by the conservation easement, such as open space, protection of views, privacy, and seclusion. The failure to take these factors into consideration or the application of improper appraisal procedures may indeed jeopardize the future benefits to those inclined to donate conservation easements for charitable purposes.

It is highly advisable that property owners seeking appraisals of conservation easements select an appraiser with experience in conservation easements. The most likely source is from among the membership of one of the recognized professional appraisal institutes or societies, including the American Institute of Real Estate Appraisers, Society of Real Estate Appraisers, and the American Society of Farm Managers and Rural Appraisers. The members of each of these organizations are bound by a strict code of ethics, which, in effect, states that if the appraiser's previous experience with respect to the subject matter of the assignment is insufficient to enable the appraiser to complete the assignment competently, it is unethical for that appraiser to accept, undertake, and complete the assignment without either associating with another appraiser who has had such previous experience or disclosing such lack of experience to the client prior to accepting the assignment.

Notes

1. Smith, Walstein, Jr., M.A.I., "Some Enchanting Easements," *The Appraisal Journal* (October 1980).

2. *Ibid.*

3. Condemnation: The act of government (federal, state, county, municipal) and of duly authorized units of government and public utility companies invested with right of eminent domain

204   PART IV: FEDERAL TAXATION

to take private property for public use and benefit, upon the payment of just compensation. It is the act of the sovereign in substituting itself in place of the owner and/or the act of taking all or a part of the right of an owner. American Institute of Real Estate Appraisers, *Real Estate Appraisal Terminology*, rev. ed.

4. Severance damages: The diminution of the market value of the remainder area, in the case of a partial taking, that arises (a) by reason of the taking (severance) and/or (b) the construc-

tion of the improvement in the manner proposed. American Institute of Real Estate Appraisers, *Real Estate Appraisal Terminology*, rev. ed.

5. American Institute of Real Estate Appraisers, *The Appraisal of Real Estate*, 7th ed.

6. American Institute of Real Estate Appraisers, *Real Estate Appraisal Terminology*, rev. ed.

7. *Ibid.*

Appraising Conservation Easements

Warren Illi

The appraisal of a conservation easement requires a written, well-documented opinion of easement value. It should be prepared by a professional real estate appraiser who is an expert in the valuation of partial interests. Acceptable partial interest appraisal principles and methods have been established by case law rulings in governmental eminent domain (condemnation) proceedings.

The federal government publishes a booklet entitled "Uniform Appraisal Standards for Federal Land Acquisitions." This publication is available from the Superintendent of Documents, U.S. Government Printing Office, Washington, D.C. 20402 (Stock No. 5259-0002). This booklet develops standards for solving partial interest appraisal problems.

A conservation easement, being a partial interest in real estate, should be appraised much like partial takings for roads, powerlines, etc. Since the easement appraisal is frequently used to support a tax deduction (charitable contribution), the appraiser should review appraisal guidelines printed by various taxing authorities. The Internal Revenue Service has available Publication 526 (Rev. Nov. 81), "Charitable Contributions"; and Publication 561 (Rev. Nov. 81), "Determining the Value of Donated Property."

In its simplest form a conservation easement can be defined as a partial interest (limited property rights) in land held by a second party (trust or government agency) to promote conservation of natural resources (scenic beauty, wildlife, water quality, etc.). If the appraisal will be used to support a charitable contribution tax deduction, it must fulfill the taxing authority's requirement to establish the *fair market value* of the easement rights donated.

What constitutes a good appraisal report? Professional appraisal groups and government agencies often use the following format.

I. **Introduction**
   1. Title page
   2. Letter of transmittal (appraiser to client)
   3. Table of contents
   4. Summary of facts and conclusions
   5. Statement of limiting conditions and assumptions
   6. References

II. **Analysis and Conclusions**
   1. Purpose of the appraisal
   2. Legal description of the property
   3. Area and local data
   4. Property data
      Land data: soil, topography, vegetation, etc.
      Improvements
      Property history
      Zoning, tax values, misc.
   5. Highest and best use analysis
   6. Analysis of appraisal approaches
   7. Before valuation
   8. After valuation
   9. Summary—conclusion of easement value
   10. Certificate of appraisal

III. *Addenda*
Property photos, maps, comparable sale data forms, copy of conservation easement, qualifications of the appraiser, etc.

The three classical approaches to determining the fair market value of a property are the cost, income, and market data approaches to value. The cost approach values a property's improvements and land separately, then combines these two estimates for a final estimate of total property value. It is most commonly used for intensively developed properties. The income approach entails the determination and capitalization of the net income stream produced by a property. But conservation easements are often placed on rural property with few structural improvements and minimal annual income. Therefore the cost and income approaches are usually not applicable to rural properties. There are occasions when they may be useful approaches to value the effects of an easement. The market data, or direct comparison, approach is most frequently used. It compares the subject property with recent sales of similar properties, known as comparable sales. Comparable sales are usually not identical to the subject property, so the appraiser must consider their differences in the appraisal. Each element of property value is analyzed, and appropriate value adjustments are made when these differences affect market value. Each of the three to eight best comparable sales is adjusted to an indication of subject value. These various indications of subject value are then correlated into a final estimate of subject value. Property characteristics that need to be considered when adjusting comparable sales to a subject value are time, location, size, topography, soil or site productivity, vegetation, view, water (creek or lake frontage), utility service, improvements, access, and any other property characteristics that affect property value. Adjustments between sales and the subject should be documented by market evidence whenever possible.

Appraisals should be dated, on or near the date of easement conveyance. When appraising conservation easements, and most other partial interests, the appraiser will not, in all likelihood, be able to locate many sales of the property rights contained in typical conservation easements. These kinds of property rights are not generally bought and sold in the open real estate market. Therefore, the appraiser must resort to the before and after appraisal method. This method values the entire property before the easement rights are conveyed—including all the property rights owned that can be legally exercised by the landowner. Then the appraiser estimates the fair market value of the "remainder" property for an "after" property value. The remainder property being valued in the after valuation is the original "before" property less the property rights conveyed in the conservation easement. The value difference (loss or gain) between the before and after valuations is the market value of the property rights conveyed in the conservation easement.

The before and after appraisal method has been universally accepted by legal authorities (courts) as the best method for valuation of partial interests because it includes the value of the property rights conveyed, plus changes in value to the remainder, if any. Changes in value to the remainder must be considered by the appraiser. These changes, if any, are referred to as damages (severance damages) or benefits (enhancement). Damages or enhancement to the remainder must be considered whenever a conservation easement covers only part of the total property owned by the landowner.

Here is a simple example that helps illustrate how the before and after method works. A 200-acre dairy farm lies eight miles from the heart of an expanding city. Excellent access into the city is provided by an interstate highway that borders the property. The most profitable use (appraisers would define this as its highest and best use) is for sale to a developer for subdivision into small suburban homesites. Comparable homesites of similar land with subdivision potential are selling for $4,000 per acre. Thus the before value of the farm is $800,000 (200 acres × $4,000 per acre). The farmer, in conjunction with a local open space trust, has agreed to convey all subdivision and residential, commercial, and industrial use property rights to the trust. After easement imposition, the land can be used only for farming. Valuation of the remainder property (200 acres with restricted use) is accomplished by comparison with farmland sales of similar agricultural productivity but little or no subdivision potential. The appraiser finds similar farm sales about forty miles farther out from the city—beyond residential commute. These farmlands sell for $2,500 per acre. Thus the after value is $500,000 (200 acres × $2,500 per acre). The conservation easement value (primarily the value of the development rights) is $300,000 ($800,000—before value, less $500,000—after value). The apparent $300,000 loss in fair market value reflects a change in the property's highest and best use from subdivision-potential land to agricultural land.

This example simplifies a very complex appraisal problem, but it does illustrate the partial interest appraisal concept. Some of the commonly occurring conservation easement complexities will be discussed later.

The ideal way to value the farm in the after condition would be to compare it with similar farms near the city, which had sold on the open market, after a conservation easement encumbered the property. This would have been an even better market documentation of the effects of the conservation easement on fair market value. Unfortunately, in most areas of the country, easement programs are too new and easement encumbered resales are too few to allow good documentation of after values using easement encumbered resales.

The first major step in appraising an individual easement is to thoroughly review the conservation easement document. Each easement provision must be analyzed for its effect on fair market value. From an appraiser's standpoint most conservation easement provisions can be placed in four categories. They are (1) provisions similar to protective covenants, (2) grantee rights provisions, (3) provisions that require a physical change to the property, and (4) provisions that limit subdivision and development of the property (changing the property's highest and best use).

Easement provisions similar to protective covenants usually require no valuation beyond the initial analysis. They usually do not change the property's highest and best use and are similar to provisions found in protective covenants for most good-quality land developments. They tend to maintain or enhance long-term property and neighborhood values. Examples of such provisions are: no dumping of trash, garbage, sewage, junk cars, or any similar unsightly or offensive material within the easement area is permitted; and the location and architectural design of new structures and facilities and the location and design of new roads shall be harmonious with the landscape and general surroundings. These kinds of provisions usually do not directly affect property value.

Provisions that convey occupancy rights to the grantee (easement holder) may impact property value. These kinds of provisions usually are very few in number; in fact, most easements contain only one or two.

Almost all easements allow the easement holder to enter the property from time to time to check for easement compliance. This type of easement provision doesn't influence property value.

Another type of grantee right that is commonly used is the right to permit public use of all or part of the easement area. An example is an easement provision that allows public use of a riverbank area for hiking or fishing. Public agencies are more apt to acquire this right than private trusts. Public use of all or part of private land can have a very significant impact on property value. The comparable sales used to make the after valuation need to reflect the loss of privacy and seclusion caused by this easement provision. One government agency has taken the position that public use of a strip of land along a creek, river, or lake renders the remainder as property without water frontage.

A midwestern state acquired a public fishing easement along a trout stream crossing a forty-acre tract of forestland. The easement included a strip of land 150 feet wide on either side of the stream. It permitted public fishing and hiking. Public hunting and camping were prohibited. The owner retained grazing, timber harvesting, hunting, and camping rights. The owner could not build any structures in the easement area. The before value for the "40" was $900 per acre, or $36,000 total. This figure was based on sales of forty-acre tracts with trout stream frontage. Similar nearby comparable sales, without stream frontage, sold for about $475 per acre. The agency's appraiser recognized that the remainder land had additional recreational value because it included a public fishing easement area. This was not as good as having exclusive use of the trout fishery but better than the after comparable sales that required a short drive to reach a fishing stream. The appraiser made a judgmental adjustment of plus 10 percent. Overall subject after value was $475 × 110 percent = $522.50 × 40 acres = $20,900. Easement value was $15,100 ($36,000 minus after value of $20,900).

The third type of easement provision requires the landowner to make some physical change in the property. This kind of provision is more frequently found in government-acquired easements where the easement provision intent is to make existing structures or uses more compatible with project objectives. The "cost-to-cure" appraisal technique is used to correct the problem. The easement payment essentially pays for this corrective action.

One such example is an easement requirement to provide fencing that will keep cattle off a river bank in order to stabilize natural vegetation on the bank and better ensure water quality. The easement provision requires fencing cattle 100 feet back from the river bank on both sides of the river as it flows through a section (640 acres) of western grazing land. Before the easement the highest and best use was for subdivision into 20-acre recreational homesites with river frontage. The river has a national reputation for good trout fishing and scenic areas. Public recreation use on the easement area is permitted. The conservation easement precludes any recreational or residential subdivision or development on the entire 640 acres. Residual use is agricultural. Stock watering is from unfenced lateral streams.

Before value: 640 acres (grazing land with river frontage and subdivision potential) at $800 per acre, or $512,000.

After value: The fenced riverbank strip of about 24 acres (no grazing) has no remaining value for the agricultural owner; 616 acres of grazing land (no subdivision permitted) at $300 per acre would make the after value when fenced $184,800; subtract the cost to meet the fencing requirement of the easement ($15,800), giving a net after value of $169,000. The value of this easement is $343,000 ($512,000 minus $169,000).

The easement payment of $343,000 includes $19,200 for eliminating all meaningful market value for the fenced 24 acres along the river ($800 per acre × 24 acres), plus $308,000 for changing the highest and best use of the remaining 616 acres from recreational subdivision land to grazing land ($800 per acre to $300 per acre = $500 per acre value loss × 616 acres), plus $15,800 to conform to the fencing requirements of the easement. A local fencing contractor supplied the fencing cost estimate.

Some argument can be made that all land has some value, so the ungrazed twenty-four acres might be assigned some minimum value. The appraiser may also want to develop the present worth to perpetually maintain the fencing along the river as the easement requires.

The fourth, and last, category of easement provisions includes those provisions that prohibit or limit subdivision and development of a property. Typically, the before valuation cites a highest and best use for subdivision and development, while the after value is a less intensive or profitable highest and best use, such as agriculture or timber production. The definition of highest and best use includes the phrase "most profitable use." Any reduction in profitability usually has a corresponding reduction in property value. While these kinds of easement provisions are few in number, they usually account for the preponderance of easement value. In the western states where government easement purchase projects have attempted to preserve nationally significant rivers and scenic areas, 90 percent of the easement costs is attributable to easement provisions prohibiting or limiting subdivision and development.

The best way to value these provisions is by direct comparison (market data approach to value) with comparable sales of property with similar easement encumbrances. These sales are few and far between. If the appraiser is fortunate enough to find such sales in the same neighborhood as the subject property, these resales can be compared directly to the subject to derive an estimate of after subject value. Besides adjusting the comparable sales for differences in access, topography, etc., the appraiser needs to evaluate the comparability of the sale's easement encumbrance and the subject easement. If there are significant differences, the appraiser can adjust the sale price in much the same way as adjustments are made for physical differences.

In most instances the few resales of easement encumbered properties are located in entirely different market areas, so direct comparison is not feasible. Then appraisers should consider using percent adjustments to reflect the effects of easement imposition, as in the following example.

A 10,000-acre Montana cattle ranch has six miles of a famous trout river flowing through it. There is a strong demand for recreational homesites to enjoy the fishing, hunting, and scenic resources of the area. The before value, considering the ranch's subdivision potential, is $500 per acre, or $5,000,000. The proposed conservation easement, covering the entire 10,000-acre ranch, will preclude all subdivision and development except for agricultural purposes. A 1,800-acre cattle ranch in Montana, with a similar easement already encumbering its title, sold in 1977 for $445,000, or $247 per acre. For various reasons, not important to this discussion, that ranch, which sold in 1974 for $525,000, cannot be compared *directly* to the subject. The restrictive conservation easement was placed on it in 1975. Market evidence shows that cattle ranches in that area appreciated at the rate of 15 percent per year between 1974 and 1977. The comparable sale, if unencumbered by an easement, should have appreciated to about $760,000 ($525,000 × 145 percent) by 1977. In addition, $40,000 of capital improvements were added to the property in 1975. Overall the 1,800-acre ranch should have sold for $800,000 in 1977. Instead, with the very restrictive easement on it, it sold for $445,000. That indicates an after value of 56 percent ($445,000—actual sale price ÷ $800,000—the projected sale price without easement). This after value indication is then applied to the subject before value.

Before value	$5,000,000
After value (56% × $5,000,000)	2,800,000
Easement value (44%)	$2,200,000

If the appraiser felt there were differences between the subject and sale easements that would influence the after value, the percentages could be adjusted.

The appraiser can also use the "paired" sales technique to measure the loss in value to the easement encumbered sale. This technique compares the easement encumbered sale with a sale of similar unencumbered property. The difference in sales price (usually a loss) will reflect the value of the easement rights. This difference, usually expressed as a percent of the before value, is applied to the before value of the subject property, thus indicating a probable easement value.

Seldom are easement appraisals as straightforward as the cattle ranch example. Easement appraisals usually are complicated in a number of ways. A common complication is for the conservation easement to cover only a part of the total property. On large properties such as the cattle ranch in the example, it is common for the easement to cover only a narrow corridor of land along the river. The remaining portion of the ranch, away from the river, could still be subdivided and developed. These backlands or nonriverfront lands (remainder) may now reflect an enhancement (increase) in value in the after condition. In the after condition these backlands will border riverfront lands that will remain undeveloped, open space lands. Most real estate markets indicate that land bordering open space or natural areas (parks, golf courses, etc.) sell for premium prices. The appraiser needs to consider possible enhancement whenever an easement encumbers only part of a property. Similarly, the appraiser needs to consider possible "damages" to the remainder when the easement covers only part of the property. Damages due to easement imposition usually occur much less frequently than enhancement situations.

Usually the lack of easement encumbered comparable sales requires the appraiser to find other ways to measure the loss of subdivision and development rights. The first example in this article, a 200-acre dairy farm, solved that problem by locating sales physically out of the residential development range of the city. Another technique is to use nearby lands that are not physically suitable for subdivision and development.

Many western rivers have relatively narrow bands of level valley land along them that are ideally suited for subdivision and development. Roads and utility lines follow these same narrow corridors, thereby providing the access and utility services needed for subdivision and development. Behind these corridors the terrain becomes steeply sloping mountain land—either forest or grassland. These steep lands usually have most of the amenities of the adjoining level land, that is, good access, utility service, proximity to population areas, and view. However, steep topography makes them physically unsuitable for subdivision and development. These steep lands sell for much less than the nearby level lands, which can be developed. The difference in sale price reflects developmental values, as demonstrated by the following example.

Before value: 50 acres of valley land (suitable for subdivision) at $2,000 per acre, or $100,000.

After value: Subject property is compared with adjoining steep land, suitable only for livestock grazing, which is similar to use permitted in easement. Steep land sells for $250 per acre. This is adjusted upward to $350 per acre to reflect the better soil and agricultural potential of the flat valley land—$350 × 50 acres, or $17,500. The value of the easement is, therefore, $82,500.

The preceding example used sale price differences between valley land and steep land to indicate subdivision and developmental values. Similar comparisons can be made to other lands with low utility, such as flood plain land or lands that cannot be legally developed due to zoning restrictions.

Frequently landowners will want to reserve some limited subdivision and development rights. That appraisal situation can be handled in the following manner.

Before value: 50 acres of valley land at $2,000 per acre, or $100,000.

After value: Two subdivisions of the 50 acres and two homes are permitted by the easement. Typical homesites in the market are 2 acres and sell for $10,000 each. The easement allows the remainder to be used for: two 2-acre homesites at $10,000 each, or $20,000, and 46 agricultural acres at $350 per acre, or $16,100, which is $36,100. The value of the easement is $63,900.

A brief word on timber valuation. Conservation easements that severely limit timber harvest on lands with a highest and best use for commercial timber production will be very expensive. Converting commercial forestlands to uses where natural appearance and scenic values have priority over economic decisions will normally leave the landowner with speculative timber values. However, in many areas where timber value is an integral part of a higher value for recreational or residential use, easement provisions that severely limit commercial timber harvest may not be costly. The prudent landowner or developer will not harvest timber if it causes a disproportionate loss in recreational values. Occasionally, some properties may have a surplus of timber that can be removed without adversely affecting remaining subdivision values; for example, perhaps some timber value could be derived when clearing road rights-of-way and homesites during development. This "bonus" may already be included in comparable sale prices if they also had similar surplus timber.

Overall the appraisal of conservation easements is a complicated and challenging undertaking. Difficulty is usually increased because easement encumbered comparable sales are few and because few conservation easements are alike. The appraiser must carefully evaluate each easement provision for its influence on fair market value, then find a way to measure the influence in the open market.

Increased Tax Penalties for Valuation Overstatements

Thomas A. Coughlin III

Determination of a property's fair market value and the factors likely to influence future market value are essential in planning a charitable gift for land conservation.[1] Fair market value is traditionally defined as the price at which property would change hands between a willing seller and a willing buyer, both of whom possess equal bargaining power and are reasonably well informed and neither of whom is acting under duress. Although the concept of fair market value is easy to state, disputes over valuation are the most common factual disputes in federal taxation.[2]

Value disputes arise most frequently when the value of property is determined indirectly by appraisal rather than by reference to cost, open market sales, or other objective standards. Appraisal is an inexact science. As one commentator observed, "[v]aluation is always an approximation. You are valuing a specific item at a specific place at a definite moment of time."[3]

The inherent imprecision in the appraisal process fuels Treasury Department and congressional concerns about the potential for taxpayer abuse. This abuse can occur through aggressively high valuations claimed in connection with charitable gifts. The Economic Recovery Tax Act of 1981 (ERTA) dealt with this subject. It increased the interest rate on tax deficiencies and the penalty for underpayments due to negligence, and it established penalties for "valuation overstatements."

The perceived opportunity for error in valuation is especially true for charitable gifts of easements and other forms of partial interests in land.[4] The absence of a market in such interests makes reliance on appraisal data essential. However, reliance on appraisal data and the nature of the easement interest itself render tax planning in the easement area more vulnerable to audit and subsequent recomputation of tax liability.[5]

Easement Appraisals

The methodology for appraising easements is similar to that used for condemnations and eminent domain proceedings involving a taking of less than the property owner's full fee interest. In both condemnation and easement appraisals the appraiser relies on traditional approaches to value—comparable market sales, replacement cost, and the capitalized income approach—to evaluate the property as it exists before the taking or the imposition of the easement and as it exists after the taking or imposition of the easement. The difference, if any, is the damage to the property for compensation purposes or the reduction in value for easement purposes.

The only distinction between the two forms of appraisal is that in condemnations the property owner is compensated directly by cash payment while in easement donations the owner receives compensation through the charitable contribution deduction. This should have no effect on the appraisal methodology. However, the absence of "bargaining" between the easement donor and the conservation organization may render donated easement valuations more difficult to monitor and value accurately. Further, although the appraisal methodology is clear, there are few guidelines from either the Internal Revenue Service or the courts to guide attorneys or appraisers in particular instances. The Service's published rulings simply state that the correct approach to valuing donated easements is the before and after approach described above.[6]

The only court decision on point is Robert H. Thayer and Virginia Thayer v. Commissioner, T.C. Memo, 1977-370. The sole issue in *Thayer* was the value of an open space easement given to the Virginia Outdoors Foundation over 59 acres of farmland adjacent to Gunston Hall in Virginia. The court observed that the principal effect of the easement was to prevent any further development or use of the property for other than a farm. The taxpayers claimed the value of the farm had been reduced from $347,005 to $199,317 as a result of the easement donation. The taxpayers' appraiser determined that it would have been possible to subdivide the farm into five to eight luxury homesites. As a result of the easement donation, the taxpayers gave up their right to develop the farm to its "highest and best use," a right the appraiser deemed worth $147,688.

The Internal Revenue Service argued that the highest and best use of the farm both before and after the easement donation was as a country estate. The IRS disputed the taxpayers' assertion that the land could be subdivided because of poor soil conditions, lack of adequate water and sewer facilities, and inadequate access. Nevertheless, the court noted that the Service's appraiser recognized "that the restriction contained in the easement would diminish the value of the property as a country gentleman's estate; hence his value of $60,000 on the easement."[7] The IRS valued the farm before the easement at $300,000 and the value after the easement at $240,000. The Tax Court, following extensive factual investigation, determined to split the difference between the two appraisals and assigned the easement a value of $113,000.

The *Thayer* decision is noteworthy for several reasons. First, it reaffirms the propriety of the Service's before and after methodology for appraising easements. Second, it provides an excellent discussion of the factors an appraiser must consider in valuing an open space easement. Finally, and of perhaps greatest significance, the Service recognized that the existence of restrictions contained in the easement would diminish the value of the property "as a country gentleman's estate," which according to the Service's appraiser was the property's highest and best use. In *Thayer*, the Service's appraiser found, and the Service agreed, that even though the farm lacked significant development potential because of its topography and other special characteristics, the easement would still diminish the market value of the property by $60,000, or fully 20 percent of its unrestricted value.

Valuation Disputes: Judicial and Congressional Concerns

The *Thayer* case is illustrative of the difficulty the Treasury Department and the courts have had in dealing with valuation disputes. The appraisal data in *Thayer* were extensive and appeared to be well documented. Nevertheless, the court found itself forced to "split the difference." The opportunity to obtain a court-sanctioned compromise with the IRS in colorable valuation claims has undoubtedly encouraged some taxpayers to overreach.

In a recent case the chief judge of the U.S. Tax Court signaled that the court might refrain from entering into compromise agreements in future valuation disputes:

> We are convinced that the valuation issue is capable of resolution by the parties themselves through an agreement which will reflect a compromise Solomon-like adjustment, thereby saving the expenditure of time, effort, and money by the parties and the Court—a process not likely to produce a better result. Indeed, the parties should keep in mind that, in the final analysis, the Court may find the evidence of one of the parties sufficiently more convincing than that of the other party, so that the final result will produce a significant financial defeat for one or the other, rather than a middle-of-the-road compromise which we suspect each of the parties expects the Court to reach.[8]

Until ERTA,[9] the rules governing tax disputes favored the taxpayer. If taxpayers prevailed in a tax dispute, they were significantly ahead. When the taxpayers lost, they were liable for interest on the tax underpayment, but they were otherwise unaffected. In effect, taxpayers who gambled over a tax dispute and lost received a loan for tax deficiencies at the statutory interest rate, which was often significantly below the prime rate. For underpayments of tax attributable to nonfraudulent negligence or intentional disregard of rules and regulations, taxpayers were also exposed to a negligence penalty equal to 5 percent of the amount of the tax underpayment.[10]

When the maximum marginal tax rate was 70 percent and the statutory interest rate for tax deficiencies was significantly below the prime rate, there was little inducement for taxpayers to settle tax disputes and every incentive to take an aggressive posture in hopes of avoiding audit. The Treasury Department has become increasingly concerned about the apparent level of taxpayer noncompliance and the extent of the audit lottery. For example, the Joint Committee on Taxation reported that in the period 1978 to 1980, the number of delinquent tax accounts increased from 886,000 to 1,204,000 while the value of delinquent accounts increased from $2.356 million to $3.631 million, a 56 percent increase in just two years. A similar pattern was discernible from cases filed in the U.S. Tax Court.[11]

Congressional Response

In ERTA Congress enacted several provisions intended to induce taxpayer compliance and to remove the incentives for delaying the settlement of outstanding tax disputes. Three are particularly germane to taxpayers and organizations seeking to promote land conservation and preservation of historic resources through voluntary preservation techniques that rely, in whole or in part, on tax incentives for charitable giving.

Increased Interest Rate for Tax Underpayments
As a first step in inducing greater taxpayer compliance,

Congress increased the interest rate on tax deficiencies to 100 percent of the prime rate. Until ERTA, the interest rate for tax underpayments was set at 90 percent of the prime rate. This rate was recomputed only once every twenty-four months.[12] Because of the substantial changes in the prime rate that occurred in the months preceding enactment of ERTA, the statutory rate was only 12 percent when ERTA was enacted, while the adjusted prime rate for that period had averaged over 15 percent.

Congress was convinced that the disparity between the tax interest rate and the commercial interest rate contributed to increasing delinquency in taxpayer accounts.[13] To redress this disparity, Congress revised the formula for computing the tax interest rate to 100 percent of the prime rate and required the Treasury Department to adjust the interest rate annually, on or before October 15 in each year in which the prime rate during the preceding September was at least a full percentage point above or below the statutory interest rate. The interest rate so determined becomes effective the following January 1.[14] For 1983 the interest rate was 16 percent.

Increase in Negligence Penalty

In a related area Congress increased the penalty for underpayments of tax due to nonfraudulent "negligence or intentional disregard of rules and regulations." Prior to ERTA, the negligence penalty was 5 percent of the amount of the underpayment of taxes.[15] The alternative civil fraud penalty is 50 percent of the tax underpayment.[16] ERTA retained the 5 percent negligence penalty and added an additional penalty equal to 50 percent of the interest rate payable on that portion of the tax deficiency attributable to negligence or intentional disregard of rules and regulations.[17]

Unlike the 5 percent negligence penalty, which applies to the entire underpayment of taxes, the additional 50 percent negligence penalty is confined to that portion of the tax underpayment that is attributable to negligence. Thus, if only part of the tax underpayment was attributable to negligence, the 50 percent penalty would be confined to that portion of the tax deficiency directly attributable to taxpayer negligence. The 5 percent penalty would be imposed against the entire amount of the tax deficiency, including the 50 percent penalty.[18]

The increased negligence penalty applies to taxes payable after December 31, 1981. As an addition to tax, the amount of the tax penalty is not deductible.

Overvaluation Penalty

The overvaluation penalty is potentially the most significant of all the penalty and tax administration reforms made by ERTA. Prior law contained no provision specifically applicable to underpayments of taxes that result from improper valuation of property. Congress and the Treasury Department were convinced that the tendency of both the courts and the Internal Revenue Service to resolve diffi-

cult valuation disputes "simply by dividing the difference" encouraged taxpayers "to overvalue certain types of property and to delay the resolution of valuation issues."[19] In an effort to induce greater taxpayer diligence in accurately valuing property, Congress established a three-tier penalty for "valuation overstatements."

The penalty for valuation overstatements is confined to individuals, closely held corporations, and personal service corporations that underpay their taxes by at least $1,000. The penalty applies only to underpayments attributable to property that the taxpayer has held for less than 5 years as of the close of the taxable year. Finally, the underpayment must be attributable to a "valuation overstatement," which occurs "if the value of any property, or the adjusted basis of any property, claimed on any return exceeds 150 percent of the amount determined to be the correct amount of such valuation or adjusted basis (as the case may be)."[20] The 150 percent threshold was adopted as "a test of the application of [the] new penalty under which only significant overvaluations will be penalized."[21]

The penalty is graduated from 10 percent to 30 percent of the amount of any tax underpayment that is attributable to a valuation overstatement. The penalty is 10 percent of the underpayment for overvaluations of 150 but not more than 200 percent of the correct valuation, 20 percent for overvaluations of 200 but not more than 250 percent of the correct valuation, and 30 percent for overvaluations in excess of 250 percent of the correct valuation.[22] The overvaluation penalty is confined to underpayments of income taxes. It does not apply to underpayments of taxes reported on estate and gift tax returns. The penalty is effective for tax returns filed after December 31, 1981. However, taxpayers who have an excess charitable contribution deduction carryforward attributable to a valuation overstatement on a return filed prior to 1981 may be exposed to the penalty for that portion of the tax underpayment attributable to the excess charitable contribution carryforward.

The Secretary of the Treasury is given discretion to waive "all or any part of the addition to the tax . . . on a showing by the taxpayer that there was a reasonable basis for the valuation or adjusted basis claimed . . . and that such claim was made in good faith."[23] The authority to waive the penalty on a showing that there was a reasonable basis for the value claimed and that the taxpayer acted in good faith underscores the need for taxpayers, their advisors, and the conservation and preservation organizations who promote voluntary preservation through tax-induced charitable gifts to rely on qualified appraisers and legal and tax counsel.

Effect on Preservation and Conservation Efforts

The overvaluation penalty and related reforms will compound the problems of land conservation and preservation organizations that rely, in whole or in part, on charitable gifts of environmentally or historically significant land areas. Unlike corporations and land investors, large landowners are frequently small taxpayers whose principal asset is the land.[24] For such taxpayers the out-of-pocket transactional costs associated with an easement donation—the cost of legal and tax counsel, the costs of appraisal, and the cash endowment requested by many organizations as a condition to accepting an easement donation—often render such donations impractical. In the open space easement area the often marginal economic incentives to easement donation may be further outweighed by the potential exposure to gift tax liability if the donation fails to meet the statutory "conservation purpose" requirements necessary to qualify as a charitable contribution deduction.[25]

Fortunately for preservation and land conservation organizations the overvaluation penalty applies only to property the taxpayer has owned for less than five years. Many owners of land holdings of interest to preservation organizations have owned their land for more than five years and, consequently, will not be affected by the penalty. Further, the Secretary of the Treasury is empowered to waive the penalty on a showing that the taxpayer acted in good faith and had a reasonable basis for the valuation claimed.

Until regulations are promulgated, it is impossible to define the circumstances in which a taxpayer might rely on the waiver authority. However, at a minimum, the taxpayer should obtain legal counsel in planning the gift and should obtain a well-documented appraisal from a professionally qualified appraiser.

The existence of the overvaluation penalty underscores the need to develop uniform procedures for valuing donated property accurately, and especially gifts of easements for conservation purposes. The penalty also reinforces the need for conservation and preservation organizations to work with potential easement donors, their appraisers, and legal advisors to ensure that the easement values claimed are supported by objective appraisal data.

Notes

1. For example, the value of a charitable contribution is generally measured by the appreciated value of the property on the date of donation. Also, the fair market value of an estate determines whether it will be subject to estate taxes, the amount of such taxes, and, in the case of lifetime gifts, whether the value of donated property qualifies for the annual $10,000 per person exclusion from gift tax.

2. In 1981 there were approximately 500,000 tax disputes outstanding involving questions of valuation. These represented approximately $2.5 billion in tax attributable to property valuation questions. Joint Committee on Taxation, General Explanation of the Economic Recovery Tax Act of 1981, at 332 [hereinafter cited as General Explanation].

3. Freeman & Freeman, The Tax Practice Deskbook 2-16 (1973).

4. The Treasury Department expressed its concern about the potential for aggressive and abusive valuation in charitable gifts of easements in its testimony opposing legislation codifying and making permanent authority for charitable gifts of easements for conservation purposes under I.R.C. §170(h). See Hearings on H.R. 4511 Before the Subcomm. on Select Revenue Measures of the House Comm. on Ways and Means, 96th Cong., 1st Sess. (Nov. 9, 1979); Hearings on H.R. 7318 Before the Subcomm. on Select Revenue Measures of the House Comm. on Ways and Means, 96th Cong., 2d Sess. (June 26, 1980). The Senate Committee on Finance, in its report accompanying the Tax Treatment Extension Act of 1980, reiterated Treasury's concerns. See S. Rep. No. 96-1007, 96th Cong., 2d Sess. (1980), reprinted in Andrews, Tax Incentives for Historic Preservation (2d ed. 1980).

5. An easement frequently does not materially interfere with the way a taxpayer currently uses property and generally guarantees that in the future the property will be used only as the taxpayer and the conservation organization wish it to be used. This fact caused considerable difficulty for the Treasury Department in the 1979–80 legislative deliberations that led to enactment of I.R.C. §170(h). Daniel Halperin, Assistant Secretary for Tax Policy in Hearings on H.R. 4511 and H.R. 7318, supra note 4.

6. Rev. Rul. 73-339, 1973-2 C.B. 68; Rev. Rul. 76-376, 1976-2 C.B. 53. Perhaps the best single analysis of appraisal methodology for valuing easements is Roddewig and Shlaes, Appraising the Best Tax Shelter in History, 50 The Appraisal J. 25 (1982). Although the article is focused on urban landmark buildings, the discussion of appraisal methodology provides useful background relevant to appraisal of open-space and conservation easements.

7. Thayer v. Comm'r, 36 T.C.M. (CCH) 1504 (1977-370) (CCH Dec. 34,708(M)) (1977).

8. Buffalo Tool & Die Mfg. Co. v. Comm'r, 74 T.C. 441 (1980).

9. Pub. L. No. 97-34, 95 Stat. 172 (1981) [hereinafter cited as ERTA].

10. I.R.C. §6653(a)(2).

11. General Explanation, supra note 2, at 328-29.

12. I.R.C. §6621(a).

13. General Explanation, supra note 2, at 328.

14. I.R.C. §6621(a); ERTA §711.

15. I.R.C. §6653(a)(2).

16. I.R.C. §6653(b).

17. I.R.C. §6553(a)(2); ERTA §722(b).

18. General Explanation, supra note 2, at 337, 333 n. 3.

19. Id. at 332.

20. I.R.C. §6659.

21. General Explanation, supra note 2, at 332. The 150 percent threshold may be too low to achieve Congress's stated purpose of penalizing only significant overvaluations. Although 150 percent appears significant in absolute terms, in difficult valuation cases it may be impossible to rely on an arbitrary percentage of value for purposes of imposing the penalty. For example, the Thayers' easement appraisal of $147,688 exceeded the Service's value of $60,000 by 246 percent. The Thayers' appraisal exceeded the "correct amount" determined by the Tax Court by 188 percent. Had the overvaluation penalty been in effect at the time the Thayer donation was made, the easement would have fallen within the penalty's ambit.

22. I.R.C. §6659.

23. Id.

24. Recent amendments in the estate and gift tax area—principally, allowance of tax-free interspousal transfers increasing the unified credit to $175,000 (thereby exempting estates up to $600,000 from taxation) and increasing the annual gift tax exclusion from $3,000 to $10,000—should reduce somewhat the forced sale and development of undeveloped or under-used family land.

25. Treasury regulations interpreting the various conservation purpose categories should clearly address the conservation purpose category governing open space, which includes the preservation of farmland and forestland. Preservation of open space is recognized as a permissible conservation purpose, "where such preservation is—(I) for the scenic enjoyment of the general public or (II) pursuant to a clearly delineated Federal, State, or local governmental conservation policy and will yield a significant public benefit." I.R.C. §170(h)(4)(A)(iii).

PART V
LAND SAVING
AND THE INDIVIDUAL
LANDOWNER

Underlying the entire private land-saving movement is the belief that each individual can act as a trustee for the natural resources he touches. When individual landowners understand the protective devices that are available and their advantages, we will have gained ground in making land stewardship accessible to all.

An array of legal options greets any landowner who attempts to institute lasting protective measures. To choose among them, he must know two things: (1) what he wishes to protect, and (2) to what degree he wishes to protect it. Similarly, individuals attempting to negotiate protections for land they do not own must persuade landowners of the advantages of particular approaches to land preservation.

The contours and requirements of property law may vary from state to state, but the basic choices and instruments remain constant. Janet Milne's article, "The Landowner's Options," describes ways of conveying land or interests in land and discusses their respective potentials for effective protection of a given parcel. Because very few conservation transactions

can be considered apart from their tax consequences, Milne's article touches on some of the tax implications of various conservation devices.

Although land ownership is affected by local taxes such as property taxes, the diversity of these taxes and of their degree of impact is so great as to preclude discussion in this book. The federal tax system, however, is a pervasive influence on a landowner's decision to restrict the use of his land. The financial benefits bestowed by the federal tax system on certain types of land-saving transactions may make conservation feasible for a landowner who believes he cannot afford to protect his land; they may also persuade an otherwise uninterested landowner to protect his property.

Within the context of a specific transaction, competent, professional guidance must be sought to ensure that all federal and state requirements are met. A general comprehension of tax planning opens the door to the intelligent use of tax incentives as a means of assisting private land saving. Relevant tax planning covers two areas: (1) income tax planning, and (2) estate and gift tax planning. Kingsbury Browne's article on income tax planning describes the process used by one landowner to determine the practicality of various conservation measures. Marion R. Fremont-Smith's article on estate and gift tax planning analyzes the process a landowner might follow with his attorney in deciding how to dispose of property through his estate or through gifts during his lifetime. The principal goal of such tax planning, and of income tax planning as well, is to structure property transfers that minimize the federal tax burden. The landowner, in dealing with professional advisors, however, must be aware that the various types of transfers can serve his substantive conservation goals as well as his tax reduction purposes. Both Kingsbury Browne and Marion R. Fremont-Smith explore tax planning strategies that can help the landowner fulfill his stewardship aims while achieving beneficial financial results.

The Landowner's Options

Janet E. Milne

The Starting Point

Why do people decide to permanently protect land that they own? John Muir, one of America's first advocates of the protection of unique areas, captured the sentiments that often dominate when he wrote of one of his experiences:

> When I was about to wander away on my long rambles, I was sorry to leave that precious meadow unprotected; therefore, I said to my brother-in-law, who then owned it, "Sell me the forty acres of lake meadow, and keep it fenced and never allow cattle or hogs to break into it, and I will gladly pay you whatever you say. I want to keep it untrampled for the sake of its ferns and flowers; and even if I should never see it again, the beauty of its lilies and orchids is so pressed into my mind I shall always enjoy looking back at them in imagination, even across seas and continents, and perhaps after I am dead."
>
> But he regarded my plan as a sentimental dream wholly impracticable. . . . Eighteen years later I found the deep water pond-lilies in fresh bloom, but the delicate gardensod of the meadow was broken up and trampled into mire.[1]

Despite the strong sentiments that are sure to be present, the decision to permanently protect land is a decision that requires careful thought, a decision that is often difficult to make. Altruism must be weighed against financial realities, personal desires against family needs, the ideal solution against the ability of a conservation agency to be involved.

Perhaps the best way for a landowner to start sorting out the many considerations involved is to ponder the following questions:

1. Is the land truly worthy of being more forcefully protected than it is now?

2. Do you wish to protect all or part of the property?

3. Do you wish to protect the land forever or for a limited term?

4. Do you want the land to be protected and to remain in individual ownership, or would you consider transferring ownership to a conservation agency?

5. Should you consider a sale or a donation?

6. If you transfer title, do you want to protect the land by restricting future use?

7. Are tax (estate, gift, income, property) implications important to you?

8. Do you wish to act immediately, over a period of years, or through your will?

9. How would your actions affect your family?

10. How would they affect your community and its land-use and tax considerations?

11. Are there conservation agencies or other institutions that might be interested in helping protect your land?

The pages that follow describe in general terms the various ways of voluntarily protecting land. The details of each may vary from state to state, but this discussion should give you an idea about which alternatives you, your family, and your attorney may want to consider in more detail. The tax considerations, which may be important to you, are covered in depth in another section of this book.

So if you own land that is indeed worthy of being permanently protected—be it an island, a unique wildlife habitat, or productive fields—and your interest is piqued, please read on. Permanent protection may not always be feasible or wise in the end, but it is usually a possibility worth exploring.

Options for Protecting Special Land

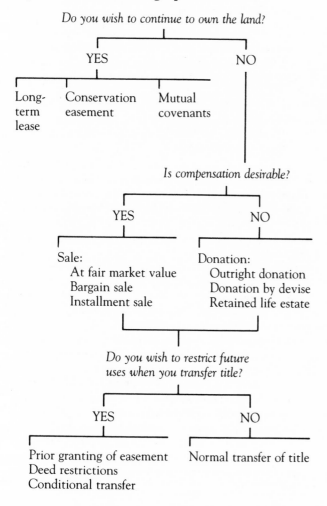

Do you wish to continue to own the land?

YES   NO

Long-term lease   Conservation easement   Mutual covenants

Is compensation desirable?

YES   NO

Sale:
   At fair market value
   Bargain sale
   Installment sale

Donation:
   Outright donation
   Donation by devise
   Retained life estate

Do you wish to restrict future uses when you transfer title?

YES   NO

Prior granting of easement
Deed restrictions
Conditional transfer

Normal transfer of title

Protection by Restriction

One of the first questions a landowner seeking to protect his land should face is whether he wishes to continue to own the land. If he does, he can consider either granting a conservation easement, which would permanently limit future development on the property, or putting restrictions on development in the deed to the property.

The Conservation Easement

A conservation easement—also known as a conservation restriction—is a legal means by which a landowner can voluntarily set permanent limitations on the future use of the land, thus protecting the land's particular attributes. The attraction of the conservation easement lies in the fact that the land remains in *private ownership*. The responsibilities and rewards of ownership continue, and unless otherwise specified, the landowner retains full control over public access, just as he did before.

The limitations set forth in conservation easements are tailored to suit the unique characteristics of individual properties as well as the different activities and interests of individual landowners. Generally, the covenants in an easement limit the number and location of structures and the types of commercial and industrial activity, and they specify what can be done to the surface of the land and its natural growth. The versatility of easements allows them to range from the "forever-wild" easement, which states that the land will remain as nature leaves it, to the easement that allows limited residential use, farming, and properly managed commercial timber harvesting, with many combinations in between.

Not only do the type of restrictions vary but also the size of the property under easement. One may place all of one's holding under easement or just the portion that has greatest significance from a conservation point of view. It may be several acres or several hundred. In sum, each easement is created in light of the particular situation, according to the values of the land and the needs and wishes of its owner.

The protection afforded by conservation easements granted in perpetuity is permanent because easements legally bind all present and future owners of the land. They are recorded in the same manner as a deed to land and burden the title to the land thereafter, whether the land is transferred by sale, by gift, or by devise.

The covenants contained in easements have lasting effect in practice because each conservation easement is granted to an organization or agency interested in preserving the natural characteristics of the land. The sole responsibility of the recipient of an easement is to ensure that neither the present nor any subsequent owners disregard the regulations on use set forth in the easement, a responsibility that is fulfilled by periodically monitoring the property and by enforcing the restrictions in court if necessary.

Because the protection created by the easement is only as good as the agency that will enforce it, a landowner will want to be sure that the agency has the resources and determination necessary to carry through on its obligation. By the same token a recipient agency or organization will want to think carefully before assuming this long-lived responsibility and will want to be sure that the protection it is making possible is in keeping with its objectives. The agencies that are interested in accepting easements will vary from state to state. They may be public or private, local, statewide, or national. It is important to note, however, that their availability as recipients will be determined not only by their interest but by the peculiarities of the particular state's law regarding conservation easements.[2]

People grant conservation easements primarily because they wish to protect land that they value, land that will be important for its natural attributes in the future. Their greatest reward is their sense of satisfaction from having protected something of value. The financial aspects of granting a conservation easement in perpetuity, however, can also be important.

A conservation easement will affect the market value of land to the extent that it limits the development and use potential of the land. It is this effect on market value that is important when considering the financial implications of easements.

Tax benefits *may* accrue from granting a conservation easement that reduces the fair market value of the land. Any diminution in value caused by the granting of a conservation easement may reduce the amount of estate tax due at the time of death by reducing the value of the landowner's estate, and it may have a similar effect on gift taxes if the landowner gives the property away during his lifetime. These benefits will result only if the value of the landowner's estate at death combined with the value of what he has given away during life exceeds the amount established by federal law to be exempt from estate and gift taxation.

The landowner may also be able to claim any loss in value as a charitable deduction for income tax purposes. If the landowner expects to get such a deduction, however, he should examine federal tax laws and regulations carefully before granting an easement because the allowances for deductions are becoming more stringent than they have been in the past. One must be aware of the fact that if the loss in value is not eligible for a deduction, it may be taxed for gift purposes as a "gift" given to the recipient agency—an effect that obviously works to the landowner's detriment.

Finally, the diminution in value may affect the assessed value of the land if the municipality is assessing properties at values near their fair market value—the assessors may be required to consider the restrictions when determining the assessed value of the land. If the assessed value of the property is reduced, property taxes should decrease proportionally.

While the granting of an easement may result in tax benefits, it may correspondingly mean that the landowner will receive less if he ever has to sell the land. In those instances where the land is an individual's primary investment and the reduction in value may be significant, the financial aspect of the easement must be taken seriously.

In summary, the most distinctive aspect of protecting land through granting a conservation easement is that the land remains in private ownership, yet its use is regulated by a means stronger than zoning or state land-use laws.

A landowner can take this voluntary measure quite easily—by discussing it with his family and his lawyer, then finding an agency that is eligible to and interested in accepting the easement. Yet the decision must be weighed carefully, for once that granting process is completed, it is difficult to reverse. The financial benefits must be weighed against the realities of a loss in market value; the protection must be weighed against the need for flexibility. In many instances, however, the range of covenants that can be contained in a conservation easement and the way they may be applied afford tremendous room for finding a proper balance of personal and conservation considerations.

Mutual Covenants

Occasionally there are situations where a conservation easement may not be feasible either because there is no recipient agency interested in accepting the easement or because the landowner does not want to enter into an agreement with the agency or organization. In such a case it may be possible to limit the future uses of the land by the imposition of mutual covenants—if there are several landowners in the immediate area interested in entering into mutually restrictive agreements.[3]

Neighboring landowners having a common conservation interest may sign and record an agreement containing mutually beneficial covenants that would control the future use of their land. The agreement would then bind subsequent owners just as an easement would, and the types of restrictions imposed would be much the same. These covenants could be enforced by any of the landowners who entered into the mutual agreement or by any future owners of the land.

Mutual covenants differ from conservation easements in three respects. First, the nature of the enforcer is quite different. Enforcement would lie with one or several of the individuals owning the benefited land rather than with a conservation agency or organization. Though the presence of restrictions of which others are acutely aware is likely to restrain forbidden acts by the owners, enforcement would ultimately depend on the determination and resources of individuals rather than on an organization.

The second difference is that mutual covenants may not be as lasting as the restrictions contained in an easement. By their legal nature they would be subject to the doctrine of changed conditions: a court would be able to refuse to enforce the covenants if it felt that it is no longer possible to achieve the benefits sought when the covenants were imposed.

Third, there are the financial considerations. Mutual covenants should receive the same treatment that easements receive when property taxes and estate and gift taxes are calculated. The similarity stops there. The imposition of mutual covenants, unlike easements, never allows the landowner to claim the loss in market value as a charitable deduction on his income tax return.

While not as strong as conservation easements, mutually restrictive covenants provide an alternative for those instances when easements may not be feasible or necessarily desirable. They do, however, require the presence of the right combination of people and circumstances.

Options Involving the Transfer of Title

Some landowners may not be interested in continuing to own the property. Rather, they may wish to give or sell important open spaces to a governmental or private conservation agency or landholding body. This may be for a number of reasons: the belief that the land should be used by the public or by a certain group, the belief that a landholding agency is better able to manage or protect the land than an individual owner, or that the taxes have climbed too high for the owner to continue to own and protect the land himself.

Whatever the cause, there are a number of ways the donation or sale may be executed. A landowner might donate the property to a conservation organization during his lifetime; he might give title but retain life use; or he might retain full title during his life and provide for donation in his will. If the landowner wishes to sell rather than donate the property to a conservation agency, he could sell the land at its fair market value, at a bargain price, or convey the land in installments. Whether donating or selling, he may create an additional tier of protection by restricting the use of the property after it has been transferred. Each of these alternatives has differing financial and personal implications, and each is discussed below.

It is important to remember, however, that donations or sales to a conservation agency are not the only ways of achieving conservation goals if a landowner no longer wishes to own the property. An individual can put his land on the open market yet protect it by granting a conservation easement prior to sale or by inserting restrictions in the deed when title passes. These alternatives, too, are discussed.

Donations

Outright donation. A donation of land is usually the simplest way to arrange outright transfers of title because no financing or negotiations about price are necessary. The landowner need only obtain the approval of the gift from the agency to which it will be given, then deed the land to that recipient.

Donations, by definition, rely on the fact that the land-

owner is willing to protect his land at the cost of giving it away without direct financial compensation. The loss in direct compensation, however, may be offset in part by the tax benefits that may accrue when the gift is given. One of the financial benefits is obvious: the donor need no longer pay the property taxes. There may also be the potential for income, estate, and gift tax advantages. If the land is given to a governmental agency or a publicly supported private charity, the donor can claim as an income tax deduction the market value of the land as determined by a qualified appraiser.[4] The transfer would not be subject to gift tax. In addition, because the transfer of the property will reduce the size of the estate retained by the donor, his liability for estate taxes at the time of death may decrease. If, however, the land is transferred to an organization that is not a governmental agency or a publicly supported private charity, the donor will be subject to a gift tax.

Because landholding agencies are becoming increasingly aware of the financial and managerial responsibilities that come with the ownership of land, they want to review proposed gifts of land carefully. They must look upon gifts in relation to their ability to care for and use the land properly. Reciprocally, the landowner will want to be sure that the agency will be capable of caring for the land as he would wish. To ensure against uncertainties of funding in the future, some agencies have encouraged the establishment of an endowment fund when a donation of land is made.

Under some conditions a landowner may wish to donate his land but not give up his use of it immediately. In that case two options exist: donation by devise or donation with a reserved life estate.

Donation by devise. A landowner may give away land at the time of death simply by providing for the gift in a will. When the will is probated, the named recipient agency will decide whether it wishes to accept the gift. Should it choose not to, the gift would go to the second named recipient, or, if none is named, to the party found to be appropriate by the court. Discussing the gift with the proposed recipient before writing the will can help determine whether the choice of recipient is realistic.

The advantage of a donation by devise is that the landowner retains full use and control of the land until his death. He may revoke his will at any time if circumstances change and a donation becomes inadvisable. If his estate is subject to taxation at the time of death, a donation to a qualified recipient will reduce taxes by removing the land from the estate. But obviously he would not benefit from the income tax deductions that would be possible if he were to make a charitable gift during his lifetime, nor is he free from the responsibility of paying real estate taxes during his lifetime.

The risk that accompanies making a gift by devise is that the named recipient or recipients may not wish to accept the gift at the time the will is probated. An organization's objectives and financial circumstances can change with the passage of time. A way of avoiding this risk entirely is to donate the land now but retain a life estate.

Donation with a reserved life estate. A landowner may donate his land and retain use of all or part of the donated land during his lifetime and/or the lifetimes of other members of his immediate family. By doing this he knows that the gift has been accepted by a recipient suitable to him, yet he can continue to use the land. This type of donation is accomplished by giving the recipient a deed that includes a provision allowing lifetime use of the land by the landowners or other specified individuals.

The donor usually must pay real estate taxes on that portion of the land he retains for his own or his family's use. If the gift of the land qualifies for treatment as a charitable deduction, the donor may take as an income tax deduction the value of what he has actually given up. This would not include the value of the life estate he has retained, as determined by actuarial tables. If the gift qualifies, its value also would be removed from the value of his estate that is subject to gift and estate taxes.[5]

From the point of view of the recipient of the gift, donation by devise or with a reserved life estate may be preferable if the agency knows that it would like to own the property but does not wish to accept the responsibilities of ownership immediately.

Sale

A landowner may need or prefer to sell his property yet wish to see it protected. To accomplish his purpose, he can place restrictions on the use of the property to secure the preservation of the land, then sell the land on the open market, an option that is discussed later in this article in "Transfer of Title with Conditions Attached" and "Combining Conservation and Development." He may, however, own land that he thinks should be sold to a conservation organization or agency. There are landholding agencies that do have funds for outright purchase of land that has special attributes, such as a bog or rookery, or that can be used for some agency's particular purpose, such as a game sanctuary or recreational land. In considering a sale to such an agency, the landowner has the option of selling at fair market value, at a bargain price, or in installments.

Sale at fair market value. Sale at fair market value needs little explanation, but two thoughts are worth keeping in mind. The desire to sell at fair market value is often hampered by the fact that most landholding agencies have limited funds available for the purchase of land and must be very particular about their choices. Also, if the land is sold for its full value and if the land has appreciated since its purchase, the seller will be liable for income tax on the capital gain. This can significantly affect the net profit of the sale.

Bargain sale. The bargain sale is an alternative that circumvents somewhat the disadvantages of a sale at fair market value. In a bargain sale the landowner sells his land to a governmental agency or a publicly supported charity for a price less than fair market value. Because the selling price is lower, the landowner is more likely to find a landholding agency willing to purchase the land.

The bargain sale may also be financially advantageous to the landowner. He not only receives some money for his land, but he can also claim an income tax deduction. The Internal Revenue Code allows him to deduct as a charitable contribution the difference between the bargain price received and the fair market value if the land is bought by a qualified agency. The cash benefit of the deduction can help compensate for the dollars foregone by selling at less than fair market value. Also, by selling at less than fair market value, there will be a smaller capital gain to be taxed.

Installment sale. The installment sale is another means of transfer that may be advantageous to both the landowner and the purchasing agency. An installment sale is based upon an agreement between the landowner and the purchaser that specifies that the landholding agency either pays for the land in annual installments or buys a portion of the land each year. Towns, where authorized by appropriate municipal ordinance or by state law, and private organizations may use either method of installment buying, but the state and federal agencies must use the latter approach because they cannot pledge the credit of government. In either case the landowner and the buyer can negotiate terms governing the use of the land and the responsibility for the payment of property taxes until the sale is complete.

The financial advantage to the landowner is that he spreads the income over a number of years. In doing so he can in some circumstances spread the taxable capital gain over a period of years, thus minimizing the amount of tax that must be paid. The primary advantage to the purchasing organization or agency is that it has to pay only a fraction of the entire cost at first. Also, depending upon the terms of the agreement, it may not have to worry about the maintenance of the property until the sale is complete.

Sale with a reserved life estate. A landowner may sell his property to a landholding agency with a reserved life estate so that he and his family may continue to use the land during his lifetime and/or the lifetimes of other members of his immediate family. The landowner would continue to pay real estate taxes on the land while he has use of the property. The federal income (capital gain) tax implications of a sale with a reserved life estate would, of course, depend on whether the sale is at fair market value, at less than fair market value, or in installments.

Transfer of Title with Conditions Attached

Whether by sale or donation, the outright transfer of land without strings attached is very straightforward, but its virtue is also its disadvantage. The landowner does not have the legal means to specify how the land will be used in the future. In many instances that may be of no concern—if the agency is likely to be long lived and has proven thus far to be faithful to its given purposes or if it seems advisable that the agency not be restricted in its use of the land. On occasion, however, it may seem wise to place limiting conditions on the use of the land at the time of transfer.

Limiting conditions may also be imposed if the land is to be sold on the open market and if the landowner wishes to influence its future use and hence protect its natural attributes.

Prior granting of a conservation easement. Because conservation easements are binding on all subsequent owners of the land, a landowner may grant a conservation easement regulating the future use of the property before he transfers ownership. (See "The Conservation Easement.")

The landowner *may* be able to take the loss in fair market value caused by the granting of the easement as a charitable deduction for income tax purposes, but on the same count, he would expect a lower price if a sale is being considered. If the land is to be donated to a qualified charitable organization or governmental agency, he may still take the value of the land after the easement as a charitable deduction. (See "Donations.")

The prior granting of a conservation easement provides an excellent way to control the future use of the land if it is to be sold on the open market. In most cases, however, it may provide more protection than is necessary when the land is to be transferred to an established private or public conservation agency that is experienced in acquiring and managing land. The use of other types of limiting conditions can be considered in those cases, as well as when a recipient of a conservation easement is not available.

Deed restrictions. Restrictive covenants guiding the future use of the property may be placed in the deed at the time of transfer. These restrictions can be much like those contained in conservation easements, but they may prove to be less permanent than those in easements because they are limited by the doctrine of changed conditions. In other words a court may refuse to enforce the restrictions if it finds that it is no longer possible to achieve the benefit sought when the restrictions were created. Deed restrictions also vary from conservation easements in that there is usually not a third party assuming the monitoring and enforcement responsibility.

The question of enforceability is key when considering deed restrictions. Depending on the circumstances, there may be limitations on who can enforce the restrictions and for how long. If a landowner conveys his land, inserts restrictions in the deed, and retains no land nearby, then only he may enforce the restrictions against the subsequent owners of the land. If the landowner conveys part of his property and burdens it with restrictions, then he and his successors in title to the remaining property may enforce the restrictions against whoever should own the covenanted property in the future. In that case the right to enforce arises from the fact that the restrictions on

the transferred property benefit the landowner's remaining land.

Deed restrictions may be imposed in another way if the land is to be given to a landholding agency. A landowner can transfer his property to an intermediary conservation agency, which then transfers it to the landholding agency that is to hold title permanently. The intermediary agency inserts the restrictive covenants in the deed at the time of the second transfer. This seemingly complex transaction is performed for good reason. By inserting the restrictions, the conservation agency obtains the right to enforce the covenants, and presumably the agency will be long lived and will be interested in seeing that the restrictions are not broken.

As in the case of all alternatives, the financial implications of deed restrictions must be considered. Deed restrictions will affect the market value of the land if they significantly limit its development potential. Thus, the presence of restrictions may lower the price if the property is to be sold or the deductible value of the gift if the land is donated to a governmental or charitable agency.

It is important to note that the Internal Revenue Service does not allow one to claim the loss in value resulting from the imposition of deed restrictions as a charitable deduction. Because this is so, a landowner may choose to donate the land to an intermediary agency, which then inserts the deed restrictions and transfers title. The landowner is able to claim an income tax deduction for the unrestricted value of the land provided that the intermediary agency is of the type that qualifies him to do so.

If the restricted land is being transferred to an individual landowner, the restrictions should be considered when the landowner's death taxes and real estate taxes are calculated, as in the case of conservation easements.

Conditional transfers. One can also govern the future use of land by using a form of deed that spells out the restrictions on use *and* states that title will transfer to a certain named party if the restrictions on use are breached. Thus, the conditions can be similar in content to deed restrictions, but they carry more force; breaking the conditions may mean loss of title rather than enforcement of the restrictions on use.

Such a conditional transfer may be constructed in one of several ways. The deed may be worded so that the original owner and his heirs reserve the right to reassert ownership *at their own choice* if the landholding agency disobeys the conditions. Or the conditional transfer may be in the form of a "possibility of reverter," in which case title would revert *automatically* to the landowner or his heirs. Finally, the landowner could choose to name another charitable landholding organization that would *automatically* assume title if the conditions for use were no longer being fulfilled.

If the land is being transferred as a gift to a qualified recipient, the landowner may claim the value of the gift as a charitable deduction. Because the existence of restrictions may reduce that value, a landowner wishing to maximize his income tax deduction may want to transfer the unrestricted land to a qualified agency, which would then impose the conditions and convey the land to the agency that is to own it permanently.

This conservation technique is not without its legal stumbling blocks. State law *may* limit the duration of the conditions, and courts, which tend to disfavor conditions, may be reluctant to enforce the conditions through forfeiture of title if litigation becomes necessary. Despite these possible limitations, conditional transfers are an appealing way of regulating future use because they are created with ease, particularly if an intermediary agency is not involved. At the same time they provide strong guidance for the use of the property: loss of title is a severe penalty for breaking the regulations set on use.

In the end, however, practical considerations may be determinative. Would the heirs take the initiative to reassert ownership if necessary? If the land reverted automatically to them, would they treat it wisely? If an intermediary or second agency ideally should be involved, is there one that is willing to participate and that would act responsibly in the future? These are considerations that must be judged against the facts of the particular situation.

Leases

Granting a long-term lease to a land management agency is another option available to the landowner. The lease, which would be recorded, would allow for unrestricted and exclusive use of the land by that agency for a given number of years. Even if rental payments are not received for the use of the land, there may be other financial incentives that accompany the leasing of the land. Although it is not possible to take as a charitable deduction the value of a lease that is donated, any impact of the lease on the value of the land would be taken into account when death taxes are calculated.

The lease provides an alternative for those who may not wish to transfer their land to a conservation agency or organization but who want to see it used or protected by such a group for a period of years.

Combining Conservation and Development

Although one tends to assume that conservation and development are mutually exclusive alternatives for the future of a parcel of land, this need not be true. If a parcel of land is large enough, the conservation options discussed thus far may be used alone or in combination to protect the important natural aspects of the land while still allowing for some commercial development of the property. The development potential may be preserved in one of two general ways.

First, a landowner might apply one of the conservation techniques to the portion of the property he most wants to protect, while leaving completely unprotected the portion that is suited for development. This approach offers the benefit of allowing the landowner complete control in the future over the disposition of the unrestricted land and will probably allow him to maximize his financial return on that portion. In doing so, however, he should consider whether the prospect of unrestricted development will diminish the real value of the protection placed on the remainder. On some parcels of land, the peculiarities of the particular values one is trying to preserve may make conservation and unrestrained development incompatible. The potential for development may also affect the extent to which a recipient agency will be willing to cooperate in the protection of the remainder.

Alternatively, a landowner might protect the entire property by using one or more conservation techniques while simultaneously allowing for development in specified portions. This could be accomplished by granting a conservation easement that covers the entire property but establishes the locations where development may take place and the limits to which development would be subject. Or one could use a combination of techniques by placing an easement[6] or deed restrictions on the lots suitable for development and preserving the remainder by transferring title to a conservation agency.

Whether one tries to integrate conservation and development by protecting the entire property or only part, one should first think carefully about the attributes of the land and how the conservation and development goals can best be intertwined so that the potential for achieving each is maximized. It may be advisable to seek professional assistance to determine the feasibility of development for each site to be considered for future development before a landowner relies on the prospect of developing. Also, professional opinions may be useful to determine how development may affect the conservation values the landowner is trying to protect. For example, the protection of a particularly sensitive wildlife habitat may require that development take place beyond a certain distance even if one would think that it could occur more closely.

This description provides only the briefest introduction to the ways in which a landowner can protect what is most important about the land and yet not completely foreclose the possibility of development. The conservation options previously discussed can be used in a number of permutations to allow for both protection and development, but as with the application of each of these options alone, the success when applied to a particular situation will depend on the characteristics of the land, the wishes of the landowner, and the availability of an agency interested in cooperating.

Finding a Partner

In the case of many of the protective arrangements discussed here, it is the presence of a strong landholding agency that guarantees that the land is indeed protected in the manner in which the landowner envisions. Although it is not possible to catalog within this article all of the agencies that might be interested in helping a landowner permanently protect his property, the following is at least a survey of the categories.

First, there is the division between private organizations and public agencies. Because the range of types of organizations and agencies within each of these two categories is so great, it would be dangerous to generalize about the advantages or disadvantages of each. It is safer to take the next step in the dissection and divide each category into its component parts: local organizations or agencies, statewide or regional organizations, and national organizations or agencies.

Starting with the smallest, one can consider working with a town. The success of this alternative will depend upon whether the townspeople are committed enough to the goal of land conservation to accept a perpetual responsibility and the financial burdens that may go along with it. Some towns may be ready; some may not. On the private side one might determine whether a local land trust exists that would be interested in undertaking the project. A local land trust is a private corporation formed and financed by a group of local people for the purpose of owning and protecting locally significant open spaces. It offers the equivalent of town ownership with the advantages that transactions need not involve town politics and decisions affecting the use of the land once it is acquired and need not be directly responsive to political pressures and tides. One has to be sure, however, that the people who are initially enthusiastic and willing to take on the responsibilities will be followed by others in subsequent years who are equally committed.

Proceeding to the statewide level, there are of course state agencies such as departments of conservation, wildlife, fisheries, forestry, and recreation. The strength of these agencies as recipients will depend on how committed the state is—philosophically and fiscally—to land conservation, whether that commitment is likely to remain constant or grow in the future, and the extent to which any particular agency is participating in land-protection programs. Statewide private organizations may exist as independent entities or as subsets of national organizations and will vary in suitability according to their financial resources and their ability to undertake long-term responsibilities.

Finally, on the national level there are the federal agencies such as the National Park Service, Fish and Wildlife Service, and Forest Service. Their counterparts in the private sector are such organizations as the National Audubon Society and The Nature Conservancy.

To sort out the proper place to start looking for an agency with which to work, the landowner might think about the characteristics of his property. Is it of national significance—a highly unusual area that has few equals in the country and might be of interest to the federal government or a national organization? Or is it more of local significance—offering resources valuable to the community but not markedly unique? Or does it lie in between? Is it of interest more to one type of group—such as birdwatchers, scientists, or people interested in recreation—than to another? The characteristics of the property are bound to determine which organizations or agencies—and at which levels—will be interested in exploring the possibility of cooperating with the landowner.

If a landowner thinks he may have more than one choice, he should consider whether he would prefer to entrust the future of his property to a local entity, a statewide organization, or an organization that is operating nationally. This consideration has several facets. Out of personal preference, a landowner may prefer to negotiate with a local government than a state or national government, or vice versa. He may have more faith in the long-term commitment of one over the others. Or for purely emotional reasons he may wish to give his "gift" to one type of organization or agency rather than to another.

Whichever agency or organization a landowner thinks he might prefer should be examined carefully. How well it will perform its obligations will depend on how it is funded, the quality of the people involved (either as volunteers or as professionals), the degree of commitment of the organization to the goal of land conservation, and the clarity with which it has defined its goals and the manner in which it intends to achieve them.

Whether public or private, local or national, an organization's characteristics are bound to change with time as its appeals for funding meet with greater or less success, as the people involved change, and as priorities for land conservation reshape themselves with changes in thought and circumstances. A landowner can only do his best to choose the organization that seems to be soundest and most committed to the goal he is trying to promote at the time he is ready to act.

By the same token the organization or agency will scrutinize the landowner and his proposal carefully. It will want to be sure that the protection to be achieved falls within the scope of its interest and that it will have the practical and financial ability to follow through on any responsibilities that will result.

The road to the final resolution—finding the right technique and matching the landowner and property with an agency interested in cooperating—may be long and may have some false turns. Do not be afraid to plunge in. There may be advisory conservation organizations in the landowner's state that are not interested in actually holding land or enforcing restrictions but may be most willing to help someone investigate his alternatives. Or if such an organization does not exist, a landowner can start by talking with someone at any one of the conservation organizations or agencies. Although that organization may not be the one that will be interested in making a long-term commitment to the property, it may be able to give an interested landowner an idea of which organizations may be suitable and the person with whom he should talk next. Do not be afraid to ask. Most individuals and organizations that are knowledgeable about land conservation will be happy to extend a helping hand to someone genuinely interested in protecting land that warrants protection.

Pondering the Choices

Many of the hardest questions that will affect the landowner's final decision must be answered by the landowner alone—questions such as whether he wants to give up the development potential of the land and how important continued ownership of the land is to him and to his family. Although the ultimate decision is his, the landowner should not explore the alternatives in isolation.

A landowner who is seriously considering protecting his property through the use of any of the legal techniques described here should discuss his plan with an attorney who is familiar with land conservation law in that particular state and with the tax implications of conservation measures. Although the final legal transaction may not be complex, a landowner needs to be sure that the alternative chosen is legally sound, that the legal instrument used will be able to fully accomplish the goal, and that the action will be wise from a tax planning perspective.

Relatedly, a landowner may wish to consult a real estate appraiser to determine the approximate effect of the proposed measure on the value of the property or the value of the gift that will be given. Only if a landowner has a realistic idea of the financial impact of the conservation measure can he determine whether he can afford to take the step and to what extent any tax benefits will counter the loss in value. The services of an accountant may be required to help with these determinations if the landowner's financial situation is complex. With this professional advice a landowner can help ensure that his decision is the proper one.

Should a landowner ponder the conservation alternatives discussed above and decide not to take action now, the subject need not be closed. Circumstances and thoughts may change with the passage of time and action may later be deemed appropriate.[7]

Theory and Experience: The Decisions of Three Maine Landowners

Surrounded by extensively developed and heavily used shorefront properties is a twenty-six-acre point, remarkably unspoiled and quietly beautiful, a haven for nesting birds. Now it is a permanently protected conservation area, a status it gained after the three individuals owning the contiguous parcels considered their alternatives and acted in concert to preserve the point.

The Maine Audubon Society had an interest in the area: it owned two other properties nearby. Therefore, by virtue of both its general concerns and its particular interest in the area, it seemed to be the conservation organization to be approached about the project.

Two of the landowners weighed the possibility of donating the land to the Maine Audubon Society and the various ways of making the gift. One chose to make an unrestricted gift of her eight acres to Audubon, a gift that was eagerly accepted. The other took a different path. He gave The Nature Conservancy a two-fifths' undivided interest in his twelve acres. The Nature Conservancy then conveyed the land to the Maine Audubon Society on condition that the premises "shall forever be held as a nature preserve, for scientific, educational and aesthetic purposes and shall be kept entirely in their natural state. . . ." The Nature Conservancy retained the right to claim title should the conditions ever be violated. Transferring the land in this way gave the landowner the assurance that the land would always be used as a nature preserve, and it also allowed him to claim the value of the land, unrestricted, as a charitable deduction. The remaining interest in his land has been willed to the Maine Audubon Society, so ultimately Audubon will become sole owner of the twelve acres as well as the eight acres.

The third owner was faced with different circumstances. Having a house on her parcel, she did not wish to transfer ownership of the land. Rather, she granted a conservation easement on the six acres forming one side of the natural area. Her easement excluded the house lot that was near the road, but it stipulated that the remaining land was to remain "forever wild." Though public use of the property did not come with the granting of the easement, the Maine Audubon Society and the public are able to enjoy the benefits of the scenic and natural protection that it provides.

Thus, three landowners seeking a common goal chose different means of accomplishing their purpose. As with all landowners facing similar decisions, they each considered their individual financial and personal needs and their desires for the land. The range of options was wide enough to allow each to find a suitable solution, and the presence of committed organizations with similar objectives enabled them to make their goal a reality.

Notes

1. Speech given by John Muir in 1894, quoted in *The Life and Letters of John Muir*, Volume 1, by William Frederic Bade.

2. Most states have statutes governing the granting of easements that establish whether governmental or private agencies can accept easements and the procedures that must be followed. Even if a state has not passed such a statute, a landowner may be able to grant a "common law" easement to an agency owning benefiting land nearby.

3. Legally speaking, mutual covenants fit within the larger category of property interests known as equitable servitudes.

4. In some instances the landowner may want to donate the land in installments to maximize the benefit of the deduction.

5. If the donor has retained a life estate only for himself, none

of the value of the property would be included in his estate at the time of death because full title would pass to the recipient. If the life estate is passed on to heirs, the value of the use of the property would be included in the donor's estate.

6. The landowner is likely to find a recipient for an easement governing just the development lots only if the lots are fairly large or are unique in some way: a recipient organization will be interested in accepting the responsibility of enforcing the easement only if it finds that the easement conservation purposes are independent of those achieved by protecting the remainder of the property.

7. In view of this, one more caveat is in order. If a landowner is interested in conservation but not ready to act and ultimately puts his property in trust, he should consider giving the trustee powers that are broad enough to allow the trustee to protect the property. Ordinarily a trustee would not be able to reduce the value of the property in trust or to give it away; his duty is to maximize the value of the trust for the beneficiaries. But if he is specifically given power to consider and execute conservation measures, the trustee may be able to effect a conservation plan. Thus, a landowner who does not think it timely to act now can allow for the possibility of imposing conservation measures in the future. To do this, however, he must explicitly define the powers of the trustee when placing the property in trust.

Federal Tax Planning: Strategies and Priorities for Landowners

Kingsbury Browne, Jr.

Working with Tax Incentives

The concerned landowner wonders whether a conservation program is financially within reach. There are family obligations and only limited resources with which to meet them. There will be death taxes to pay that will deplete the liquid assets needed to support the surviving spouse and to provide educational assistance for the grandchildren. The landowner is vaguely aware that a charitable gift of land can produce immediate and future tax savings as well as assure the preservation of open space, but his understanding is incomplete and he postpones any decision. He needs assistance in appraising his resources, in identifying and estimating the expenses of meeting family objectives and the probable cost of dying, and in comparing both his resources and expenses. The various ways of conserving open space and their relative tax benefits must be explained to him. The example that follows is intended to illustrate an approach pattern that will provide such an explanation and identify the specialized assistance required. It is a hypothetical composite of actual encounters with landowners whose eventual conservation programs depended in large measure on the tax benefits involved.

Grandfather George was born in 1916. He plans to retire from active law practice in two years at age seventy. His wife, Mehitabel, is ten years younger, in good health, and has a normal life expectancy. He, too, has a life expectancy of many years. They have four grown children and eleven grandchildren. Two of the children are neighbors. The others live in distant parts of the country but return for summer visits. All have reasonably productive jobs but inadequate means of providing college educations for their children.

During the Depression, George was able with a modest inheritance to buy a summer home at the end of a coastal promontory north of Boston. The property included a barn, various farm buildings, a tennis court, and greenhouse, all of which were in a state of disrepair. Accompanying the buildings were four hundred acres of land, on which were located a salt pond separated from the sea by a narrow barrier beach, a sizable marsh, a high hill of pine woods, overgrown pastures, and granite outcroppings. It is a typical New England farmscape except for the large Victorian house and the spectacular scenic qualities of the property. George and Hetty over the years have restored the farm buildings, winterized the main house, cleared the pastures, and cut trails through the pine woods.

George owns marketable securities that are worth $300,000 and earn $15,000 annually. As a self-employed lawyer he has a modest, funded retirement plan. He has only a rough idea of his family's annual expenses, but he suspects, rightly as it turns out, that spendable income after retirement will not sustain the family's present scale of living. He is aware of recent sales of small land parcels in the neighborhood at $5,000 an acre and has concluded, wrongly, that the family land is worth $2,000,000 without consideration of the buildings. He has no idea of the amount of death taxes that will be due on his death and Hetty's. The only land-use objectives articulated by the family boil down to a desire to keep the place "as is" and "forever."

To develop the facts presented above requires at the outset the skills of an appraiser to provide some rough idea of the value of the land. It turns out that George's estimate of $2,000,000 proves to be $400,000 high because the value of a large tract of land generally cannot be determined on the basis of sales of small parcels. The facts, to be useful, must be arranged in some financial presentation that will permit comparison of spendable income with expenditures at several critical points in time. George's first thought concerns his income during retirement, but he must also consider the financial picture during the period Hetty survives him and thereafter the assets available for the education of the grandchildren. At each critical point the essential financial presentation involves a simplified balance sheet on the one hand and a spendable income and estimated expenditure statement on the other. The balance sheet forecast at the time of George's retirement will change at his death and again at Hetty's death when marketable securities must be sold in order to pay death taxes. Spendable income will drop as income-producing securities are sold. The extent of the drop in assets and spendable income depends upon the magnitude of death taxes. Consequently, George needs the assistance of a person skilled in making income and estate tax computations.

George compares estimated annual expenditures during retirement with his projected spendable income. The result is a deficit. Continuing inflation, a setback in the economy, or extraordinary family medical expenses would enlarge that deficit.

After George's death, spendable income drops again because payment of death taxes, especially with respect to the land, will consume most of his securities. Hetty's annual cash needs may decline somewhat but will still exceed the projected spendable income by a substantial margin. Death tax obligations on her death and the educational needs of grandchildren will force the sale of the land. George's first reaction to these projections is to put his affairs in order at once by selling the land, reinvesting the proceeds in marketable securities, and moving to the Sunbelt. His family, however, persuades him to reexamine all objectives, especially those about the land itself.

When George studies the flow of spendable income in the various critical periods, he realizes that much of the deficit problem traces to the high value of the land, which is not producing income and is the source of a substantial annual real estate tax liability and eventually will give rise to heavy death taxes. He asks what the effect would be if he gave half the land to a charitable organization engaged in land conservation.

The appraiser estimates the value of the gift, then the tax expert recomputes the various taxes involved. A charitable gift of half the land gives rise to an immediate income tax deduction and an income tax saving that increase spendable income for a period of time. Real estate taxes are cut in half. If George eliminates half the land from his estate, the death taxes will drop and fewer of his marketable securities will need to be sold. After analysis, it still does not appear, however, that spendable income is adequate. George then asks about the effect of selling half the land.

The real estate appraiser knows that development as a residential subdivision constitutes the highest and best use of the property. The cost of subdividing, laying out roads, and putting in utilities; the retail value of lots; and the speed with which the market can absorb the lots are all factors affecting his estimate of the present fair market value of the land proposed for sale. After the real estate expert's rough figure is reduced by selling expenses and after the various tax computations are redone, it appears that George's spendable income problem during retirement is resolved and that after his death spendable income will remain adequate to meet the needs of his widow.

The thought, however, of losing open space to real estate development shocks the family, and they ask whether a sale to a private or governmental entity interested in open space conservation could be arranged. At this point the help of a local land conservation organization is sought to identify possible conservation-minded buyers.

At the suggestion of the conservation organization, various federal and state agencies are contacted, among them the Fish and Wildlife Service in the Department of the Interior. That agency is initially interested in the salt pond and marsh as a possible resting area for migrating waterfowl but loses interest when its biologist reports that the pond will not provide adequate natural food.

The Commonwealth of Massachusetts is also considering the area for public recreation but has no available state funds. It does, however, have access to federal funds, provided George is willing to bargain sell the land at 50 percent of its fair market value. According to this proposal, George would sell 200 acres, worth $800,000, for $400,000. The land conservation organization points out to George that the $400,000 value of the given portion may be deducted as a charitable contribution for federal income tax purposes. The income tax benefit of the charitable gift plus the net cash from the sale might possibly meet George's financial requirements. Spendable income is accordingly recomputed (the tax computations have to be redone) on the basis of a 50 percent bargain sale. While spendable income appears to be adequate during George's retirement, it remains marginal after his death. Consequently the charitable bargain sale route is abandoned in favor of selling 200 acres to a developer.

When George first considered a sale for residential development, the financial analysis indicated that half the land had to be sold to meet spendable income needs. After dropping the bargain sale idea in favor of a sale for residential use, George asks whether cost savings could be achieved if he acts as his own developer. The real estate expert describes the large front-end investment of cash that will be required of George, the cost of borrowing money, the months that will pass before the first sale is completed, and the fact that his profit will be taxable as ordinary income. George quickly agrees to sell to a single buyer.

Since some residential development now seems to be the likely solution, George seeks out a land-use planner for advice on how to best preserve the buildings and surrounding 200 acres and at the same time maximize the value of the 200 acres to be sold. The entire family wishes to maintain the essential scenic qualities of the promontory and as many of the various natural wildlife and plant species habitats as possible. The family is also concerned about its privacy.

The land-use planner presents several options, all of which for aesthetic reasons limit subdivision by the purchasing developer to lots of at least five acres. The real estate expert interjects that his original estimate of the value of the 200 acres was premised on lot sizes of two acres, the minimum size permitted by the town zoning laws. A reduction in the number of salable lots would reduce the value of the 200 acres to be sold. A rerun of the balance sheet and spendable income projections and a rerun of tax computations to reflect this change indicate a need to sell an additional 50 acres to meet objectives.

At this juncture the land conservation organization suggests that instead of selling an additional 50 acres, George consider putting a conservation easement on the retained 200 acres. The easement would be given to the conservation organization and would have the effect of preventing any future development of the retained lands. It would also substantially reduce their fair market value. That reduction would be a charitable gift deductible for federal income tax purposes. The deduction would substantially reduce the income taxes otherwise payable on the gain from the sale of the other 200 acres. It would also reduce future death taxes. Again the figures are rerun, and the results appear favorable in all respects. The family agrees to sell 200 acres for limited 5-acre development and to place a conservation easement on the retained lands, thus ensuring the protection of important habitat and scenic qualities of the land.

Federal Estate and Gift Tax Planning: Strategies and Priorities for the Landowner

Marion R. Fremont-Smith

The task of an estate planner is to translate his client's wishes for the transmission of his property into a plan that reduces estate, gift, and income taxes as much as possible. In some cases reduction of income tax will be most important; in others it will be estate tax. Kingsbury Browne's description (in the preceding article) of George's and Hetty's family situation and the choices they face in planning their estate is a perfect introduction to the planning process. The purpose of this article is to describe the appropriate provisions of the federal estate, gift, and income tax laws, with particular attention to their application to estates that include valuable real property.

Often the person with unusual property holdings already has formulated the preservation of his real property as one of his estate planning goals. For him any alternative that combines preservation with substantial tax savings will be an optimum choice. Another individual may not have thought of conservation and preservation as being within his purview. He may adopt these as goals only after learning of the potential tax savings that are available.

What then are the basic federal gift and estate tax rules within which the estate planner operates? To start, each person has a credit against the federal gift and estate tax that permits a certain amount of property to be given during life or, if not given then, to pass at death free of tax. Between 1977 and 1981 this credit was the equivalent of an exemption for $175,000 worth of property passing from one person to others. Under the Economic Recovery Tax Act of 1981 (ERTA), the credit was increased to $225,000 for gifts made in 1982 and for estates of persons dying in that year. The law also provided for a further increase in the credit in each year between 1983 and 1987 until it will offset all tax on $600,000. For amounts in excess of the credit, the tax is imposed at a graduated rate, with the marginal rate starting at approximately 34 percent. Until 1982 the maximum top marginal rate was 70 percent, and it was imposed on taxable estates of $5,000,000 or more. ERTA also modified this aspect of the gift and estate tax law, again over a period of years starting in 1982. When the law is fully phased in, in 1985, the top marginal rate will be reduced to 50 percent, applicable to all transfers in excess of $2,500,000.

The gift tax laws have always contained provisions under which a minimum amount could be given each year to any number of individuals without incurring tax or using up a credit (or, before the credit was in effect, an exclusion). ERTA increased this annual exclusion amount from $3,000 per gift to $10,000. Accordingly, a donor can now give up to $10,000 to each of as many persons as he or she wishes (or can afford to); in addition, expenditures for medical needs and education can be made without limit.

It has always been possible for a husband and wife to agree that a gift made by one of them will be treated as made by both for purposes of determining the amount of a taxable gift. Thus one spouse can make gifts of $20,000, not $10,000, to each of his children so long as the other spouse agrees. This same pooling (or gift-splitting) concept applies to the gift tax credit so that if one spouse has no funds but is willing to join in a major lifetime transfer, his or her credit can be used up with gifts from the other spouse. Thus, for example, after 1986, a spouse could transfer $1,200,000 as a split gift without incurring tax.

ERTA also made a major change in the deductions that are allowed before computing the estate and gift tax. Spouses can now give unlimited amounts to each other and incur neither gift nor estate tax on the transfer. This change was accomplished through enactment of an unlimited marital deduction. Furthermore, the deduction became available for a gift that was limited to providing income only to the surviving spouse for life; this is in contrast to prior law under which a deduction was available only if the gift was outright or included a power of disposition over the principal that was essentially the equivalent of outright ownership.

There has been a deduction for gifts for charitable, religious, educational, and scientific purposes since the first estate tax law was enacted. Conservation purposes are considered charitable if they meet the strict requirements described in the article by Stephen Small in the section on federal taxation. Both the marital and charitable deductions permit individuals to transfer large amounts of property without incurring estate or gift tax, quite apart from the credit and exclusions already described. They are, thus, basic to the planning process. For example, George could leave all his property to Hetty, and there would be no estate tax at his death whether his estate was $200,000 or $20,000,000; he could also give, or leave by will, all his property to his local conservation land trust and avoid all tax; or he could leave part to the land trust and part to his wife with the same result. This is because of the deductions. Another alternative, which takes advantage of both the deduction and the credit, allows him to leave all his property in excess of $600,000 (which is the amount offset by the credit after 1986) to his wife or to a land trust or to both and leave $600,000 to his children (or any other individuals he chose), and there would still be no gift or estate tax.

Another important tool for the estate planner is the establishment of trusts to hold property in such a manner that the beneficiary of the trust will not be taxed as the owner of the property at his death, even though he had the right to all income, could receive principal at the discretion of the trustee, and had the ability to direct within some limits the disposition of the property at death. If the property ultimately passes to a qualified charitable organization after the individual interests cease and if the trust meets fairly stringent requirements as to the annual amount the individual beneficiary can receive, the value of the charitable interest can be deducted from the value of the total gift before the tax on the transfer is determined. Conservation organizations are eligible beneficiaries of such trusts. For example, George could leave $1,000,000 in trust for his seventy-year-old sister for life and provide that on her death the principal would pass to conservation organizations. The value of the sister's life estate, as determined under Internal Revenue Service tables that are based on life expectancy, is 47.5 percent. Therefore, George would get a deduction for 52.5

percent. If George's wife were the life beneficiary of the trust, a deduction would be available not just for the charitable interest but for the full value of the property, both when it is given and then again at his wife's death, because the transfer qualified first for the marital and then for the charitable deduction.

These gifts in trust are really gifts of partial interest (i.e., a right to income). There are other forms of partial interests that, when given away, also qualify for the charitable deduction. One is a legal life estate in real property; this is the right to live on or lease the property for life (but not sell it) and, when this right terminates, have title pass to a charity. One can create such a deductible interest during life or so provide at death. One can also retain the life estate and give away only the remainder. In either case a gift or estate tax charitable deduction will be available for the remainder gift. Another partial gift that may be the subject of a living or testamentary gift is one that splits the property not in terms of time (i.e., the life of an individual) but by the nature of the interest in it. The most common interest of this type is a conservation easement, which in effect provides that all individuals who hold legal title to the property, whether they obtain it by gift or by purchase, are restricted in the manner in which they can use the property. The easement may prohibit development or require that there will always be public access to those who wish to use it. Conservation easements can last for a period of time or forever; only perpetual easements are eligible for the charitable deduction.

As noted earlier, the gift and estate tax rates are graduated, with the marginal rate running from 34 percent to 50 percent. Thus any reduction in the amount of one's taxable estate means a relative reduction in the tax to be imposed. Accordingly, even in situations where it is not possible to avoid all tax, the "cost" of charitable gifts that are deductible will be less than the dollar amount of the property given. For someone with a projected taxable estate of $2,500,000 or more, where all additional property will be taxed at 50 percent, each charitable gift will reduce the tax by an amount equal to one-half of the value of the property given to charity. At the lower level of the scale, with a taxable estate of $1,100,000, the cost of a $100,000 gift will be $59,000. For an estate that is under $600,000 (and death after 1986), the cost of the gift will equal the value of the property. However, there may well be state estate tax savings for estates of this size that should also be considered.

The discussion thus far has been confined to estate and gift taxes, but proper estate planning cannot be done without considering the income tax. This tax is also a graduated tax with a maximum marginal rate of 50 percent. A deduction is permitted for charitable gifts, but, unlike the estate and gift tax laws, the Internal Revenue Code places limitations on the amount of the charitable deduction. Furthermore, the extent of the limits varies depending on the nature of the charitable donee, with stricter limits on gifts to certain private foundations. (Because of the complexity of the rules relating to gifts to private foundations and their lack of general application, they will not be described here.) As to gifts to publicly supported charities, a category that includes most land trusts and conservation organizations, a donor can deduct up to 50 percent of adjusted gross income for gifts of cash and 30 percent for gifts of appreciated property that, if sold, would give rise to long-term capital gain. Amounts in excess of these limits can be carried forward and used as deductions for five additional years after the year of gift. If the property has long-term capital appreciation, the deduction will be equal to its fair market value on the date of the gift.

The techniques for reducing income taxes, therefore, include removing from the tax base property that either produces a large taxable income or that is likely to appreciate in value. There is a tradeoff, however, for gifts, as opposed to testamentary dispositions of property that has appreciated since its acquisition and that is likely to be sold by a donee or devisee. This is so because the donee of the gift takes the donor's basis (plus any gift tax paid on the transfer) as his own. When property passes at death, however, it receives a new basis equal to the value at which it is reported for estate tax purposes (either date of death or value six months after death). For example, if George gave his son land worth $100,000 on the date of gift that had a cost to George of $10,000 and ten years later the son sold the land for $200,000, the son's gain would be $190,000. If George left the same property to his son under his will and if its value at George's death was $100,000, and if it was worth $200,000 when his son sold it, the son's gain would be $100,000. So, in the cases of property that is to be sold immediately, it may be advantageous financially to wait until death to make a current gift.

A brief reference must be made to still another tax on transfers that was enacted in 1976. This is the generation-skipping tax; it is imposed on any transfer of property from a member of an older generation to a member of a younger generation, if there is no estate or gift tax imposed at the termination of the older generation's interest. For example, if father gives his son a life estate in real property and on son's death title passes to a grandson, the transfer will not be subject to estate tax at the son's death. However, unless it meets a special exclusion for gifts to grandchildren, it will be subject to the generation-skipping tax. The purpose behind enactment of the tax was to discourage the use of techniques that permitted property to pass through successive generations without being subject to any transfer tax. It has served to complicate the estate planner's task. It has also served to encourage gifts of property to charitable organizations because there is a deduction for such gifts similar to that found in the estate and gift tax laws. In other words, a gift of a legal life estate to a son, with the remainder to charity, will not be subject to the generation-skipping tax because the charitable interest would be deductible.

The foregoing is only a summary of some of the most basic tax rules applicable to owners of valuable real property. It should be sufficient, however, to indicate some of the choices available to them in planning their estates. The initial set of choices concerns lifetime transfers. Obviously, the first option is to do nothing and hope that the family will have cash from other sources to pay taxes and expenses and avoid any forced sale of the property. A second choice, and one of the most appealing, is to reduce the value of the real property by subjecting it to a conservation easement. If the property is suitable for development and the easement effectively prevents it, the property's value will be substantially reduced, and this may well make the difference between enabling the family to keep the property and having to sell it. In all events the easement will assure its conservation. As already noted, the tax laws delineating conservation purposes are exceedingly strict, and it is important that proper evaluation techniques be used in order to assure the deduction. Furthermore, if an easement does not meet the income tax requirements, its creation will be treated as a taxable gift to the governmental unit or charitable organization that is given the right to enforce it, thereby making the transfer a tax-paying rather than a tax-saving one.

A third type of transfer is one that removes the property entirely from the tax base. This can be done without tax cost by transferring fractional interests, each within the $10,000 per donee limit. If an easement has previously been placed on the property and the easement reduced its value, transfer of the donor's interest can obviously be achieved more quickly than otherwise. Another possibility is for a donor to use part or all of his unified credit during lifetime to make a present gift. In families where only one spouse has assets, it is possible for the other to join in the gift and thereby assure that the credit available to each person is not lost. For a couple in this situation, unless a split gift is made during their joint lives, for all practical purposes the credit will be lost.

Gifts of remainder interests in real property to charitable organizations are suitable for donors who can use an income tax deduction but need to retain the property during life or until the death of a spouse or another person. Naturally, one can assure complete preservation by an outright gift to a land trust or similar conservation organization. A difficulty for many donors contemplating such a transfer is that often the donee organization will require a cash contribution as a condition of accepting the real estate in order to ensure the continued upkeep of the property. A final choice for a lifetime transfer is a part-gift/part-sale whereby the charity pays a reduced price for the property, thereby permitting the donor to receive a charitable deduction equal to the amount of the reduction.

The choice for testamentary dispositions is not different, except that the income tax considerations will be less important at that time. There is no question but that when Congress adopted the unlimited marital deduction and the provisions permitting qualified terminable interest property trusts to qualify for the deduction, it removed a large incentive to married couples to create charitable remainder trusts or retained life estates. The technique is useful, however, if one wants to create a life interest for others, and it will continue to be an important tool for the estate planner.

It should be apparent from the foregoing that the tax laws are replete with incentives for charitable gifts, including those directed toward preservation and conservation of real property. Knowledge of the basic rules and an understanding of a client's goals are the two crucial ingredients for assuring that the incentives will be properly used. There is much that can be done by charitable organizations such as local land trusts to educate themselves and potential donors as to the benefits available and the techniques for assuring that they are achieved. In many instances it is possible to combine preservation with added benefit to family members, but, unless donors understand this, it is unlikely that the goal of preservation will be achieved.

Author Biographies

Sarah M. Bates

Sarah M. Bates is a graduate of the University of Pennsylvania, Yale University School of Forestry and Environmental Studies, and the University of Connecticut School of Law. From 1976 to 1980 she served as counsel to the Conservation Law Foundation of New England.

Terry Bremer

Terry Bremer was educated at Harvard University. She is on the board of directors of Plymouth County Wildlands Trust in Massachusetts and has written articles for *Private Options: Tools and Concepts for Land Conservation*. She co-compiled, for the Lincoln Institute of Land Policy in Cambridge, the first *National Directory of Local Land Conservation Organizations*.

Russell L. Brenneman

Russell L. Brenneman received a B.A. from Ohio State University in 1950 and an LL.B. from the Harvard Law School in 1953. He is the author of *Private Approaches to the Preservation of Open Land* and numerous articles on land conservation and historic preservation. Mr. Brenneman is a partner in the Hartford firm of Murtha, Cullina, Richter & Pinney. Active as a volunteer in land conservation, Mr. Brenneman is a director of the Connecticut chapter of The Nature Conservancy and is vice-president of the Connecticut Forest and Park Association. He teaches environmental policy courses at the University of Connecticut School of Law and Trinity College. He is a member of the International Council of Environmental Law. Mr. Brenneman is chairman of the Committee on Historic Preservation and Easements, Section on Real Property, Probate, and Trust, American Bar Association.

Kingsbury Browne, Jr.

Kingsbury Browne received an A.B. cum laude from Harvard College in 1944 and an LL.B. from Harvard Law School in 1950. Mr. Browne is a partner in the Boston law firm of Hill & Barlow and a tax specialist by training and practice. He is a member of the American Law Institute and a Fellow of the American Bar Foundation. From July 1 to December 31, 1980, he was a Fellow of the Lincoln Institute of Land Policy in Cambridge, Massachusetts, and a Visiting Scholar at the Harvard Law School, studying federal tax policy and land preservation.

Richard W. Carbin

Richard W. Carbin is a graduate of Rutgers University. He cofounded the Ottauquechee Regional Land Trust in 1977 and since 1980 has served as its executive director. Prior to joining the trust, Mr. Carbin served for six years as executive director of the Ottauquechee Regional Planning and Development Commission. Currently, Mr. Carbin is chairman of the Barnard, Vermont, town planning commission; a board member of the Connecticut River Watershed Council; and an appointed member of Vermont's Task Force on Agricultural Land Conservation.

Thomas A. Coughlin III

Thomas A. Coughlin III is a graduate of Brandeis University and Boston College Law School and is an assistant general counsel at the National Trust for Historic Preservation in Washington, D.C. His principal areas of practice are tax, real estate, and historic preservation law. Prior to coming to the trust, Mr. Coughlin was employed as an attorney-advisor in the Department of Housing and Urban Development's Office of General Counsel. He has authored several articles on easements and federal tax incentives for historic preservation.

Benjamin R. Emory

Benjamin R. Emory was executive director of Maine Coast Heritage Trust from 1976 to 1982 and has been associated with the trust in other capacities since 1971. He has worked for the University of Maine in economic development and for the New England Natural Resources Center studying offshore oil issues. Mr. Emory holds an M.B.A. from Dartmouth College and an A.B. from Harvard College.

Marion R. Fremont-Smith

Marion R. Fremont-Smith is a graduate of Wellesley College and Boston University School of Law. She is a partner in the Boston law firm of Choate, Hall & Stewart, specializing in estate planning, the tax and legal problems of exempt organizations, and charitable giving. She is the author of *Foundations and Government, State and Federal Law and Supervision* and *Philanthropy and the Business Organization,* as well as numerous articles on philanthropy and estate planning.

Jennie Gerard

Jennie Gerard, since 1978 the director of The Trust for Public Land's land trust program, has assisted the formation of more than two dozen land trusts in seven states. Among these are the nation's first five local agricultural land trusts and land trusts in scenic areas of national and state significance. She brought to TPL eight years of experience as a city planning consultant for small towns and agricultural counties.

Hank Goetz

Hank Goetz graduated in 1963 from the University of Montana with a B.S. in forest management. From 1967 until 1969, he was a forester for the Northern Pacific Railway land office in Seeley Lake, Montana. Since 1969, he has been the resident manager of the 28,000-acre Lubrecht Experimental Forest for the School of Forestry, University of Montana, Missoula.

Davis Hartwell

Davis Hartwell succeeded Benjamin R. Emory as executive director of Maine Coast Heritage Trust. He attended Bowdoin College in Brunswick, Maine. Mr. Hartwell holds a J.D. from the Yale Law School and an M.F.S. from the Yale School of Forestry and Environmental Studies.

M. Eugene Hoffman

M. Eugene Hoffman graduated with a B.S. in range management from Utah State University in 1955 and from the Weaver School of Real Estate in 1968. He has also done graduate work in law and forestry. Mr. Hoffman has worked for the Bureau of Land Management and the U.S. Forest Service and is a licensed real estate broker in Wyoming and Idaho. He has been particularly active in land-use planning in Teton Valley, Wyoming.

Warren A. Illi

Warren A. Illi graduated from the University of Minnesota in 1961 with a B.S. in forest management. From 1967 to 1972, he served as staff appraiser and negotiator for land purchase and exchange programs on national forests in Minnesota and Pennsylvania for the U.S. Forest Service. From 1973 to 1977, he served as land purchase, land exchange, and appraisal specialist for the U.S. Forest Service in Montana and Idaho. Currently, he serves as Lands and Minerals Staff Officer for the Flathead National Forest, Kalispell, Montana.

Roger E. Koontz

Roger E. Koontz received a B.S. from the University of Illinois and an LL.B. from Yale University. He is the former executive director of Connecticut Legal Services and, most recently, Connecticut counsel for the Conservation Law Foundation of New England. In that position he coauthored the *Connecticut Land Trust Handbook.* Currently, Mr. Koontz is in private practice in Connecticut.

Robert A. Lemire

Robert A. Lemire received a B.A. from Yale University and an M.B.A. from the Harvard Business School. He is the author of *Creative Land Development: Bridge to the Future* and served as chairman of the Lincoln, Massachusetts, Conservation Commission from 1966 to 1981. He serves on the Massachusetts Agricultural Land Preservation Committee and the executive committee of the Commonwealth's Water Supply Citizens' Advisory Committee.

Mary Lester

Mary Lester was formerly a land trust assistant with The Trust for Public Land, where she provided land trusts with information, coordinated regional workshops, and prepared bulletins on technical issues relevant to land trusts. She has had seven years' experience with the day-to-day operation of nonprofit community organizations—writing proposals, installing management systems, and developing service programs. She is currently the business manager for a research and education organization.

Charles Matthei

Charles Matthei is the director of the Institute for Community Economics, which provides technical, financial, and construction assistance to both rural and urban community land trusts. Mr. Matthei is a coauthor of ICE's *Community Land Trust Handbook* and a variety of articles; he has spent the past seventeen years working full time in community service.

Jan W. McClure

Jan W. McClure is a graduate of Williams College and the author of several articles on land protection. Ms. McClure is now land protection program manager at the Society for the Protection of New Hampshire Forests. Previously, she worked with the State of New Hampshire as an environmentalist in the Department of Public Works and Highways.

Janet E. Milne

Janet E. Milne was associate director of Maine Coast Heritage Trust when she wrote the first edition of "The Landowner's Options," a pamphlet jointly funded by Maine Coast Heritage Trust and the Maine State Planning Office. After leaving Maine Coast Heritage Trust, she attended the Georgetown University Law Center and clerked for the Hon. Frank M. Coffin, who was then Chief Judge of the U.S. Court of Appeals for the First Circuit. She is now an attorney for the *Washington Post.*

William F. Morrill

William F. Morrill is a graduate of Cornell University with a B.A. in economics and has a J.D. from Columbia University. He is now a lawyer in private practice in Lakeville, Connecticut. For the last thirteen years he has been involved in conservation and environmental law, with a particular emphasis on land preservation.

Ross D. Netherton

Ross D. Netherton was educated at the law schools of the Universities of Chicago, Michigan, and Wisconsin. During the 1960s and 1970s he conducted research for the National Academy of Sciences, Department of the Interior, Federal Highway Administration, and a congressional study commission on highway beautification. As chairman of the American Bar Association's Committee on Historic Preservation and Easements from 1976 to 1982, he served as an advisor in the development of the Uniform Conservation Easement Act.

Russell K. Osgood

Russell K. Osgood received a B.A. from Yale College in 1969 and a J.D from the Yale Law School in 1974. He is an associate professor of law at Cornell University, the editor of *Cornell Law Forum,* and the editor of *Law and History Review.* Mr. Osgood is the author of taxation and legal history articles.

Stephen J. Small

Stephen J. Small is an attorney with the Boston law firm of Powers & Hall Professional Corporation. He has a J.D.

and an LL.M. in taxation from the Georgetown University Law Center. Before joining Powers & Hall, Small was an attorney-advisor in the Office of Chief Counsel at the Internal Revenue Service in Washington, D.C., where he was the principal draftsman of proposed income tax regulations on the charitable donation of easements for conservation purposes.

Peter R. Stein

Peter Stein is vice-president of The Trust for Public Land, where he directs a national program to provide technical assistance in land acquisition and land management to community development groups and local public agencies. Mr. Stein is trained as an environmental planner and has written extensively about abandoned urban wastelands, urban open space protection, community gardening, and private-sector land preservation techniques. During 1980–81, Mr. Stein was a Loeb Fellow in advanced environmental studies at Harvard University and Adjunct Lecturer in the Department of Urban and Environmental Policy at Tufts University. In addition, Mr. Stein was a founding director and remains a member of the governing council of Partners for Livable Places, a nonprofit organization engaged in urban livability issues.

Robert E. Suminsby

Robert E. Suminsby graduated from the University of Maine with a B.S. in 1958. He is a licensed Maine real estate broker and an instructor in real property valuation at the University of Maine at Machias. Mr. Suminsby was the supervising appraiser for the revaluation of eighteen municipalities in Maine and Vermont from 1960 to 1970. He specializes in property appraisals for ad valorem tax, estate tax, mortgage loan, and investment purposes.

Edward Thompson, Jr.

Edward Thompson, Jr., received a J.D. in 1974 from the George Washington University Law Center and an A.B. from Cornell University in 1971 and is counsel to the American Farmland Trust. Prior to his association with AFT, Mr. Thompson served as director of the Agricultural Lands Project of the National Association of Counties Research Foundation and as Washington, D.C., counsel for the Environmental Defense Fund.

Glenn F. Tiedt

Glenn F. Tiedt received a B.A. from the University of Washington and a J.D. from George Washington University. He has served the National Park Service in a variety of positions, including those with the Bureau of Outdoor Recreation and the Heritage Conservation and Recreation Service. He has written several articles on conservation easements and served as an advisor to the National Conference of Commissioners on Uniform State Laws during the drafting of the Uniform Conservation Easement Act.

Suzanne C. Wilkins

Suzanne C. Wilkins is director of the Connecticut Land Trust Service Bureau, which assists the eighty-two local land conservation trusts in the state. She is the coauthor of the *Connecticut Land Trust Handbook.* Ms. Wilkins is the former executive director of the Long Island Sound Task Force, a regional chapter of the Oceanic Society. Currently, she serves as vice-chair of the Connecticut Environmental Caucus and is on the boards of the Conservationists of Stamford and the Stamford Land Trust.

Steele Wotkyns

Steele Wotkyns graduated from the University of California at Los Angeles in 1944 and also received a degree in architecture from the University of California at Berkeley in 1950. He has since practiced architecture, interior design, and planning in California and Colorado. He is associated with the graduate group in ecology at the University of California at Davis and remains active in land conservation efforts in Trinidad, California.

Selected Readings

Readers who wish to consult additional texts concerning private land conservation are directed to the following group of selected publications. Prepared by the Land Trust Exchange, a national network of private land conservation organizations, this list is intended to introduce interested individuals to a basic collection of works and not to provide exhaustive references. These publications are available from their respective publishers or from the Land Trust Exchange, Mount Desert, Maine 04660.

The American Cropland Crisis: Why U.S. Farmland Is Being Lost and How Citizens and Governments Are Trying to Save What Is Left. W. Wendell Fletcher and Charles E. Little. Bethesda, Md.: American Land Forum, 1982.

Building an Ark: Tools for the Preservation of Natural Diversity Through Land Protection. Phillip M. Hoose. Covelo, Ca.: Island Press, 1981.

Charitable Gifts of Land: A Landowner's Guide to Vermont and Federal Tax Incentives. Darby Bradley. Woodstock, Vt.: Ottauquechee Regional Land Trust, 1982.

The Community Land Trust Handbook. The Institute for Community Economics. Emmaus, Pa.: Rodale Press, 1982.

Connecticut Land Trust Handbook. Suzanne C. Wilkins and Roger E. Koontz. Middletown, Conn.: Connecticut Land Trust Service Bureau, 1982.

The Conservation Easement in California. Thomas S. Barrett and Putnam Livermore for The Trust for Public Land. Covelo, Ca.: Island Press, 1983.

A Supplement to The Conservation Easement in California: Proposed Federal Tax Regulations with Commentary by Thomas S. Barrett. Covelo, Ca.: Island Press, 1983.

Creative Land Development: Bridge to the Future. Robert A. Lemire. Boston: Houghton Mifflin Co., 1979.

Creative Solutions to Development Conflicts: Proceedings of the Negotiated Land Development Seminar. D. Ernest Cook, ed., 1981.

Exchange, quarterly journal of the Land Trust Exchange, Mount Desert, Maine.

The Landowner's Options: A Guide to the Voluntary Protection of Land in Iowa. Iowa Natural Heritage Foundation. Des Moines, Iowa: Iowa Natural Heritage Foundation, 1982.

On Common Ground: Caring for Shared Land from Town Common to Urban Park. Ronald Lee Fleming and Lauri A. Haldeman. Boston: Harvard Common Press, n.d.

Private Options: Tools and Concepts for Land Conservation. The Montana Land Reliance and the Land Trust Exchange. Covelo, Ca.: Island Press, 1982.

The Use and Protection of Privately Held Natural Lands: A Handbook for the Landowner. The Natural Lands Trust. Philadelphia, Pa.: The Natural Lands Trust, 1982.

Index

Also Available from Island Press

Land-Saving Action is the latest volume in a series of books published by Island Press that make available state-of-the-art information on all aspects of conservation and land use to professionals and laypeople at work in these fields. Other titles in this series as well as titles of related interest are available directly from Island Press, Star Route 1, Box 38, Covelo, California 95428.

The Conservation Easement in California, by Thomas S. Barrett and Putnam Livermore for The Trust for Public Land. Cloth, $44.95; paper, $24.95

The authoritative legal handbook for the use of conservation easements in California. This book puts the conservation easement in context, discusses the historical and legal background of the conservation easement in California, its state and federal tax implications, and the problems involved in drafting easements.

A Supplement to The Conservation Easement in California: Proposed Federal Tax Regulations with Commentary by Thomas S. Barrett. $6.00

The complete text of the draft regulations governing federal tax deductions for gifts of conservation easements, published by the Internal Revenue Service in May 1983, with commentary by author Thomas S. Barrett.

Private Options: Tools and Concepts for Land Conservation, by the Montana Land Reliance and the Land Trust Exchange. $25.00

This volume presents practical methods of preserving land, based on the experience of more than thirty experts. Topics include income tax incentives for preserving agricultural land, marketing land conservation, management of conserved land areas, and the real estate business as a conservation tool.

Building an Ark: Tools for the Preservation of Natural Diversity Through Land Protection, by Phillip M. Hoose. Illustrations. $12.00

The author is national protection planner for The Nature Conservancy, and this book presents a comprehensive plan that can be used to identify and protect what remains of each state's natural ecological diversity. Case studies augment this blueprint for conservation.

Tree Talk: The People and Politics of Timber, by Ray Raphael. Illustrations by Mark Livingston. $12.00

A probing analysis of modern forestry practices and philosophies. In a balanced and informed text, *Tree Talk* presents the views of loggers, environmentalists, timber industry executives, and forest farmers and goes beyond the politics of "production versus protection" to propose new ways to harvest trees and preserve forest habitats in a healthy economy and a thriving environment.

Pocket Flora of the Redwood Forest, by Dr. Rudolf W. Becking. Illustrations. $15.00

The most useful and comprehensive guidebook available for the plants of the world-famous redwood forest. Dr. Rudolf W. Becking, a noted botanist and professor of natural resources, is also a gifted artist. The *Pocket Flora* includes detailed drawings, a complete key, and simple, accurate descriptions for 212 of the most common species of this unique plant community, as well as eight pages of color photographs. Plasticized cover for field use.

A Citizen's Guide to Timber Harvest Plans, by Marylee Bytheriver. Illustrations. $1.50

California state law permits any interested citizen to learn the details of proposed timber cutting on private or public lands. This report instructs citizens on their rights concerning timber harvesting, the procedures for influencing the details of proposed logging operations, and the specialized vocabulary surrounding the Timber Harvest Plan. A resource for action.

An Everyday History of Somewhere, by Ray Raphael. Illustrations by Mark Livingston. $8.00

This work of history and documentation embraces the lives and work of ordinary people, from the Indians who inhabited the coastal forests of northern California to the loggers, tanbark strippers, and farmers who came after them. This loving look at history takes us full circle, leading to the everyday life of us all.

Two Californias: The Truth About the Split-State Movement, by Michael DiLeo and Eleanor Smith. $10.95

A timely and provocative examination of the issues that underlie the split-state movement in California, with special focus on the question of resources. A book that is likely to change the ways we think about living together and sharing resources in the 1980s.

The Trail North, by Hawk Greenway. Illustrations. $7.50

The summer adventure of a young man who traveled the spine of coastal mountains from California to Washington with only his horse for a companion. The book he has made from this journey reveals his coming of age as he studies, reflects, and greets the world that is awakening within and around him.

America Without Violence: Why Violence Persists and How You Can Stop It, by Michael N. Nagler. Foreword by Louis Jolyon West, M.D. $8.00

Challenging the widespread assumption that violence is an inevitable part of human existence, *America Without Violence* asserts that it *is* possible to live in a nonviolent society. The choice, Michael Nagler says, begins with each individual. In personal, practical language, *America Without Violence* explains how to make the changes in our private lives that can counteract the forces of violence throughout our society.

The Book of the Vision Quest: Personal Transformation in the Wilderness, by Steven Foster with Meredith E. Little. Photographs. $10.00

The inspiring record of modern people enacting an ancient, archetypal rite of passage. This book shares the wisdom and the seeking of many persons who have known the opportunity to face themselves, their fears, and their courage, and to live in harmony with nature through the experience of the traditional Vision Quest. Excerpts from participants' journals add an intimate dimension to this unique account of human challenge.

Wellspring: A Story from the Deep Country, by Barbara Dean. Illustrations. $6.00

The moving, first-person account of a contemporary woman's life at the edge of wilderness. Since 1971, Barbara Dean has lived in a handmade yurt on land she shares with fifteen friends. Their struggles, both hilarious and poignant, form the background for this inspiring story of personal growth and deep love for nature.

Headwaters: Tales of the Wilderness, by Ash, Russell, Doog, and Del Rio. Preface by Edward Abbey. Photographs and illustrations. $6.00

Four bridge-playing buddies tackle the wilderness—they go in separately, meet on top of a rock, and come out talking. These four are as different as the suits in their deck of cards, as ragged as a three-day beard, and as eager as sparks.

No Substitute for Madness: A Teacher, His Kids & The Lessons of Real Life, by Ron Jones. Illustrations. $8.00

Seven magnificent glimpses of life as it is. Ron Jones is a teacher with the gift of translating human beauty into words and knowing where to find it in the first place. This collection of true experiences includes "The Acorn People," the moving story of a summer camp for handicapped kids, and "The Third Wave," a harrowing experiment in Nazi training in a high school class—both of which were adapted for television movies.

Perfection Perception, with the Brothers O. and Joe de Vivre. $5.00

Notes from a metaphysical journey through the mountains of Patagonia. The authors share their experiences and discoveries in using their powers of perception to change the world. Their thoughts are mystical at times, but their basis is firmly experiential and parallels the most theoretically advanced works in modern physics.

The Search for Goodbye-to-Rains, by Paul McHugh. $7.50

Steve Gertane takes to the road in an American odyssey that is part fantasy and part real—a haphazard pursuit that includes Faulkner's Mississippi, the rarefied New Mexico air, and a motorcycle named Frank. "A rich, resonant novel of the interior world. Overtones of Whitman, Kerouac."—Robert Anton Wilson

---

Please enclose $1.00 with each order for postage and handling.

California residents, add 6% sales tax.

A catalog of current and forthcoming titles is available free of charge.